EVERGREEN
WITH READINGS

A Guide to Writing

SIXTH EDITION

Susan Fawcett

Alvin Sandburg

HOUGHTON MIFFLIN COMPANY
Boston   New York

Senior Sponsoring Editor: Mary Jo Southern
Senior Associate Editor: Ellen Darion
Senior Project Editor: Chere Bemelmans
Senior Production/Design Coordinator: Sarah Ambrose
Senior Manufacturing Coordinator: Priscilla Bailey
Senior Marketing Manager: Nancy Lyman
Senior Designer: Henry Rachlin
Editorial Assistants: Danielle Richardson and Joy Park
Custom Publishing Editor: Peter Nowka
Custom Publishing Production Manager: Kathleen McCourt
Project Coordinator: Kyle Sarofeen
Cover Designer: Kelly Mannion
Cover Photograph: Artville

This book contains select works from existing Houghton Mifflin Company resources and was produced by Houghton Mifflin Custom Publishing for collegiate use. As such, those adopting and/or contributing to this work are responsible for editorial content, accuracy, continuity and completeness.

Printed in the United States of America.

ISBN: 0-618-18862-2
N00400

1 2 3 4 5 6 7 8 9 – DS – 04 03 02 01

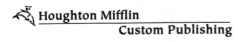

222 Berkeley Street • Boston, MA 02116
Address all correspondence and order information to the above address.

Contents

Preface

"*Evergreen* works." Again and again, we hear this comment from instructors and students alike, and we consider it the greatest possible compliment. *Evergreen with Readings* combines in one volume the new Sixth Edition of our popular college writing text *Evergreen* and fourteen high-interest reading selections. Based on our classroom experience at Bronx Community College of the City University of New York, *Evergreen* was designed for students who need to improve the writing skills so necessary to success in college and in most careers. The text's clear, paced lessons, numerous high-interest practices, and engaging writing assignments have guided more than one and a half million students through the process of writing effectively, from prewriting to final draft.

By choosing *Evergreen with Readings*, those instructors who wish to include reading in their writing classes may select from richly varied and provocative readings by such authors as Sandra Cisneros, Arthur Ashe, Russell Baker, Anna Quindlen, Alice Walker, and Dave Barry. Each selection is accompanied by a headnote, glosses, critical thinking questions, and writing assignments, some of them collaborative.

In this exciting Sixth Edition—marking both the year 2000 and *Evergreen*'s twentieth birthday—we have kept the carefully honed lessons, flow of practices, and overall organization that have served students so well over the years. However, we have extensively reviewed and updated the text, replacing numerous activities and models and occasionally adjusting instructional priorities.

In doing so, we listened closely to the suggestions of college faculty across the country and weighed the kinds of academic and job-related challenges that our students will face once they complete this course. Our goal has been to take an excellent book and make it even more motivating, useful, and engaging than before.

Specifically, we have enhanced *Evergreen*'s academic focus with a new chapter on cause and effect, a much-expanded and reorganized chapter on summarizing and quoting, and more wide-ranging content (research on twins, underwater archeology, job search techniques, date rape, comets and asteroids, and more). In addition, we have included more samples of inspiring student writing; added more collaborative and critical thinking activities; selectively enriched writing, revising, and proofreading coverage; and replaced more models, practices, and writing assignments than ever before. Other changes include weaving references to writing on computers throughout the text, reversing Units 4 and 5 so that paragraph instruction flows directly into essay instruction, adding more practice on sentence errors plus a sentence fragment chart, and upgrading many photographs, cartoons, and other visual prompts for thinking and writing.

Special Features of *Evergreen*, Sixth Edition

Expanded Academic Focus

■ **New Coverage of Cause and Effect Writing.** Unit 3 now includes a chapter on cause and effect paragraphs. A corresponding section in Chapter 15, "Types of Essays," teaches students to write essays analyzing causes and effects.

■ **New Chapter on Summary and Quotation.** Chapter 18, "Special College Skills: Summary and Quotation," defines plagiarism and includes much-expanded material on how to summarize and quote from outside sources.

More Student Writing

■ **New Writers' Workshops.** This versatile feature at the end of every unit show-cases a student-authored paragraph or essay, carefully processed with peer-editing questions and followed by group work and writing ideas. Keyed to the subject matter of each unit and ideal for group discussion, these workshops reinforce writing and revising skills and inspire student writers by example.

■ **More Student Models.** Because students are often motivated by the fine work of their peers, more student models, in addition to professional models, are used throughout the text. These represent a range of levels, from finished writing to work needing revision.

Enriched Coverage of the Writing Process

■ **New Material on Controlling Idea and Revising for Support.** New coverage of the controlling idea has been added to our paragraph- and essay-writing instruction, with emphasis on the controlling idea in the topic sentence or thesis statement. At the urging of instructors, we also have added more practices in which students revise poorly developed paragraphs and essays.

■ **New Chapter, "Putting Your Proofreading Skills to Work."** A new chapter of mixed-error proofreading practice now concludes Unit 6, "Reviewing the Basics." Here students correct six high-interest selections, each containing a random, real-world mix of errors.

More New High-Interest Content Than Ever Before

■ **High-Interest Models and Practices.** Guided by our Faculty Advisory Board and users of the text, we have carefully reviewed and replaced many of the models and content-based practice sets so important to *Evergreen*'s effectiveness. Fresh subjects include young entrepreneurs, James Escalante's student math stars, how technology helps Stephen Hawking, insect sexual attraction, high schools of the twenty-first century, Oprah's book club, *Latina* magazine's founder, the moon as a tourist destination, soul and hip-hop, how famous authors beat writer's block, Mexico's Day of the Dead, and the Guggenheim Museum's recent motorcycle show.

■ **Four New Reading Selections.** We have replaced four readings with strong new selections, according to instructor and student feedback: Sandra Cisneros on becoming a writer, Andrew Ferguson on the epidemic of road rage, Dave Barry on school science projects, and Rene Denfeld on the lessons she learned from boxing.

New Collaborative and Critical-Thinking Activities

■ **Peer Revising.** Chapter 3 now includes instruction on peer editing, with a Peer Feedback Sheet to help students respond specifically to each other's work. In addition, the Writers' Workshops offer multiple opportunities for collaborative work.

■ **Improved Visual Prompts for Thinking and Writing.** This edition includes more stimulating visual images for critical analysis and writing, such as a billboard campaign to stop teen smoking, a British cartoon about America's armed children, and several paintings by contemporary artists.

Extensive Ancillary Package

Available on adoption of the text, the following ancillaries provide the instructor with excellent support material and expand teaching options. New to this edition is the Evergreen Web Site, which includes the Evergreen Community (a bulletin board where users can exchange ideas about teaching with *Evergreen*), additional tests and exercises, links, and tips on teaching developmental English.

■ *Instructor's Annotated Edition*

■ *Test Bank*

■ *Computerized Test Bank (Diagnostic/Mastery/Chapter Tests)*

■ *Evergreen Web Site including the Evergreen Community*

■ *Answer Key*

Organization of the Text

Evergreen's self-contained chapters and units can be taught in any order. Unit 1 provides an overview of the writing process, audience, and purpose and then introduces five prewriting techniques. Unit 2 guides students through the paragraph-writing process: planning, writing topic sentences, generating ideas, organizing, making smooth transitions, and revising. Unit 3 moves on to the rhetorical modes most often required in college writing (illustration, narration, description, process, definition, comparison/contrast, classification, cause/effect, and persuasion). In Unit 4, the techniques of paragraph writing are applied step by step to the process of writing essays, answering essay examination questions, and summarizing and quoting from sources. Unit 5 covers the more subtle skills of revising for consistency, sentence variety, and language awareness. Unit 6 thoroughly reviews basic grammar, highlighting such major problem areas as verbs, sentence boundaries, punctuation, and mechanics; Unit 7 covers spelling and homonyms. A reader containing fourteen professional selections and a Quotation Bank—a mini-reader of great short quotations for student use—conclude the text. *Evergreen*'s full range of materials and flexible organization adapt easily to almost any course design and to a wide range of student needs. Because each chapter is self-contained, the text also works well for tutorials, laboratory work, and self-teaching.

Acknowledgments

We wish to thank those people whose thoughtful comments and suggestions helped us develop this Sixth Edition.

Carlo Annese, Bergen Community College

Kathleen Beauchene, Community College of Rhode Island

Kathleen S. Britton, Florence-Darlington Technical College

Kathryn L. Cid, Lincoln Technical Institute

Nancy B. Culberson, Georgia College & State University

Donald Edge, Camden County College

Donna M. Farrow, Miami-Dade Community College–Kendall Campus

Eddye Gallagher, Tarrant County Junior College

Cliff Gardiner, Augusta State University

Elizabeth Boote Griffey, Florida Community College at Jacksonville

Sandra K. Hall, Corning Community College

Bonita Hilton, Broward Community College

Michael Hricik, Westmoreland County Community College

Brenda Kelly, Pensacola Junior College

Qian Lu, Pima Community College

Patricia A. Malinowski, Finger Lakes Community College

Dorothy Reade, North Harris College

David Rollison, College of Marin

Sharon Shapiro, Naugatuck Valley Community Technical College

Linda Whisnant, Guilford Technical Community College

We are grateful to our exceptional editors at Houghton Mifflin, who always go the distance to create the best possible book. Special thanks to Mary Jo Southern, Senior Sponsoring Editor, who has long believed in *Evergreen* and its mission; to Ellen Darion, Senior Associate Editor, whose many gifts include expert problem solving, a wicked sense of humor, and the ability to steer us all smoothly through the inevitable snags; and to Chere Bemelmans, our superb Senior Project Editor, who sees all—or almost all—as she manages the transformation of messy manuscript into beautiful printed pages. We are the happy beneficiaries of Chere's high standards and keen eye and share her devotion to the Chocolate Force. Harriett Prentiss, our Development Editor, enthusiastically stepped into this complicated revision and helped it evolve, contributing organizational skills, wisdom, and sometimes her formidable writing talents.

In addition, Marilyn Weissman and Nancy Brandwein helped with high-quality research and writing for some of the content-based exercises.

To the English Department faculty and students of Bronx Community College, we owe a special debt of gratitude. Many of the excellent student paragraphs and essays in this book were written in BCC classrooms and later won the college newspaper's "Writer of the Month" contest; each year, winners and finalists are published in booklet form with the help of Dr. Larraine Fergenson. Dr.

Bernard Witlieb read *Evergreen* pages for accuracy, lending his sharp eye and rich store of knowledge, and Carol Zavin kindly helped us track student authors.

We thank Bruce Carson for expert assistance in securing art permissions; watercolorist Patricia Hansen for the use of her painting and for her extraordinary efforts to take an excellent photograph of it; the Crispin Porter & Bogusky advertising agency for the use of its witty truth-or-lies billboard photograph; and Harriet Fawcett, whose art books inspired several of our selections.

Susan Fawcett thanks her husband, Richard Donovan, for sharing his love, humor, and invigorating thoughts over many good years. She dedicates her work on this revision to her beloved father, Millard F. Fawcett, who died on February 21, 1999. He was vivid and courageous—an inventor, photographer, small business owner, sportsman, and stylish wearer of hats.

Alvin Sandberg thanks Beth for her encouragement and support and Miriam for her many suggestions for improvements to the manuscript. He also thanks Marilyn Weissman for her editorial assistance.

S. F.
A. S.

Evergreen

A GUIDE TO WRITING

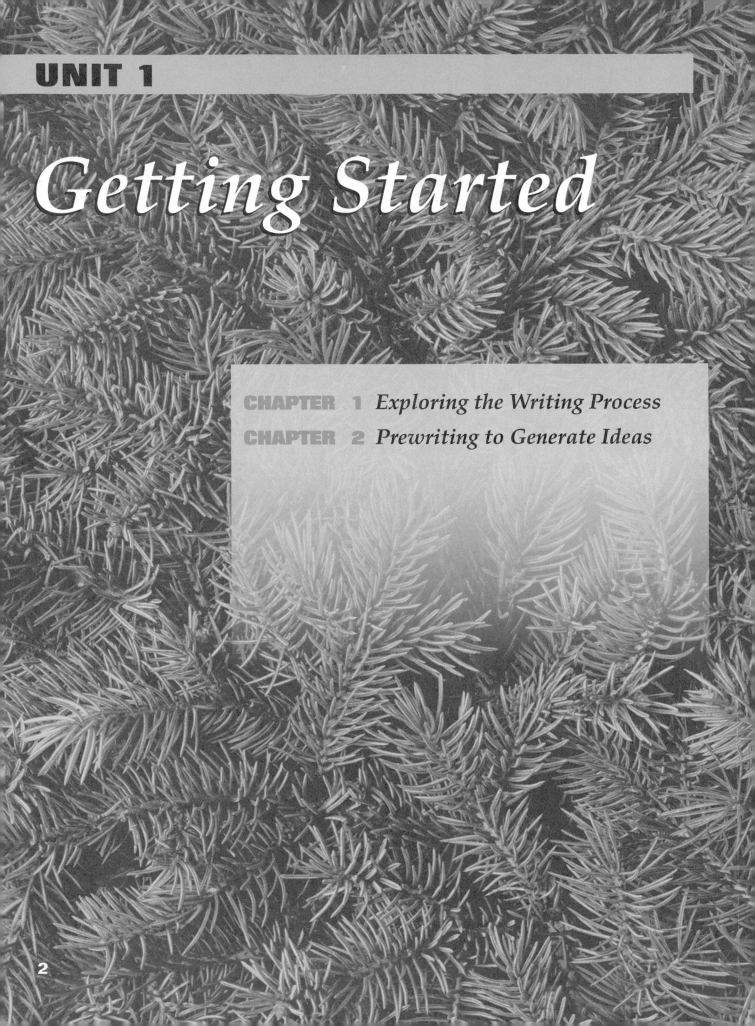

UNIT 1

Getting Started

CHAPTER 1

Exploring the Writing Process

PART A	The Writing Process
PART B	Subject, Audience, and Purpose

This chapter will give you a brief overview of the writing process, which is explored in greater depth throughout this book. By surveying the steps that many writers take and some of the factors they consider, you will see that writing is not a magic ability some are born with, but a skill that can be learned—the result of planning, hard work, and a positive attitude.

PART A   The Writing Process

Many students mistakenly think that good writers simply sit down and write out a perfect letter, paragraph, or essay from start to finish. In fact, writing is a **process** consisting of a number of steps:

1 Prewriting
- Thinking about possible subjects
- Freely jotting down ideas on paper or computer
- Narrowing the subject and writing it as one sentence
- Deciding which ideas to include
- Arranging ideas in a plan or an outline

2 Writing
- Writing a first draft

3 Revising
- Rethinking, rearranging, and rewriting as necessary
- Writing one or more new drafts
- Proofreading for grammar and spelling errors

Not all writers perform all the steps in this order, but most prewrite, write, revise, and proofread. Actually, writing can be a messy process of thinking, writing, reading what has been written, and rewriting. Sometimes steps overlap or must be repeated. The important thing is that writing the first draft is just one stage in the process. "I love being a writer," jokes Peter De Vries. "What I can't stand is the paperwork."

Before they write, good writers spend time **prewriting**—thinking about and planning for a paper. The first five steps on page 3 are all prewriting steps. Here writers think, let their imaginations run free, jot down ideas or list ideas on the computer, decide which ideas to use, and come up with a plan. Many beginning writers get into trouble by skipping the prewriting phase. They don't realize that doing this early work saves time and frustration later and usually creates a much better piece of writing than when students just sit down to write.

Next comes **writing** the first draft. Writers who have planned ahead are now free to concentrate on writing the best possible draft. The focus now is on presenting ideas, feelings, and experiences as convincingly as possible, rather than on correcting.

The next phase of the process—and one that many writers rush through or omit altogether—is **revising.** Experienced writers do not accept the first words that flow from their pens; they are like sculptors, shaping and reworking rough material into something meaningful. Writers do this by letting the first draft sit for five minutes, an hour, or a day. Then they read it again with a fresh, critical eye and rewrite—adding, dropping, or rearranging ideas; changing words to achieve more clarity and punch; and so on. Many writers revise two or three times until they get it right—until their writing says clearly and effectively what they want it to say. Finally, they **proofread** for grammar and spelling errors, so that their writing seems to say, "I am proud to put my name on this work."

PART B   Subject, Audience, and Purpose

Early in the prewriting phase, you should give some thought to your subject, audience, and purpose.

Whenever possible, choose a **subject** that you know and care about: life in Cleveland, working with learning-disabled children, repairing motorcycles, overcoming shyness, watching a friend struggle with drug addiction, succeeding in college. You may not realize how many subjects you do know or have strong opinions about. What special experience or expertise do you have? What angers you, inspires you, saddens you? What do you love to do? The answers to these questions will suggest good subjects to write about. In college courses, instructors often assign a broad subject. Try to narrow this subject toward some specific aspect that intrigues you. If you have interest, energy, and passion about a topic, then probably your readers will, too.

Just how you approach your subject will depend on your readers—your **audience.** Ask yourself who these readers are: your classmates, your professor, other students at your college, your boss, youngsters in your community, people who probably agree with you, people who don't. Keeping your audience in mind will help you know what information to include and what to leave out. For example, if you are writing about rap music for an audience of middle-aged parents, you will explain your subject differently than you will to an audience of eighteen-year-old rap fans. What do your readers already know about your subject? What may they need or want to learn?

Next you will want to think about your **purpose** in writing. Do you want to explain something to your readers, persuade them that a certain view is correct, entertain them, tell a good story, or some combination of these? Keeping your purpose in mind will help you write more effectively. For example, if your purpose is to persuade your company to recycle its paper and glass, you may want to write about ways in which recycling will benefit the company: Recycling can earn or save money, improve the company's image, or make employees proud to work there.

PRACTICE 1

List five subjects that you might like to write about. For ideas, reread the list of possible subjects and the questions in Part B, page 4. Consider your audience and purpose: For whom are you writing? What do you want them to know about your subject? Notice how the audience and purpose will help shape your paper.

	Subject	Audience	Purpose
EXAMPLE	my recipe for chili	inexperienced cooks	to show how easy it is to make chili
1.			
2.			
3.			
4.			
5.			

PRACTICE 2

Jot down ideas for these three assignments, by yourself or with a group of classmates. Notice how your ideas and details differ, depending on the audience and purpose.

1. You have been asked to write a description of your college for local high school students. Your purpose is to encourage them to enroll in your college after graduating from high school. What kinds of information should you include? What will your audience want to know?

2. You have been asked to write a description of your college for the governor of your state. Your purpose is to persuade her or him to spend more money to improve your college. What information should you include? What will your audience want to know?

3. You have been asked to write a description of your college for your best friend, who attends a college out of state. Your purpose is to share your personal impressions and experiences. What information should you include? What will your audience want to know?

CHAPTER 2

Prewriting to Generate Ideas

PART A	Freewriting
PART B	Brainstorming
PART C	Clustering
PART D	Asking Questions
PART E	Keeping a Journal

This chapter presents five effective prewriting techniques that will help you get your ideas onto paper (or onto the computer). These techniques can help you overcome the "blank-page jitters" that many people face when they first sit down to write. You also can use them to generate new ideas at any point in the writing process. Try all five to see which ones work best for you.

In addition, if you write on a computer, try prewriting in different ways: on paper and on computer. Some writers feel they produce better work if they prewrite by hand and only later transfer their best ideas onto the computer. Every writer has personal preferences, so don't be afraid to experiment.

PART A   Freewriting

Freewriting is an excellent method that many writers use to warm up and to generate ideas. These are the guidelines: for five, ten, or fifteen minutes, write rapidly, without stopping, about anything that comes into your head. If you feel stuck, just repeat or rhyme the last word you wrote, but *don't stop writing*. And don't worry about grammar, logic, complete sentences, or grades.

The point of freewriting is to write so quickly that ideas can flow without comments from your inner critic. The *inner critic* is the voice inside that says, every time you have an idea, "That's dumb; that's no good; cross that out." Freewriting helps you tell this voice, "Thank you for your opinion. Once I have lots of ideas and words on paper, I'll invite you back for comment."

After you freewrite, read what you have written, underlining or marking any parts you like.

Here is one student's first freewriting, with his own underlinings:

> Boy I wish this class was over and I could go home and get out of this building, boy was my day miserable and this sure is a crazy thing to do <u>if a shrink could see us now</u>. My I just remember I've got to buy that CD my my my I am running out of stuff to write but dont worry teach because this is really the nuttiest thing but lots of fun you probably like reading this mixed up thing That girl's remark sounded dumb but impressing. You know <u>this writing sure puts muscles in your fingers</u> if I stop writing oh boy this is the most incredible assignment in the world think and write without worrying about sentence structure and other English garbage to stall you down boy that guy next to me is writing like crazy so he looks crazy you know this is outrageous I'm writing and writing I never realized the extent of mental and physical concentration it takes to do this constantly <u>dont mind the legibility of my hand my hand oh my hand is ready to drop off</u> please this is crazy crazy and too much work for a poor guy like myself. Imagine me putting on paper all I have to say and faster than a speeding bullet.

■ This example has the lively energy of many freewritings. Why do you think the student underlined what he did? Would you have underlined other words or phrases? Why?

Freewriting is a powerful tool for helping you turn thoughts and feelings into words, especially when you are unsure about what you want to say. Sometimes freewriting produces only nonsense; often, however, it can help you zoom in on possible topics, interests, and worthwhile writing you can use later.

If you are freewriting on a computer, try turning off the monitor and writing "blind." Some students find that this helps them forget about making mistakes and concentrate on getting words and ideas out fast.

PRACTICE 1

1. Set a timer for ten minutes or have someone time you. Freewrite without stopping for the full ten minutes. If you get stuck, repeat or rhyme the last word you wrote until words start flowing again but *don't stop writing!*

2. When you finish, write down one or two words that describe how you felt while freewriting.

   _____

   _____

3. Next, read your freewriting. Underline any words or lines you like—anything that strikes you as interesting, thoughtful, or funny. If nothing strikes you, that's okay.

PRACTICE 2

Try three more freewritings at home—each one ten minutes long. Do them at different times of day or night when you have a quiet moment. If possible, use a timer. Set it for ten minutes; then write quickly and freely until it rings. Later, read over your freewritings and underline any striking lines or ideas.

Focused Freewriting

In **focused freewriting**, you simply try to focus your thoughts on one subject as you freewrite. The subject might be one assigned by your instructor, one you choose, or one you have discovered in unfocused freewriting. The goal of most writing is a polished, organized piece of writing; focused freewriting can help you generate ideas or narrow a topic to one aspect that interests you.

Here is one student's focused freewriting on the topic *someone who strongly influenced you:*

Mr. Martin, the reason I'm interested in science. Wiry, five-foot-four-inch, hyperactive guy. A darting bird in the classroom, a circling teacher-bird, now jabbing at the knee bone of a skeleton, now banging on the jar with the brain in it. Like my brain used to feel, pickled, before I took his class. I always liked science but everything else was too hard. I almost dropped out of school, discouraged, but Martin was fun, crazy, made me think. Encouragement was his thing. Whacking his pencil against the plastic model of an eyeball in his office, he would bellow at me, "Taking too many courses! Working too many hours in that restaurant! Living everyone else's life but your own!" Gradually, I slowed down, got myself focused. Saw him last at graduation, where he thwacked my diploma with his pencil, shouting, "Keep up the good work! Live your own life! Follow your dreams!"

■ This student later used this focused freewriting—its vivid details about Mr. Martin and his influence—as the basis for an effective paper. Underline any words or lines that you find especially striking or appealing. Be prepared to explain why you like what you underline.

PRACTICE 3

Do a three-minute focused freewriting on three of these topics:

beach	body piercing
friendship	parent (*or* child)
news	tests

Underline as usual. Did you surprise yourself by having so much to say about any one topic? Perhaps you would like to write more about that topic.

1. Read over your earlier freewritings and notice your underlinings. Would you like to write more about any underlined words or ideas? Write two or three such words or ideas here:

    _____

    _____

    _____

2. Now choose one word or idea. Focus your thoughts on it and do a ten-minute focused freewriting. Try to stick to the topic as you write but don't worry too much about keeping on track; just keep writing.

PART B   Brainstorming

Another prewriting technique that may work for you is **brainstorming** or freely jotting down ideas about a topic. As in freewriting, the purpose is to generate lots of ideas so you have something to work with and choose from. Write everything that comes to you about a topic—words and phrases, ideas, details, examples.

After you have brainstormed, read over your list, underlining interesting or exciting ideas you might develop further. As with freewriting, many writers brainstorm on a general subject, underline, and then brainstorm again as they focus on one aspect of that subject.

Here is one student's brainstorm list on the topic *e-mail:*

> everyone has it—really neat
>
> can send mail day or night
>
> not like snail mail—so slow
>
> I hate to write letters but I love to e-mail
>
> I e-mail my friends at their colleges all the time
>
> I even e-mail my little brother at home
>
> more intimate than phone calls—you can share inner thoughts
>
> Mom's always sending me e-mails
>
> she e-mails her old college friends, too
>
> people are more in touch with each other now

With brainstorming, this writer generated many ideas and started to move toward a more focused topic: *People are more in touch with each other now because of e-mail*. With a narrowed topic, brainstorming once more can help the writer generate details and reasons to support the idea.

Choose one of the following topics that interests you and write it at the top of your paper or computer screen. Then brainstorm. Write anything that comes into your head about the topic. Just let ideas pour out fast!

1. a place I want to go back to
2. dealing with difficult people
3. an unforgettable person in politics, sports, or religious life

4. growing up
5. my best/worst job
6. a first or blind date

Once you fill a page with your list, read it over, marking the most interesting ideas. Draw arrows or highlight and move text on your screen to connect related ideas. Is there one idea that might be the subject of a paper?

PART C Clustering

Some writers use still another method—called **clustering** or **mapping**—to get their ideas onto paper. To begin clustering, simply write an idea or a topic, usually one word, in the center of a piece of paper. Then let your mind make associations, and write these associations branching out from the center.

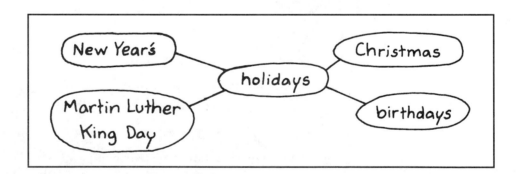

When one idea suggests other ideas, details, and examples, write these around it in a "cluster." After you finish, pick the cluster that most interests you. You may wish to freewrite for more ideas.

Choose one of these topics or another topic that interests you. Write it in the center of a piece of paper and then try clustering. Keep writing down associations until you have filled most of the page.

1. heroes   4. inspiration

2. holidays   5. a dream

3. food   6. movies

PART D   Asking Questions

Many writers get ideas about a subject by asking questions and trying to answer them. This section describes two ways of doing this.

The Reporter's Six Questions

Newspaper reporters often answer six basic questions at the beginning of an article: **Who? What? Where? When? Why? How?** Here is the way one student used these questions to explore the general subject of *sports* assigned by his instructor:

Who?	Players, basketball and football players, coaches, fans. Violence—I'm tired of that subject. Loyal crazy screaming fans—Giants fans.
What?	Excitement. Stadium on the day of a game. Tailgate parties. Cookouts. Incredible spreads—Italian families with peppers, stuff to spread on sandwiches. All day partying. Radios, TVs, grills, Giants caps.
Where?	Giants Stadium parking lot. People gather in certain areas—meet me in 10-B. Stadiums all over the country, same thing. People party on tailgates, in cars, on cars, plastic chairs, blankets.
When?	People arrive early morning—cook breakfast, lunch. After the game, many stay on in parking lot, talking, drinking beer. Year after year they come back.
Why?	Big social occasion, emotional outlet.
How?	They come early to get space. Some stadiums now rent parking spaces. Some families pass on season tickets in their wills!

Notice the way this writer uses the questions to focus his ideas about tailgate parties at Giants Stadium. He has already come up with many interesting details for a good paper.

Ask Your Own Questions

If the reporter's six questions seem too confining, just ask the questions *you* want answered about a subject. Let each answer suggest the next question.

Here is how one student responded to the subject of *teenage pregnancy:*

What do I know about teenage pregnancy? I saw my sister's plans for her future cut short by pregnancy. She won a high-school fashion design award, was spunky, full of fun. Now, with a child to raise, she works in a diner. The father of the child disappeared two years ago.

What would I like to know? Why do teenagers get pregnant? Teenage girls think they can't get pregnant. Teenage boys think it's macho to get a girl pregnant. Lack of knowledge of birth control methods. Teenage girls think that having a baby will keep their boyfriends from leaving them. They think that babies are fun to have around, to play with.

Where can I get more information? Guidance counselors at my old school. Planned Parenthood. Interview my friends who had babies when they were still teenagers. Talk to my sister.

What would I like to focus on? What interests me? I would like to know what pressures, fears, and hopes teenage girls feel that would allow them to take the chance of becoming pregnant.

What is my point of view? I would like teenagers to be aware of how their lives will be forever changed by a pregnancy.

Who is my audience? I would like to write for teenagers—primarily girls—to help them understand the problems of teenage pregnancy.

PRACTICE 7

Answer the reporter's six questions on one of the following topics or on a topic of your own choice.

1. drug addiction
2. sports
3. career goals
4. neighbors/neighborhood

5. music
6. family get-togethers
7. living a simple life
8. choosing a major or concentration

PRACTICE 8

Ask and answer at least five questions of your own about one of the topics in Practice 7. Use these questions if you wish: What do I know about this subject? What would I like to know? Where can I find answers to my questions? What would I like to focus on? What is my point of view about this subject? Who is my audience?

PART E   Keeping a Journal

Keeping a journal is an excellent way to practice your writing skills and discover ideas for further writing. Your journal is mostly for you—a private place where you record your experiences and your inner life; it is the place where, as one writer says, "I discover what I really think by writing it down."

You can keep a journal in a notebook or on a computer. If you prefer handwriting, get yourself an attractive notebook with 8½-by-11-inch paper. If you prefer to work on a computer, just open a "Journal" folder or keep a "Journal" disk. Then every morning or night, or several times a week, write for at least fifteen minutes in this journal. Don't just record the day's events. ("I went to the store. It rained. I came home.") Instead, write in detail about what most angered, moved, or amused you that day.

Write about what you really care about—motorcycles, loneliness, working in a doughnut shop, family relationships, grades, ending or starting a relationship. You may be surprised by how much you know. Write, think, and write some more. Your journal is private, so don't worry about grammar or correctness. Instead, aim to capture your truth so exactly that someone reading your words might experience it too.

You might also carry a little 3-by-5-inch pad with you during the day for "fast sketches," jotting down things that catch your attention: a man playing drums in the street; a baby wearing a bib that reads *Spit Happens*; a compliment you receive at work; something your child just learned to do.

Every journal is unique—and usually private—but here are two sample journal entries to suggest possibilities. The first student links a quotation he has just learned to a disturbing "lesson of love":

Apr. 11. Two weeks ago, our professor mentioned a famous quote: "It is better to have loved and lost than never to have loved at all." The words had no particular meaning for me. How wrong I was. Last Sunday I received some very distressing news that will change my life from now on.

My wife has asked me why I never notified any family members except my mother of the birth of our children. My reply has been an argument or an angry stare. Our daughter Angelica is now two months shy of her second birthday, and we were also blessed with the birth of a son, who is five months old. I don't know whether it was maturity or my conscience, but last Sunday I decided it was time to let past grievances be forgotten. Nothing on this green earth would shelter me from what I was to hear that day.

I went to my father's address, knocked on his door, but got no response. Nervous but excited, I knocked again. Silence. On leaving the building, I bumped into his neighbor and asked for the possible whereabouts of my father. I couldn't brace myself for the cold shock of hearing from him that my father had died. I was angry as well as saddened, for my father was a quiet and gentle man whose love of women, liquor, and good times exceeded the love of his son.

Yes, it would have been better to have loved my father as he was than never to have gotten the opportunity to love such a man. A lesson of love truly woke me up to the need to hold dearly the ones you care for and overcome unnecessary grudges. "I love you, Pop, and may you rest in peace. Que Díos te guide."

—Anthony Falu (Student)

In the more freely written journal entry that follows, another student writes in order to sort out her feelings. As you read, ask yourself what seems to be bothering her. Is it really a cold? Is it the cat?

Nov. 5. The coffee and the donut can wait—not particularly in the mood for that now. Not in the mood for this journal either, but maybe I'll find out what's going on or why I feel so bad. I'm a little sleepy, have less patience lately, especially stupidity—questions asked without thinking. Why do I feel my time's wasted? Shouldn't. Just a little irritable, worried about this cold I'm getting and why Don seemed upset when I asked him about visiting his sister. I didn't sleep very well last night. Maybe the cat's at fault. She must have been cold and crawled under the covers, so I pushed her out and Don woke up. Or he shoved her off the bed when her whiskers tickled his nose and that woke me up. So we fought again. Now I'm the one who gets up at 7 a.m., and he's the one in the beautiful picture of a tired sleeping male form under the covers, calico cat curled up, sleeping off the breakfast I just gave her. Wish I didn't have to leave.

The uses of a journal are limited only by your imagination. Here are some ideas:

■ Write down your career goals and dreams; then brainstorm steps you can take to make them reality. (Notice negative thoughts—"I can't do that. That will never work." Focus on positive thoughts—"Of course I can! If X can do it, so can I.")

■ Write about a problem you are having and creative ways in which you might solve it.

■ Analyze yourself as a student. What are your strengths and weaknesses? What can you do to build on the strengths and overcome the weaknesses?

■ What college course have you most enjoyed? Why?

■ Who believes in you? Who seems not to believe in you? How do these attitudes make you feel?

■ Imagine five other lives you might want to live. Who would you be: a figure skater? an inventor? a surgeon?

■ If you could change one thing about yourself, what would it be? What might you do to change it?

■ If you could spend time with one famous person, living or dead, who would it be? Why?

■ List five things you would love to do if they didn't seem so crazy.

■ Do you have an important secret? Kept from whom? How do you feel about keeping this secret? Why *do* people have secrets?

■ Name three people you are supposed to admire; then name three you really do admire. Do the differences teach you anything about yourself?

■ If money were no object, what place in the world would you visit and why? What would you do there, whom would you take, and how long would you stay?

■ Use your journal as a place to think about material that you have read in a text-book, newspaper, magazine, or the Internet.

■ What news story most upset you in the past month? Why?

■ Write down facts that impress you—the average young American watches 18,000 TV murders before graduating from high school! Analyzing that one fact could produce a good paper.

■ Record quotations that spark your interest. Suppose you jot down Abe Lincoln's statement that "most folks are as happy as they make up their minds to be." Later, thinking and writing about that thought could produce a whole paragraph or composition.

■ Read through the Quotation Bank at the end of this book, and copy your five favorite quotations into your journal.

PRACTICE 9

Get a notebook or set up your computer journal. Write for at least fifteen minutes three times a week.

At the end of each week, reread what you have written or typed. Underline sections or ideas you like and put a check mark next to subjects you might like to write more about.

PRACTICE 10

Choose one passage in your journal that you would like to rewrite and let others read. Mark the parts you like best. Now rewrite and polish the passage so you would be proud to show it to someone else.

Using Just One of Your Five Senses, Describe a Place

Readers of a finished paper can easily forget that they are reading the *end result* of someone else's writing process. The writer has already thought about audience and purpose, zoomed in on a subject, and prewritten to get ideas.

Here is one student's response to the following assignment: "Using just one of the five senses—smell, hearing, taste, touch, or sight—describe a special place." In your class or group, read the paper, aloud if possible. As you read, underline words or lines that strike you as especially well written or powerful.

Noises in My Village

Orlu, my village in Nigeria, has a population of about five hundred sounds. The sounds range from the clucking of the rooster in the morning to the rumbling of people getting ready for market. You hear the shrill cry of the widow and the squeaking of the rats. At the farm, two men start a fight over land and slam each other on the ground with great thuds. Water flows with a rushing sound from the rocks into the river, and the trees whisper themselves. People fill their earthen pots with water while children splash into the water after washing their clothes. From a distance, a lost goat bleats, "Meeee, meee." At the village square, bamboo drums sound, "Drooom, drooom." This signifies a curfew for the women. A young man tells how his friend bought a car that sounded "Vrooom, vrooom." At dusk people return from the market. One woman shouts at the top of her voice, "I forgot my palm oil keg!" and rushes to get it. After supper children gather at the village square. They clap their hands and listen to folk tales. From distance, the town crier announces the arrival of the new moon.

—Chinwe Okorie (Student)

1. How effective is Ms. Okorie's paper?

   _____ Good topic for a college audience?   _____ Clear main idea?

   _____ Rich supporting details?   _____ Logical organization?

2. Does the first sentence make you want to read on? Why or why not?

3. Which of the five senses does the writer emphasize? What words reveal this?

4. Discuss your underlinings with the group or class. Try to explain why a particular word or sentence is effective. For instance, the fourth sentence contains such precise words that we can almost hear the two men "*slam* each other *on the ground* with great *thuds*."

5. Would you suggest that the writer make any improvements? For instance, does the word *cluck* accurately describe the sound roosters make?

6. Last, proofread for grammar, spelling, and omitted words. Do you spot any error patterns (the same type of error made two or more times) that this student should watch out for?

> Of her prewriting process, Chinwe Okorie writes: "I decided to write about my village in Africa because I thought my American classmates (my audience) would find that more interesting than the local neighborhood. This paper also taught me the importance of brainstorming. I filled two whole pages with my brainstorming list, and then it was easy to pick the best details."

GROUP WORK

Imagine that you have been given this assignment: *Using just one of the five senses, describe a special place.* Your audience will be your college writing class. Working as a group, plan a paper and prewrite. First, choose a place that your group will describe; if it is a place on campus, your instructor might even want you to go there. Second, decide whether you will emphasize sound, smell, taste, touch, or sight. Choose someone to write down the group's ideas, and then brainstorm. List as many sounds (or smells, etc.) as your group can think of. Fill at least one page. Now read back the list and put a check next to the best details; does your group agree or disagree about which ones are best?

You are well on your way to an excellent paper. Each group member can now complete the assignment, based on the list. If necessary, prewrite again for more details.

 ## WRITING AND REVISING IDEAS

1. Using one of your five senses, describe a place. You might use a first sentence like this:

   _____ has a population of about five hundred _____.
   (place)   (smells, tastes, etc.)

2. List unusual experiences you have had that your classmates and professor might like to read about (a job, time in another country, and so on). Choose one of these and prewrite; use the prewriting method of your choice and fill at least a page with ideas.

UNIT 2

Discovering the Paragraph

CHAPTER 3

The Process of Writing Paragraphs

PART A	Defining and Looking at the Paragraph
PART B	Narrowing the Topic and Writing the Topic Sentence
PART C	Generating Ideas for the Body
PART D	Selecting and Dropping Ideas
PART E	Arranging Ideas in a Plan or an Outline
PART F	Writing and Revising the Paragraph

This chapter will guide you step by step from examining basic paragraphs to writing them. The paragraph makes a good learning model because it is short yet contains many of the elements found in longer compositions. Therefore, you easily can transfer the skills you gain by writing paragraphs to longer essays, reports, and letters.

In this chapter, you will first look at finished paragraphs and then move through the process of writing paragraphs of your own.

PART A   Defining and Looking at the Paragraph

A **paragraph** is a group of related sentences that develops one main idea. Although there is no definite length for a paragraph, it is often from five to twelve sentences long. A paragraph usually occurs with other paragraphs in a longer piece of writing—an essay, an article, or a letter, for example. Before studying longer compositions, however, we will look at single paragraphs.

A paragraph looks like this on the page:

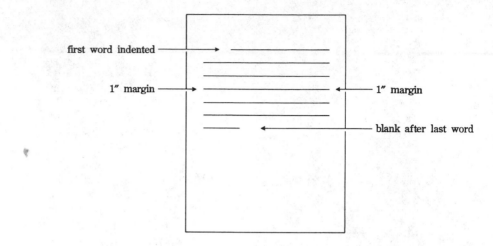

■ Clearly **indent** the first word of every paragraph about 1 inch (five spaces on the computer).

■ Extend every line of a paragraph as close to the right-hand margin as possible.

■ However, if the last word of the paragraph comes before the end of the line, leave the rest of the line blank.

Topic Sentence and Body

Most paragraphs contain one main idea to which all the sentences relate.

The **topic sentence** states this main idea.

The **body** of the paragraph develops and supports this main idea with particular facts, details, and examples:

I allow the spiders the run of the house. I figure that any predator that hopes to make a living on whatever smaller creatures might blunder into a four-inch-square bit of space in the corner of the bathroom where the tub meets the floor needs every bit of my support. They catch flies and even field crickets in those webs. Large spiders in barns have been known to trap, wrap, and suck hummingbirds, but there's no danger of that here. I tolerate the webs, only occasionally sweeping away the very dirtiest of them after the spider itself has scrambled to safety. I'm always leaving a bath towel draped over the tub so that the big, haired spiders, who are constantly getting trapped by the tub's smooth sides, can use its rough surface as an exit ramp. Inside the house the spiders have only given me one mild surprise. I washed some dishes and set them to dry over a plastic drainer. Then I wanted a cup of coffee, so I picked from the drainer my mug, which was still warm from the hot rinse water, and across the rim of the mug, strand after strand, was a spider web.

—Annie Dillard, *Pilgrim at Tinker Creek*

■ The first sentence of Dillard's paragraph is the **topic sentence.** It states the main idea of the paragraph: that *the spiders are allowed the run of the house.*

■ The rest of the paragraph, the **body,** fully explains and supports this statement. The writer first gives a reason for her attitude toward spiders and then gives particular examples of her tolerance of spiders.

The topic sentence is more *general* than the other sentences in the paragraph. The other sentences in the paragraph provide specific information relating to the topic sentence. Because the topic sentence tells what the entire paragraph is about, *it is usually the first sentence,* as in the example. Sometimes the topic sentence occurs elsewhere in the paragraph, for example, as the sentence after an introduction or as the last sentence. Some paragraphs contain only an implied topic sentence but no stated topic sentence at all.

As you develop your writing skills, however, it is a good idea to write paragraphs that *begin* with the topic sentence. Once you have mastered this pattern, you can try variations.

PRACTICE 1

Find and underline the **topic sentence** in each of the following paragraphs. Look for the sentence that states the **main idea** of the entire paragraph. Be careful: the topic sentence is not always the first sentence.

Paragraph a   The summer picnic gave ladies a chance to show off their baking hands. On the barbecue pit, chickens and spareribs sputtered in their own fat and in a sauce whose recipe was guarded in the family like a scandalous affair. However, every true baking artist could reveal her prize to the delight and criticism of the town. Orange sponge cakes and dark brown mounds dripping Hershey's chocolate stood layer to layer with ice-white coconuts and light brown caramels. Pound cakes sagged with their buttery weight and small children could no more resist licking the icings than their mothers could avoid slapping the sticky fingers.

—Maya Angelou, *I Know Why the Caged Bird Sings*

Paragraph b   Something strange and wonderful has happened, and it challenges much of what we thought we knew about living to be very old. All over the country, the number of people who last to and beyond the age of 100—the centenarians—has been soaring. There are more than 52,000 in America today, almost three times the number in 1980. They have become the fastest-growing age group not only in this country but throughout the industrialized world. New studies show that Americans live longer after the age of 80 than other national groups. In fact, after the age of 85, the odds that you will die in the next year or two actually level off. And half of today's centenarians are in good health, both physically and mentally.

—Caryl Stern, "Who Is Old?" *Parade*

Paragraph c   Eating sugar can be worse than eating nothing. Refined sugar provides only empty calories. It contributes none of the protein, fat, vitamins or minerals needed for its own metabolism in the body, so these nutrients must be obtained elsewhere. Sugar tends to replace nourishing food in the diet. It is a thief that robs us of nutrients. A dietary emphasis on sugar can deplete the body of nutrients. If adequate nutrients are not supplied by the diet—and they tend not to be in a sugar-rich diet—they must be leached from other body tissues before sugar can be metabolized. For this reason, a U.S. Senate committee labeled sugar as an "antinutrient."

—Janice Fillip, "The Sweet Thief," *Medical Self-Care*

Paragraph d   At local noontime on the Moon, surface temperatures rise above the boiling point of water. But at night or in the shade, the temperature plummets to well below water's freezing point. Warmth does not spread on the Moon's surface, for lunar soil is made of pulverized dust that does not conduct heat well. Nor does heat move through lunar air, for the Moon has no air. Without an artificial Earth habitat such as a spacecraft or spacesuit, humans could not survive on the Moon.

—Eric Chaisson and Steve McMillan, *Astronomy Today*

PRACTICE 2

Each group of sentences below could be unscrambled and written as a paragraph. Circle the letter of the **topic sentence** in each group of sentences. Remember: The topic sentence should state the main idea of the entire paragraph and should be general enough to include all the ideas in the body.

EXAMPLE
a. Rubies were supposed to stimulate circulation and restore lost vitality.
b. Clear quartz was believed to promote sweet sleep and good dreams.
c. For centuries, minerals and precious stones were thought to possess healing powers.
d. Amethysts were thought to prevent drunkenness.
(Sentence c includes the ideas in all the other sentences.)

1. a. Tiger Woods first appeared on television at the age of two, winning a putting contest against comedian Bob Hope.

    b. The world took note in 1997 when he won the famous Masters Golf Championship by twelve strokes, the largest margin of victory in any major golf championship of the twentieth century.

    c. At age twenty-one, Tiger Woods was not only the youngest person but the first person of color to win the Masters.

    d. Coached by his father, Earl Woods, Tiger Woods spent his teen years honing his skills and winning one junior and amateur golf title after another.

    e. Nike featured him in a series of stylish commercials that helped give golf a younger, "cooler" image.

    f. Tiger Woods has become a sports legend through his exceptional talent and his role in attracting young people and minorities to the game of golf.

2. a. Though they often wield their powerful trunks aggressively, elephants are just as likely to use their trunks to offer greetings by entwining them in a "trunk shake."

    b. One of the trunk's many functions is to suck up gallons of water, which it carries to the mouth for drinking or sprays on the back like a flexible showerhead.

    c. An elephant's trunk is a marvel of engineering.

    d. The trunk is sensitive enough to pick up a thin dime off a concrete floor and strong enough to carry several hundred pounds of mahogany logs.

3. a. Albert Einstein, whose scientific genius awed the world, did not speak until he was four and could not read until he was nine.

   b. Inventor Thomas Edison had such severe problems reading, writing, and spelling that he was called "defective from birth," taken out of school, and taught at home.

   c. Many famous people have suffered from learning disabilities.

   d. Olympic diving champion Greg Louganis was teased and laughed at for his speech delay, stutter, and perceptual problems.

4. a. Here at Kensington College, without our student numbers, we would hardly exist.

   b. We must display our student numbers and IDs just to get onto campus.

   c. We must pencil our student numbers on computer cards in order to register for courses.

   d. When our grades are posted, the A's and F's go not to Felicia Watson and Bill Jenkins, Jr., but to 237–002 and 235–1147.

5. a. The left side of the human brain controls spoken and written language.

   b. The right side, on the other hand, seems to control artistic, musical, and spatial skills.

   c. Emotion is also thought to be controlled by the right hemisphere.

   d. The human brain has two distinct halves, or hemispheres, and in most people, each one controls different functions.

   e. Logical reasoning and mathematics are left-brain skills.

   f. Interestingly, the left brain controls the right hand and vice versa.

6. a. The better skaters glided in wide circles, playing tag or crack the whip.

   b. Every winter, the lake was the center of activity.

   c. People talked and shoveled snow, exposing the dark, satiny ice.

   d. Children on double runners skated in the center of the cleared area.

   e. Dogs raced and skidded among the skaters.

7. a. This college student from Los Angeles could not find pastel nail polish in the stores, so she started mixing her own.

   b. When Mohajer took samples to a trendy shop in 1995, one customer snapped up four bottles at $18 apiece.

   c. Celebrities like Alicia Silverstone started buying the polish in colors like pea green and black, with offbeat names like "Geek," "Tantrum," and "Trailer Trash."

   d. Mohajer received so many compliments that she decided to start selling her product.

   e. Soon the business was so big that Mohajer hired someone to handle the finances.

   f. With only a fine sense of style and a knack for mixing colors, twenty-two-year-old Dineh Mohajer created a $10-million company.

8. a. Male and female insects are attracted to each other by visual, auditory, and chemical means.

   b. Through its chirping call, the male cricket attracts a mate and drives other males out of its territory.

   c. Butterflies attract by sight, and their brightly colored wings play an important role in courtship.

   d. Some female insects, flies among them, release chemicals called *pheromones* that attract males of the species.

9. a. At the University of Michigan, he helped develop a flu vaccine.

   b. He served as a consultant to the World Health Organization, a branch of the United Nations that brings medical help to developing countries.

   c. Dr. Jonas Salk contributed much to the cure of disease.

   d. After years of research, he finally created the first effective polio vaccine.

   e. When Dr. Salk died in 1995, he was working on an AIDS vaccine.

10. a. Believe it or not, the first contact lens was drawn by Leonardo da Vinci in 1508.

    b. However, not until 1877 was the first thick glass contact actually made by a Swiss doctor.

    c. The journey of contact lenses from an idea to a comfortable, safe reality took nearly five hundred years.

    d. In 1948, smaller, more comfortable plastic lenses were introduced to enthusiastic American eyeglass wearers.

    e. These early glass lenses were enormous, covering the whites of the eyes.

    f. Today, contact lens wearers can choose ultra-thin, colored, or even disposable lenses.

PART B   Narrowing the Topic and Writing the Topic Sentence

A writer can arrive at the goal—a finished paragraph—in several ways. However, before writing a paragraph, most writers go through a process that includes these important steps:

1. Narrowing the topic

2. Writing the topic sentence

3. Generating ideas for the body

4. Selecting and dropping ideas

5. Arranging ideas in a plan or an outline

The rest of this chapter will explain these steps and guide you through the process of writing basic paragraphs.

Narrowing the Topic

As a student, you may be assigned broad writing topics by your instructor—success, cheating in schools, a description of a person. Your instructor is giving you the chance to cut the topic down to size and choose one aspect of the topic *that interests you*.

Suppose, for example, that your instructor gives this assignment: "Write a paragraph describing a person you know." The challenge is to pick someone you would *like* to write about, someone who interests you and also would probably interest your readers.

Thinking about your *audience* and *purpose* may help you narrow the topic. In this case, your audience probably will be your instructor and classmates; your purpose is to inform or perhaps to entertain them by describing a person you want to write about.

Many writers find it useful at this point—on paper or on computer—to brainstorm, freewrite, or ask themselves questions: "What person do I love or hate or admire? Is there a family member I would enjoy writing about? Who is the funniest, most unusual, or most talented person I know?"

Let's suppose you choose Pete, an unusual person and one about whom you have something to say. But Pete is still too broad a subject for one paragraph; you could probably write pages and pages about him. To narrow the topic further, you might ask yourself, "What is unusual about him? What might interest others?" Pete's room is the messiest place you have ever seen; in fact, Pete's whole life is sloppy, and you decide that you could write a good paragraph about that. You have now narrowed the topic to just one of Pete's qualities: *his sloppiness*.

Writing the Topic Sentence

The next important step is to state your topic clearly *in sentence form*. Writing the topic sentence helps you further narrow your topic by forcing you to make a statement about it. The simplest possible topic sentence about Pete might read *Pete is sloppy*, but you might wish to strengthen it by saying, for instance, *Pete's sloppiness is a terrible habit*.

Writing a good topic sentence is an important step toward an effective paragraph because the topic sentence controls the direction and scope of the body. A topic sentence should have a clear *controlling idea* and should be a *complete sentence*.

You can think of the topic sentence as having two parts, a **topic** and a **controlling idea.** The controlling idea states the writer's point of view or attitude about the topic.

topic   controlling idea

Topic sentence: Pete's sloppiness is a terrible habit.

The controlling idea helps you focus on just one aspect or point. Here are three possible topic sentences about the topic *a memorable job*.

1. My job in the complaint department taught me how to calm down angry people.

2. Two years in the complaint department persuaded me to become an assistant manager.

3. Working in the complaint department persuaded me to become a veterinarian.

■ These topic sentences all explore the same topic—working in a complaint department—but each controlling idea is different. The controlling idea in 1 is *taught me how to calm down angry people*.

■ What is the controlling idea in 2? _____

What is the controlling idea in 3? _____

■ Notice the way in which the controlling idea lets the reader know what the paragraph will be about. There are many possible topic sentences for any topic, depending on the writer's interests and point of view. If you were assigned the topic *a memorable job*, what would your topic sentence be?

_____

_____

PRACTICE 3

Read each topic sentence below. Circle the topic and underline the controlling idea.

1. A low-fat diet provides many health benefits.
2. MTV's *Road Rules* is both entertaining and educational.
3. Our football coach works to build players' self-esteem.
4. This campus offers many peaceful places where students can relax.
5. My cousin's truck looks like something out of *Star Wars*.

As a rule, the more specific and clear your topic and controlling idea, the better the paragraph; in other words, your topic sentence should not be so broad that it cannot be developed in one paragraph. Which of these topic sentences do you think will produce the best paragraphs?

4. Five wet, bug-filled days at Camp Nirvana made me a fan of the great indoors.
5. This town has problems.
6. Road rage is on the rise for three reasons.

■ Topic sentences 4 and 6 are both specific enough to write a good paragraph about. In each, the topic sentence is carefully worded to suggest clearly what ideas will follow. From topic sentence 4, what do you expect the paragraph to include?

_____

■ What do you expect paragraph 6 to include?

_____

■ Topic sentence 5, on the other hand, is so broad that a paragraph could include almost anything. Just what problems does the town have? Strained relations between police and the community? Litter in public parks? Termites? The writer needs to rewrite the controlling idea, focusing on just one problem for an effective paragraph.

The topic sentence also must be a **complete sentence.** It must contain a subject and a verb, and express a complete thought.* Do not confuse a topic with a

---

* For practice in correcting fragments, see Chapter 25, "Avoiding Sentence Errors," Part B.

topic sentence. For instance, *a celebrity I would like to meet* cannot be a topic sentence because it is not a sentence; however, it could be a title* because topics and titles need not be complete sentences. One possible topic sentence might read, *A celebrity I would like to meet is writer Julia Alvarez.*

Do not write *This paragraph will be about . . .* or *In this paper I will write about. . . .* Instead, craft your topic sentence carefully to focus the topic and let your reader know what the paragraph will contain. Make every word count.

PRACTICE 4

Put a check beside each topic sentence that is focused enough to allow you to write a good paragraph. If a topic sentence is too broad, narrow the topic according to your own interests and write a new topic sentence with a clear controlling idea.

EXAMPLES

✓ Keeping a journal can improve a student's writing.

Rewrite: _____

___ This paper will be about my family.

Rewrite: My brother Mark has a unique sense of humor._____

1. ___ Eugene's hot temper causes problems at work.

   Rewrite: _____

   _____

2. ___ This paragraph will discuss study techniques.

   Rewrite: _____

   _____

3. ___ Bilingualism is a great asset in the workplace.

   Rewrite: _____

   _____

4. ___ Many beer commercials on TV imply that people need to drink in order to have a good time.

   Rewrite: _____

   _____

_____

*For practice in writing titles, see Chapter 16, "The Introduction, the Conclusion, and the Title," Part C.

5. ___ Child abuse is something to think about.

Rewrite: _____

_____

6. ___ Students should not be allowed to wear short shorts or revealing clothing on campus.

Rewrite: _____

_____

7. ___ Learning karate increased my self-confidence.

Rewrite: _____

_____

8. ___ Companies should not read employees' e-mail.

Rewrite: _____

_____

PRACTICE 5

Here is a list of broad topics. Choose three that interest you from this list or from your own list on page 5. Narrow each topic, choose your controlling idea, and write a topic sentence focused enough to write a good paragraph about. Make sure that each topic sentence has a clear controlling idea and is a complete sentence.

Overcoming fears	Insider's tour of your community
Popular music	Balancing work and play
Credit cards	A person you like or dislike
An act of cowardice or courage	A time when you were (or were not) in control

1. Narrowed topic: _____

Controlling idea: _____

Topic sentence: _____

_____

_____

2. Narrowed topic: _____

   Controlling idea: _____

   Topic sentence: _____

3. Narrowed topic: _____

   Controlling idea: _____

   Topic sentence: _____

   _____

PRACTICE 6

Many writers adjust the topic sentence after they have finished drafting the paragraph. In a group of three or four classmates, study the body of each of these paragraphs to find the main, or controlling, idea. Then, working together, write the most exact and interesting topic sentence you can for each paragraph.

Paragraph a   _____

_____

In 1981, fewer than 300 computers were linked to the Internet. By 1989, the number of Internet users was fewer than 90,000. However, by 1993, more than 1 million computer users had logged on and were sending e-mail, doing research, working, and shopping in cyberspace. According to a survey conducted by *Business Week* magazine in 1997, about 60 million people in the United States alone were hooked up to the Internet. As the twenty-first century dawned, that number topped 100 million, with no end to the explosive growth in sight.

Paragraph b   _____

_____

A pet parrot recently saved his owner's life. Harry Becker was watching TV in his living room when he suddenly slumped over with a heart attack. The parrot screamed loudly until Mr. Becker's wife awoke and called 911. In another reported case of animal rescue, a family cat saved six-week-old Stacey Rogers. When the cat heard the baby gasping for breath in her crib, it ran howling to alert the baby's mother, who called paramedics. Even more surprising was an event reported in newspapers around the world. In 1996 in a Chicago zoo, a female gorilla rushed to save a three-year-old boy who fell accidentally into the gorilla enclosure. Still carrying her own baby on her back, the 150-pound gorilla gently picked up the unconscious child and carried him to the cage door to be rescued. Though we might not understand why, animals sometimes help and even save us.

PART C   Generating Ideas for the Body

One good way to generate ideas for the body of a paragraph is **brainstorming**—freely jotting on paper or computer anything that relates to your topic sentence: facts, details, examples, little stories. This step might take just a few minutes, but it is one of the most important elements of the writing process. Brainstorming can provide you with specific ideas to support your topic sentence. Later you can choose from these ideas as you compose your paragraph.

Here, for example, is a possible brainstorm list for the topic sentence *Pete's sloppiness is a terrible habit:*

1. His apartment is full of dirty clothes, books, candy wrappers

2. His favorite candy—M&Ms

3. He is often a latecomer or a no-show

4. He jots time-and-place information for dates and appointments on scraps of paper that are soon forgotten

5. Stacks of old newspapers sit on chair seats

6. Socks are on the lampshades

7. Papers for classes wrinkled and carelessly scrawled

8. I met Pete for the first time in math class

9. His sister is just the opposite, very neat

10. Always late for classes, out of breath

11. He is one messy person

12. Papers stained with coffee or M&Ms

Instead of brainstorming, some writers freewrite or ask themselves questions to generate ideas for their paragraphs. Some like to perform this step on paper whereas others use a computer. Do what works best for you. If you need more practice in any of these methods, reread Chapter 2, "Prewriting to Generate Ideas."

PRACTICE 7

Now choose the topic from Part B, Practice 5, that most interests you. Write your narrowed topic, controlling idea, and topic sentence here.

Narrowed topic: _____

Controlling idea: _____

Topic sentence: _____

_____

Next, brainstorm. On paper or on computer, write anything that comes to you about your topic sentence. Just let your ideas pour out. Try to fill at least one page.

PART D   Selecting and Dropping Ideas

Next, simply read over what you have written, **selecting** those ideas that relate to and support the topic sentence and **dropping** those that do not. That is, keep the facts, examples, or little stories that provide specific information about your topic sentence. Drop ideas that just **repeat** the topic sentence but that add nothing new to the paragraph.

If you are not sure which ideas to select or drop, underline the **key word** or **words** of the topic sentence, the ones that indicate the real point of your paragraph. Then make sure that the ideas that you select are related to those key words.

Here again is the brainstorm list for the topic sentence *Pete's sloppiness is a terrible habit*. The key word in the topic sentence is *sloppiness*. Which ideas would you keep? Why? Which would you drop? Why?

1. His apartment is full of dirty clothes, books, candy wrappers

2. His favorite candy—M&Ms

3. He is often a latecomer or a no-show

4. He jots time-and-place information for dates and appointments on scraps of paper that are soon forgotten

5. Stacks of old newspapers sit on chair seats

6. Socks are on the lampshades

7. Papers for classes wrinkled and carelessly scrawled

8. I met Pete for the first time in math class

9. His sister is just the opposite, very neat

10. Always late for classes, out of breath

11. He is one messy person

12. Papers stained with coffee or M&Ms

You probably dropped ideas 2, 8, and 9 because they do not relate to the topic—Pete's sloppiness. You should also have dropped idea 11 because it merely repeats the topic sentence.

PRACTICE 8

Read through your own brainstorm list from Part C, Practice 7. Select the ideas that relate to your topic sentence and drop those that do not. In addition, drop any ideas that just repeat your topic sentence. Be prepared to explain why you drop or keep each idea.

PART E   Arranging Ideas in a Plan or an Outline

After you have selected the ideas you wish to include in your paragraph, you can begin to make a plan or an outline. A plan briefly lists and arranges the ideas you wish to present in your paragraph. An outline does the same thing a bit more formally, but in an outline, letters or numbers indicate the main groupings of ideas.

First, group together ideas that have something in common, that are related or alike in some way. Then order your ideas by choosing which one you want to come first, which one second, and so on.

Below is a plan for a paragraph about Pete's sloppiness:

Topic sentence: Pete's sloppiness is a terrible habit.

His apartment is full of dirty clothes, books, candy wrappers

Stacks of old newspapers sit on chair seats

Socks are on the lampshades

He jots time-and-place information for dates and appointments on scraps of paper that are soon forgotten

He is often a latecomer or a no-show

Always late for classes, out of breath

Papers for classes wrinkled and carelessly scrawled

Papers stained with coffee or M&Ms

■ Do you see the logic in this arrangement? How are the ideas in each group

above related? _____

_____

_____

■ Does it make sense to discuss Pete's apartment first, his lateness second,

and his written work third? Why? _____

_____

_____

■ Once you have finished arranging ideas, you should have a clear **plan** from which to write your paragraph.*

PRACTICE 9

On paper or on computer, arrange the ideas from your brainstorm list according to some plan or outline. First, group together related ideas; then decide which ideas will come first, which second, and so on.

Keep in mind that there is more than one way to group ideas. Think about what you want to say; then group ideas according to what your point is.

_____

* For more work on order, see Chapter 4, "Achieving Coherence," Part A.

PART F Writing and Revising the Paragraph

Writing the First Draft

The first draft should contain all the ideas you have decided to use in the order you have chosen in your plan. Be sure to start with your topic sentence. Try to write the best, most interesting, or most amusing paragraph you can, but avoid getting stuck on any one word, sentence, or idea. If you are unsure about something, put a check in the margin and come back to it later. Writing on every other line or double spacing if you write on computer will leave room for later corrections.

Once you have included all the ideas from your plan, think about adding a concluding sentence that summarizes your main point or adds a final idea. Not all paragraphs need concluding sentences. For example, if you are telling a story, the paragraph can end when the story does. Write a concluding sentence if it will help to bring your thoughts to an end for your reader.

If possible, once you have finished the first draft, set the paper aside for several hours or several days.

PRACTICE 10

Write a first draft of the paragraph you have been working on.

Revising

Revising means rethinking and rewriting your first draft and then making whatever changes, additions, or corrections are necessary to improve the paragraph. You may cross out and rewrite words or entire sentences. You may add, drop, or rearrange details.

As you revise, keep the *reader* in mind. Ask yourself these questions:

■ Is my topic sentence clear?

■ Can a reader understand and follow my ideas?

■ Does the paragraph follow a logical order and guide the reader from point to point?

■ Will the paragraph keep the reader interested?

In addition, check your paragraph for adequate support and unity, characteristics that we'll consider in the following pages.

Revising for Support

As you revise, make sure your paragraph contains excellent **support**—that is, specific facts, details, and examples that fully explain your topic sentence.

Be careful, too, that you have not simply repeated ideas—especially the topic sentence. Even if they are in different words, repeated ideas only make the reader suspect that your paragraph is padded and that you do not have enough facts and details to support your main idea properly.

Which of the following paragraphs contains the most convincing support?

Paragraph a   (1) Our run-down city block was made special by a once-vacant lot called The Community Garden. (2) The lot was planted with all sorts of plants, vegetables, and flowers. (3) There was a path curving through it. (4) We went there to think. (5) The Community Garden made our block special. (6) Though our neighborhood was known as "tough," no one ever vandalized the garden.

Paragraph b   (1) Our run-down city block was made special by a once-vacant lot called The Community Garden. (2) I'm not sure who first had the idea, but the thin soil had been fertilized, raked, and planted with a surprising assortment of vegetables and flowers. (3) Anyone interested in gardening could tend green pepper plants, string beans, fresh herbs, even corn. (4) Others planted flowers, which changed with the seasons—tall red dahlias, white and purple irises, and taxi-yellow marigolds to discourage the insects. (5) Paved with bricks no doubt left over from the building that once stood here, a narrow path curved gracefully among the plants. (6) The Community Garden was our pride, the place we went to think and to be still. (7) Though the neighborhood was known as "tough," no one ever vandalized the garden.

■ *Paragraph a* contains general statements but little specific information to support the topic sentence.

■ *Paragraph a* also contains needless repetition. What is the number of the sentence or sentences that just repeat the topic sentence?

_____

■ *Paragraph b*, however, supports the topic sentence with specific details and examples: *thin soil, fertilized, raked and planted, green pepper plants, string beans, fresh herbs, corn, red dahlias.* What other specific support does it give?

_____

_____

_____

_____

_____

PRACTICE 11

Check the following paragraphs for adequate support. As you read each one, decide which places need more or better support—specific facts, details, and examples. Then rewrite the paragraphs, inventing facts and details whenever necessary and dropping repetitious words and sentences.

Paragraph a   (1) My uncle can always be counted on when the family faces hardship. (2) Last year, when my mother was very ill, he was there, ready to help in every way. (3) He never has to be called twice. (4) When my father became seriously depressed, my uncle's caring made a difference. (5) Everyone respects him for his willingness to be a real "family man." (6) He is always there for us.

Paragraph b   (1) Loaning money to a friend can have negative consequences. (2) For example, Ashley, a student at Tornado Community College, agreed to lend $200 to her best friend, Jan. (3) This was a bad decision even though Ashley meant well. (4) The results of this loan were surprising and negative for Ashley, for Jan, and for the friendship. (5) Both women felt bad about it but in different ways. (6) Yes, loaning money to a friend can have very negative consequences, like anger and hurt.

Paragraph c   (1) Many television talk shows don't really present a discussion of ideas. (2) Some people who appear on these shows don't know what they are talking about; they just like to sound off about something. (3) I don't like these shows at all. (4) Guests shout their opinions out loud but never give any proof for what they say. (5) Guests sometimes expose their most intimate personal and family problems before millions of viewers—I feel embarrassed. (6) I have even heard hosts insult their guests and guests insult them back. (7) Why do people watch this junk? (8) You never learn anything from these dumb shows.

Revising for Unity

It is sometimes easy, in the process of writing, to drift away from the topic under discussion. Guard against doing so by checking your paragraph for unity; that is, make sure the topic sentence, every sentence in the body, and the concluding sentence all relate to one main idea.*

This paragraph lacks unity:

> (1) John Bryant is a prime example of someone who has used his success and expertise to help others. (2) In 1992, Bryant was a successful financial consultant in Los Angeles. (3) After the riots, Bryant, an African American, was moved to tears by the sight of South Central L.A. in ruins. (4) With $5,000 of his personal savings, he set up Operation Hope, a non-profit banking group dedicated to rebuilding inner-city Los Angeles. (5) Since that day, Bryant has personally escorted dozens of bankers through South Central L.A. (6) Compton, California, was his birthplace. (7) His passionate appeals have persuaded forty financial institutions to fund $13 million in home loans. (8) In addition, Bryant has worked one-on-one with people who want to buy homes, teaching them to solve the personal credit problems that have stood in their way.

■ What is the number of the topic sentence in this paragraph?

_____

—————————

* For more work on revising, see Chapter 22, "Putting Your Revision Skills to Work."

■ Which sentence in the paragraph does not clearly relate to the topic sentence?

_____

This paragraph also lacks unity:

> (1) Quitting smoking was very difficult for me. (2) When I was thirteen, my friend Janice and I smoked in front of a mirror. (3) We practiced holding the cigarette in different ways and tried French inhaling, letting the smoke roll slowly out of our mouths and drawing it back through our noses. (4) I thought this move, when it didn't incite a fit of coughing, was particularly sexy. (5) At first I smoked only to give myself confidence on dates and at parties. (6) Soon, however, I was smoking all the time.

■ Here the topic sentence itself, sentence 1, does not relate to the rest of the paragraph. The main idea in sentence 1, that quitting smoking was difficult, is not developed by the other sentences. Since the rest of the paragraph *is* unified, a more appropriate topic sentence might read, *As a teenager, I developed the bad habit of smoking.*

PRACTICE 12

Check the following paragraphs for unity. If a paragraph has unity, write U in the blank. If not, write the number of the sentence that does not belong in the paragraph.

Paragraph a ____ (1) The first batch of one of the world's most popular soft drinks was mixed in a backyard kettle over a hundred years ago. (2) On May 6, 1886, Dr. John Styth Pemberton heated a mixture of melted sugar, water, cocoa leaves, kola nuts, and other ingredients. (3) He planned to make one of the home-brewed medical syrups so popular at that time. (4) However, this one tasted so good that Dr. Pemberton decided to sell it as a soda fountain drink for five cents a glass. (5) The first glass of this new drink was sold at Jacob's Pharmacy in Atlanta, Georgia. (6) Atlanta was and still is a wonderful place to live. (7) Pemberton's tasty invention, Coca-Cola, caught on. (8) Today, Coca-Cola is consumed by 140,000 people every minute.

Paragraph b ____ (1) At Paradise Produce, attractive displays of fruit and vegetables caught my eye. (2) On the left, oranges, lemons, and apples were stacked in neat pyramids. (3) In the center of the store, baskets of ripe peaches, plums, and raspberries were grouped in a kind of still life. (4) Many nutritionists believe that berries help prevent certain diseases. (5) On the right, the leafy green vegetables had been arranged according to intensity of color: dark green spinach, then romaine lettuce and parsley, next the lighter iceberg lettuce, and finally the nearly white Chinese cabbage. (6) On the wall above the greens hung braided ropes of garlic.

Paragraph c ____ (1) Technology enables people like the famous physicist Dr. Stephen Hawking to continue working despite serious physical disabilities. (2) For thirty-five years, Dr. Hawking has lived with Lou Gehrig's disease, which attacks the muscles, but his brilliant mind works perfectly. (3) He can no longer walk, speak, or feed himself. (4) Nevertheless, a high-tech wheelchair with computer attachments allows him to continue his research and stay in touch with friends and colleagues around the world. (5) His computer is hooked up full-time to the Internet. (6) To speak, he chooses words displayed on the computer screen, and then an electronic voice machine pronounces each word. (7) A pressure-sensitive joystick even lets Dr. Hawking make his way through traffic. (8) In his home, infrared remote control operates doors, lights, and his personal entertainment center. (9) He had two children with his first wife, Jane. (10) Dr. Hawking continues to search for new ways to overcome his problems through technology.

Revising with Peer Feedback

You may wish to show or read your first draft to a respected friend. Ask this person to give an honest response, *not* to rewrite your work. Ask specific questions of your own or use this peer feedback sheet.

PEER FEEDBACK SHEET

To _____   From _____   Date _____

1. What I like about this piece of writing is _____

   _____

2. Your main point seems to be _____

   _____

3. These particular words or lines struck me as powerful:

   Words or lines   I like them because

   _____   _____

   _____   _____

   _____   _____

4. Some things aren't clear to me. These lines or parts could be improved (meaning not clear, supporting points missing, order seems mixed up, writing not lively):

   Lines or parts   Need improving because

   _____   _____

   _____   _____

   _____   _____

   _____   _____

5. The one change you could make that would make the biggest

   improvement in this piece of writing is _____

   _____

Writing the Final Draft

When you are satisfied with your revisions, recopy your paper or print a fresh copy. If you are writing in class, the second draft will usually be the last one. Be sure to include all your corrections, writing neatly and legibly.

The first draft of the paragraph about Pete, showing the writer's changes, and the revised, final draft follow. Compare them.

First Draft with Revisions

Pete's sloppiness is a terrible habit. He lives by him-

Add details to show his sloppiness!

self in a small apartment ^carpeted^ with dirty clothes, books, and

how small?—better word needed

candy wrappers. Stacks of papers cover the chair seats.

^bake!^

Socks ~~are~~ on the lampshades. When Pete makes a date or

an appointment, he may jot down the time and place on

a scrap of paper that is soon ^tucked into a pocket and^ forgotten, or—more likely—

he doesn't jot down the information at all. ^As a result,^ Pete often

Show consequences

arrives late, or he completely forgets to appear. His

grades have suffered, too, ^because^ ~~F~~ew instructors will put up

with a student who arrives out of breath ^ten minutes after class has begun^ and whose

Add more details— better support

~~messy~~ ^wrinkled, scrawled^ papers arrive (late, of course) ^punctuated with coffee stains and melted M&Ms.^ with ~~stains~~ on them.

~~Pete's sloppiness really is a terrible habit.~~

This repeats t.s. Better conclusion needed.

Final Draft

Pete's sloppiness is a terrible habit. He lives by himself in a one-room apartment carpeted with dirty clothes, books, and crumpled candy wrappers. Stacks of papers cover the chair seats. Socks bake on the lampshades. When Pete makes a date or an appointment, he may jot down the time and place on a scrap of paper that is soon tucked into a pocket and forgotten, or—more likely—he doesn't jot down the information at all. As a result, Pete often arrives late, or he completely forgets to appear. His grades have suffered, too, because few instructors will put up with a student who arrives out of breath ten minutes after the class has begun and whose wrinkled, carelessly scrawled papers arrive (late, of course) punctuated with coffee stains and melted M&Ms. The less Pete controls his sloppiness, the more it seems to control him.

■ Note that the paragraph contains good support—specific facts, details, and examples that explain the topic sentence.

■ Note that the paragraph has unity—every idea relates to the topic sentence.

■ Note that the final sentence provides a brief conclusion, so that the paragraph *feels finished*.

Proofreading

Whether you write by hand or on computer, be sure to **proofread** your final draft carefully for grammar and spelling errors. Pointing to each word as you read it will help you catch errors or words you might have left out, especially small words like *to*, *the*, or *a*. If you are unsure of the spelling of a word, consult a dictionary and run spell check if you work on a computer.* Make neat corrections in pen or print a corrected copy of your paper. Chapter 36, "Putting Your Proofreading Skills to Work," and all of Units 6 and 7 in this book are devoted to improving your proofreading skills.

PRACTICE 13

Now read the first draft of your paragraph with a critical eye. Revise and rewrite it, checking especially for a clear topic sentence, strong support, and unity.

PRACTICE 14

Exchange *revised* paragraphs with a classmate. Ask specific questions or use the Peer Feedback Sheet.

When you *give* feedback, try to be as honest and specific as possible; saying a paper is "good," "nice," or "bad" doesn't really help the writer. When you *receive* feedback, think over your classmate's responses; do they ring true?

Now **revise** a second time, with the aim of writing a fine paragraph. Proofread carefully for grammar errors, spelling errors, and omitted words.

 ## WRITING ASSIGNMENTS

The assignments that follow will give you practice in writing basic paragraphs. In each, aim for (1) a topic sentence with a clear controlling idea and (2) a body that fully supports and develops the topic sentence.

Remember to **narrow the topic, write the topic sentence, freewrite or brainstorm, select,** and **arrange ideas** in a plan or an outline before you write. Rethink and **revise** as necessary before composing the final version of the paragraph. As you work, refer to the checklist at the end of this chapter.

Paragraph 1   *Discuss an important day in your life*

Think back to a day when you learned something important. In the topic sentence, tell what you learned. Freewrite or brainstorm to gather ideas. Then describe the lesson in detail, including only the most important steps or events in the learning process. Conclude with an insight.

---

* For tips and cautions on using a computer spell checker, see Chapter 37, Part B.

Paragraph 2 *Examine campus fashion*

What clothing and hair styles are currently in fashion on your campus? Update your readers on the look—or looks—of the moment. Focus your topic: You might write about a certain group of students who share one look, hair only, clothing styles only, and so forth. Use humor if you wish. Vivid supporting details, descriptions, and examples will help make your point. Revise your work for good support, unity, and all-around excellent writing.

Paragraph 3 *Interview a classmate about an achievement*

Write about a time when your classmate achieved something important, like winning an award for a musical performance, getting an *A* in a difficult course, or helping a friend through a hard time. To gather interesting facts and details, ask your classmate questions like these and take notes: *Is there one accomplishment of which you are very proud? Why was this achievement so important?* Keep asking questions until you feel you can give the reader a vivid sense of your classmate's triumph. In your first sentence, state the person's achievement—for instance, *Being accepted in the honors program improved Gabe's self-esteem.* Then explain specifically why the achievement was so meaningful.

Paragraph 4 *Choose an ideal job*

Decide what kind of job you are best suited for and, in your topic sentence, tell what this job is. Then give three or four reasons that will convince readers of the wisdom of your choice. Discuss any special qualifications, talents, skills, or attitudes that would make you an excellent _____. Revise your work, checking for support and unity.

Paragraph 5 *Discuss a quotation*

Look through the quotations in the Quotation Bank before the indexes in this book. Pick a quotation you especially agree or disagree with. In your topic sentence, state how you feel about the quotation. Then explain why you feel the way you do, giving examples from your own experience to support or contradict the quotation. Make sure your reader knows exactly how you feel.

Paragraph 6 *Explain a sports or music fanatic*

Do you know a sports or music fan who takes his or her loyalty and enthusiasm to an extreme? Explain this person's behavior to your readers. You might choose several details or actions that best capture his or her fanatic behavior. Or you might wish to discuss why you think a team or musical group is so important to this person. Use humor if you wish. State your controlling idea in the topic sentence and support this idea fully with details, facts, and examples.

Paragraph 7 *Discuss a childhood experience*

Choose an experience that deeply affected you. First tell exactly what happened, giving important details. Then explain the meaning this experience had for you.

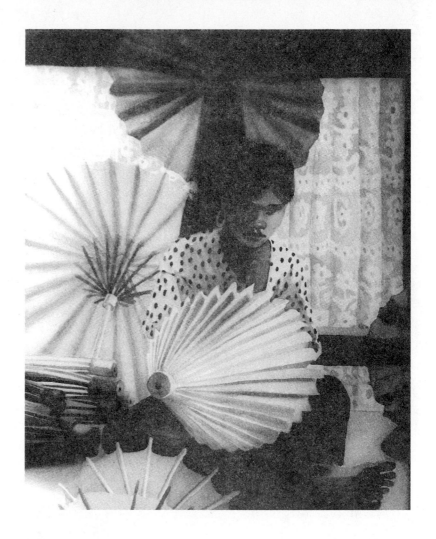

Paragraph 8   *Describe a portrait*

Look closely at this painting of a young woman, "Umbrella Maker" by artist Patricia Hansen. Study the woman in the painting—her eyes, mouth, expression, and other important details. Notice the room and the umbrellas that surround her. Then write a paragraph in which you describe the painting for a reader who has never seen it. In your topic sentence, state your overall impression of the painting. Support this impression with details.

✔ CHECKLIST: The Process of Writing Basic Paragraphs

_____ 1. Narrow the topic in light of your audience and purpose.

_____ 2. Write a topic sentence that has a clear controlling idea and is a complete sentence. If you have trouble, freewrite or brainstorm first; then narrow the topic and write the topic sentence.

_____ 3. Freewrite or brainstorm, generating facts, details, and examples to develop your topic sentence.

_____ 4. Select and drop ideas for the body of the paragraph.

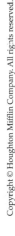

_____ 5. Arrange ideas in a plan or an outline, deciding which ideas will come first, which will come second, and so forth.

_____ 6. Write the best first draft you can.

_____ 7. Conclude. Don't just leave the paragraph hanging.

_____ 8. Revise as necessary, checking your paragraph for support and unity.

_____ 9. Proofread for grammar and spelling errors.

Achieving Coherence

Every composition should have **coherence.** A paragraph *coheres*—holds together—when the sentences are arranged in a clear, logical *order* and when the sentences are *related* like links in a chain.

PART A   Coherence Through Order

An orderly presentation of ideas within the paragraph is easier to follow and more pleasant to read than a jumble. *After* jotting down ideas but *before* writing the paragraph, the writer should decide which ideas to discuss first, which second, which third, and so on, according to a logical order.

There are many possible orders, depending on the subject and the writer's purpose. This section will explain three basic ways of ordering ideas: **time order, space order,** and **order of importance.**

Time Order

One of the most common methods of ordering sentences in a paragraph is through **time,** or **chronological, order**, which moves from present to past or from past to present. Most stories, histories, and instructions follow the logical order of time.* The following paragraph employs time order:

---

* For work on narrative paragraphs, see Chapter 6, "Narration," and for work on process paragraphs, see Chapter 8, "Process."

43

(1) Most Westerners are fascinated by Japanese sumo wrestling, but few understand the elaborate ritual that begins every bout. (2) *First*, the two *rikishi* (the Japanese term for "sumo wrestlers") step to the edge of the ring opposite each other, squat on their haunches, extend their arms, and clap once. (3) *Then* they go to the center of the ring; each lifts one leg sideways and stomps down on the mat. (4) *Next*, each opponent returns to his side of the ring and receives a dipper of "power-water" to rinse his mouth. (5) *At this point*, an attendant offers each a basket of unrefined salt. (6) The wrestlers walk toward the center of the ring, scattering salt to purify the ring. (7) They stop in the center, squat on their haunches with their fists on their knees, and lean toward each other, eyeball to eyeball. (8) As the fans scream and shout, the wrestlers return to the edge of the ring *one more time*. (9) The referee raises his war fan. (10) *Finally*, the fighters approach each other and begin fighting.

■ The events in this paragraph are clearly arranged in the order of time. They are presented as they happen, *chronologically*.

■ Throughout the paragraph, key words like *first*, *then*, *next*, and *at this point* emphasize time order and guide the reader from event to event.

Careful use of time order helps prevent confusing writing like this: *Oops, I forgot to mention that before the wrestlers scatter salt, they rinse their mouths.*

Occasionally, when the sentences in a paragraph follow a very clear time order, the topic sentence is only implied, not stated directly, as in this example:

(1) In 1905, a poor washerwoman with a homemade hair product started a business—with $1.50! (2) In just five years, Madame C. J. Walker established offices and manufacturing centers in Denver, Pittsburgh, and Indianapolis. (3) The Madame C. J. Walker Manufacturing Company specialized in hair supplies, but Madame Walker specialized in independence for herself and for others. (4) Although she was not formally educated, she developed an international sales force, teaching her African-American agents the most sophisticated business skills. (5) Eight years after starting her business, Madame Walker was the first African-American woman to become a self-made millionaire. (6) In addition, she drew thousands of former farm and domestic workers into the business world. (7) One of her most original ideas was to establish "Walker Clubs," and she awarded cash prizes to the clubs with the most educational and philanthropic projects in their African-American communities. (8) When she died in 1919, Madame Walker left two-thirds of her fortune to schools and charities. (9) Another of her contributions also lived on. (10) After her death, many of her former employees used their experience to start businesses throughout the United States and the Caribbean.

■ Time order gives coherence to this paragraph. Sentence 1 tells us about the beginning of Madame Walker's career as a businessperson. However, it does not express the main idea of the entire paragraph.

■ What is the implied topic sentence or main idea developed by the paragraph?

_____

_____

_____

■ The implied topic sentence or main idea of the paragraph might read, *With nothing but natural business ability and vision, Madame C. J. Walker achieved history-making success for herself and others.*

■ Because the writer arranges the paragraph in chronological order, the reader can easily follow the order of events in Madame Walker's life. What words and phrases indicate time order? Underline them and list them here:

_____

_____

_____

PRACTICE 1

Arrange each set of sentences in logical time order, numbering the sentences 1, 2, 3, and so on, as if you were preparing to write a paragraph. Underline any words and phrases, like *first*, *next*, and *in 1692*, that give time clues.

1. _____ First, turn off the appliance that caused the fuse to blow.

   _____ Finally, replace with a new fuse of the same amperage.

   _____ Remove the blown fuse by turning it from right to left.

   _____ Changing a fuse is not difficult.

   _____ Then identify the blown fuse by its clouded glass cap.

2. _____ The judge later deeply regretted his part, but this sorry chapter in American history has never been forgotten.

   _____ Two books "proving" that witches existed, by the famous Puritan ministers Increase Mather and his son Cotton Mather, further fanned the hysteria in 1693.

   _____ The stage was set for the terrible Salem witchcraft trials.

   _____ Nineteen so-called "witches and wizards" were hanged; one was pressed to death.

   _____ In 1692, when two girls in Salem Village, Massachusetts, had fits, they blamed the townspeople for bewitching them.

3. ____ Therefore, they decided to produce the reissues themselves, including three LPs by early rock legend Ritchie Valens.

____ In 1978 Richard Foos and Harold Bronson decided to turn their hobby of recording novelty tunes into a business, Rhino Records, Inc.

____ After this initial success, however, Foos and Bronson realized that many old favorites were out of print and that the original labels did not want to reissue them.

____ The king of reissues, Rhino Records is known today as Rhino Entertainment and includes Rhino Home Video, Rhino Movie Music, Rhino Films, and the family division Kid Rhino.

____ Rhino continued to produce even more reissues, including a classic seven-CD John Coltrane box set and the hugely successful twenty-five-volume *Have a Nice Day: Super Hits of the '70s.*

____ At first, Rhino Records was known for its unusual records and compilations, like "Pencil Neck Geek" and *The World's Worst Recordings.*

WRITING ASSIGNMENT 1

Use **time order** to give coherence to a paragraph. Choose one of the following three paragraphs. Compose a topic sentence, freewrite or brainstorm to generate ideas, and then arrange your ideas *chronologically.* You may wish to use transitional words and phrases like these to guide the reader from point to point.*

first, second	before	soon	suddenly
then	during	when	moments later
next	after	while	finally

Paragraph 1   *Narrate the first hour of your average day*

Start with getting up in the morning and continue to describe what you do for that first hour. Record your activities, your conversations, if any, and possibly your moods as you go through this hour of the morning. As you revise, make sure that events clearly follow time order.

Paragraph 2   *Record an unforgettable event*

Choose a moment in sports or in some other activity that you vividly remember, either as a participant or as a spectator. In the topic sentence, tell in a general way

---

* For a more complete list of transitional expressions, see p. 62.

what happened. *(It was the most exciting touchdown I have ever seen,* or *Ninety embarrassing seconds marked the end of my brief surfing career.)* Then record the experience, arranging details in time order.

Paragraph 3   *Relate an accident or a close call*

Focus on just a few critical moments of an accident or a close call that you experienced or witnessed, depicting the most important events in detail. Try to capture your thoughts and perceptions at the time as honestly and exactly as possible. Arrange them in time order.

Space Order

Another useful way to arrange ideas in writing is through **space order**—describing a person, a thing, or a place from top to bottom, from left to right, from foreground to background, and so on. Space order is often used in descriptive writing because it moves from detail to detail like a movie camera's eye:*

> (1) We lived on the top floor of a five-story tenement in Williamsburg, facing the BMT elevated train, or as everyone called it, the El. (2) Our floors and windows would vibrate from the El, which shook the house like a giant, roaring as if his eyes were being poked out. (3) When we went down into the street, we played on a checkerboard of sunspots and shadows, which rhymed the railroad ties above our heads. (4) Even the brightest summer day could not lift the darkness and burnt-rubber smell of our street. (5) I would hold my breath when I passed under the El's long shadow. (6) It was the spinal column of my childhood, both oppressor and liberator, the monster who had taken away all our daylight, but on whose back alone one could ride out of the neighborhood into the big broad world.
>
> —Philip Lopate, *Bachelorhood: Tales of the Metropolis*

■ This paragraph uses space order.

■ Sentence 1 clearly places the scene: on the *top floor* of a tenement, *facing* the elevated train.

■ In sentences 3 and 4, the paragraph moves downstairs, from the apartment to the street. These sentences describe the pattern made by the sun through the tracks overhead.

■ Sentence 5 moves directly *under* the railroad.

Note how words and phrases like *on the top floor, facing, down into the street, above our heads,* and *passed under* help locate the action as the paragraph *moves* from place to place.

Some paragraphs that are clearly arranged according to space order have only an implied topic sentence:

---

* For more work on space order, see Chapter 7, "Description."

(1) On my right a woods thickly overgrown with creeper descended the hill's slope to Tinker Creek. (2) On my left was a planting of large shade trees on the ridge of the hill. (3) Before me the grassy hill pitched abruptly and gave way to a large, level field fringed in trees where it bordered the creek. (4) Beyond the creek I could see with effort the vertical sliced rock where men had long ago quarried the mountain under the forest. (5) Beyond that I saw Hollins Pond and all its woods and pastures; then I saw in a blue haze the world poured flat and pale between the mountains.

—Annie Dillard, *Pilgrim at Tinker Creek*

■ The main idea of this paragraph is *implied*, not stated by a topic sentence.

What is the main idea? _____

_____

■ The implied topic sentence or main idea of this paragraph might read, *This was the scene all around me*. Because the paragraph is so clearly arranged according to space order, the reader can easily follow it.

■ Transitional phrases like *on my right* and *on my left* guide the reader from sentence to sentence. What phrases in sentences 3, 4, and 5 help guide the

reader? _____

_____

PRACTICE 2

Arrange each group of details here according to **space order,** numbering them 1, 2, 3, and so on, as if in preparation for a descriptive paragraph. Be prepared to explain your choices.

1. Describe an ostrich.

   ____ on each foot, two clawed toes of unequal length

   ____ long neck lightly covered with down

   ____ muscular legs that can deliver tremendously strong kicks

   ____ sharp eyes, which spot enemies a long way off

   ____ toenails so sharp they can disembowel prey

2. Describe an old bike.

   ____ wide seat, adjustable in height

   ____ nearly bald front tire, with inner tube of soft rubber

_____ scratched handlebars, with bell and brake levers

_____ back tire nearly flat

_____ pedals fixed to the chain wheel

3. Describe a gift.

_____ white rectangular box

_____ big blue bow

_____ flannel nightgown with Minnie Mouse designs

_____ white tissue paper, the innermost wrapping

_____ flowered wrapping paper

WRITING ASSIGNMENT 2

Use **space order** to give coherence to one of the following paragraphs. Compose a topic sentence, freewrite or brainstorm for more details, and then arrange them in space order. Use transitional words and phrases like these if you wish:*

on the left	above	next to
on the right	below	behind
in the middle	beside	farther out

Paragraph 1 *Describe an ostrich, a bike, or a gift*

Choose one group of details from Practice 2, formulate a topic sentence that sets the scene for them all, and use them as the basis of a paragraph. Convert the details into complete sentences, adding words if you wish.

Paragraph 2 *Describe a room in your home*

Describe a room in your home that has special meaning to you—the bedroom, the kitchen, a workroom or den. Write a topic sentence that gives the reader a sense of what the room is like. Then choose details that capture the special feeling or purpose of the room. Before you write the paragraph, arrange your details in space order.

_____

* For a more complete list of transitional expressions, see p. 62.

Paragraph 3   *Describe a photograph*

Describe this unusual beach scene as clearly and exactly as you can. First, jot down the four or five most important details in the scene. Then, before you write your paragraph, arrange these details according to space order—moving from background to foreground, perhaps, or from top to bottom.

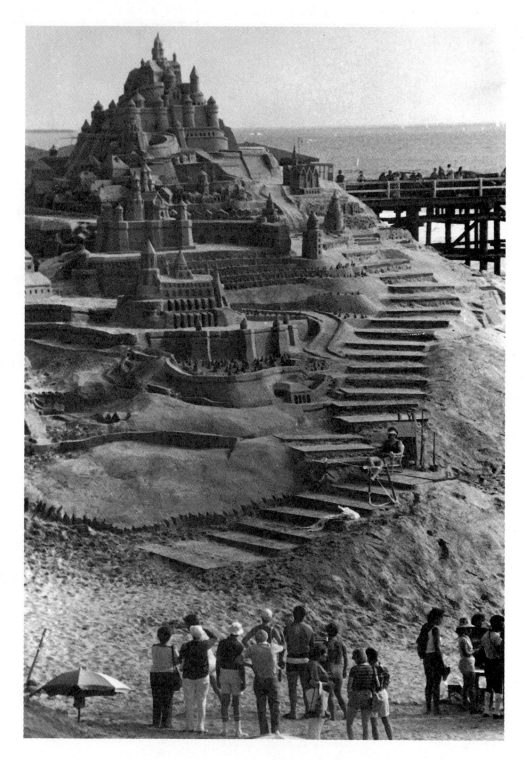

Paragraph 4 *Describe a public figure*

Choose someone you admire or like—for example, a person in the news or a television personality. Working from memory or from a photograph, choose five or six striking details to use as the basis of a paragraph that employs space order. Move from head to toe, or from face to hands, but follow a logical plan.

Order of Importance

Ideas in a paragraph can also be arranged in the **order of importance.** You may start with the most important ideas and end with the least, or you may begin with the least important idea and build to a climax with the most important one. If you wish to persuade your reader with arguments or examples, beginning with the most important points impresses the reader with the force of your ideas and persuades him or her to continue reading.*

On essay examinations and in business correspondence, be especially careful to begin with the most important idea. In those situations the reader definitely wants your important points first.

Read the following paragraph and note the order of ideas.

> (1) Louis Pasteur is revered as a great scientist for his three major discoveries. (2) Most important, this Frenchman created vaccines that have saved millions of human and animal lives. (3) The vaccines grew out of his discovery that weakened forms of a disease could help the person or animal build up antibodies that would prevent the disease. (4) The vaccines used today to protect children from serious illnesses owe their existence to Pasteur's work. (5) Almost as important was Pasteur's brilliant idea that tiny living beings, not chemical reactions, spoiled beverages. (6) He developed a process, pasteurization, that keeps milk, wine, vinegar, and beer from spoiling. (7) Finally, Pasteur found ways to stop a silkworm disease that threatened to ruin France's profitable silk industry. (8) Many medical researchers regard him as "the father of modern medicine."

■ The ideas in this paragraph are explained in the **order of importance,** from the *most important to the least important:*

What was Pasteur's most important discovery? _____

What was his next most important discovery? _____

What was his least important one? _____

■ Note how the words *most important, almost as important,* and *finally* guide the reader from one idea to another.

---

* See Chapter 5, "Illustration," and Chapter 13, "Persuasion."

Sometimes, if you wish to add drama and surprise to your paragraphs, you may want to begin with the least important idea and build toward a climax by saving the most important idea for last. This kind of order can help counter the tendency of some writers to state the most important idea first and then let the rest of the paragraph dwindle away.

Read the following paragraph and note the order of ideas.

> (1) El Niño, an unusual flow of warm ocean water in the Pacific, has many destructive effects. (2) Peruvian fishermen usually are the first to know that El Niño is back. (3) The warm currents prevent plankton—tiny plants and animals on which fish feed—from forming on the surface of the ocean. (4) When the plankton supply goes down, so does the fish supply. (5) Even more devastating, however, are the rainstorms that are caused by the change in water temperature. (6) Rains that normally move west "follow" the warm water east, bringing severe storms—and flooding—to North and South America. (7) But the most destructive effects of El Niño are unrelenting heat and drought. (8) Some areas in the United States, for example, have suffered temperatures of more than a hundred degrees for several months at a time. (9) Crops have been ruined, herds have been destroyed, and hundreds of people have died of heat-related causes.

■ The destructive effects of El Niño that develop the topic sentence in this paragraph are discussed in the **order of importance:** *from the least to the most harmful*.

■ The effects of the rainstorms are more destructive than the effects of the lessened fish supply. However, the destructive effects of heat and drought—which result in lost crops and the deaths of animals and people—are the most destructive effects of all.

■ Transitional words like *more* and *most* help the reader follow clearly from one set of destructive effects to the next.

PRACTICE 3

Arrange the ideas that develop each topic sentence in their **order of importance,** numbering them 1, 2, 3, and so on. *Begin with the most important* (or largest, most severe, most surprising) and continue to the *least* important. Or reverse the order if you think that the paragraph would be more dramatic by beginning with the *least* important ideas and building toward a climax, with the most important last.

1. Cynthia Lopez's first year of college brought many unexpected expenses.

    _____ Her English professor wanted her to own a college dictionary.

    _____ All those term papers to write required a computer.

    _____ She had to spend $90 for textbooks.

    _____ Her solid geometry class required various colored pencils and felt-tipped pens.

2. Alcoholic beverages should not be sold at sporting events.

_____ Injuries and even deaths caused by alcohol-induced crowd violence would be eliminated.

_____ Fans could save money by buying soft drinks instead of beer.

_____ Games and matches would be much more pleasant without the yelling, swearing, and rudeness often caused by alcohol.

3. The apartment needed work before the new tenants could move in.

_____ The handles on the kitchen cabinets were loose.

_____ Every room needed plastering and painting.

_____ Grime marred the appearance of the bathroom sink.

_____ Two closet doors hung off the hinges.

WRITING ASSIGNMENT 3

Use **order of importance** to give coherence to one of the paragraphs that follow. Use transitional words and phrases like these to guide the reader along:*

first	even more	another
next	last	least of all
above all	especially	most of all

Paragraph 1 *Describe a day in which everything went right (or wrong)*

Freewrite or brainstorm to generate ideas. Choose three or four of the day's best (or worst) events and write a paragraph in which you present them in order of importance—either from the most to the least important, or from the least to the most important.

Paragraph 2 *Describe an unusual person*

Choose a person you know whose looks or actions are unusual. Write your topic sentence and generate ideas; choose three to five details about the person's looks or behavior. Arrange the details according to the order of importance—either from the most to the least important or from the least to the most important.

Paragraph 3 *Explain a goal*

Write a paragraph that begins *I want a college education* (or name some other goal) *for three reasons*. Choose the three reasons that matter most to you and arrange them in the order of importance—either from the most to the least important or from the least to the most important.

_____

* For a more complete list of transitional expressions, see page 62.

PRACTICE 4	**Review**

Decide how you would develop each of the following topic sentences into a paragraph and choose an appropriate **order** of ideas. In the blanks, state what order you would use and briefly describe your approach.

There are no "right" answers. Some topics can be developed in several ways, depending on the writer.

EXAMPLE   The fields behind the barn are vibrant with color.

Order: _Space_   Approach: _Describe the colors of the fields_

from foreground to background.

Order: _Time_   Approach: _Describe the different colors at_

three different times of day.

Order: _Importance_   Approach: _Describe the details of color from_

most to least striking—or the reverse.

1. The Peruvian band Inca Son stunned the crowd with its show-stopping performance.

   Order: _____   Approach: _____

   _____

2. The attic was filled with unusual objects.

   Order: _____   Approach: _____

   _____

3. Three influences formed my decision to major in _____.

   Order: _____   Approach: _____

   _____

4. During my first year at college, I had to make three important changes in my life.

   Order: _____   Approach: _____

   _____

   _____

5. One look at my dog reveals his mixed background.

   Order: _____   Approach: _____

   _____

6. Gregor Mendel, an Austrian monk, performed many experiments before he discovered the laws of heredity.

Order: _____   Approach: _____

PART B   Coherence Through Related Sentences

In addition to arranging ideas in a logical order, the writer can ensure paragraph coherence by linking one sentence to the next. This section will present four basic ways to link sentences: **repetition of important words, substitution of pronouns, substitution of synonyms,** and **transitional expressions.**

Repetition of Important Words and Pronouns

Link sentences within a paragraph by *repeating important words and ideas.*

> (1) A grand jury is an investigative body composed of members elected from the community. (2) It serves as a buffer between the state and the citizen. (3) The prosecutor, in many cases, brings before the grand jury the evidence gathered on a particular case. (4) The grand jury must then decide if sufficient evidence exists to hand down an indictment—the indictment being a formal charge against an accused person written by the prosecutor and submitted to a court by the grand jury. (5) With the indictment issued, the prosecutor can proceed to the arraignment.
>
> —Ronald J. Waldron et al., *The Criminal Justice System: An Introduction*

■ What important words are repeated in this paragraph?

■ The words *grand jury* appear four times, in sentences 1, 3, and 4. The word *indictment*, introduced near the end of the paragraph, appears three times, in sentences 4 and 5. The word *prosecutor* appears three times, in sentences 3, 4, and 5.

■ Repetition of these key words helps the reader follow from sentence to sentence as these terms are defined and the relationships between them are explained.

Although repetition of important words can be effective, it can also become boring if overused.* To avoid *unnecessary* repetition, substitute *pronouns* for words already mentioned in the paragraph, as this author does:

---

* For practice in eliminating wordiness (repetition of unimportant words), see Chapter 21, "Revising for Language Awareness," Part B.

(1) For several months, Julia "Butterfly" Hill has been living in Northern California—at the top of a two-hundred-foot, one-thousand-year-old redwood. (2) A logging company wants to cut down the ancient tree, but *it* has not done so because of *her*. (3) Hill says *she* will stay atop the tree until the loggers agree to allow *it* to live out a natural life.

■ The use of pronouns in this paragraph avoids unnecessary repetition. In sentence 2, the pronoun *it* refers to the antecedent* *a logging company*, and the pronoun *her* refers to *Julia "Butterfly" Hill.*

■ The pronoun *she* in sentence 3 gives further coherence to the paragraph by

referring to what antecedent? _____

■ The pronoun *it* in sentence 3 refers to what antecedent? _____

Use pronoun substitution together with the repetition of important words for a smooth presentation of ideas.

PRACTICE 5

What important words are repeated in the following paragraph? Underline them. Circle any pronouns that replace them. Notice the varied pattern of repetitions and pronoun replacements.

I have always considered my father a very intelligent person. His intelligence is not the type usually tested in schools; perhaps he would have done well on such tests, but the fact is that he never finished high school. Rather, my father's intelligence is his ability to solve problems creatively as they arise. Once when I was very young, we were driving through the desert at night when the oil line broke. My father improvised a light, squeezed under the car, found the break, and managed to whittle a connection to join the two severed pieces of tubing; then he added more oil and drove us over a hundred miles to the nearest town. Such intelligent solutions to unforeseen problems were typical of him. In fact, my father's brand of brains—accurate insight, followed by creative action—is the kind of intelligence that I admire and most aspire to.

_____

* For more work on pronouns and antecedents, see Chapter 30, "Pronouns," Parts A, B, and C.

WRITING ASSIGNMENT 4

Paragraph 1   *Discuss success*

How do you measure *success?* By the money you make, the number or quality of friends you have? Freewrite or brainstorm for ideas. Then answer this question in a thoughtful paragraph. Give the paragraph coherence by repeating important words and using pronouns.

Paragraph 2   *Discuss a public figure*

Choose a public figure whom you admire—from the arts, politics, media, or sports—and write a paragraph discussing *one quality* that makes that person special. Name the person in your topic sentence. Vary repetition of the person's name with pronouns to give the paragraph coherence.

Synonyms and Substitutions

When you do not wish to repeat a word or use a pronoun, give coherence to your paragraph with a **synonym** or **substitution**. **Synonyms** are two or more words that mean nearly the same thing. For instance, if you do not wish to repeat the word *car*, you might use the synonym *automobile* or *vehicle*. If you are describing a sky and have already used the word *bright*, try the synonym *radiant*.

Or instead of a synonym, **substitute** other words that describe the subject. If you are writing about José Canseco, for example, refer to him as *this powerful slugger* or *this versatile outfielder*. Such substitutions provide a change from constant repetition of a person's name or a single pronoun.*

Use synonyms and substitutions together with repetition and pronouns to give coherence to your writing:

> (1) On September 10, 1990, *the main building of Ellis Island* in New York Harbor reopened as a museum. (2) Restoration of *the huge red brick and limestone structure* took eight years and cost $156 million. (3) From 1900 to 1924, *this famous immigrant station* was the first stop of millions of newcomers to American shores. (4) *The building* was finally abandoned in 1954; by 1980, *it* was in such bad condition that snow and rain fell on its floor. (5) Today, visitors can follow the path of immigrants: from a ferryboat, through the great arched doorway, into the room where the weary travelers left their baggage, up the stairway where doctors kept watch, and into the registry room. (6) Here questions were asked that determined if each immigrant could stay in the United States. (7) *This magnificent monument to the American people* contains exhibits that tell the whole immigration history of the United States.

- This paragraph effectively mixes repetition, pronouns, and substitutions. The important word *building* is stated in sentence 1 and repeated in sentence 4.

- Sentence 4 also substitutes the pronoun *it*.

- In sentence 2, *the huge red brick and limestone structure* is substituted for *building*, and a second substitution, *this famous immigrant station*, occurs in sentence 3. Sentence 7 refers to the building as *this magnificent monument to the American people* and concludes the paragraph.

---

* For more work on exact language, see Chapter 21, "Revising for Language Awareness," Part A.

Sometimes the dictionary lists synonyms. For instance, the entry for *smart* might list *clever, witty, intelligent*. An even better source of synonyms is the **thesaurus,** a book of synonyms. For example, if you are describing a city street and cannot think of other words meaning "noisy," look in the thesaurus. The number of choices will amaze you.

PRACTICE 6

Read each paragraph carefully. Then write on the lines any synonyms and substitutions that the writer has used to replace the word(s) in italics.

Paragraph 1   *Rocky Mountain bighorn sheep* use their massive horns as percussion instruments. During the fall rutting season, when hormone changes bring on the breeding urge, 250-pound rams square off in violent, head-butting matches to determine which gains leadership of the herd and pick of the ewes. Duelists rear on hind legs, then drop to all fours and, heads down, charge at full speed.

—*National Geographic*

Rocky Mountain bighorn sheep are also referred to as _____

_____ and _____.

Paragraph 2   According to sports writer Ian Stafford, the British hold the record for winning the world's *oddest competitions*. In one of these bizarre events, contestants contort their faces and are judged on their ugliness. One competitor removed half his dentures and reversed the other half, rolled his eyes, and tucked his nose into his mustache and upper lip to achieve prize-winning ugliness. Another of these eccentric contests is snail racing. Opponents in this case are, of course, snails, which are placed in the center of a thirteen-inch cloth circle. The first to reach the edge of the circle wins. The race often takes four to five minutes, although the all-time champion (owned and trained by an English seven-year-old) finished the course in two minutes. Toe wrestling, bog snorkeling, worm charming—the British have emerged as unconquered rivals in all of these so-called sports. Perhaps you think that sports writer Ian Stafford should win first prize in the Biggest Liar in the World Competition. No, every one of these outlandish games exists. You can check them all out on the Internet.

Oddest competitions are also referred to as _____, _____,

_____, and _____.

Paragraph 3   When Lewis and Clark made their way through what is now North Dakota, the Shoshone Indian woman named *Sacajawea* and her French-Canadian husband joined the team of explorers. Because the expedition was traveling with a Native American, other tribes did not attack the group. In fact, one tribe even supplied horses to help the explorers and their interpreter cross the Rocky Mountains. This invaluable team member taught the men how to find medicine and food in the wilderness and once even saved the records of the journey when a canoe overturned during a storm. Sacajawea reached the Pacific Ocean with Lewis and Clark in 1805. Her fame eventually spread; one of the best-known monuments to her is a statue in Portland, Oregon.

Sacajawea is also referred to as _____,

_____, and _____.

PRACTICE 7

Give coherence to the following paragraphs by thinking of appropriate synonyms or substitutions for the words in italics. Then write them in the blanks.

Paragraph 1   Christopher Reeve's story includes an extraordinary twist of fate. This *star* played Superman, the fictional hero who inspired fans with his ability to overcome obstacles and save others from harm. How ironic that this

_____ was paralyzed from the neck down in a horse-jumping accident in 1995 and now personifies that superhuman perseverance himself. Before his accident, Reeve was not only a(n) _____ but a pianist, an athlete who performed his own film stunts, a pilot, and an all-round outdoorsman. Now he depends on a ventilator to breathe and operates his wheelchair by sipping or puffing on a straw. Since his accident, however, this

_____ has directed and narrated award-winning films, written the best-selling autobiography *Still Me*, and inspired thousands of people through speeches and interviews. He also has raised millions of dollars for research on spinal cord injuries. Christopher Reeve has become a(n)

_____ of a different kind; his heroism depends not on physical strength but on courage, optimism, and a sense of purpose.

Paragraph 2   Much evidence shows that the urge to take a midafternoon *nap* is natural to humans. Sleep researchers have found that volunteer subjects, kept in underground rooms where they cannot tell the time, need a

_____ about twelve hours after the halfway point of their main sleep. For example, if people sleep from midnight till 6:00 A.M., they'll be ready for a _____ at 3:00 the next afternoon. Other studies show that people have less trouble taking a

_____ in midafternoon than at any other daylight time. In many countries with warm climates, citizens take their daily

_____ in the afternoon. Even stressed Americans take an average of two afternoon naps a week.

Paragraph 3   According to the experts, those who learn about *money* early in life usually

make sound financial decisions as adults. How then can parents give children

the knowledge and experience they need? Well, even preschoolers can feed

_____ into parking meters and pay phones. Young

children will become interested in clipping coupons if parents give them the

_____ saved off the regular prices. Children of seven

and eight can learn about _____ by managing an

allowance. By the age of ten or so, kids become fascinated by the idea of

having a bank account of their own and earning interest on their

_____. In other words, parents can provide children

with learning experiences about money at almost every age and stage of their

lives. However, if your children won't accept any gift but stocks for their birthday

presents, you may have carried the concept too far!

WRITING ASSIGNMENT 5

As you do the following assignments, try to achieve paragraph coherence by
using repetition, pronouns, synonyms, and substitutions.

Paragraph 1   *Discuss your favorite form of relaxation*

Tell what you like to do when you have free time. Do you like to get together
with friends? Do you like to go to a movie or to some sporting event? Or do you
prefer to spend your time alone, perhaps listening to music or reading? Maybe
you like to get outdoors and do something active, like play a game of pickup basketball or go rollerblading.

Whatever your favorite free-time activity, name it in your topic sentence. Be
sure to tell what makes your choice of activity *relaxing*. Then give your paragraph
coherence by using pronouns and synonyms such as *take it easy, rest,* and *unwind.*

Paragraph 2   *Describe your ideal mate*

Decide on three or four crucial qualities that your ideal husband, wife, or friend
would possess, and write a paragraph describing this extraordinary person. Use
repetition, pronouns, and word substitutions to give coherence to the paragraph.
For example, *My ideal husband . . . he . . . my companion.*

Paragraph 3   *React to a quotation*

Choose a quotation from the Quotation Bank before the indexes in this book, one
you strongly agree or disagree with. Write a paragraph explaining why you feel
that way. As you write, refer to the quotation as a *wise insight* or a *silly idea*—
depending on what you think of it. Use other substitutions to refer to the quotation without repeating it or calling it *the quotation.*

Transitional Expressions

Skill in using transitional expressions is vital to coherent writing. **Transitional expressions** are words and phrases that point out the exact relation between one idea and another, one sentence and another. Words like *therefore*, *however*, *for example*, and *finally* are signals that guide the reader from sentence to sentence. Without them, even orderly and well-written paragraphs can be confusing and hard to follow.

The transitional expressions in this paragraph are italicized:

> (1) Zoos in the past often contributed to the disappearance of animal populations. (2) Animals were cheap, and getting new ones was easier than providing the special diet and shelter necessary to keep captive animals alive. (3) *Recently*, *however*, zoo directors have begun to realize that if zoos themselves are to continue, they must help save many species from extinction. (4) *As a result*, some zoos have begun to redefine themselves as places where endangered species can be protected and even revived. (5) The Basel Zoo in Switzerland, *for example*, selects endangered species and encourages captive breeding. (6) If zoos continue such work, perhaps they can, like Noah's ark, save some of earth's wonderful creatures from extinction.

- Each transitional expression in the previous paragraph links, in a precise way, the sentence in which it appears to the sentence before. The paragraph begins by explaining the destructive policies of zoos in the past.

- In sentence 3, two transitional expressions of contrast—*recently* (as opposed to the past) and *however*—introduce the idea that zoo policies have *changed*.

- The phrase *as a result* makes clear that sentence 4 is a *consequence* of events described in the previous sentence(s).

- In sentence 5, *for example* tells us that the Basel Zoo is *one particular illustration* of the previous general statement.

As you write, use various transitional expressions, together with the other linking devices, to connect one sentence to the next. Well-chosen transitional words also help stress the purpose and order of the paragraph.

Particular groups of transitional expressions are further explained and demonstrated in each chapter of Unit 3. However, here is a combined partial list for handy reference as you write.

Purpose	Transitional Expressions
to add	also, and, and then, as well, besides, beyond that, first (second, third, last, and so on), for one thing, furthermore, in addition, moreover, next, what is more
to compare	also, as well, both (neither), in the same way, likewise, similarly
to contrast	although, be that as it may, but, even though, however, in contrast, nevertheless, on the contrary, on the other hand, whereas, yet
to concede (a point)	certainly, granted that, of course, no doubt, to be sure
to emphasize	above all, especially, indeed, in fact, in particular, most important, surely
to illustrate	as a case in point, as an illustration, for example, for instance, in particular, one such, yet another
to place	above, below, beside, beyond, farther, here, inside, nearby, next to, on the far side, opposite, outside, to the east (south, and so on)
to qualify	perhaps, maybe
to give a reason or cause	as, because, for, since
to show a result or effect	and so, as a consequence, as a result, because of this, consequently, for this reason, hence, so, therefore, thus
to summarize	all in all, finally, in brief, in other words, lastly, on the whole, to sum up
to place in time	after a while, afterward, at last, at present, briefly, currently, during, eventually, finally, first (second, and so on), gradually, immediately, in the future, later, meanwhile, next, now, recently, soon, suddenly, then

PRACTICE 8

Carefully determine the *exact relationship* between the sentences in each pair below. Then choose from the list a **transitional expression** that clearly expresses this relationship and write it in the blank. Pay attention to punctuation and capitalize the first word of every sentence.*

1. No one inquired about the money found in the lobby. _____, it was given to charity.

_____

* For practice using conjunctions to join ideas, see Chapter 24, "Coordination and Subordination."

2. First, cut off the outer, fibrous husk of the coconut. _____ poke a hole through one of the dark "eyes" and sip the milk through a straw.

3. The English Department office is on the fifth floor. _____ to it is a small reading room.

4. Some mountains under the sea soar almost as high as those on land. One underwater mountain in the Pacific, _____, is only 500 feet shorter than Mount Everest.

5. All citizens should vote. Many do not, _____.

6. Mrs. Dalworth enjoys shopping in out-of-the-way thrift shops. _____, she loves bargaining with the vendors at outdoor flea markets.

7. In 1887, Native Americans owned nearly 138 million acres of land. By 1932, _____, 90 million of those acres were owned by whites.

8. Kansas corn towered over the fence. _____ the fence, a red tractor stood baking in the sun.

9. Most street crime occurs between 2:00 and 5:00 A.M. _____, do not go out alone during those hours.

10. Dr. Leff took great pride in his work at the clinic. _____, his long hours often left him exhausted.

11. Few scientists have worked so creatively with a single agricultural product. _____ peanut oil and peanut butter, George Washington Carver developed literally hundreds of uses for the peanut.

12. We waited in our seats for over an hour. _____ the lights dimmed, and the Fabulous String Band bounded on stage.

PRACTICE 9

Add **transitional expressions** to this essay to guide the reader smoothly from sentence to sentence. To do so, consider the relationship between sentences (shown in parentheses). Then write the transitional word or phrase that best expresses this relationship.

Math Stars

James Escalante was teaching physics in his native Bolivia when political unrest made him flee to the United States. In East Los Angeles, where he settled, he learned English and _____ found a job teaching
(time)
mathematics at Garfield High School. Garfield was known for its gangs, drugs, and low academic ratings. Teaching in this environment was difficult, _____ Escalante persisted, taking a tough, humorous
(contrast)
approach to motivate his classes. _____, many stu-
(illustration)
dents remember the day he chopped up an apple with a meat cleaver to teach percentages.

Only five students showed up for his first calculus class, but four of them went on to pass the advanced placement test for college credit. Escalante's students continued to succeed. Suddenly, _____, fourteen
(contrast)
of them were accused of cheating. Twelve agreed to take an even more difficult test; _____, all twelve passed. The incident
(addition)
received considerable media attention and _____,
(result)
became the subject of the film *Stand and Deliver*. _____,
(emphasis)
at a time when only 2 percent of U.S. seniors were taking the advanced placement test, all of Escalante's students were taking it—and 80 percent of them
were passing.

PRACTICE 10   Review

Most paragraphs achieve coherence through a variety of linking devices: repetition, pronouns, substitutions, and transitional expressions. Read the following
paragraphs with care, noting the kinds of linking devices used by each writer.
Answer the questions after each paragraph.

Paragraph 1   (1) The blues is the one truly American music. (2) Born in the Mississippi
Delta, this twelve-bar cry of anguish found its durable, classic form in the searing
soliloquies of poor black men and women who used it to ventilate all the aches
and pains of their condition—the great Bessie Smith, Robert Johnson, Ma Rainey,
Lightnin' Hopkins and Son House, Mississippi John Hurt, John Lee Hooker and

Blind Lemon Jefferson. (3) And, ever since, the blues has served as the wellspring of every major movement in this country's popular music.

—Paul D. Zimmerman with Peter Barnes et al.,
"Rebirth of the Blues," *Newsweek*

1. What important words appear in both the first and the last sentence?

   _____

2. In sentence 2, *the blues* is referred to as _____

   _____

3. What transitional expressions are used in sentence 3? _____

   _____

Paragraph 2   (1) Mrs. Zajac seemed to have a frightening amount of energy. (2) She strode across the room, her arms swinging high and her hands in small fists. (3) Taking her stand in front of the green chalkboard, discussing the rules with her new class, she repeated sentences, and her lips held the shapes of certain words, such as "homework," after she had said them. (4) Her hands kept very busy. (5) They sliced the air and made karate chops to mark off boundaries. (6) They extended straight out like a traffic cop's, halting illegal maneuvers yet to be perpetrated. (7) When they rested momentarily on her hips, her hands looked as if they were in holsters. (8) She told the children, "One thing Mrs. Zajac expects from each of you is that you do *your* best." (9) She said, "Mrs. Zajac gives homework. (10) I'm sure you've all heard. (11) The old meanie gives homework." (12) *Mrs. Zajac.* (13) It was in part a role. (14) She worked her way into it every September.

—Tracy Kidder, *Among Schoolchildren*

1. What important words are repeated in this paragraph? _____

   _____

2. What word does *they* in sentences 5 and 6 refer to? _____

Paragraph 3   (1) More important perhaps than the recipes and ideas that flowed into the home through cookbooks and magazines were the conveniences that began more and more to appear in the kitchen. (2) First it was the icebox. (3) Next it was running hot water, along with the cold. (4) Then it was the gas stove, a frightening apparatus for the uninitiated—and then, just as soon as mastery of its dials and heat had been achieved, along came the electric stove to sow confusion again. (5) The icebox gave way to the refrigerator and the freezer. (6) And out of Clarence Birdseye's observation that Eskimos in Labrador froze their meat and fish evolved the quick-freezing of various foodstuffs, a revolution of the first order in American cooking.

—*Foods of the World/American Cooking,*
Time-Life Books Inc.

1. Underline the transitional expressions in this paragraph.

2. What *order* of ideas does the paragraph employ? _____

   _____

Pay Tribute to an Exceptional Person

In this unit, you learned that most good paragraphs have a clear topic sentence, convincing support, and an order that makes sense. In your group or class, read this student's paragraph, aloud if possible. Underline any parts you find especially well written. Put a check next to anything that might be improved.

Making Mittens Out of Sweaters

This paper will be about my grandmother. My grandmother, Mary Bell Auld, was exceptional in her ability to "make do." She made tasty meals out of the cheapest ingredients and grew fresh vegetables in coffee cans on the fire escape. She could fix just about anything. Once I watched her take our kitchen clock apart and repair it. When she couldn't afford a new mop head, she made one out of rags. She sewed our clothes by hand and was always darning someone's shirt or socks. One winter, we didn't have any gloves, and it was bitterly cold outside. I remember her taking an old wool sweater from the hamper, placing my hands over one of the sleeves, and drawing a pattern for mittens. She cut them out, sewed them with tiny stitches, turned them on the other side, and presto, I had mittens. She cut off the other sleeve, tied the top, rolled and stitched the edge, and there was my matching hat. Today my grandmother lives on in me. From her, I learned to be independent and creative, and if ever I am overcome by one of the curves that life throws me, I am not down for long.

—Crystal Standish (Student)

1. How effective is this paragraph?

    _____ Clear topic sentence?   _____ Good supporting details?

    _____ Logical organization?   _____ Effective conclusion?

2. Which sentence, if any, is the topic sentence? Is sentence 1 as good as the rest of the paragraph? If not, what revision advice would you give the writer?

3. Does this student provide adequate support for her main idea? Why or why not?

4. Discuss your underlinings with the group or class. Which parts of this paragraph did you find most powerful? Explain as specifically as possible why. For example, the detail about growing vegetables on a fire escape vividly supports the topic sentence.

5. Although the subject of the paragraph is the writer's grandmother, the two concluding sentences focus on the writer herself. Has Ms. Standish drifted away from her main idea or written an interesting conclusion? Justify your position.

6. Do you see any error patterns (one error made two or more times) that this student needs to watch out for)?

GROUP WORK

In your group or class, make a plan of Ms. Standish's paragraph. How many points does she use to support her topic sentence? Which point is developed more fully than the others? Why do you think the writer does this? Is this effective or not? How can a writer know whether a paragraph has good support or needs better support? List three ways.

 ## WRITING AND REVISING IDEAS

1. Pay tribute to an exceptional person.

2. Discuss the ways in which someone from the past lives on in you.

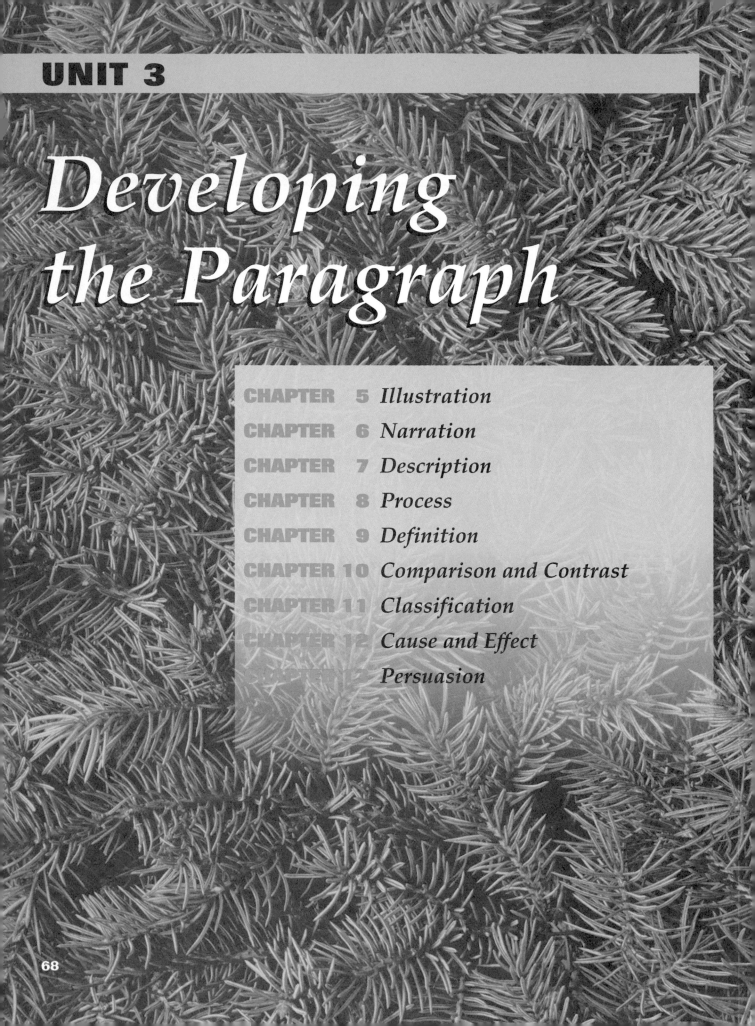

UNIT 3

Developing the Paragraph

CHAPTER 5

Illustration

To **illustrate** is to explain a general statement by means of one or more specific *examples*.

Illustration makes what we say more vivid and more exact. Someone might say, "My math professor is always finding crazy ways to get our attention. Just yesterday, for example, he wore a high silk hat to class." The first sentence is a general statement about this professor's unusual ways of getting attention. The second sentence, however, gives a specific example of something he did that *clearly shows* what the writer means.

Writers often use illustration to develop a paragraph. They explain a general topic sentence with one, two, three, or more specific examples. Detailed and well-chosen examples add interest, liveliness, and power to your writing.

Topic Sentence

Here is the topic sentence of a paragraph that is later developed by examples:

> Great athletes do not reach the top by talent alone but by pushing themselves to the limit and beyond.

- The writer begins an illustration paragraph with a topic sentence that makes a general statement.

- This generalization may be obvious to the writer, but if he or she wishes to convince the reader, some specific examples would be helpful.

Paragraph and Plan

Here is the entire paragraph:

> Great athletes do not reach the top by talent alone but by pushing themselves to the limit and beyond. For instance, champion figure skater Michelle Kwan is her own worst critic, studying every practice on video in order to perfect her performance. During one practice, when she flubbed a double axel, she repeated the jump over and over until the ice cleaners urged her off the ice. "Winning isn't about miracles on ice," she says. "It's all about training." Another example is tennis great Pete Sampras, whose relaxed attitude hides a punishing work ethic. For 90 to 150 minutes a day, he rallies with a tennis pro and then works out with a strength and conditioning coach for another 60 to 90 minutes. Even Chicago Bulls superstar Michael Jordan, who has been called the most gifted athlete of all time, was a relentlessly hard worker and perfectionist. He and two teammates practiced *before* every team practice. Each day from pre-season camp to the last Finals game, Jordan was in his gym with a trainer by 8 A.M., sweating through a tough routine created by exercise scientists; then he hit the court. Like many top athletes, he turned his talent into greatness through sheer hard work.

■ How many examples does the writer use to develop the topic sentence?

_____

■ Who are they?

_____

Before completing this illustration paragraph, the writer probably made an outline or plan like this:

Topic Sentence: Great athletes do not reach the top by talent alone but by pushing themselves to the limit and beyond.

Example 1:   Michelle Kwan

—studies practices on video

—repeated one jump until thrown off the ice

—quote ("not about miracles but training")

Example 2:   Pete Sampras

—relaxed attitude hides work ethic

—90–150 minutes rallying with a pro

—then 60–90 minutes working out

Example 3:   Michael Jordan

—most gifted but also relentlessly hard worker

—practiced before practice!

—8 A.M. scientific workout, then practice on the court

■ Note that each example clearly relates to and supports the topic sentence.

Instead of using three or four examples to support the topic sentence, the writer may prefer instead to discuss one single example:

> Many schools in the twenty-first century will look more like elegant shopping malls than like old-fashioned school buildings. The new Carl Sandburg High School in Chicago is just one example. Now being redesigned, the school will feature a main library with the comfortable, open layout of a super-bookstore like Barnes & Noble or Borders. The physical education facilities will include rock-climbing walls and other features now seen in health clubs. Carl Sandburg's cafeteria will be laid out like a food court, not only giving students more choices, but eliminating the long lunch lines that caused delays in the old high school. Retailers have learned how to create attractive, practical public spaces, and many modern school planners think it's time that school officials learned the same lessons.

■ What is the general statement? _____

_____

■ What specific example does the writer give to support the general statement?

_____

The single example may also be a **narrative**,* a *story* that illustrates the topic sentence.

> Aggressive drivers not only are stressed out and dangerous, but often they save no time getting where they want to go. Recently I was driving south from Oakland to San Jose. Traffic was heavy but moving. I noticed an extremely aggressive driver jumping lanes, speeding up and slowing down. Clearly, he was in a hurry. For the most part, I remained in one lane for the entire forty-mile journey. I was listening to a new audiotape and daydreaming. I enjoyed the trip because driving gives me a chance to be alone. As I was exiting off the freeway, the aggressive driver crowded up behind me and raced on by. Without realizing it, I had arrived in San Jose ahead of him. All his weaving, rapid acceleration, and putting families at risk had earned him nothing except perhaps some high blood pressure and a great deal of wear and tear on his vehicle.
>
> —Adapted from Richard Carlson, *Don't Sweat the Small Stuff*

■ What general statement does the aggressive driver story illustrate?

_____

_____

■ Note that this narrative follows time order.†

_____

* For more on narrative, see Chapter 6, "Narration," and Chapter 15, "Types of Essays," Part B.

† For more work on time order, see Chapter 4, "Achieving Coherence," Part A.

Transitional Expressions

The simplest way to tell your reader that an example is going to follow is to say so: "*For instance*, Michelle Kwan . . ." or "The new Carl Sandburg High School is *just one example*." This partial list should help you vary your use of **transitional expressions** that introduce an illustration:

Transitional Expressions for Illustration	
for instance	another instance of
for example	another example of
an illustration of this	another illustration of
a case in point is	here are a few examples
to illustrate	(illustrations, instances)

■ Be careful not to use more than two or three of these transitional expressions in a single paragraph.*

PRACTICE 1

Read each of the following paragraphs of illustration. Underline each topic sentence. Note in the margin how many examples are provided to illustrate each general statement.

Paragraph 1   Random acts of kindness are those little sweet or grand lovely things we do for no reason except that, momentarily, the best of our humanity has sprung . . . into full bloom. When you spontaneously give an old woman the bouquet of red carnations you had meant to take home to your own dinner table, when you give your lunch to the guitar-playing beggar who makes music at the corner between your two subway stops, when you anonymously put coins in someone else's parking meter because you see the red "Expired" medallion signalling to a meter maid—you are doing not what life requires of you, but what the best of your human soul invites you to do.

—Daphne Rose Kingma, *Random Acts of Kindness*

Paragraph 2   There are many quirky variations to lightning. A "bolt from the blue" occurs when a long horizontal flash suddenly turns toward the earth, many miles from the storm. "St. Elmo's Fire," often seen by sailors and mountain climbers, is a pale blue or green light caused by weak electrical discharges that cling to trees, airplanes, and ships' masts. "Pearl lightning" occurs when flashes are broken into segments. "Ball lightning" can be from an inch to several feet in diameter. Pearls and balls are often mistaken for flying saucers or UFOs, and many scientists believe they are only optical illusions.

—Reed McManus, *Sierra Magazine*

---

*For a complete essay developed by illustration, see "Libraries of the Future—Now," Chapter 15, Part A.

PRACTICE 2

Each example in a paragraph of illustration must clearly relate to and support the general statement. Each general statement in this practice is followed by several examples. Circle the letter of any example that does *not* clearly illustrate the generalization. Be prepared to explain your choices.

EXAMPLE The museum contains many fascinating examples of African art.

    a. It houses a fine collection of Ashanti fertility dolls.

    b. Drums and shamans' costumes are displayed on the second floor.

    (c.) The museum building was once the home of Frederick Douglass. (The fact that the building was once the home of Frederick Douglass is *not an example of African art.*)

1. Amelia Earhart dared to act beyond the limits of what society thought a woman could or should do.

    a. She saw her first plane at the Iowa State Fair.

    b. She became a pilot and mechanic, entering the all-male world of aviation.

    c. She presented her new husband with a marriage contract that gave both partners considerable freedom.

2. Today's global companies sometimes find that their product names and slogans can translate into embarrassing bloopers.

    a. Pepsi's slogan "Come alive with the Pepsi Generation" didn't work in Taiwan, where it meant "Pepsi will bring your ancestors back from the dead."

    b. When General Motors introduced its Chevy Nova in South America, company officials didn't realize that *no va* in Spanish means "it won't go."

    c. In Chinese, the Kentucky Fried Chicken slogan "finger-lickin' good" means "eat your fingers off."

    d. Nike runs the same ad campaign in several countries, changing the ad slightly to fit each culture.

3. Stone Age cave dwellers left amazing paintings on the walls of over two hundred European caves.

    a. The walls of the now-famous cave at Lascaux, France, glow with multi-colored animals and human figures painted some 25,000 years ago.

    b. Cave dwellers in China left evidence of the human use of fire 400,000 years ago.

    c. Using mineral pigments mixed with fat, Stone Age artists also adorned the cave walls at Altamira, Spain, with graceful animal paintings.

4. Some writers use strange tricks to overcome writer's block and keep their ideas flowing.

    a. To help himself choose the right word, the German playwright and poet Schiller sniffed rotten apples that he kept inside his desk.

    b. Benjamin Franklin believed that he had to write in the nude to do his best work, and he often wrote in the bathtub.

    c. Argentinian writer Jorge Luis Borges went blind, but he kept creating brilliant stories packed with learning, philosophy, and magic.

    d. To inspire herself before she started writing, Dame Edith Sitwell would lie for a while each morning in an open coffin.

5. In the Arizona desert, one sees many colorful plants and flowers.
   a. Here and there are patches of pink clover.
   b. Gray-green saguaro cacti rise up like giant candelabra.
   c. Colorful birds dart through the landscape.
   d. Bright yellow poppies bloom by the road.

6. Many important inventions were rejected when they were first introduced.
   a. Chester Carlson was laughed at for his dry copy process, xerography, but it later made him rich and gave a company its name, Xerox.
   b. The invention of NutraSweet happened accidentally in 1965 when a chemist noticed that a chemical he had spilled tasted sweet.
   c. When John Holland first invented the submarine in the late 1800s, the Navy saw no use for it and treated him like a kook.

7. The United States offers many unusual tourist attractions for those who venture off the beaten path.
   a. Visitors to Mitchell, South Dakota, can stop at the Mitchell Corn Palace, a castle covered with murals made of corn, grass, and grain.
   b. One of the most popular tourist stops in the country is the Washington Monument in Washington, D.C.
   c. Hard-core Elvis fans can visit the Elvis Museum in Pigeon Forge, Tennessee, to see Elvis's razor, hair dryer, and nasal spray applicator.
   d. On Route 115 in Colorado, drivers can gawk at the World's Largest Hercules Beetle, a giant bug made of plaster.

8. Many months in our calendar take their names from Roman gods or heroes.
   a. Mars, the Roman war god, gave his name to March.
   b. January was named for Janus, the god of doorways, whose two faces looked both forward and back.
   c. August honors Augustus, the first Roman emperor and the second Caesar.
   d. December took its name from *decem*, the Latin word meaning "ten," and was the tenth month in the Roman calendar.

PRACTICE 3

The secret of good illustration lies in well-chosen, well-written examples. Think of one example that illustrates each of the following general statements. Write out the example in sentence form (one to three sentences) as clearly and exactly as possible.

1. A few contemporary singers work hard to send a positive message.

   Example: _____

   _____

2. In a number of ways, this college makes it easy for working students to attend.

Example: _____

_____

_____

3. Believing in yourself is 90 percent of success.

Example: _____

_____

_____

4. Many teenagers believe they must have expensive designer clothing.

Example: _____

_____

_____

5. Growing up in a large family can teach the value of compromise.

Example: _____

_____

_____

6. A number of shiny classic cars cruised up and down Ocean Drive.

Example: _____

_____

_____

7. Children say surprising things.

Example: _____

_____

_____

8. Sadly, gun violence has affected many Americans.

Example: _____

_____

✔ CHECKLIST: **The Process of Writing an Illustration Paragraph**

Refer to this checklist of steps as you write an illustration paragraph of your own.

___ 1. Narrow the topic in light of your audience and purpose.

___ 2. Compose a topic sentence that can honestly and easily be supported by examples.

___ 3. Freewrite or brainstorm to find six to eight examples that support the topic sentence. If you wish to use only one example or a narrative, sketch out your idea. (You may want to freewrite or brainstorm before you narrow the topic.)

___ 4. Select only the best two to four examples and drop any examples that do not relate to or support the topic sentence.

___ 5. Make a plan or an outline for your paragraph, numbering the examples in the order in which you will present them.

___ 6. Write a draft of your illustration paragraph, using transitional expressions to show that an example or examples will follow.

___ 7. Revise as necessary, checking for support, unity, logic, and coherence.

___ 8. Proofread for errors in grammar, punctuation, sentence structure, spelling, and mechanics.

Suggested Topic Sentences for Illustration Paragraphs

1. Some lucky people love their jobs.

2. In my family, certain traditions (or values or beliefs) are very important.

3. Painful experiences can sometimes teach valuable lessons.

4. Using animated animals and humor, some beer commercials seem to target minors.

5. Some unusual characters live in my neighborhood.

6. Soap operas "hook" viewers in several ways.

7. Many enjoyable activities in this area are inexpensive or even free.

8. Celebrities who have overcome illness or tragedy can inspire others.

9. A sense of humor can make difficult times easier to bear.

10. Sexual harassment is a fact of life for some employees.

11. Some professors are masters at helping their students learn.

12. Many sites on the Internet offer free grammar help (greeting cards, medical information, and so on).

13. Sometimes a chance meeting can change a person's life.

14. Choose a quotation from the Quotation Bank at the end of this book. First, state whether you think this saying is true; then use an example from your own or others' experience to support your view.

15. Writer's choice: _____

CHAPTER 6

Narration

To **narrate** is to tell a story that explains what happened, when it happened, and who was involved.

A news report may be a narrative about how Congress voted, what the president did, or how a man was rescued from a burning building. When you read a bedtime story to your children, you are reading them a narrative.

In a letter to a friend, you might want to write a narrative detailing how you were hired for your new job; your narrative could emphasize the fact that your relaxed and confident manner throughout the interview impressed your future employer. Or you might wish to retell what happened on your first skiing trip, when a minor accident proved to you that you prefer tamer recreation.

However, no matter what your narrative is about, it must make a *point:* It must clearly tell what you want your reader to learn or take away from the story.

Topic Sentence

Here is the topic sentence of a **narrative** paragraph:

> A birthday gift I received years ago has become a lasting symbol of love.

■ The writer begins a narrative paragraph with a topic sentence that tells the point of the narrative.

■ What is the point of this narrative? _____

_____

Paragraph and Plan

Here is the entire paragraph:

A birthday gift I received years ago has become a lasting symbol of love. It was a cold day during my first year in college. My birthday had just passed, and I hadn't heard from my best friend, Linda, who had moved away two years before. A card and a present would have been nice, but what I really wanted from her was a hug. Suddenly the doorbell rang. I ran downstairs and signed the receipt that the letter carrier held out—in return for a package from Linda! I pulled off all the wrappings—and stared. Then, because I didn't know whether to laugh or cry, I ended up doing some of each. Linda's gift was a sweater, but this sweater had something extra. Attached to each cuff was a cutout of one of Linda's hands, and the hands in the box were arranged in a hug around the sweater. I loved the sweater, but I didn't wear it for months because I couldn't bear to unpin the hands, which would have looked pretty silly just dangling from my cuffs. Then I got an idea. I'm not an artist, but I decided to make a collage. I got hours of pleasure painting a background and then cutting, arranging, and pasting photographs and magazine pictures, along with the hands, into what is surely a unique piece of artwork. I eventually wore out the sweater, but the collage has hung in every place I've ever lived. Every time I look at it, I feel hugged, loved, and comforted.

■ The body of a narrative paragraph is developed according to time, or chronological, order.* That is, the writer explains the narrative—the entire incident—as a series of small events or actions in the order in which they occurred. By keeping to strict chronological order, the writer helps the reader follow the story more easily and avoids interrupting the narrative with *But I forgot to mention that before this happened. . . .*

■ What smaller events make up this narrative? _____

_____

_____

_____

Before writing this narrative paragraph, the writer may have brainstormed or freewritten to gather ideas, and then she may have made an outline or a plan like this:

Topic sentence: A birthday gift I received years ago has become a lasting symbol of love.

    Event 1:   My birthday passed.

    Event 2:   I didn't hear from best friend, Linda.

                —would have liked card or present

                —really wanted hug

_____

*For more work on time, see Chapter 4, "Achieving Coherence," Part A.

Event 3:	The letter carrier came with a package.
Event 4:	The present was from Linda.
	—laughed and cried
	—sweater had hands
	—hands were arranged in a hug
Event 5:	I didn't wear the sweater.
Event 6:	I made a collage.
Event 7:	I wore out the sweater.
Event 8:	I've hung the collage everywhere I've lived.

■ Note that all of the events occur in chronological order.

■ Also note that the first two events present background information: They tell what led up to receiving the gift.

■ Finally, note that the specific details of certain events (like events 2 and 4) make the narrative more vivid.

Transitional Expressions

Because narrative paragraphs tell a story in **chronological** or **time order,** transitional expressions that indicate time can be useful.*

Transitional Expressions for Narratives		
after	finally	soon
as (soon as)	later	then
before	meanwhile	upon
during	next	when
first	now	while

PRACTICE 1

Read the following narrative paragraph carefully and answer the questions.

Horace Bristol might be the only photographer to owe his fame to his child's book report. Before he became an architect, Bristol had been a documentary journalist. One day his teenage son was writing a book report on *The Grapes of Wrath,* John Steinbeck's novel about an Oklahoma farm family forced off their drought-stricken land during the 1930s. He asked his father if he'd ever read the book. Not

---

* For a complete essay developed by narration, see "Maya Lin's Vietnam War Memorial," Chapter 15, "Types of Essays," Part B.

only had he read it, Bristol replied, he had dreamed up the idea for it, recruited Steinbeck to write it, and photographed thousands of real farm families forced to leave their homes. After revealing his past to his son, Bristol the photographer came out of hiding. Hoping to sell a few of his photographs, he was soon astounded by the prices they commanded. Encouraged, he took up his camera once again. Since then the photographs of Horace Bristol have become famous. His images of despair during the Depression, heroism in the Pacific during World War II, and postwar poverty and hope in rural Korea are among the greatest photographs of the twentieth century.

1. What is the point of the narrative? _____

   _____

2. What events make up this narrative paragraph? _____

   _____

   _____

   _____

   _____

   _____

   _____

   _____

PRACTICE 2

Here are three plans for narrative paragraphs. The events in the plans are not in correct chronological order. The plans also contain events that do not belong in each story. Number the events in the proper time sequence and cross out any irrelevant ones.

1. Aesop's fable about a dog and his reflection teaches a lesson about greed.

   _____ He thought he saw another dog with another piece of meat in his mouth, so he decided to get that one too.

   _____ Now the dog had nothing at all to eat.

   _____ A dog was happily carrying a piece of meat in his mouth.

   _____ The dog was brown with white spots.

_____ While crossing a bridge, he saw his reflection in the water of a running brook.

_____ When he snapped at the reflection, the meat dropped from his mouth into the water and sank.

2. In 1897, Lena Jordan performed the first triple somersault on the flying trapeze, but for years she did not get credit.

   _____ For the next sixty-six years, all the record books listed Clarke as the record holder, not Jordan.

   _____ When a second person, a man named Ernest Clarke, managed a triple somersault in 1909, he received national attention.

   _____ Only recently did the _Guinness Book of World Records_ give Jordan sole credit for the first triple somersault in circus history.

   _____ The first free-fall parachute jump from an airplane was also made by a woman.

   _____ In 1975, the _Guinness Book of World Records_ finally listed Lena Jordan's achievement, but only in addition to Clarke's.

3. The Civil War battle between two iron-covered ships, on March 9, 1862, changed sea warfare forever.

   _____ Two hours into the battle, the _Monitor_ ran out of ammunition and moved into shallow water to reload.

   _____ After four hours, the _Merrimack,_ her hull leaking and her smokestack broken, escaped from the scene of battle.

   _____ When the _Monitor_ returned with guns loaded, the _Merrimack_ lured her into deep water and then suddenly swung around and rammed her, leaving barely a dent.

   _____ The Civil War lasted from 1861 to 1865.

   _____ At the end of the conflict, neither ironclad ship had really won, but the wooden fighting ship was a thing of the past.

   _____ At first, the two ships—the North's _Monitor_ and the South's _Merrimack_— just circled each other like prehistoric monsters, firing at close range but causing no damage.

PRACTICE 3

Here are topic sentences for three narrative paragraphs. Make a plan for each paragraph, placing the events of the narrative in the proper time sequence.

1. When I was _____, help came from an unexpected source.

2. Sometimes, seemingly unimportant events can prove to be of great importance.

3. Last year, _____ learned something surprising about himself/herself.

You have been given the photo below and asked to tell the story behind it. That is, you must invent a brief narrative that explains this mysterious picture. What are these people looking at so intently and why? Your narrative can be serious, funny, or otherwordly. First, list the main events and include them in chronological order. State the point of your narrative in the topic sentence, which you may wish to place last rather than first in your paragraph.

✔ CHECKLIST: The Process of Writing a Narrative Paragraph

Refer to this checklist of steps as you write a narrative paragraph of your own.

_____ 1. Narrow the topic in light of your audience and purpose.

_____ 2. Compose a topic sentence that tells the point of the story.

_____ 3. Freewrite or brainstorm for all of the events and details that might be part of the story. (You may want to freewrite or brainstorm before you narrow the topic.)

_____ 4. Select the important events and details; drop any that do not clearly relate to the point in your topic sentence.

_____ 5. Make a plan or an outline for the paragraph, numbering the events in the correct time (chronological) sequence.

_____ 6. Write a draft of your narrative paragraph, using transitional expressions to indicate time sequence.

_____ 7. Revise as necessary, checking for support, unity, logic, and coherence.

_____ 8. Proofread for errors in grammar, punctuation, sentence structure, spelling, and mechanics.

Suggested Topics for Narrative Paragraphs

1. A favorite family story

2. A lesson in tolerance

3. A fulfilled ambition

4. A few moments that changed someone's life

5. A laugh at yourself

6. A breakthrough (emotional, physical, or spiritual)

7. An experience in another country

8. A first day at college (or at a new job)

9. A triumphant (or embarrassing) moment

10. The first time you met an important friend

11. A serious decision

12. A strange dream

13. Something you or another person dared to do

14. An incident that made you happy (or proud)

15. Writer's choice: _____

CHAPTER 7

Description

To **describe** something—a person, a place, or an object—is to capture it in words so others can imagine it or see it in their mind's eye.

The best way for a writer to help the reader get a clear impression is to use language that appeals to the senses: sight, sound, smell, taste, and touch. For it is through the senses that human beings experience the physical world around them, and it is through the senses that the world is most vividly described.

Imagine, for instance, that you have just gone boating on a lake at sunset. You may not have taken a photograph, yet your friends and family can receive an accurate picture of what you have experienced if you *describe* the pink sky reflected in smooth water, the creak of the wooden boat, the soothing drip of water from the oars, the occasional splash of a large bass jumping, the faint fish smells, the cool and darkening air. Writing down what your senses experience will teach you to see, hear, smell, taste, and touch more acutely than ever before.

Description is useful in English class, the sciences, psychology—anywhere that keen observation is important.

Topic Sentence

Here is the topic sentence of a descriptive paragraph:

> On November 27, 1922, when archaeologist Howard Carter unsealed the door to the ancient Egyptian tomb of King Tut, he stared in amazement at the fantastic objects heaped all around him.

■ The writer begins a descriptive paragraph by pointing out what will be described. What will be described in this paragraph?

■ The writer can also give a general impression of this scene, object, or person. What overall impression of the tomb does the writer provide?

_____

_____

Paragraph and Plan

Here is the entire paragraph:

> On November 27, 1922, when archaeologist Howard Carter unsealed the door to the ancient Egyptian tomb of King Tut, he stared in amazement at the fantastic objects heaped all around him. On his left lay the wrecks of at least four golden chariots. Against the wall on his right sat a gorgeous chest brightly painted with hunting and battle scenes. Across from him was a gilded throne with cat-shaped legs, arms like winged serpents, and a back showing King Tut and his queen. Behind the throne rose a tall couch decorated with animal faces that were half hippopotamus and half crocodile. The couch was loaded with more treasures. To the right of the couch, two life-sized statues faced each other like guards. They were black, wore gold skirts and sandals, and had cobras carved on their foreheads. Between them was a second sealed doorway. Carter's heart beat loudly. Would the mummy of King Tut lie beyond it?

■ The overall impression given by the topic sentence is that the tomb's many objects were amazing. List three specific details that support this impression.

_____

_____

_____

■ Note the importance of words that indicate richness and unusual decoration in helping the reader visualize the scene.* List as many of these words as you can:

_____

_____

_____

_____

* For more work on vivid language, see Chapter 21, "Revising for Language Awareness."

■ This paragraph, like many descriptive paragraphs, is organized according to space order.* The author uses transitional expressions that show where things are. Underline the transitional expressions that indicate place or position.

Before composing this descriptive paragraph, the writer probably brainstormed and freewrote to gather ideas and then made an outline or a plan like this:

Topic sentence: On November 27, 1922, when archaeologist Howard Carter unsealed the door to the ancient Egyptian tomb of King Tut, he stared in amazement at the fantastic objects heaped all around him.

1. **To the left:**   chariots
—wrecked
—golden

2. **To the right:**   a gorgeous chest
—brightly painted with hunting and battle scenes

3. **Across the room:**   a throne
—gilded
—cat-shaped legs
—arms like winged serpents

4. **Behind the throne:**   a couch
—decorated with faces that were half hippopotamus and half crocodile

5. **To the right of the couch:**   two life-sized statues
—black
—gold skirts and sandals
—cobras carved on foreheads

6. **Between the two statues:**   a second sealed doorway

7. **Conclusion:**   expectation that King Tut's mummy was beyond the second door

■ Note how each detail supports the topic sentence.

Transitional Expressions

Since space order is often used in description, **transitional expressions** indicating place or position can be useful:

Transitional Expressions Indicating Place	
next to, near	on top, beneath
close, far	toward, away
up, down, between	left, right, center
above, below	front, back, middle

* For more work on space order and other kinds of order, see Chapter 4, "Achieving Coherence," Part A.

Of course, other kinds of order are possible. For example, a description of a person might have two parts: details of physical appearance and details of behavior.*

PRACTICE 1

Read the following paragraph carefully and answer the questions.

The woman who met us had an imposing beauty. She was tall and large-boned. Her face was strongly molded, with high cheekbones and skin the color of mahogany. She greeted us politely but did not smile and seemed to hold her head very high, an effect exaggerated by the abundant black hair slicked up and rolled on the top of her head. Her clothing was simple, a black sweater and skirt, and I remember thinking that dressed in showier garments, this woman would have seemed overwhelming.

1. What overall impression does the writer give of the woman?

   _____

   _____

   _____

2. What specific details support this general impression? _____

   _____

   _____

   _____

   _____

3. What kind of order does the writer use? _____

   _____

   _____

PRACTICE 2

It is important that the details in a descriptive paragraph support the overall impression given in the topic sentence. In each of the following plans, one detail has nothing to do with the topic sentence; it is merely a bit of irrelevant information. Find the irrelevant detail and circle the letter.

_____

* For a complete essay developed by description, see "The Day of the Dead," Chapter 15, Part C.

1. Miami's Calle Ocho Festival, named after S.W. 8th Street in Little Havana, is a giant Latino street party.
   a. as far as the eye can see on S.W. 8th Street, thousands of people stroll, eat, and dance
   b. on the left, vendors sell hot pork sandwiches, *pasteles* (spiced meat pies), and fried sweets dusted with powdered sugar
   c. up close, the press of bare-limbed people, blaring music, and rich smells
   d. during the 1980s, Dominican merengue music hit the dance clubs of New York
   e. on the right, two of many bands play mambo or merengue music

2. In my mind's eye is a plan for the perfect workout room.
   a. complete Nautilus set in center
   b. StairMaster near the door
   c. on shelf above the StairMaster, a color TV
   d. exercise helps me think more clearly
   e. hot tub with view of woods through one-way glass
   f. spotless blue carpet

3. In the photograph from 1877, Chief Joseph looks sad and dignified.
   a. long hair pulled back, touched with gray
   b. dark eyes gaze off to one side, as if seeing a bleak future
   c. strong mouth frowns at the corners
   d. ceremonial shell necklaces cover his chest
   e. Nez Percé tribe once occupied much of the Pacific Northwest

4. On the plate lay an unappetizing hamburger.
   a. burned bun, black on the edges
   b. burger cost two dollars
   c. fat dripping from the hamburger onto the plate
   d. parts of burger uncooked and partially frozen
   e. sour smell of the meat

5. An illegal dump site has spoiled the field near the edge of town.
   a. fifty or more rusting metal drums, some leaking
   b. pools of green-black liquid on the ground
   c. in the distance, view of the mountains
   d. wildflowers and cottonwood trees dead or dying
   e. large sign reading "Keep Out—Toxic Chemicals"

PRACTICE 3

Here is a list of topic sentences for descriptive paragraphs. Give five specific details that would support the overall impression given in each topic sentence. Appeal to as many of the senses as possible. Be careful not to list irrelevant bits of information.

EXAMPLE | Stopped in time by the photographer, my mother appears confident.

Details: a. _her hair swept up in a sophisticated pompadour_

b. _a determined look in her young eyes_

c. _wide, self-assured smile_

d. _her chin held high_

e. _well-padded shoulders_

(These five details support *confident* in the topic sentence.)

1. This was clearly a music lover's room.

   a. _____

   _____

   b. _____

   _____

   c. _____

   _____

   d. _____

   _____

   e. _____

   _____

2. The prizefighter looked tough and fearless.

   a. _____

   _____

   b. _____

   _____

   c. _____

   _____

   d. _____

   _____

   e. _____

   _____

3. Spaghetti and meatballs were splattered all over the white kitchen.

a. _____

_____

b. _____

_____

c. _____

_____

d. _____

_____

e. _____

_____

4. The auto repair shop was alive with activity.

a. _____

_____

b. _____

_____

c. _____

_____

d. _____

_____

e. _____

_____

5. The buildings on that street look sadly rundown.

a. _____

_____

b. _____

_____

c. _____

_____

d. _____

_____

e. _____

_____

6. The beach on a hot summer day presented a constant show.

a. _____

_____

b. _____

_____

c. _____

_____

d. _____

_____

e. _____

_____

7. During the first week of classes, the college bookstore is wall-to-wall confusion.

a. _____

_____

b. _____

_____

c. _____

_____

d. _____

_____

e. _____

_____

8. The automobile seemed like something from the next century.

a. _____

_____

b. _____

_____

c. _____

_____

d. _____

_____

e. _____

_____

PRACTICE 4

Pick the description you like best from Practice 3. Prewrite for more details if you wish. Choose a logical order in which to present the best details, make a plan or an outline, and then write an excellent descriptive paragraph.

PRACTICE 5

Describe the photograph on page 94. In your topic sentence state your overall impression of the scene and those in it. What do you think they are watching—what is the mood? Then support this impression with a detailed description—facial expressions, clothing, and so on.

Make your description as vivid as you can, so that readers who have not seen the photograph can visualize it in their minds' eye.

You may wish to use space order to organize these details, moving from left to right, top to bottom, or front to back.

CHECKLIST: The Process of Writing a Descriptive Paragraph

Refer to this checklist of steps as you write a descriptive paragraph of your own.

_____ 1. Narrow the topic in light of your audience and purpose.

_____ 2. Compose a topic sentence that clearly points to what you will describe or gives an overall impression of the person, object, or scene.

_____ 3. Freewrite or brainstorm to find as many specific details as you can to capture your subject in words. Remember to appeal to your readers' senses. (You may want to freewrite or brainstorm before you narrow the topic.)

_____ 4. Select the best details and drop any irrelevant ones.

_____ 5. Make a plan or an outline for the paragraph, numbering the details in the order in which you will present them.

_____ 6. Write a draft of your descriptive paragraph, using transitional expressions wherever they might be helpful.

_____ 7. Revise as necessary, checking for support, unity, logic, and coherence.

_____ 8. Proofread for errors in grammar, punctuation, sentence structure, spelling, and mechanics.

Suggested Topics for Descriptive Paragraphs

1. An unusual man or woman: for example, an athlete, an entertainer, someone with amazing hair or clothing, or a teacher you won't forget

2. A public place: emergency room, library, fast-food restaurant, town square, or theater lobby

3. The face of someone in the news

4. A shop that sells only one type of item: cheese, computer software, Western boots, car parts, flowers

5. An animal, a bird, or an insect you have observed closely

6. Someone or something you found yourself staring at

7. A photograph of yourself as a child

8. A scene of peace (or of conflict)

9. A room that reveals something about its owner

10. An intriguing outdoor scene

11. A possession you value

12. An interesting person you have seen on campus

13. Your favorite dinner

14. A neighborhood personality

15. Writer's choice: _____

CHAPTER 8

Process

Two kinds of **process paragraphs** will be explained in this chapter: the how-to paragraph and the explanation paragraph.

The **how-to paragraph** gives the reader directions on how he or she can do something: how to install a software program, how to get to the airport, or how to make tasty barbecued ribs. The goals of such directions are the installed software, the arrival at the airport, or the great barbecued ribs. In other words, the reader should be able to do something after reading the paragraph.

The **explanation paragraph**, on the other hand, tells the reader how a particular event occurred or how something works. For example, an explanation paragraph might explain how an internal combustion engine works or how palm trees reproduce. After reading an explanation paragraph, the reader is not expected to be able to do anything, just to understand how it happened or how it works.

Process writing is useful in history, business, the sciences, psychology, and many other areas.

Topic Sentence

Here is the topic sentence of a *how-to paragraph:*

> Careful preparation before an interview is the key to getting the job you want.

■ The writer begins a how-to paragraph with a topic sentence that clearly states the goal of the process—what the reader should be able to do.

■ What should the reader be able to do after he or she has read the paragraph following this topic sentence?

_____

Paragraph and Plan

Here is the entire paragraph:

> "Luck is preparation meeting opportunity," it has been said, and this is true for a job interview. Careful preparation before an interview is the key to getting the job you want. The first step is to learn all you can about the employer. Read about the company in its brochures or in newspaper and magazine articles. A reference librarian can point you to the best sources of company information. You can also find company web sites and other useful material on the Internet. Second, as you read, think about the ways your talents match the company's goals. Third, put yourself in the interviewer's place, and make a list of questions that he or she will probably ask. Employers want to know about your experience, training, and special skills, like foreign languages. Remember, every employer looks for a capable and enthusiastic team player who will help the firm succeed. Fourth, rehearse your answers to the questions out loud. Practice with a friend or a tape recorder until your responses sound well prepared and confident. Finally, select and prepare a professional-looking interview outfit well in advance to avoid the last-minute panic of a torn hem or stained shirt. When a job candidate has made the effort to prepare, the interviewer is much more likely to be impressed.

■ The topic sentence is the second sentence. In the first sentence, the writer has used a quotation to open the paragraph and spark the reader's interest.

■ The body of the how-to paragraph is developed according to time, or chronological, order.* That is, the writer gives directions in the order in which the reader is to complete them. Keeping to a strict chronological order avoids the necessity of saying, *By the way, I forgot to tell you . . .* , or *Whoops, a previous step should have been to. . . .*

■ How many steps are there in this how-to paragraph and what are they?

_____

_____

_____

_____

_____

Before writing this how-to paragraph, the writer probably brainstormed or freewrote to gather ideas and then made an outline or a plan like this:

---

* For more work on order, see Chapter 4, "Achieving Coherence," Part A.

Topic sentence: Careful preparation before an interview is the key to getting the job you want.

Step 1:	Learn about the employer
	—read company brochures, papers, magazines
	—reference librarian can help
	—check company web site
Step 2:	Think how your talents match company goals
Step 3:	List interviewer questions
	—think about experience, training, special skills
	—employers want capable team players
Step 4:	Rehearse your answers out loud
	—practice with friend or tape recorder
Step 5:	Select your interview outfit
	—avoid last-minute panic
	—avoid torn hem, stained shirt
Conclusion:	interviewer more likely to be impressed

■ Note that each step clearly relates to the goal stated in the topic sentence.

The second kind of process paragraph, the *explanation paragraph*, tells how something works, how it happens, or how it came to be:

> Many experts believe that recovery from addiction, whether to alcohol or other drugs, has four main stages. The first stage begins when the user finally admits that he or she has a substance abuse problem and wants to quit. At this point, most people seek help from groups like Alcoholics Anonymous or treatment programs because few addicts can "get clean" by themselves. The next stage is withdrawal, when the addict stops using the substance. Withdrawal can be a painful physical and emotional experience, but luckily, it does not last long. After withdrawal comes the most challenging stage—making positive changes in one's life. Recovering addicts have to learn new ways of spending their time, finding pleasure and relaxation, caring for their bodies, and relating to spouses, lovers, family, and friends. The fourth and final stage is staying off drugs. This open-ended part of the process often calls for ongoing support or therapy. For people once defeated by addiction, the rewards of self-esteem and a new life are well worth the effort.

■ What process does the writer explain in this paragraph? _____

_____

■ How many stages or steps are explained in this paragraph? _____

■ What are they? _____

_____

■ Make a plan of the paragraph in your notebook.

Just as the photographs on this page show each stage in the process of a chick hatching, so your process paragraph should clearly describe each step or stage for the reader. Before you write, try to visualize the process as if it were a series of photographs.*

_____

* For complete essays developed by process, see "How to Prepare for a Final Exam," Chapter 15, Part D, and "Bottle Watching," page 172.

Transitional Expressions

Since process paragraphs rely on **chronological order,** or **time sequence,** words and expressions that locate the steps of the process in time are extremely helpful.

Transitional Expressions for Process			
Beginning a Process	**Continuing a Process**		**Ending a Process**
(at) first	second, third step	when	finally
initially	until	while	at last
begin by	after(ward)	as soon as	
	then	as	
	next	upon	
	later	during	
	before	meanwhile	

PRACTICE 1

Read the following how-to paragraph carefully and answer the questions.

If your dog barks too much, the Humane Society recommends an easy way to solve the problem. All you need is a plant mister—a small spray bottle—filled with water and kept handy. First and most important, respond immediately every time your dog barks unnecessarily. Instantly say, "Quiet, Pluto," or whatever the dog's name is, giving one or two squirts of water in the dog's face. Be sure to do this while the dog is barking. Waiting until the dog stops barking may confuse it. If the dog moves away, say, "Quiet" again as you move toward the dog and give it one more squirt of water. Second, repeat this procedure every time the dog barks without a good reason. The dog will soon learn that your saying "Quiet" comes with a squirt of water. Usually two days—about five to ten water treatments—are enough. Third, as time goes by, use the spray bottle only if the dog forgets—that is, rarely. Throughout the training process, remember to be consistent, using the spray technique every single time, and don't forget to reassure your dog that you two are still friends by petting it when it is quiet.

—Eleanor Steiger (Student)

1. What should you be able to do after reading this paragraph?

   _____

   _____

2. Are any "materials" necessary for this process? _____

   _____

3. How many steps are there in this paragraph? List them.

_____

_____

_____

4. What order does the writer employ? _____

PRACTICE 2

Here are five plans for process paragraphs. The steps for the plans are not in the correct chronological order. The plans also contain irrelevant details that are not part of the process. Number the steps in the proper time sequence and cross out any irrelevant details.

1. Starting your own rock band is a difficult process.

   _____ After the group has mastered five songs, it should make a demo tape.

   _____ The first step is finding friends and local musicians with the same musical taste and vision.

   _____ Send the demo tapes to local clubs, bars, and DJs, and follow up in person to try to line up some gigs.

   _____ Each band member should choose a main instrument, and only one or two should sing, to avoid chaos on stage.

   _____ When Ginger Spice left the Spice Girls, it definitely shook up the whole group.

   _____ With persistence, multiple performances, and a small dose of talent, your band might develop a following.

2. Stress, which is your body's response to physical or mental pressures, occurs in three stages.

   _____ In the resistance stage, your body works hard to resist or handle the threat, but you may become more vulnerable to other stressors, like flu or colds.

   _____ If the stress continues for too long, your body uses up its defenses and enters the exhaustion stage.

   _____ Trying to balance college courses, parenthood, and work is sure to cause stress.

   _____ During the alarm stage (also called *fight or flight*), your body first reacts to a threat by releasing hormones that increase your heart rate and blood pressure, create muscle tension, and supply quick energy.

3. Chewing gum is made entirely by machine.

_____ Then the warm mass is pressed into thin ribbons by pairs of rollers.

_____ First, the gum base is melted and pumped through a high-speed spinner that throws out all impurities.

_____ The gum base makes the gum chewy.

_____ Huge machines mix the purified gum with sugar, corn syrup, and flavoring, such as spearmint, peppermint, or cinnamon.

_____ Finally, machines wrap the sticks individually and then package them.

_____ Knives attached to the last rollers cut the ribbons into sticks.

4. Many psychologists claim that marriage is a dynamic process consisting of several phases.

_____ Sooner or later, romance gives way to disappointment as both partners really see each other's faults.

_____ Idealization is the first phase, when two people fall romantically in love, each thinking the other is perfect.

_____ The last phase occurs as the couple face their late years as a twosome once again.

_____ The third phase is sometimes called the productivity period, when two people work at parenting and career development.

_____ Men and women may have different expectations in a marriage.

_____ As the children leave home and careers mature, couples may enter a stage when they rethink their lives and goals.

5. Because turtles are cold-blooded animals, they hibernate during the winter.

_____ After finding the right place, they dig their winter home, bury themselves in the mud, and fall into a deep sleep.

_____ As the weather turns cold, turtles begin to seek a spot in the mud near a pond to spend the winter.

_____ Contrary to popular opinion, turtles make charming pets.

_____ With the onset of spring, the ice on the pond melts and the thawing mud awakens these buried creatures to new life.

_____ Throughout the winter, their metabolism remains low.

Here are topic sentences for five process paragraphs. Make a plan for each paragraph, listing in proper time sequence all the steps that would be necessary to complete the process. Now choose one plan and write an excellent process paragraph.

1. Although I'm still not the life of the party, I took these steps to overcome my shyness at parties.

   _____

   _____

   _____

   _____

   _____

2. _____ is/was a very complicated (or simple) process.

   _____

   _____

   _____

   _____

   _____

3. Ted learned _____ in stages over a period of time.

   _____

   _____

   _____

   _____

   _____

4. Good kids turning bad: it is a process occurring all over the country.

_____

_____

_____

_____

_____

_____

_____

5. My morning routine gets me out of the house in twenty minutes.

_____

_____

_____

_____

_____

_____

✔ CHECKLIST: **The Process of Writing a Process Paragraph**

Refer to this checklist of steps as you write a process paragraph of your own.

_____ 1. Narrow the topic in light of your audience and purpose.

_____ 2. Compose a topic sentence that clearly states the goal or end result of the process you wish to describe.

_____ 3. Freewrite or brainstorm to generate steps that might be part of the process. (You may want to freewrite or brainstorm before you narrow the topic.)

_____ 4. Drop any irrelevant information or steps that are not really necessary for your explanation of the process.

_____ 5. Make an outline or a plan for your paragraph, numbering the steps in the correct time (chronological) sequence.

_____ 6. Write a draft of your process paragraph, using transitional expressions to indicate time (chronological) sequence.

_____ 7. Revise as necessary, checking for support, unity, logic, and coherence.

_____ 8. Proofread for errors in grammar, punctuation, sentence structure, spelling, and mechanics.

Suggested Topics for Process Paragraphs

1. How to relax or meditate

2. How to establish credit

3. How to break up with (or attract) someone

4. How an important discovery was made

5. How to find information in the library's electronic card catalogue (or reference book section)

6. How to be a good friend

7. How someone landed a wonderful job

8. How to prepare your favorite dish

9. How to shop on a budget for a computer (or clothes, school supplies, and so on)

10. How to appear smarter than you really are

11. How to break an unhealthy habit

12. How a team won an important game

13. How to get the most out of a visit to the doctor

14. How to choose a major

15. Writer's choice: _____

CHAPTER 9

Definition

| PART A | Single-Sentence Definitions |
| PART B | The Definition Paragraph |

To **define** is to explain clearly what a word or term means.

As you write, you will sometimes find it necessary to explain words or terms that you suspect your reader may not know. For example, *net profit* is the profit remaining after all deductions have been taken; a *bonsai* is a dwarfed, ornamentally shaped tree. Such terms can often be defined in just a few carefully chosen words. However, other terms—like *courage, racism,* or *a good marriage*—are more difficult to define. They will test your ability to explain them clearly so that your reader knows exactly what you mean when you use them in your writing. They may require an entire paragraph for a complete and thorough definition.

In this chapter, you will learn to write one-sentence definitions and then whole paragraphs of definition. The skill of defining clearly will be useful in such courses as psychology, business, the sciences, history, and English.

PART A   Single-Sentence Definitions

There are many ways to define a word or term. Three basic ways are **definition by synonym, definition by class,** and **definition by negation.**

Definition by Synonym

The simplest way to define a term is to supply a **synonym,** a word that means the same thing. A good synonym definition always uses an easier and more familiar word than the one being defined.

1. *Gregarious* means *sociable*.

2. *To procrastinate* means *to postpone needlessly*.

3. A *wraith* is a *ghost* or *phantom*.

4. *Adroitly* means *skillfully*.

Although you may not have known the words *gregarious, procrastination, wraith,* and *adroitly* before, the synonym definitions make it very clear what they mean.

A synonym should usually be the same part of speech as the word being defined, so it could be used as a substitute. *Gregarious* and *sociable* are both adjectives; *to procrastinate* and *to postpone* are verb forms; *wraith, ghost,* and *phantom* are nouns; *adroitly* and *skillfully* are adverbs.

5. Quarterback Payton Manning *adroitly* moved his team up the field.

6. Quarterback Payton Manning *skillfully* moved his team up the field.

■ In this sentence *skillfully* can be substituted for *adroitly*.

Unfortunately, it is not always possible to come up with a good synonym definition.

Definition by Class

The **class** definition is the one most often required in college and formal writing —in examinations, papers, and reports.

The class definition has two parts. First, the writer places the word to be defined into the larger **category,** or **class,** to which it belongs.

7. *Lemonade* is a *drink* . . .

8. An *orphan* is a *child* . . .

9. A *dictatorship* is a *form of government* . . .

Second, the writer provides the **distinguishing characteristics** or **details** that make this person, object, or idea *different* from all others in that category. What the reader wants to know is what *kind* of drink is lemonade? What *specific* type of child is an orphan? What *particular* form of government is a dictatorship?

10. *Lemonade* is a drink *made of lemons, sugar, and water*.

11. An *orphan* is a child *without living parents*.

12. A *dictatorship* is a form of government *in which one person has absolute control over his or her subjects*.

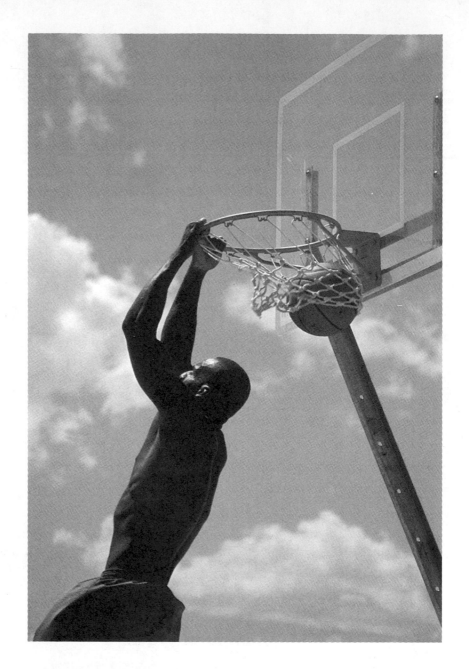

Here is a class definition for the action pictured: A slam-dunk is a basket that is scored when the shooter leaps high, forcefully throwing the basketball through the rim from above.

Think of class definitions as if they were in chart form:

Word	Category or Class	Distinguishing Facts or Details
lemonade	drink	made of lemons, sugar, and water
orphan	child	without living parents
dictatorship	form of government	one person has absolute control over his or her subjects

When you write a class definition, be careful not to place the word or term in too broad or vague a category. For instance, saying that lemonade is a *food* or that an orphan is a *person* will make your job of zeroing in on a distinguishing detail more difficult.

Besides making the category or class as limited as possible, be sure to make your distinguishing facts as specific and exact as you can. Saying that lemonade is a drink *made with water* or that an orphan is a child *who has lost family members* is not specific enough to give your reader an accurate definition.

Definition by Negation

A definition by **negation** means that the writer first says what something is not, and then says what it is.

13. A *good parent* does not just feed and clothe a child but loves, accepts, and supports that child for who he or she is.

14. *College* is not just a place to have a good time but a place to grow intellectually and emotionally.

15. *Liberty* does not mean having the right to do whatever you please but carries the obligation to respect the rights of others.

Definitions by negation are extremely helpful when you think that the reader has a preconceived idea about the word you wish to define. You say that *it is not* what the reader thought, but that *it is* something else entirely.

Here is a definition by negation: The fax machine is not the revolutionary new office machine that people think but an invention patented in 1863 and used to send words and pictures between the United States and France.

PRACTICE 1

Write a one-sentence definition by **synonym** for each of the following terms. Remember, the synonym should be more familiar than the term being defined.

1. *irate:* _____

2. *to elude:* _____

3. *pragmatic:* _____

4. *fiasco:* _____

5. *elated:* _____

PRACTICE 2

Here are five **class definitions.** Circle the category and underline the distinguishing characteristics in each. You may find it helpful to make a chart.

1. A *haiku* is a Japanese poem that has seventeen syllables.
2. A *homer* is a referee who unconsciously favors the home team.
3. An *ophthalmologist* is a doctor who specializes in diseases of the eye.
4. The *tango* is a ballroom dance that originated in Latin America and is in 2/4 or 4/4 time.
5. *Plagiarism* is stealing writing or ideas that are not one's own.

PRACTICE 3

Define the following words by **class definition.** You may find it helpful to use this form: "A _____ is a _____
(noun)   (class or category)

that _____."
(distinguishing characteristic)

1. *hamburger:* _____

_____

_____

2. *bikini:* _____

_____

_____

3. *snob:* _____

_____

_____

4. *mentor:* _____

_____

_____

5. *adolescence:* _____

_____

_____

PRACTICE 4

Write a one-sentence definition by **negation** for each of the following terms. First say what each term is not; then say what it is.

1. *hero:* _____

_____

_____

2. *final exam:* _____

_____

_____

3. *self-esteem:* _____

_____

_____

4. *intelligence:* _____

_____

_____

5. *freedom of speech:* _____

_____

_____

PART B   The Definition Paragraph

Sometimes a single-sentence definition may not be enough to define a word or term adequately. In such cases, the writer may need an entire paragraph in which he or she develops the definition by means of examples, descriptions, comparisons, contrasts, and so forth.

Topic Sentence

The topic sentence of a definition paragraph is often one of the single-sentence definitions discussed in Part A: definition by synonym, definition by class, definition by negation.

Here is the topic sentence of a definition paragraph:

> *Ambivalence* can be defined as a feeling or attitude that is both positive and negative at the same time.

- What kind of definition does the topic sentence use?

  _____

- To what larger category or class does *ambivalence* belong?

  _____

- What are the distinguishing details about *ambivalence* that make it different from all other feelings or attitudes?

  _____

Paragraph and Plan

Here is the entire paragraph:

> *Ambivalence* can be defined as a feeling or attitude that is both positive and negative at the same time. For instance, a young woman might feel *ambivalent* about motherhood. She may want to have a child yet fear that motherhood will use up energy she would like to spend on her career. Or a Michigan man who is offered a slightly higher salary in Arizona might be ambivalent about moving. He and his family don't want to leave their friends, their schools, and a city they love. On the other hand, they are tempted by a larger income and by Arizona's warm climate and clean air. Finally, two people may have ambivalent feelings about each other, loving and disliking each other at the same time. It hurts to be together, and it hurts to be apart; neither situation makes them happy. As these examples show, the double tug of ambivalence can complicate decision making.

■ One effective way for a writer to develop the body of a definition paragraph is to provide examples.*

■ What three examples does this writer give to develop the definition in the topic sentence?

_____

_____

■ By repeating the word being defined—or a form of it—in the context of each example, the writer helps the reader understand the definition better: A young woman might feel *ambivalent*, a Michigan man might be *ambivalent*, and two people may have *ambivalent* feelings.

Before writing the paragraph, the writer probably brainstormed or freewrote to gather ideas and then made an outline or a plan like this:

Topic sentence: *Ambivalence* can be defined as a feeling or attitude that is both positive and negative at the same time.

Example 1: A young woman

—wants to have a child

—yet fears motherhood will use up career energy

Example 2: Michigan man and his family

—don't want to leave friends, schools, city

—are tempted by income, climate, clean air

Example 3: Two people

—love each other

—also dislike each other

Conclusion: Ambivalence can complicate decisions.

■ Note that each example in the body of the paragraph clearly relates to the definition in the topic sentence.

Although examples are an excellent way to develop a definition paragraph, other methods of development are also possible. For instance, you might compare and contrast† *love* and *lust*, *assertiveness* and *aggressiveness*, or *the leader* and *the follower*. You could also combine definition and persuasion.‡ Such a paragraph might begin *College is a dating service* or *Alcoholism is not a moral weakness but a disease.* The rest of the paragraph would have to persuade readers that this definition is valid.

There are no transitional expressions used specifically for definition paragraphs. Sometimes phrases like *can be defined as* or *can be considered* or *means that* can help alert the reader that a definition paragraph will follow.§

---

* For more work on examples, see Chapter 5, "Illustration."

† For more work on contrast, see Chapter 10, "Comparison and Contrast."

‡ For more work on persuasion, see Chapter 13, "Persuasion."

§ For an entire essay developed by definition, see "Winning," Chapter 15, Part E.

Read the following paragraph carefully and then answer the questions.

A feminist is *not* a man-hater, a masculine woman, a demanding shrew, or someone who dislikes housewives. A feminist is simply a woman or man who believes that women should enjoy the same rights, privileges, opportunities, and pay as men. Because society has deprived women of many equal rights, feminists have fought for equality. For instance, Susan B. Anthony, a famous nineteenth-century feminist, worked to get women the right to vote. Today, feminists want women to receive equal pay for equal work. They support a woman's right to pursue her goals and dreams, whether she wants to be an astronaut, athlete, banker, or full-time homemaker. On the home front, feminists believe that two partners who work should equally share the housework and child care. Because the term is often misunderstood, some people don't call themselves feminists even though they share feminist values. But courageous feminists of both sexes continue to speak out for equality.

1. The definition here spans two sentences. What kind of definition does the writer use in sentence 1? _____

    _____

2. What kind of definition appears in sentence 2? _____

    _____

3. The paragraph is developed by describing some key beliefs of feminists. What are these? _____

    _____

    _____

4. Which point is supported by an example? _____

    _____

5. Make a plan or an outline of the paragraph.

    _____

    _____

    _____

    _____

    _____

    _____

    _____

_____

_____

_____

PRACTICE 6

Read the following paragraphs and answer the questions.

Induction is reasoning from particular cases to general principles; that is, the scientific method: you look at a number of examples, then come to a general conclusion based on the evidence. For instance, having known twenty-five people named Glenn, all of whom were men, you might naturally conclude, through induction, that all people named Glenn are men. The problem with inductive reasoning here, however, is Glenn Close, the movie actress.

Deduction is reasoning from the general to the particular. One starts from a statement known or merely assumed to be true and uses it to come to a conclusion about the matter at hand. Once you know that all people have to die sometime and that you are a person, you can logically deduce that you, too, will have to die sometime.

—Judy Jones and William Wilson, "100 Things Every
College Graduate Should Know," *Esquire*

1. What two terms are defined? _____

   _____

2. What kind of definition is used in both topic sentences? _____

   _____

3. In what larger category do the writers place both induction and deduction?

   _____

4. What example of induction do the writers give? _____

   _____

5. What example shows the *problem* with induction? _____

   _____

6. What example of deduction do the writers give? _____

   _____

PRACTICE 7

Here are some topic sentences for definition paragraphs. Choose one that interests you and make a plan for a paragraph, using whatever method of development seems appropriate.

1. An optimist is someone who usually expects the best from life and from people.

2. Prejudice means prejudging people on the basis of race, creed, age, or sex—not on their merits as individuals.

3. A wealthy person does not necessarily have money and possessions, but he or she might possess inner wealth—a loving heart and a creative mind.

4. Registration is a ritual torture that students must go through before they can attend their classes.

5. Bravery and bravado are very different character traits.

PRACTICE 8

The Martians have landed. You have been chosen to answer their questions about several things they have noticed on Earth. Since they can read English but cannot speak it, you must write a clear paragraph defining one of the following: *money, clothes, computers, cars, the president of the United States.* Begin with a one-sentence definition; then discuss, giving examples and details that fully define the word or term for your Martian readers.

✔ CHECKLIST: **The Process of Writing a Definition Paragraph**

Refer to this checklist of steps as you write a definition paragraph of your own.

____ 1. Narrow the topic in light of your audience and purpose.

____ 2. Compose a topic sentence that uses one of the three basic methods of definition discussed in this chapter: synonym, class, or negation.

____ 3. Decide on the method of paragraph development that is best suited to what you want to say.

____ 4. Freewrite or brainstorm to generate ideas that may be useful in your definition paragraph. (You may want to freewrite or brainstorm before you narrow the topic.)

____ 5. Select the best ideas and drop any ideas that do not clearly relate to the definition in your topic sentence.

____ 6. Make a plan or an outline for your paragraph, numbering the ideas in the order in which you will present them.

____ 7. Write a draft of your definition paragraph, using transitional expressions wherever they might be helpful.

____ 8. Revise as necessary, checking for support, unity, logic, and coherence.

____ 9. Proofread for errors in grammar, punctuation, sentence structure, spelling, and mechanics.

Suggested Topics for Definition Paragraphs

1. A self-starter

2. The loner (or life of the party, perfectionist, big mouth, Internet addict)

3. Country and western music (or rock, gospel, Celtic, or some other type of music)

4. Confidence

5. A dead-end job

6. A good marriage (or a good partner, parent, or friend)

7. The racing-car (or fashion, football, credit-card, computer-game, or other) fanatic

8. An interesting term you know from reading (*placebo, UFO, apartheid, hubris,* and so forth)

9. Spring break

10. A racist (sexist, terrorist, artist, philanthropist, or other *-ist*)

11. The night person (or morning person)

12. Integrity

13. A technical term you know from work or a hobby

14. A slang term you or your friends use

15. Writer's choice: _____

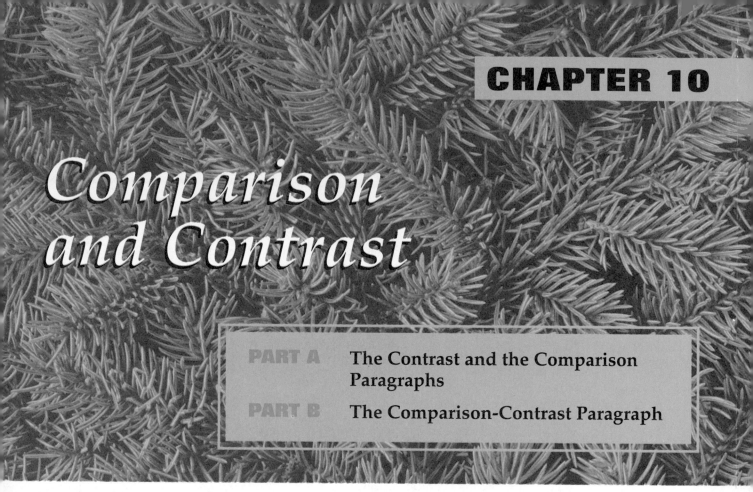

CHAPTER 10

Comparison and Contrast

PART A	The Contrast and the Comparison Paragraphs
PART B	The Comparison-Contrast Paragraph

To **contrast** two persons, places, or things is to examine the ways in which they are different. To **compare** them is to examine the ways in which they are similar.

Contrast and comparison are useful skills in daily life, work, and college. When you shop, you often compare and contrast. For instance, you might compare and contrast two dishwashers to get the better value. In fact, the magazine *Consumer Reports* was created to help consumers compare and contrast different product brands.

Your employer might ask you to compare and contrast two computers, two telephone services, or two shipping crates. Your job is to gather information about the similarities and differences to help your employer choose one over the other. In nearly every college course, you will be expected to compare and contrast—two generals, two types of storm systems, two minerals, or two painters of the same school.

PART A   The Contrast and the Comparison Paragraphs

Topic Sentence

Here is the topic sentence of a contrast paragraph:

> Although soul and hip-hop both spring from African-American roots, they are very different musical expressions.

■ The writer begins a contrast paragraph with a topic sentence that clearly states what two persons, things, or ideas will be contrasted.

■ What two things will be contrasted?

_____

■ What word or words in the topic sentence make it clear that the writer will contrast soul and hip-hop?

_____

Paragraph and Plan

Here is the entire paragraph:

> Although soul and hip-hop both spring from African-American roots, they are very different musical expressions. Soul music borrows from gospel and rhythm and blues. The singer's voice, backed up by live instruments, soars with emotion, with soul. This music captures the optimism of its time—the civil rights movement of the 1960s and hope for social change. There are two types of soul—the smooth Detroit style of the Supremes, Stevie Wonder, and the Temptations and the more gritty, gospel-driven Memphis style of Otis Redding and Booker T and the MGs. Soul music is upbeat and often joyful; its subjects are love and affirmation of the human condition. On the other hand, hip-hop (or rap) draws on hard rock, funk, and techno. The rapper chants rhymes against a driving instrumental background that may be prerecorded. Rap grew out of the New York ghettos in the late 1970s and the 1980s, when crack and guns flooded "the hood" and many dreams seemed broken. Of the rival East and West Coast rappers, New Yorkers include Grandmaster Flash, LL Cool J, and the murdered Biggie Smalls, while Los Angeles rappers include Ice Cube and the murdered Tupac Shakur. The subjects of hip-hop are racism, crime, and poverty. Both soul and hip-hop claim to "tell it like it is." Hip-hop's answer to the soulful Four Tops is the Furious Four. What's in a name? Perhaps the way the listener experiences reality.
>
> —Maurice Bosco (Student)

■ The writer first provides information about (A) soul music and then gives contrasting parallel information about (B) hip-hop.

■ What information about (A) soul does the writer provide in the first half of the

paragraph? _____

_____

_____

■ What contrasting parallel information does the writer provide about hip-hop

in the second half of the paragraph? _____

_____

_____

■ Why do you think the writer chose to present the points of contrast in this

order? _____

_____

■ Note that the last four sentences provide a thoughtful conclusion. What final

point does the writer make? _____

_____

Before composing the paragraph, the writer probably brainstormed or freewrote to gather ideas and then made an outline or a plan like this:

Topic sentence: Although soul and hip-hop both spring from African-American roots, they are very different musical expressions.

Points of Contrast	A. Soul	B. Hip-Hop
1. influences	gospel, R&B	rock, funk, techno
2. sound	soaring voice, live instruments	chanted rhymes; instrumentals may be prerecorded
3. time period	1960s, civil rights, hope for change	1970s–80s, crack, guns
4. types	Detroit, Memphis	New York, Los Angeles
5. subjects	love, affirmation	racism, crime, poverty

Organized in this manner, the plan for this contrast paragraph helps the writer make sure that the paragraph will be complete. That is, if the historical period of soul is discussed, that of hip-hop must also be discussed, and so on, for every point of contrast.

Here is another way to write the same paragraph:

Although soul and hip-hop both spring from African-American roots, they are very different musical expressions. Soul music borrows from gospel and rhythm and blues, whereas hip-hop (or rap) draws on hard rock, funk, and techno. The soul singer's voice, backed up by live instruments, soars with emotion, with soul; however, the rapper chants rhymes against a driving instrumental background that may be prerecorded. Soul music captures the optimism of its time—the civil rights movement of the 1960s and hope for social change. On the other hand, hip-hop grew out of the New York ghettos in the late 1970s and the 1980s, when crack and guns flooded "the hood" and many dreams seemed broken. There are two types of soul—the smooth Detroit style of the Supremes, Stevie Wonder, and the Temptations and the more gritty, gospel-driven Memphis style of Otis Redding and Booker T and the MGs. Of the rival East and West Coast rappers, New Yorkers include Grandmaster Flash, LL Cool J, and the murdered Biggie Smalls, while Los Angeles rappers include Ice Cube and the murdered Tupac Shakur. Whereas soul music's subjects are love and affirmation of the human condition, the subjects of hip-hop are racism, crime, and poverty. Both soul and hip-hop claim to "tell it like it is." Hip-hop's answer to the soulful Four Tops is the Furious Four. What's in a name? Perhaps the way the listener experiences reality.

■ Instead of giving all the information about soul music and then going on to hip-hop, this paragraph moves back and forth between soul and hip-hop, dealing with *each point of contrast separately.*

Use either one of these two patterns when writing a contrast or a comparison paragraph:

1. Present all the information about **A** and then provide parallel information about **B:**

   First all A: point 1
                        point 2
                        point 3

   Then all B: point 1
                      point 2
                      point 3

■ This pattern is good for paragraphs and for short compositions. The reader can easily remember what was said about *A* by the time he or she gets to *B.*

2. Move back and forth between **A** and **B.** Present one point about **A** and then go to the parallel point about **B.** Then move to the next point and do the same:

   First A, point 1;   **then B,** point 1

   First A, point 2;   **then B,** point 2

   First A, point 3;   **then B,** point 3

■ The second pattern is better for longer papers, where it might be hard for the reader to remember what the writer said about *A* by the time he or she gets to *B* a few paragraphs later. By going back and forth, the writer makes it easier for the reader to keep the contrasts or comparisons in mind.

What you have learned so far about planning a contrast paragraph holds true for a comparison paragraph as well. Just remember that a **contrast** *stresses differences* whereas a **comparison** *stresses similarities.*

Here is a comparison paragraph:

"Two birds of a feather," so the family describes my mother and me, and it's true that we have much in common. We share the same honey-colored skin, hazel eyes, and pouting mouth. I like to think I've inherited her creative flair. Though we were poor, she taught me that beauty requires style, not money, and I see her influence in my small apartment, which I have decorated with colorful fabrics and my own paintings. One similarity alarms me, however: both my mother and I were battered wives. She believed a woman's place is with her husband, so she stayed with my father despite the abuse. Eventually, he left us. Soon after I married, my husband hit me for the first time. Shocked to think that the secret pain of my mother's life would now be mine, I took the initiative, got counseling, and left him. Two birds of a feather, my mother and I, but not in this.

—Janice Wilson (Student)

■ What words in the topic sentence does the writer use to indicate that a comparison will follow? _____

_____

■ In what ways are the writer and her mother similar? _____

_____

_____

■ What transitional words stress the similarities? _____

_____

■ What pattern of presentation does the writer use? _____

_____

■ What one point of *contrast* serves as a strong punch line for the paragraph?

_____

_____

■ Make a plan or an outline of this comparison paragraph.

Transitional Expressions

Transitional expressions in contrast paragraphs stress opposition and difference:

Transitional Expressions for Contrast	
although	on the other hand
whereas	in contrast
but	while
however	yet
conversely	unlike

Transitional expressions in comparison paragraphs stress similarities:

Transitional Expressions for Comparison	
in the same way	just as . . . so
and, also, in addition	similarly
as well as	like
both, neither	too
each of	the same

As you write, avoid using just one or two of these transitional expressions. Learn new ones from the list and practice them in your paragraphs.*

PRACTICE 1

Read the following paragraph carefully and answer the questions.

Certain personality traits, like whether a person is more reactive or proactive, can predict success or its opposite. In his book *The Seven Habits of Highly Effective People*, Steven Covey writes that reactive people tend to sit back and wait for life or circumstances to bring them opportunities. They react instead of act. When good things happen, they are happy, but when bad things happen, they feel like victims. Reactive people often say things like, "There's nothing I can do," "I can't because . . . ," and "If only." In the short term, reactive people might feel comfortable playing it safe, holding back, and avoiding challenges; in the long term, though, they are often left dreaming. On the other hand, proactive people know that they have the power to choose their responses to whatever life brings. They act instead of react: If things aren't going their way, they take action to help create the outcome they desire. Proactive people can be recognized by their tendency to say things like "Let's consider the alternatives," "I prefer," "We can," and "I will." In the short term, proactive people might face the discomfort of failing because they take on challenges, set goals, and work toward them. But in the long term, Covey says, proactive people are the ones who achieve their dreams.

1. Can you tell from the topic sentence whether a contrast or comparison will

   follow? _____

   _____

2. What two personality types are being contrasted? _____

3. What information does the writer provide about reactive people? _____

   _____

   _____

4. What parallel information does the writer provide about proactive people?

   _____

   _____

5. What pattern does the writer of this paragraph use to present the contrasts?

   _____

6. What transitional expression does the writer use to stress the shift from *A* to

   B? _____

---

*For an entire essay developed by comparison-contrast, see "Two Childhoods," Chapter 15, Part F.

PRACTICE 2

This paragraph is hard to follow because it lacks transitional expressions that emphasize contrast. Revise the paragraph, adding transitional expressions of contrast. Strive for variety.

The city of Bangalore, India, is a jarring mixture of new and old. Bangalore has become a world center of the computer software industry, and companies like IBM, Dell, and Hewlett Packard have built dozens of gleaming new buildings. The rutted dirt roads are choked with oxcarts, and three-wheeled taxis belch black fumes. Over breakfast each morning at the Taj Residency Hotel, Indian programmers chat with American engineers about the latest piece of computer code. Sandal-clad women carry baskets of tools on their heads at a nearby construction site, and workers drag a huge pipe into place, using only ropes. Each night, teams of programmers send their work by satellite uplink to teams on the other side of the earth. They must rely on diesel generators because power outages lasting two to three hours occur almost every day.

PRACTICE 3

Below are three plans for contrast paragraphs. The points of contrast in the second column do not follow the same order as the points in the first column. In addition, one detail is missing. First, number the points in the second column to match those in the first. Then fill in the missing detail.

1. Shopping at a Supermarket

1. carries all brands

2. lower prices

3. open seven days a week

4. little personal service

5. no credit

Shopping at a Local Grocery

____ personal service

____ closed on Sundays

____ prices often higher

____ _____

____ credit available for steady customers

2. My Son

1. fifteen years old

2. likes to be alone

My Daughter

____ good at making minor household repairs

____ likes to be with friends

3. reads a lot   ____ doesn't like to read

4. is an excellent cook   ____ expects to attend a technical college

5. wants to go to chef school   ____ _____

3. Job A   **Job B**

1. good salary   ____ three-week vacation

2. office within walking distance   ____ work on a team with others

3. two-week vacation   ____ one-hour bus ride to office

4. work alone   ____ health insurance

5. lots of overtime   ____ no overtime

6. no health insurance   ____ _____

PRACTICE 4

Here are five topics for either contrast or comparison paragraphs. Compose two topic sentences for each topic, one for a possible contrast paragraph and one for a possible comparison paragraph.

Topic	Topic Sentences
EXAMPLE Two members of my family	A. My brother and sister have different attitudes toward exercise.
	B. My parents are alike in that they're easygoing.
1. Two friends or coworkers	A. _____
	_____
	_____
	B. _____
	_____
	_____
2. Two kinds of music or dancing	A. _____
	_____
	_____
	B. _____

3. You as a child and you as an adult   A. _____

_____

_____

B. _____

_____

4. Two vacations   A. _____

_____

_____

B. _____

_____

5. Two teachers   A. _____

_____

_____

B. _____

_____

_____

PRACTICE 5

Here are four topic sentences for comparison or contrast paragraphs. For each topic sentence, think of one supporting point of comparison or contrast and explain that point in one or two sentences.

1. When it comes to movies (TV shows, books, entertainment), Demetrios and Arlene have totally different tastes.

_____

_____

2. The average bowl of chili and my family's Texas chili have little in common besides beans.

_____

3. Although there are obvious differences, the two neighborhoods (blocks, homes) have much in common.

_____

_____

4. Paying taxes is like having a tooth pulled.*

_____

_____

PRACTICE 6

Now choose one of the topic sentences you wrote in Practice 4, or write a new topic sentence. Develop three or four points of comparison or contrast to support your topic sentence, and make a plan for the paragraph, numbering points in the order you wish to present them.

 ## WRITING ASSIGNMENT 1

Study this photograph of a sunbather at the Indiana Dunes National Lakeshore. Then write a paragraph *contrasting* the man and his rather unusual surroundings.

_____

* For more work on this kind of comparison, see Chapter 21, "Revising for Language Awareness," Part D.

Notice the man's posture, clothing, and apparent mood. How do these differ from the scene on the dunes behind him? In your topic sentence, state your overall impression. Then support this main idea with details. Remember to conclude your paragraph; don't just stop abruptly.

✔ CHECKLIST: The Process of Writing a Contrast or Comparison Paragraph

Refer to this checklist of steps as you write a contrast or comparison paragraph of your own.

_____ 1. Narrow the topic in light of your audience and purpose.

_____ 2. Compose a topic sentence that clearly states that a contrast or a comparison will follow.

_____ 3. Freewrite or brainstorm to generate as many points of contrast or comparison as you can think of. (You may want to freewrite or brainstorm before you narrow the topic.)

_____ 4. Choose the points you will use, and drop any details that are not really part of the contrast or the comparison.

_____ 5. List parallel points of contrast or of comparison for both *A* and *B*.

_____ 6. Make a plan or an outline, numbering all the points of contrast or comparison in the order in which you will present them in the paragraph.

_____ 7. Write a draft of your contrast or comparison paragraph, using transitional expressions that stress either differences or similarities.

_____ 8. Revise as necessary, checking for support, unity, logic, and coherence.

_____ 9. Proofread for errors in grammar, punctuation, sentence structure, spelling, and mechanics.

Suggested Topics for Contrast or Comparison Paragraphs

1. Compare or contrast two attitudes toward money (the spendthrift and the miser) or marriage (the confirmed single and the committed partner).

2. Compare or contrast two young children parented in different ways.

3. Compare or contrast a job you hated and a job you loved.

4. Compare or contrast two athletes in the same sport.

5. Compare or contrast the same scene at two times of day.

6. Compare or contrast two high schools or colleges that you have attended (perhaps one in the United States and one in a different country).

7. Compare or contrast two ways to treat a cold, flu, or headache—Western medicine and some alternative.

8. Compare or contrast your *expectations* of a person, place, or situation and *reality*.

9. Compare or contrast your best friend and your spouse or partner.

10. Writer's choice: _____

PART B The Comparison-Contrast Paragraph

Sometimes an assignment will call for you to write a paragraph that both compares and contrasts, one that stresses both similarities and differences.

Here is a comparison-contrast paragraph:

> Although contemporary fans would find the game played by the Knickerbockers—the first organized baseball club—similar to modern baseball, they would also note some startling differences. In 1845, as now, the four bases of the playing field were set in a diamond shape, ninety feet from one another. Nine players took the field. The object of the game was to score points by hitting a pitched ball and running around the bases. The teams changed sides after three outs. However, the earlier game was also different. The umpire sat at a table along the third base line instead of standing behind home plate. Unlike the modern game, the players wore no gloves. Rather than firing the ball over the plate at ninety miles an hour, the pitcher gently tossed it underhand to the batter. Since there were no balls and strikes, the batter could wait for the pitch he wanted. The game ended, not when nine innings were completed, but when one team scored twenty-one runs, which were called "aces."

■ How are the Knickerbockers' game and modern baseball similar?

_____

_____

_____

■ How are these two versions of the game different? _____

_____

_____

_____

_____

_____

_____

■ What transitional expressions in the paragraph emphasize similarities and

differences? _____

_____

Before composing this comparison-contrast paragraph, the writer probably brainstormed or freewrote to gather ideas and then made a plan like this:

Topic sentence: Although contemporary fans would find the game played by the Knickerbockers—the first organized baseball club—similar to modern baseball, they would also note some startling differences.

Comparisons	Knickerbockers	Modern Game
Point 1	four bases, ninety feet apart, in diamond shape	
Point 2	nine players	
Point 3	scoring points	
Point 4	three outs	
Contrasts		
Point 1	umpire sat at third base line	umpire at home plate
Point 2	no gloves	gloves
Point 3	pitcher gently tossed ball	pitcher fires ball at plate
Point 4	no balls and strikes	balls and strikes
Point 5	twenty-one "aces" to win, no innings	most runs to win, nine innings

■ A plan such as this makes it easier for the writer to organize a great deal of material.

■ The writer begins by listing all the points of comparison—how the Knicker-bockers' game and modern baseball are similar. Then the writer lists all the points of contrast—how they are different.

PRACTICE 7

Here is a somewhat longer comparison and contrast (two paragraphs). Read it carefully and answer the questions.

No meal eaten in the Middle East ends without coffee or tea, but coffee takes precedence most of the time. Coffee is a social beverage, offered to guests by housewives and to customers by merchants; to refuse it borders upon insult.

There are two distinct but similar ways of preparing it, Turkish and Arabic. Both are served black, in cups the size of a demitasse or smaller. And both are brewed by starting with green beans, roasting them to a chocolate brown color, pulverizing them at once, either with mortar and pestle or in a handsome cylindrical coffee mill of chased brass, and quickly steeping them in boiling water.

The Turkish version is made in a coffee pot that has a long handle to protect the fingers from the fire and a shape narrowing from the bottom to the open neck to intensify the foaming action as the coffee boils up. Water, sugar and coffee are stirred together to your taste; then, at the first bubbling surge, the pot is whisked from the fire. It is returned briefly one or two more times to build up the foamy head, which is poured into each cup in equal amounts, to be followed by the rest of the brew, grounds and all. The dregs soon settle to the bottom, and the rich, brown coffee that covers them is ready to be enjoyed, with more sugar if you like. The Arabs prepare coffee in a single boil; they almost never use sugar; they pour the liquid into a second pot, leaving the sediment in the first, and then add such heady spices as cloves or cardamon seeds.

—*Foods of the World/Middle Eastern Cooking,*
Time-Life Books

1. What two things does this writer contrast and compare? _____

_____

_____

2. What words indicate that both contrast *and* comparison will follow?

_____

3. How are Arabic and Turkish coffee similar? _____

_____

_____

_____

_____

4. How are Arabic and Turkish coffee different? _____

_____

_____

_____

5. On a separate sheet of paper, make a plan or an outline for these paragraphs.

WRITING ASSIGNMENT 2

On this page and the next are photos of two couples. Study closely the details of facial expression, gesture, clothing, and so forth. For a paragraph that both *compares and contrasts* the two couples, jot down possible similarities and differences. Ask yourself, "What is my impression of each pair? How do they seem to be getting along with each other? How are the couples alike and how are they different?" Then plan and write your paragraph.

If you prefer, write a paragraph comparing and contrasting the two women *or* the two men.

✔ WORKING THROUGH THE COMPARISON-CONTRAST PARAGRAPH

You can work through the comparison-contrast paragraph in the same way that you do a comparison or a contrast paragraph. Follow the steps in the earlier checklist, but make certain that your paragraph shows both similarities and differences.

Suggested Topics for Comparison-Contrast Paragraphs

1. Compare and contrast two ways to prepare for an examination.

2. Compare and contrast the requirements for two jobs or careers.

3. Compare and contrast your life now with your life five years ago.

4. Compare and contrast two films on similar subjects.

5. Compare and contrast learning something from experience and learning something from books.

6. Compare and contrast two singers or musicians.

7. Compare and contrast parties, weddings, or funerals in two different cultures.

8. Compare and contrast two popular television programs of the same type (newscasts, situation comedies, talk shows, and so on).

9. Compare and contrast two attitudes toward one subject (firearms, education, immigration, welfare, and so forth).

10. Writer's choice: _____

CHAPTER 11

Classification

To **classify** is to gather into types, kinds, or categories according to a single basis of division.

Mailroom personnel, for example, might separate incoming mail into four piles: orders, bills, payments, and inquiries. Once the mail has been divided in this manner—according to which department should receive each pile—it can be efficiently delivered.

The same information can be classified in more than one way. The Census Bureau collects a variety of data about the people living in the United States. One way to classify the data is by age group—the number of people under eighteen, between eighteen and fifty-five, over fifty-five, and over seventy. Such information might be useful in developing programs for college-bound youth or for the elderly. Other ways of dividing the population are by geographic location, occupation, family size, level of education, and so on.

Whether you classify rocks by their origin for a geology course or children by their stages of growth for a psychology course, you will be organizing large groups into smaller, more manageable units that can be explained to your reader.

Topic Sentence

Here is the topic sentence for a classification paragraph:

> Gym-goers can be classified according to their priorities at the gym as sweaty fanatics, fashionites, busybodies, or fit normals.

- The writer begins a classification paragraph with a topic sentence that clearly states what group of people or things will be classified.
- What group of people will be classified? _____
- Into how many categories will they be divided? What are the categories?

_____

Paragraph and Plan

Here is the entire paragraph:

> Gym-goers can be classified according to their priorities at the gym as sweaty fanatics, fashionites, busybodies, and fit normals. Sweaty fanatics take gym-going to the extreme. They hog the machines, drip sweat everywhere, and barely look up if someone falls off the treadmill beside them. Occasionally, they will stare at the mirror, admiring the muscle group they are working on. The fashionites also admire their own reflections, but they barely break a sweat. For them, the gym is just another excuse to buy clothes. They wear perfectly matched workout clothes with color-coordinated sweat bands and gym shoes. The third group, the busybodies, can't stop talking. Whether it's making idle chitchat or correcting another exerciser's form on a machine, they seem unable to shut up. Not even headphones and one-word answers can stop the busybodies from babbling. Luckily, the fit normals keep things from getting too far out of control. They come to the gym to work out, stay healthy, and go home, but they remember that basic good manners apply in every setting.
>
> —Laurie Zamot (Student)

■ On what basis does the writer classify gym-goers? _____

_____

■ What information does the writer provide about the first type, sweaty fanatics?

_____

_____

■ What information does the writer provide about the second type, fashionites?

_____

_____

■ What information does the writer provide about the third type, busybodies?

_____

_____

■ What information does the writer provide about the fourth type, the fit normals? _____

_____

■ Why do you think the writer discusses fit normals last? _____

_____

Before composing the paragraph, the writer probably brainstormed or free-wrote to gather ideas and then made a plan like this:

Topic sentence: Gym-goers can be classified according to their priorities at the gym as sweaty fanatics, fashionites, busybodies, or fit normals.

Type 1:	Sweaty fanatics
	—hog machines; drip sweat
	—barely look if someone falls
	—stare in mirror, admiring muscles
Type 2:	Fashionites
	—admire themselves but don't sweat
	—excuse to buy clothes
	—matched workout clothes
	—coordinating sweat bands and gym shoes
Type 3:	Busybodies
	—can't stop talking, advising
	—headphones, short answers don't work
Type 4:	Fit normals
	—keep things from going out of control
	—work out, go home
	—remember good manners even in gym

■ Note that the body of the paragraph discusses all four types of gym-goers mentioned in the topic sentence and does not add any new ones.

This classification paragraph sticks to a single method of classification: *the priorities of gym-goers at the gym*. If the paragraph had also discussed a fourth category—*left-handed gym-goers*—the initial basis of classification would fall apart because *left-handedness* has nothing to do with *the priorities of different gym-goers.*

The topic sentence of a classification paragraph usually has two parts: the *topic* and the *basis of classification*. The basis of classification is the controlling idea: it *controls* how the writer will approach the topic. Stating it in writing will help keep the paragraph on track.

There is no set rule about which category to present first, second, or last in a classification paragraph. However, the paragraph should follow some kind of **logical sequence** from the most to least outrageous, least to most expensive, from the largest to the smallest category, and so on.*

Transitional Expressions

Transitional expressions in classification paragraphs stress divisions and categories:

---

* For more work on order, see Chapter 4, "Achieving Coherence," Part A. For a complete essay developed by classification, see "The Potato Scale," Chapter 15, Part G.

Transitional Expressions for Classification	
can be divided	the first type
can be classified	the second kind
can be categorized	the last category

PRACTICE 1

Read the following paragraph carefully and answer the questions.

Judges can be divided, on the basis of their written opinions, into three categories: conservative, liberal, and centrist. Although all judges respect the law, conservative judges have an especially strong belief in the importance of the law and the history surrounding it. They believe that real justice comes only from strictly applying the law to the facts of a case, whether or not the outcome seems fair to an individual. On the other hand, liberal judges look beyond a rigid reading to the "spirit of the law" in their search for real justice in a case. They might broadly interpret the law in order to champion individual rights. The outcome of the case matters more to them than the letter of the law. Finally, centrist judges walk the middle ground between conservative and liberal. They do not apply the law as rigidly as conservative judges, yet they are not as willing as liberal judges to apply the law loosely. Having different types of judges helps balance our legal system; their differing views help protect both the law and individual rights.

1. How many categories are there, and what are they?

   _____

2. On what basis does the writer classify judges?

   _____

3. Make a plan of the paragraph on a separate sheet of paper.

PRACTICE 2

Each group of things or persons on the following page has been divided according to a single basis of classification. However, one item in each group does not belong—it does not fit that single basis of classification.

Read each group of items carefully; then circle the letter of the one item that does *not* belong. Next write the single basis of classification that includes the rest of the group.

EXAMPLE Shirts
a. cotton
b. suede
c. short-sleeved
d. polyester

material they are made of
_____

1. Shoes
   a. flat heels
   b. 2-inch heels
   c. patent leather heels
   d. 3-inch heels

   _____

2. Beds
   a. double
   b. twin
   c. feather
   d. king

   _____

3. Students
   a. talkative in class
   b. very hard working
   c. goof-offs
   d. moderately hard working

   _____

4. Contact lenses
   a. soft
   b. green
   c. brown
   d. lavender

   _____

5. Apartments
   a. two-bedroom
   b. three-bedroom
   c. penthouse
   d. studio apartment

   _____

6. Dates
   a. very good-looking
   b. sometimes pay
   c. always pay
   d. expect me to pay

   _____

7. Milk
   a. 2 percent fat
   b. whole
   c. chocolate
   d. 1 percent fat

   _____

8. Drivers
   a. obey the speed limit
   b. teenage drivers
   c. speeders
   d. creepers

   _____

PRACTICE 3

Any group of persons, things, or ideas can be classified in more than one way, depending on the basis of classification. For instance, students in your class can be classified on the basis of height (short, average, tall) or on the basis of class participation (often participate, sometimes participate, never participate). Both of these groupings are valid classifications of the same group of people.

Think of two ways in which each of the following groups could be classified.

EXAMPLE

Group	Basis of Classification
Bosses	(A) how demanding they are
	(B) how generous they are
1. Members of my family	(A) _____
	(B) _____
2. Hurricanes	(A) _____
	(B) _____
3. Fans of a certain sport	(A) _____
	(B) _____
4. Vacations	(A) _____
	(B) _____
5. Fitness magazines	(A) _____
	(B) _____

PRACTICE 4

Listed below are three groups of people or things. Decide on a single basis of classification for each group and the categories that would develop from your basis of classification. Finally, write a topic sentence for each of your classifications.

EXAMPLE

Group	Basis of Classification	Categories
Professors at Pell College	methods of instruction	1. lectures
		2. class discussions
		3. both

Topic Sentence: Professors at Pell College can be classified according to their

methods of instruction: those who lecture, those who encourage class discussion,

and those who do both.

Group	Basis of Classification	Categories
1. Car owners	_____	_____
	_____	_____
		_____
		_____

Topic sentence: _____

_____

_____

_____

2. Credit-card users	_____	_____
	_____	_____
		_____
		_____

Topic sentence: _____

_____

_____

_____

3. Ways of reacting to crisis	_____	_____
	_____	_____
		_____
		_____

Topic sentence: _____

_____

_____

_____

PRACTICE 5

Now choose the classification in Practice 4 that most interests you and make a plan or outline for a paragraph on a separate sheet of paper. As you work, make sure that you have listed all possible categories for your basis of classification. Remember, every car owner or credit card user should fit into one of your categories. Finally, write your paragraph, describing each category briefly and perhaps giving an example of each.

PRACTICE 6

In a group of four or five classmates, choose one of these topics:

> friends
> restaurants (or food sources) on or near campus
> places to study

Now discuss various ways in which you could classify the members of this group; list at least ten ways. For example, you could classify *friends* on the basis of their generosity, loyalty, or supportiveness. Now, from your list, choose the classification that most interests your group and make a plan for a paragraph. Write down a clear *basis of classification* and three to five possible *categories or groups* based on that classification; make sure your categories include every person or place in the larger group. Your instructor may want each group to explain its classification plan to the whole class.

Next, each group member can write a paragraph based on the plan. As you draft and revise, adjust your topic sentence and categories, and refer to the checklist.

✔ **CHECKLIST: The Process of Writing a Classification Paragraph**

Refer to this checklist of steps as you write a classification paragraph.

—— 1. Narrow the topic in light of your audience and purpose. Think in terms of a group of people or things that can be classified easily into types or categories.

—— 2. Decide on a single basis of classification. This basis will depend on what information you wish to give your audience.

—— 3. Compose a topic sentence that clearly shows what you are dividing into categories or types. If you wish, your topic sentence can state the basis on which you are making the classification and the types that will be discussed in the paragraph.

—— 4. List the categories into which the group is being classified. Be sure that your categories cover all the possibilities. Do not add any new categories that are not logically part of your original basis of classification.

_____ 5. Freewrite, cluster, or brainstorm to generate information, details, and examples for each of the categories. (You may want to prewrite before you narrow the topic.)

_____ 6. Select the best details and examples, and drop those that are not relevant to your classification.

_____ 7. Make a plan or an outline for your paragraph, numbering the categories in the order in which you will present them.

_____ 8. Write a draft of your classification paragraph, using transitional expressions wherever they may be helpful.

_____ 9. Revise as necessary, checking for support, unity, logic, and coherence.

_____ 10. Proofread for errors in grammar, punctuation, sentence structure, spelling, and mechanics.

Suggested Topics for Classification Paragraphs

1. People waiting in a line

2. Jobs

3. Women or men you date

4. Clothing in your closet

5. Friends

6. Students in a particular class

7. Problems facing college freshmen or someone new to a job

8. College classes or instructors

9. Ways to prevent school violence

10. Neighbors or coworkers

11. Kinds of success

12. Performers of one type of music

13. Kinds of marriages

14. Brands of jeans, backpacks, cola drinks, or some other product

15. Writer's choice: _____

CHAPTER 12

Cause and Effect

The ability to think through **causes and effects** is a key to success in many college courses, jobs, and everyday situations. Daily we puzzle over the **causes** of, or reasons for, events: What caused one brother to drop out of school and another to succeed brilliantly? What causes Jenine's asthma attacks? Why did the stock market plunge 300 points?

Effects are the *results* of a cause or causes. Does playing violent computer games affect a child's behavior? What are the effects of being a twin, keeping a secret, or winning the lottery?

Most events worth examining have complex, not simple, causes and effects. That is, they may have several causes and several effects. Certainly, in many fields, questions of cause and effect challenge even the experts: *What will be the long-term effects of the breakup of the former Soviet Union? What causes the HIV virus to disappear from the blood of some infected babies?* (This one answer could help save millions of lives.)

Topic Sentence

Here is the topic statement of a cause and effect paragraph; the writer has chosen to break the information into two sentences.

> What killed off the dinosaurs—and 70 percent of life on earth—65 million years ago? According to recent research, this massive destruction had three causes.

■ The writer begins a cause and effect paragraph by clearly stating the subject and indicating whether causes or effects will be discussed. What is the subject

of this paragraph? Will causes or effects be the focus? _____

_____

■ The writer states the topic in two sentences rather than one. Is this effective? Why or why not? (A single sentence might read, "According to recent research, the massive destruction of dinosaurs and other creatures 65 million years ago

had three causes.") _____

■ Words like *causes, reasons,* and *factors* are useful to show causes. Words like *effects, results,* and *consequences* are useful to show effects.

Paragraph and Plan

Here is the entire paragraph:

> What killed off the dinosaurs—and 70 percent of life on earth—65 million years ago? According to recent research, this massive destruction had three causes. Dr. Peter Ward of the University of Washington reports that the first cause was simple "background extinction." This is the normal disappearance of some animals and plants that goes on all the time. Second, a drop in sea level during this period slowly destroyed about 25 percent more of the world's species. Last and most dramatic, a comet as big as Manhattan smashed into the earth near Mexico's Yucatan peninsula, literally shaking the world. The huge buried crater left by this comet was found in 1991. Now Dr. Ward has proved that ash and a rare metal from that fiery crash fell around the globe. This means that the impact, fires, smoke, and ash quickly wiped out the dinosaurs and much of life on earth. This great "die-off" cleared the way for mammals to dominate the earth.

■ How many causes does this writer give for the destruction of the dinosaurs

and other species? What are they? _____

_____

■ Did the writer make up these ideas? If not, who or what is the source of the

information? _____

■ What transitional words introduce each of the three causes? _____

_____

■ What kind of order is used in this paragraph?* _____

Before writing the paragraph, the writer probably jotted a plan like this:

   Topic sentence: According to recent research, this massive destruction had three causes.

            —write a catchy introductory sentence?

            —mention time, 65 million years ago

_____
* For more work on order, see Chapter 4, "Achieving Coherence," Part A.

Cause 1:   "background extinction"

—normal disappearance of animals and plants

—give credit to Dr. Ward

Cause 2:   drop in sea level

—25 percent more species destroyed

Cause 3:   giant comet hit earth

—big as Manhattan

—crater found in 1991 near Yucatan peninsula

—now Ward proves ash and rare metal circled globe

—this comet destroyed dinosaurs and others

Conclusion: "die-off" cleared way for mammals

—OR tie to current news and films about comet danger

Other paragraphs examine *effects,* not causes. Either they try to predict future effects of something happening now, or they analyze past effects of something that happened earlier, as does this paragraph:

> For Christy Haubegger, the lack of Latina role models had life-changing consequences. As a Mexican-American girl adopted by Anglo parents, Christy found no reflection of herself in teen magazines or books. One result of seeing mostly blonde, blue-eyed models was an increase in her adolescent insecurities. A more damaging effect was Christy's confusion as she wondered what career to pursue; there were no Hispanic role models in schoolbooks to suggest possible futures for this excellent student. Even at Stanford Law School, Christy and her friends missed the inspiration and encouragement of professional Latina role models. At Stanford, Christy began to see this problem as an opportunity. She decided to start a national magazine that would showcase talented and successful Latinas. The 27-year-old made a detailed business plan and, incredibly, won the financial backing of the CEO of *Essence* magazine. In 1996, the first issue of *Latina* hit the newsstands—the very positive consequence of an old loneliness.

■ Underline the topic sentence in this paragraph.

■ For Ms. Haubegger, the lack of Latina role models caused "life-changing consefquences." What effects are discussed? _____

_____

_____

■ What order does the writer follow? _____

■ Notice that the paragraph first discusses negative effects and then a positive one.

Before you write about causes or effects, do some mental detective work. First, search out the three most important causes or effects. For example, if you are trying to understand the causes of a friend's skiing accident, you might consider the snow conditions that day, whether he took unnecessary risks, and whether he had been drinking.

Causes	Effect	Further Effects
ice on the ski slope		can't drive
J. took steep course	J. breaks his leg	can't play sports
had two beers		decides to read more

In exploring the effects of something, consider both short-term and long-term effects and both negative and positive effects. (Although Jay could *not* do many things, perhaps he took advantage of his recovery time to read more or to learn a new computer program.)

Avoiding Problems in Cause and Effect Writing

1. **Do not oversimplify.** Avoid the trap of naming one cause for a complex problem: *Why did they divorce? Because she is a hothead.* Or *The reason that reading scores have fallen in the school is television.* Searching for the three most important causes or effects is a good way to avoid oversimplifying.

2. **Do not confuse time order with causation.** If your eye starts watering seconds after the doorbell rings, you cannot assume that the doorbell made your eye water. Were you peeling onions? Is it allergy season? Do you need to wet your contact lenses?

3. **Do not confuse causes and effects.** This sounds obvious, but separating causes and effects can be tricky. (Is Rita's positive attitude the cause of her success in sales or the result of it?)

Transitional Expressions

These transitional expressions are helpful in cause and effect paragraphs, which often imply order of importance or time order:*

Transitional Expressions	
To Show Causes	**To Show Effects**
the first cause (second, third)	one important effect
the first reason (second, third)	another result
yet another factor	a third outcome
because	as a result
is caused by	consequently
results from	then, next, therefore, thus, so

* To read an essay of cause and effect, see "Why I Stayed and Stayed," Chapter 15, Part H.

PRACTICE 1

Read this paragraph and answer the questions.

Sadly, this college is part of a national trend: Date rape is on the rise. To stop date rape, college administrators and students must understand and deal with its possible causes. First, some fraternities and male peer groups on campus promote an attitude of disrespect toward women. This mentality sets the stage for date rape. Second, alcohol and drugs erode good judgment and self-control. The kegs, barrels, and bags consumed at many parties here put students at risk, including the risk of date rape. A third cause of date rape is miscommunication between men and women. Men and women often have different ideas of what date rape is or even if it exists. We need campus workshops in which we can discuss this issue openly and come to some understanding between the sexes. Date rape is a serious problem that can ruin lives. We can make a difference by addressing the causes of date rape: the male mentality of disrespect, heavy campus use of alcohol and drugs, and the differing views of men and women.

—Michael White Moon (Student)

1. Underline the topic sentence. Does this paragraph discuss the causes or effects of date rape? _____

2. Do you agree with this student's analysis of the problem? Would you name other causes, and if so, which? _____

   _____

3. On a separate sheet of paper, make a plan of this paragraph.

4. Does Mr. White Moon discuss the three causes in a logical order? Why or why not? _____

   _____

PRACTICE 2

To practice separating cause from effect, write the cause and the effect contained in each item below.

EXAMPLE Fewer people are attending concerts at the Boxcar Theater because ticket prices have nearly doubled.

Cause: _ticket prices nearly doubled_____

Effect: _fewer people attending concerts_____

1. A thunderstorm was approaching, so we moved our picnic into the van.

   Cause: _____

   Effect: _____

2. Seeing my father suffer because he could not read motivated me to excel in school.

   Cause: _____

   Effect: _____

3. One study showed that laughter extended the lives of cancer patients.

   Cause: _____

   Effect: _____

4. Americans are having fewer children and doing so later in life. Some experts believe this is why they are spending more money every year on their pets.

   Cause: _____

   Effect: _____

5. According to Celtics coach Rick Pitino, what turns talent into greatness is hard work.

   Cause: _____

   Effect: _____

6. Many doctors urged that trampolines be banned because of an "epidemic" of injuries to children playing on them.

   Cause: _____

   Effect: _____

7. I bought this glow-in-the-dark fish lamp for one reason only: it was on sale.

   Cause: _____

   Effect: _____

8. As more people spend time surfing the Internet, television viewing is declining for the first time in fifty years.

   Cause: _____

   Effect: _____

9. Wild animals in South African game parks can bring in millions of tourist dollars; consequently, the government is trying to save many species.

   Cause: _____

   Effect: _____

10. For years, Charboro cigarettes outsold all competitors as a result of added ammonia. This ammonia gave smokers' brains an extra "kick."

    Cause: _____

    First effect: _____

    Second effect: _____

PRACTICE 3

List three causes *or* three effects to support each topic sentence below. First, read the topic sentence to see whether causes or effects are called for. Then think, jot, and list your three best ideas.

1. The huge success of Barbie (or some other toy, game, or product) has a number of causes. _____

    _____

    _____

2. There are several reasons why AIDS continues to spread among teenagers, despite widespread knowledge about the deadly nature of the disease. _____

    _____

    _____

    _____

3. Reading books by authors of many nationalities, instead of just American and English authors, has many positive (or negative) effects on American students. _____

    _____

    _____

    _____

PRACTICE 4

Now choose one topic from Practice 3 that interests you and write a paragraph of cause or effect on notebook paper. Before you write a draft, think and make a plan. Have you chosen the three most important causes or effects and decided on an effective order in which to present them? As you write, use transitional expressions to help the reader follow your ideas.

PRACTICE 5

In a group of four or five classmates, read this passage aloud. Then follow the directions below.

Creative risk takers are often high achievers who tend to start their own businesses or become leaders in some other way. Researchers have identified two different types of home environments that tend to produce creative risk takers: (1) "high expectation families" who enthusiastically support the child and expect great things from him or her and (2) very poor, alcoholic, or broken homes where the child receives almost no support and few positive expectations.

Your group should analyze possible reasons why households of the *second* type tend to produce creative risk takers. Write down your three best reasons. Your instructor might wish to have you report your theories to the class.

✔ **CHECKLIST: The Process of Writing a Cause and Effect Paragraph**

Refer to this checklist as you write a cause and effect paragraph.

—— 1. Narrow the topic in light of your audience and purpose. Think of a subject that can be analyzed for clear causes or effects.

—— 2. Decide whether you will emphasize causes or effects. What information would be most interesting to your audience?

—— 3. Compose a topic sentence that states the subject and indicates whether causes or effects will be discussed.

—— 4. Now freewrite, brainstorm, or cluster to find at least three possible causes or effects. Do your mental detective work. At this stage, think of all possible causes; think of short- and long-term effects, as well as positive and negative effects.

—— 5. Select the best causes or effects with which to develop your paragraph. Drop those that are not relevant.

—— 6. Make a plan or an outline for your paragraph, numbering the causes or effects in the order in which you will present them.

—— 7. Write a first draft of your cause and effect paragraph, explaining each point fully so that your reader understands just how X caused Y. Use transitional expressions to emphasize these relationships.

—— 8. Revise as necessary, checking for good support, unity, logic, and coherence. Does your paragraph have an interesting opening sentence?

_____ 9. Proofread for errors in grammar, punctuation, sentence structure, spelling, and mechanics. Especially watch for your personal error patterns.

Suggested Topics for Cause and Effect Paragraphs

1. Reasons why someone made an important decision

2. Reasons why some people cheat in college

3. Causes of an act of courage or cowardice

4. Causes of a marriage or divorce (friendship or end of a friendship)

5. Reasons for doing volunteer work

6. Causes or effects of membership in a group (choir, band, sports team, church, or gang)

7. Causes or effects of dropping out of school (or attending college)

8. Effects of e-mail or a computer on a person's life

9. Effects of having a certain boss (or teacher, parent, or leader)

10. Effects of a superstition or prejudice

11. Effects of the death of a loved one

12. Effects (positive or negative) of a habit or practice

13. Effects of living in a repressive country or home

14. Effects of living in a rural (or urban, mountainous, flat, rich, poor, or ethnically diverse) place

15. Writer's choice: _____

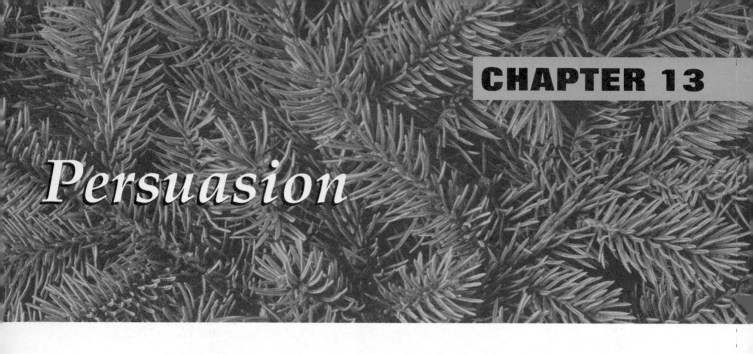

CHAPTER 13

Persuasion

To persuade is to convince someone that a particular opinion or point of view is the correct one.

Any time you argue with a friend, you are each trying to persuade, to convince, the other that your opinion is the right one. Commercials on television are another form of persuasion. Advertisers attempt to convince viewers that the product they sell—whether a deodorant, a soft drink, or an automobile—is the best one to purchase.

You will often have to persuade in writing. For instance, if you want a raise, you will have to write a persuasive memo to convince your employer that you deserve one. You will have to back up, or support, your request with proof, listing important projects you have completed, noting new responsibilities you have taken upon yourself, or showing how you have increased sales.

Once you learn how to persuade logically and rationally, you will be less likely to accept the false, misleading, and emotional arguments that you hear and read every day. Persuasion is vital in daily life, in nearly all college courses, and in most careers.

Topic Sentence

Here is the topic sentence of a persuasive paragraph:

> Passengers should refuse to ride in any vehicle driven by someone who has been drinking.

■ The writer begins a persuasive paragraph by stating clearly what he or she is arguing for or against. What will this persuasive paragraph argue against?

_____

_____

■ Words like *should, ought*, and *must* (and the negatives *should not, ought not*, and *must not*) are especially effective in the topic sentence of a persuasive paragraph.

Paragraph and Plan

Here is the entire paragraph:

> Passengers should refuse to ride in any vehicle driven by someone who has been drinking. First and most important, such a refusal could save lives. The National Council on Alcoholism reports that drunk driving causes 25,000 deaths and 50 percent of all traffic accidents each year. Not only the drivers but the passengers who agree to travel with them are responsible. Second, riders might tell themselves that some people drive well even after a few drinks, but this is just not true. Dr. Burton Belloc of the local Alcoholism Treatment Center explains that even one drink can lengthen the reflex time and weaken the judgment needed for safe driving. Other riders might feel foolish to ruin a social occasion or inconvenience themselves or others by speaking up, but risking their lives is even more foolish. Finally, by refusing to ride with a drinker, one passenger could influence other passengers or the driver. Marie Furillo, a student at Central High School, is an example. When three friends who had obviously been drinking offered her a ride home from school, she refused, despite the driver's teasing. Hearing Marie's refusal, two of her friends got out of the car. Until the laws are changed and a vast re-education takes place, the bloodshed on American highways will probably continue. But there is one thing people can do: They can refuse to risk their lives for the sake of a party.

■ The first reason in the argument **predicts the consequence.** If passengers refuse to ride with drinkers, what will the consequence be?

_____

■ The writer also supports this reason with **facts.** What are the facts?

_____

_____

■ The second reason in the argument is really an **answer to the opposition.** That is, the writer anticipates the critics. What point is the writer answering?

_____

_____

■ The writer supports this reason by **referring to an authority.** That is, the writer gives the opinion of someone who can provide unbiased and valuable information about the subject. Who is the authority and what does this person say?

_____

_____

■ The third reason in the argument is that risking your life is foolish. This reason is really another **answer to the opposition.** What point is the writer answering?

_____

_____

■ The final reason in the argument is that one passenger could influence others. What **example** does the writer supply to back up this reason?

_____

_____

■ Persuasive paragraphs either can begin with the most important reason and then continue with less important ones, or they can begin with the least important reasons, saving the most important for last.* This paragraph begins with what the author considers *most* important. How can you tell?

_____

Before composing this persuasive paragraph, the writer probably brainstormed or freewrote to gather ideas and then made an outline or a plan like this:

Topic sentence: Passengers should refuse to ride in any vehicle driven by someone who has been drinking.

Reason 1:   Refusal could save lives (**predicting a consequence**).
—statistics on deaths and accidents (**facts**)
—passengers are equally responsible

Reason 2:   Riders might say some drinkers drive well—not true (**answering the opposition**).
—Dr. Belloc's explanation (**referring to authority**)

Reason 3:   Others might feel foolish speaking up, but risking lives is more foolish (**answering the opposition**).

Reason 4:   One rider might influence other passengers.
—Marie Furillo (**example**)

Conclusion: Bloodshed will probably continue, but people can refuse to risk their lives.

■ Note how each reason clearly supports the topic sentence.

Transitional Expressions

The following transitional expressions are helpful in persuasive paragraphs:

Transitional Expressions for Persuasion		
Give Reasons	**Answer the Opposition**	**Draw Conclusions**
first (second, third)	of course	therefore
another, next	some may say	thus
last, finally	nevertheless	hence
because, since, for	on the other hand	consequently
	although	

_____

* For work on order of importance, see Chapter 4, "Achieving Coherence," Part A.

Methods of Persuasion

The drinking-and-driving example showed the basic kinds of support used in persuasive paragraphs: **facts, referring to an authority, examples, predicting the consequences,** and **answering the opposition.** Although you will rarely use all of them in one paragraph, you should be familiar with them all. Here are some more details:

1. **Facts: Facts** are simply statements of *what is.* They should appeal to the reader's mind, not just to the emotions. The source of your facts should be clear to the reader. If you wish to prove that children's eyesight should be checked every year by a doctor, you might look for supporting facts in appropriate books and magazines, or you might ask your eye doctor for information. Your paper might say, "Many people suffer serious visual impairment later in life because they received insufficient or inadequate eye care when they were children, according to an article in *Better Vision.*"*

   Avoid the vague "everyone knows that" or "it is common knowledge that" or "they all say." Such statements will make your reader justifiably suspicious of your "facts."

2. **Referring to an authority:** An **authority** is an expert, someone who can be relied on to give unbiased facts and information. If you wish to convince your readers that asthma is a far more serious illness than most people realize, you might speak with an emergency-room physician about the numbers of patients treated for asthma attacks, or you might quote experts from the literature of national organizations like the Asthma and Allergy Foundation of America or the American Lung Association. These are all excellent and knowledgeable authorities whose opinions on medical matters would be considered valid and unbiased.

   Avoid appealing to "authorities" who are interesting or glamorous but who are not experts. A basketball player certainly knows about sports, but probably knows little about cameras or cookware.

3. **Examples:** An **example** should clearly relate to the argument and should be typical enough to support it.† If you wish to convince your reader that high schools should provide more funds than they do for women's sports, you might say, "Jefferson High School, for instance, has received inquiries from sixty female students who would be willing to join a women's basketball or baseball team if the school could provide the uniforms, the space, and a coach."

   Avoid examples that are not typical enough to support your general statement. That your friend was once bitten by a dog does not adequately prove that all dogs are dangerous pets.

4. **Predicting the consequence: Predicting the consequence** helps the reader visualize what will occur if *something does or does not happen.* To convince your readers that a college education should be free to all qualified students, you might say, "If bright but economically deprived students cannot attend college because they cannot afford it, our society will be robbed of their talents."

   Avoid exaggerating the consequence. For instance, telling the reader, "If you don't eat fresh fruit every day, you will never be truly healthy," exaggerates the consequences of not eating fresh fruit and makes the reader understandably suspicious.

---

* For more work on summarizing and quoting outside sources, see Chapter 18.
† For more work on examples, see Chapter 5, "Illustration."

5. **Answering the opposition: Answering possible critics** shows that you are aware of the opposition's argument and are able to respond to it. If you wish to convince your readers that your candidate is the best on the ballot, you might say, "Some have criticized him for running a low-key campaign, but he feels that the issues and his stand on them should speak for themselves."

   Avoid calling the opposition "fools" or "crooks." Attack their ideas, not them.

Considering the Audience

In addition to providing adequate proof for your argument, pay special attention to the **audience** as you write persuasively. In general, we assume that our audience is much like us—reasonable people who wish to learn the truth. But because argument can evoke strong feelings, directing your persuasive paper toward a particular audience can be helpful. Consider just *what kind of evidence* this audience would respond to. For instance, if you were attempting to persuade parents to volunteer their time to establish a local Scout troop, you might explain to them the various ways in which their children would benefit from the troop. In other words, show these parents how the troop is important to *them*. You might also say that you realize how much time they already spend on family matters and how little spare time they have. By doing so, you let them know that you understand their resistance to the argument and that you are sympathetic to their doubts. When you take your audience into consideration, you will make your persuasive paragraph more convincing.*†

PRACTICE 1

Read the following persuasive paragraph carefully and answer the questions.

American women should stop buying so-called women's magazines because these publications lower their self-esteem. First of all, publications like *Glamour* and *Cosmo* appeal to women's insecurities and make millions doing it. Topics like "Ten Days to Sexier Cleavage" and "How to Attract Mr. Right" lure women to buy seven million copies a month, reports Claire Ito in *The Tulsa Chronicle*, May 4, 1999. The message: women need to be improved. Second, although many people—especially magazine publishers—claim these periodicals build self-esteem, they really do the opposite. One expert in readers' reactions, Deborah Then, says that almost all women, regardless of age or education, feel worse about themselves after reading one of these magazines. Alice, one of the women I spoke with, is a good example: "I flip through pictures of world-class beauties and six-foot-tall skinny women, comparing myself to them. In more ways than one, I come up short." Finally, if women spent the money and time these magazines take on more self-loving activities—studying new subjects, developing mental or physical fitness, setting goals and daring to achieve them—they would really build self-worth. Sisters, seek wisdom, create what you envision, and above all, know that you can.

—Rochelle Revard (Student)

---

* For more work on audience, see Chapter 1, "Exploring the Writing Process," Part B.

† For a complete essay developed by persuasion, see "Stopping Youth Violence: An Inside Job," Chapter 15, Part I.

1. What is this paragraph arguing for or against? _____

   _____

2. What audience is the writer addressing? _____

3. Which reason is supported by facts? _____

   What are the facts, and where did the writer get them? _____

   _____

   _____

4. Which reason answers the opposition? _____

5. Which reason is supported by an example? _____

   What is the example? _____

   _____

6. Which reason appeals to an authority? _____

   Who is the authority? _____

PRACTICE 2

Read the following paragraph carefully and answer the questions.

This state should offer free parenting classes, taught by experts, to anyone who wishes to become a parent. First and most important, such parenting classes could save children's lives. Every year, over two million American children are hurt, maimed, or killed by their own parents, according to the National Physicians Association. Some of these tragedies could be prevented by showing parents how to recognize and deal with their frustration and anger. Next, good parenting skills do not come naturally, but must be learned. Dr. Phillip Graham, chairman of England's National Children's Bureau, says that most parents have "no good role models" and simply parent the way they were parented. The courses would not only improve parenting skills but might also identify people at high risk of abusing their children. Third, critics might argue that the state has no business getting involved in parenting, which is a private responsibility. However, the state already makes decisions about who is a fit parent—in the courts, child-protection services, and adoption agencies—but often this is too late for the well-being of the child. Finally, if we do nothing, the hidden epidemic of child abuse and neglect will continue. We train our children's teachers, doctors, day-care workers, and bus drivers. We must also educate parents.

1. What is this paragraph arguing for or against? _____

   _____

2. Which reason appeals to an authority for support? _____

   Who is the authority? _____

   _____

3. Which reason answers the opposition? _____

4. Which reason includes facts? What is the source of these facts?_____

   _____

5. What consequence does the writer predict will occur if parenting classes are

   not offered? _____

   _____

6. Does this writer convince you that parenting classes might make a difference? If you were writing a persuasion paragraph to oppose or support this

   writer, what would your topic sentence be? _____

   _____

PRACTICE 3

So far you have learned five basic methods of persuasion: **facts, referring to an authority, examples, predicting the consequence,** and **answering the opposi-tion.** Ten topic sentences for persuasive paragraphs follow. Write one reason in support of each topic sentence, using the method of persuasion indicated.

Facts

1. A stop sign should be placed at the busy intersection of Hoover and Palm streets.

   Reason: _____

   _____

   _____

   _____

2. People should not get married until they are at least twenty-five years old.

   Reason: _____

   _____

   _____

   _____

Referring to an Authority

(If you cannot think of an authority offhand, name the kind of person who would be an authority on the subject.)

3. These new Sluggo bats will definitely raise your batting average.

   Reason: _____

   _____

   _____

   _____

4. Most people should get at least one hour of vigorous exercise three times a week.

   Reason: _____

   _____

   _____

   _____

Examples

5. Pet animals should be allowed in children's hospital rooms because they speed healing.

   Reason: _____

   _____

   _____

   _____

6. Mace and pepper spray should be legalized because they can prevent crime without causing permanent injury.

   Reason: _____

   _____

   _____

   _____

Predicting the Consequence

7. Companies should (should not) be allowed to conduct random drug testing on employees.

   Reason: _____

   _____

   _____

8. The federal government should (should not) prohibit the sale of handguns through the mail.

Reason: _____

_____

_____

_____

Answering the Opposition

(State the opposition's point of view and then refute it.)

9. This college should (should not) drop its required-attendance policy.

Reason: _____

_____

_____

_____

10. Teenagers should (should not) be required to get their parents' permission before being allowed to have an abortion.

Reason: _____

_____

_____

_____

PRACTICE 4

Each of the following sentences tells what you are trying to persuade someone to do. Beneath each sentence are four reasons that attempt to convince the reader that he or she should take this particular course of action. Circle the letter of the reason that seems *irrelevant, illogical,* or *untrue.*

1. If you wanted to persuade someone to do holiday shopping earlier, you might say that

    a. shopping earlier saves time.
    b. more gifts will be in stock.
    c. stores will not be overly crowded.
    d. the Back Street Boys shop early.

2. If you wanted to persuade someone to buy a particular brand of cereal, you might say that

    a. it is inexpensive.
    b. it contains vitamins and minerals.

      c. it comes in an attractive box.

      d. it makes a hearty breakfast.

3. If you wanted to persuade someone to move to your town, you might say that

      a. two new companies have made jobs available.

      b. by moving to this town, he or she will become the happiest person in the world.

      c. there is a wide selection of housing.

      d. the area is lovely and still unpolluted.

4. If you wanted to persuade someone to vote for a particular candidate, you might say that

      a. she has always kept her promises to the voters.

      b. she has lived in the district for thirty years.

      c. she has substantial knowledge of the issues.

      d. she dresses very fashionably.

5. If you wanted to persuade someone to learn to read and speak a foreign language, you might say that

      a. knowledge of a foreign language can be helpful in the business world.

      b. he or she may want to travel in the country where the language is spoken.

      c. Ricky Martin sings in two languages.

      d. being able to read great literature in the original is a rewarding experience.

6. If you wanted to persuade someone to quit smoking, you might say that

      a. smoking is a major cause of lung cancer.

      b. smoking stains teeth and softens gums.

      c. ashtrays are often hard to find.

      d. this bad habit has become increasingly expensive.

PRACTICE 5

As you write persuasive paragraphs, make sure that your reasons can withstand close examination. Here are some examples of *invalid* arguments. Read them carefully. Decide which method of persuasion is being used and explain why you think the argument is invalid. Refer to the list on pages 155–156.

1. Men make terrible drivers. That one just cut right in front of me without looking.

   Method of persuasion: _____

   Invalid because _____

   _____

2. Many people have become vegetarians during the past ten or fifteen years, but such people have lettuce for brains.

   Method of persuasion: _____

Invalid because _____

_____

3. Candy does not really harm children's teeth. Tests made by scientists at the Gooey Candy Company have proved that candy does not cause tooth decay.

   Method of persuasion: _____

   Invalid because _____

   _____

4. Stealing pens and pads from the office is perfectly all right. Everyone does it.

   Method of persuasion: _____

   Invalid because _____

   _____

5. We don't want _____ in our neighborhood. We had a

   _____ family once, and they made a lot of noise.

   Method of persuasion: _____

   Invalid because _____

   _____

6. If our city doesn't build more playgrounds, a crime wave will destroy our homes and businesses.

   Method of persuasion: _____

   Invalid because _____

   _____

7. Studying has nothing to do with grades. My brother never studies and still gets *A*'s all the time.

   Method of persuasion: _____

   Invalid because _____

   _____

8. Women bosses work their employees too hard. I had one once, and she never let me rest for a moment.

   Method of persuasion: _____

   Invalid because _____

   _____

9. The Big Deal Supermarket has the lowest prices in town. This must be true because the manager said on the radio last week, "We have the lowest prices in town."

Method of persuasion: _____

Invalid because _____

_____

10. If little girls are allowed to play with cars and trucks, they will grow up wanting to be men.

Method of persuasion: _____

Invalid because _____

_____

PRACTICE 6

In a group of four or five classmates, discuss the meaning of this cartoon. Like many cartoons, this one expresses a strong point of view. What issue in American life is this British cartoonist commenting on? What point is he making? Working together, write down the cartoon's "topic sentence" and argument. How effective— how persuasive—is this cartoon?

CARTOONISTS & WRITERS SYNDICATE http://CartoonWeb.com

To help you take a stand for a persuasive paragraph of your own, try the following exercises on notebook paper:

1. List five things you would like to see changed at your college.

2. List five things you would like to see changed in your home *or* at your job.

3. List five things that annoy you or make you angry. What can be done about them?

4. Imagine yourself giving a speech on national television. What message would you like to convey?

From your lists, pick one topic you would like to write a persuasive paragraph about and write the topic sentence here:

_____

_____

Now make a plan or an outline for a paragraph on a separate sheet of paper. Use at least two of the five methods of persuasion. Arrange your reasons in a logical order, and write the most persuasive paragraph you can.

 CHECKLIST: **The Process of Writing a Persuasive Paragraph**

Refer to this checklist of steps as you write a persuasive paragraph of your own.

—— 1. Narrow the topic in light of your audience and purpose. What do you wish to persuade your reader to believe or do?

—— 2. Compose a topic sentence that clearly states your position for or against. Use *should, ought, must,* or their negatives.

—— 3. Freewrite or brainstorm to generate all the reasons you can think of. (You may want to freewrite or brainstorm before you narrow the topic.)

—— 4. Select the best three or four reasons and drop those that do not relate to your topic sentence.

—— 5. If you use *facts,* be sure that they are accurate and that the source of your facts is clear. If you use an *example,* be sure that it is a valid one and adequately supports your argument. If you *refer to an authority,* be sure that he or she is really an authority and *not biased.* If one of your reasons *predicts the consequence,* be sure that the consequence flows logically from your statement. If one of your reasons *answers the opposition,* be sure to state the opposition's point of view fairly and refute it adequately.

—— 6. Make a plan or an outline for the paragraph, numbering the reasons in the order in which you will present them.

—— 7. Write a draft of your persuasive paragraph, using transitional expressions wherever they may be helpful.

_____ 8. Revise as necessary, checking for support, unity, logic, and coherence.

_____ 9. Proofread for errors in grammar, punctuation, sentence structure, spelling, and mechanics.

Suggested Topics for Persuasive Paragraphs

A list of possible topic sentences for persuasive paragraphs follows. Pick one statement and decide whether you agree or disagree with it. Modify the topic sentence accordingly. Then write a persuasive paragraph that supports your view, explaining and illustrating from your own experience, your observations of others, or your reading.

1. Companies should not be allowed to read their employees' e-mail.

2. Occasional arguments are good for friendship.

3. A required course at this college should be _____ (Great American Success Stories, Survey of World Art, How to Use the Internet, or another).

4. The families of AIDS patients are the hidden victims of AIDS.

5. Condom machines should be permitted on campus.

6. People should laugh more because laughter heals.

7. Expensive weddings are an obscene waste of money.

8. Single people should not be allowed to adopt children.

9. Some college football (soccer, basketball, and so on) programs send the message that academic excellence is not important.

10. TV talk shows trivialize important social issues.

11. _____ is the most _____ (hilarious, educational, mindless, racist) show on television.

12. To improve academic achievement, this town should create same-sex high schools (all boys, all girls).

13. People convicted of drunk driving should lose their licenses for one year.

14. _____ (writer, singer, or actor) has a message that more people need to hear.

15. Writer's choice: _____

Give Advice to College Writers

When you are assigned a writing task, take a few minutes to think about the different types of paragraphs you have studied in this unit. Could a certain type of paragraph help you present your ideas more forcefully? You might ask yourself, "Would a paragraph developed by examples work well for this topic? How about a paragraph of cause and effect?"

When he received the assignment "Give advice to other college writers," this student not only made use of one paragraph pattern he had learned, but he added something of his own—humor. In your class or group, read his work, aloud if possible, underlining any lines that you find especially funny or effective.

English Students, Listen Up!

You may think that years of school have taught you how to put off writing a paper; however, true procrastination is an art form, and certain steps must be followed to achieve the status of Master Procrastinator. The first step is to come up with a good reason to put off writing the paper. Reasons prevent others from hassling you about your procrastination. A reason should not be confused with an excuse. An excuse would be, "I am too tired." A reason would be, "It is important that I rest in order to do the best possible job." The second step is to come up with a worthwhile task to do before starting the paper. If you put off writing your paper by watching Baywatch. You will feel guilty. On the other hand, if you put off writing your paper by helping your child do his or her homework or by doing three weeks' worth of laundry or by organizing your sock drawer, there will be no guilt. After completing your worthwhile task. You will be hungry. In order to have the energy necessary to write the paper, you will need to eat something. The true artist can make this third step last even longer by either cooking a meal or going out for food. It is important not to risk your energy level by simply eating a bowl of cereal or a ketchup sandwich. After you eat, the fourth step is to prepare the space in which you will write the paper. This includes cleaning all the surfaces, sharpening pencils. And making sure the lighting is exactly right. You may think that after this fourth step is completed, you will have no choice but to start your paper, but you do if you have done the other steps correctly. It is now too late in the day to start your paper. The fifth step is, of course, to go to bed and start over with step one in the morning.

—Thomas Capra (Student)

1. How effective is this paragraph?

_____ Clear topic sentence?   _____ Good supporting details?

_____ Logical organization?   _____ Effective conclusion?

2. What type of paragraph development does Mr. Capra use here? How do you know? Does the topic sentence indicate what kind of paragraph will follow?

3. One step in the process of becoming a Master Procrastinator contains a *contrast*. Which step? What two things are contrasted?

4. Discuss your underlinings with the group or class. Tell what parts of the paragraph you like best, explaining as specifically as possible why. For example, the mention of a ketchup sandwich in step three adds an extra dash of humor.

5. Although this writer is having fun, procrastination is a serious problem for some people. Do you think Mr. Capra is writing from experience? Why or why not?

6. This otherwise excellent writer makes the same grammar error three times. Can you spot and correct the error pattern that he needs to avoid?

GROUP WORK

In your group or class, make a chart like the one below, listing all the types of paragraph development that you have studied. Now suppose that you have been assigned the topic *procrastination*. Discuss how different paragraphs could be developed on the subject of procrastination, each one using a different paragraph pattern. For instance, you could *illustrate* procrastination by discussing examples of procrastinators you have known. Fill in the chart with one idea per paragraph type. Then share your group's ideas with the whole class.

Topic: Procrastination

Method of development: A paragraph could

Illustration	*give two to three examples of procrastinators.*
Narration	
Description	
Process	
Definition	
Comparison and Contrast	
Classification	
Cause and Effect	
Persuasion	

 ## WRITING AND REVISING IDEAS

1. Give advice to college writers. Use humor if you wish.

2. Discuss procrastination, using one kind of paragraph development that you studied this term.

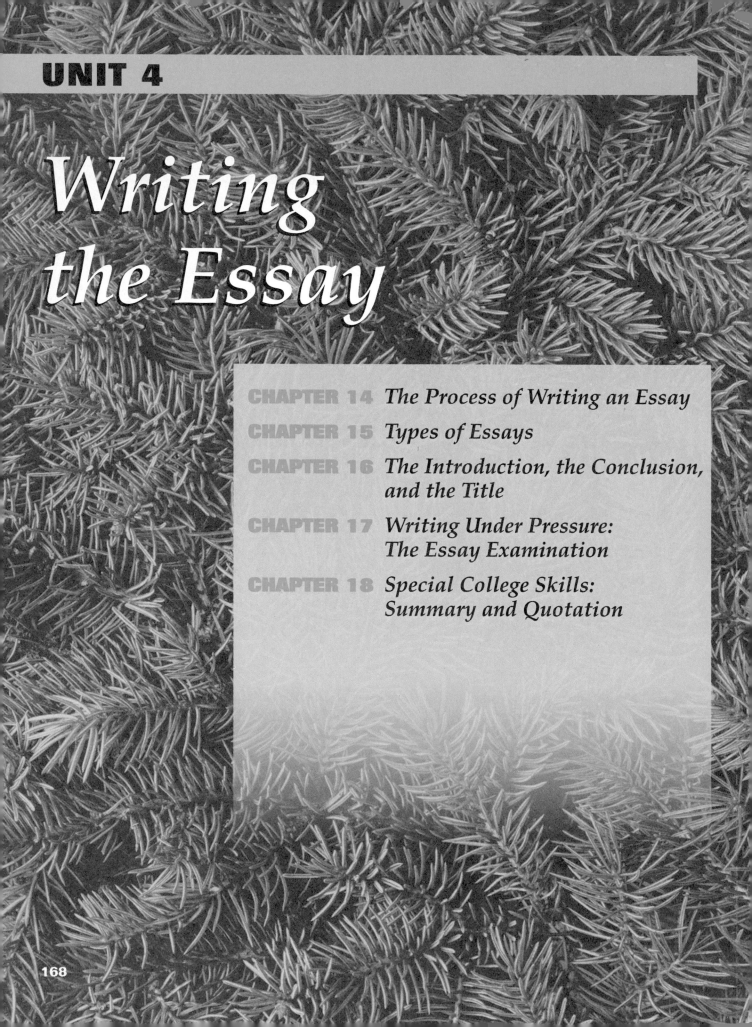

UNIT 4

Writing the Essay

The Process of Writing an Essay

Although writing effective paragraphs will help you complete short-answer exams and do brief writing assignments, much of the time—in college and in the business world—you will be required to write essays and reports several paragraphs long. Essays are longer and contain more ideas than the single paragraphs you have practiced so far, but they require many of the same skills that paragraphs do.

This chapter will help you apply the skills of paragraph writing to the writing of short essays. It will guide you from a look at the essay and its parts through the planning and writing of essays.

PART A   Looking at the Essay

An **essay** is a group of paragraphs about one subject. In many ways, an essay is like a paragraph in longer, fuller form. Both have an introduction, a body, and a conclusion. Both explain one main, or controlling, idea with details, facts, and examples. An essay is not just a padded paragraph, however. An essay is longer because it contains more ideas.

The paragraphs in an essay are part of a larger whole, so each one has a special purpose.

■ The **introductory paragraph*** opens the essay and tries to catch the reader's interest. It usually contains a **thesis statement,** one sentence that states the main idea of the entire essay.

■ The **body** of an essay consists of one, two, three, or more paragraphs, each one making a different point about the main idea.

■ The **conclusion†** brings the essay to a close. It might be a sentence or a paragraph long.

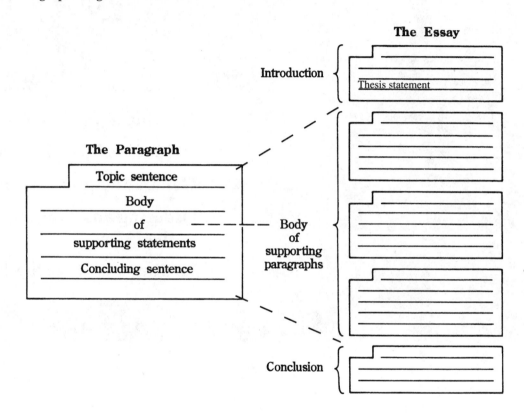

Here is a student essay:

Sunlight

(1) An old proverb says, "He who brings sunlight into the lives of others cannot keep it from himself." Students who volunteer through the Center for Community Service often experience this wisdom firsthand. By giving their time and talents to the local community, these students not only enrich the lives of others, but they receive many surprising benefits for themselves.

(2) Most important, volunteering can bring a sense of empowerment, a knowledge that we can make a difference. This is significant because many students feel passive and hopeless about "the way things are." My first volunteer assignment was working with a group of troubled teenagers. Together we transformed a dismal vacant lot into a thriving business. The three-acre lot in the

---

* For more work on introductions, see Chapter 16, "The Introduction, the Conclusion, and the Title."

† For more work on conclusions, see Chapter 16, "The Introduction, the Conclusion, and the Title."

South Bronx, surrounded by abandoned buildings, was full of junk and heaps of wood. One teenager kicked a piece of wood and said, "Why don't we chop this up and sell it?" We surprised him by taking his idea seriously. We helped these young men, some of whom already had rap sheets, to chop up the wood, bundle it, contact restaurants with wood-burning ovens, and make deliveries. The restaurants, most of them very elegant, were happy to get cheap firewood, and the teenagers were thrilled to be treated like businesspeople. Most rewarding for me was seeing the changes in Raymond, "Mr. Apathy," as he took on a leading role in our project.

(3) Second, the volunteer often gains a deeper understanding of others. Another student, Shirley Miranda, worked with SHARE, a food cooperative that distributes bulk food once a month to its members. SHARE does not give food as charity; rather, each person does a job like unloading trucks at 5 a.m. on delivery day or packing boxes in exchange for healthy, inexpensive food. For Shirley, SHARE was a lesson in human relationships. Reflecting on her service, she wrote: "I learned that people may sometimes need guidance with dignity rather than total dependency on others. I saw that true teamwork is based on people's similarities, not their differences." SHARE so impressed Shirley that she worked in the program through her graduation.

(4) Finally, volunteering can be a way to "try on" a work environment. Sam Mukarji, an engineering student, volunteers on Saturdays as a docent, or guide, at the Museum of Science and Industry, which he describes as "my favorite place on the planet." Sam admires the creative uses of science in this museum, such as the virtual-reality experience of piloting an airplane. When many visitors asked Sam how the exhibit was put together, he suggested that the museum include signs explaining the technology. His idea was accepted, and he was asked to help implement it. Struggling to explain the exhibit in a clear way taught Sam how important writing skills are, even for an engineering major. Now he is paying closer attention to his English assignments and has discovered that working in a science museum would be his "dream job."

(5) Stories like these are not unusual at the Center for Community Service. Whenever the volunteers meet there, we always seem to end up talking about the positive ways in which volunteering has changed our lives. The Center is in a cinder-block basement without a single window, but it is filled with sunlight.

■ The last sentence in the introduction is the *thesis statement.* Just as a topic sentence sets forth the main idea of a paragraph, so the thesis statement sets forth the main idea of the whole essay. It must be *general enough to include the topic sentence of every paragraph in the body.*

■ Underline the topic sentence of each supporting paragraph. Each topic sentence introduces one *benefit* that volunteers receive.

■ Note that the thesis and topic sentences of paragraphs 2, 3, and 4 make a rough *plan* of the entire essay:

1. INTRODUCTION and Thesis statement: By giving their time and talents to the local community, these students not only enrich the lives of others, but they receive many surprising benefits for themselves.

2. Topic sentence: Most important, volunteering can bring a sense of empowerment, a knowledge that we can make a difference.

3. Topic sentence: Second, the volunteer often gains a deeper understanding of others.

4. Topic sentence: Finally, volunteering can be a way to "try on" a work environment.

5. CONCLUSION

■ Note that every topic sentence supports the thesis statement. Every paragraph in the body discusses in detail one *benefit* that students receive from volunteering. Each paragraph also provides an *example* to explain that benefit.

■ The last paragraph *concludes* the essay by mentioning sunlight, a reference to the proverb in paragraph 1.

PRACTICE 1

Read this student essay carefully and then answer the questions.

Bottle Watching

(1) Every time I see a beer bottle, I feel grateful. This reaction has nothing to do with beer. The sight reminds me of the year I spent inspecting bottles at a brewery. That was the most boring and painful job I've ever had, but it motivated me to change my life.

(2) My job consisted of sitting on a stool and watching empty bottles pass by. A glaring light behind the conveyor belt helped me to spot cracked bottles or bottles with something extra—a dead grasshopper, for example, or a mouse foot. I was supposed to grab such bottles with my hooked cane and break them before they went into the washer. For eight or nine hours a day that was all I did. I got dizzy and sore in the eyes. I longed to fall asleep. I prayed that the conveyor would break down so the bottles would stop.

(3) After a while, to put some excitement into the job, I began inventing little games. I would count the number of minutes that passed before a broken bottle would come by, and I would compete against my own past record. Or I would see how many broken bottles I could spot in one minute. Once, I organized a contest for all the bottle watchers with a prize for the best dead insect or animal found in a bottle—anything to break the monotony of the job.

(4) After six months at the brewery, I began to think hard about my goals for the future. Did I want to spend the rest of my life looking in beer bottles? I realized that I wanted a job I could believe in. I wanted to use my mind for better things than planning contests for bleary-eyed bottle watchers. I knew I had to hand in my hook and go back to school.

(5) Today I feel grateful to that terrible job because it motivated me to attend college.

—Pat Barnum (Student)

1. Which sentence in the introductory paragraph is the thesis statement? _____

   _____

   _____

2. Did Mr. Barnum's introduction catch and hold your interest? Why or why not?

   _____

3. Underline the topic sentences in paragraphs 2, 3, and 4.

4. What is the controlling idea of paragraph 2? _____

5. What is the controlling idea of paragraph 3? What examples support this idea?

   _____

   _____

6. What do you like best about this essay? What, if anything, would you

   change? _____

PART B   Writing the Thesis Statement

The steps in the essay-writing process are the same as those in the paragraph-writing process: **narrow the topic, write the thesis statement, generate ideas for the body,** and **organize them.** However, in essay writing, planning on paper and prewriting are especially important because an essay is longer than a paragraph and more difficult to organize.

Narrowing the Topic

The essay writer usually starts with a broad subject and then narrows it to a manageable size. An essay is longer than a paragraph and gives the writer more room to develop ideas; nevertheless, the best essays, like the best paragraphs, are often quite specific. For example, if you are assigned a four-hundred-word essay titled "A Trip I Won't Forget," a description of your recent trip to Florida would be too broad a subject. You would need to *narrow* the topic to just one aspect of the trip. Many writers list possible narrowed subjects on paper or on computer:

1. huge job of packing, more tiring than the trip
2. how to pack for a trip with the children without exhausting yourself
3. Disney World, more fun for adults than for children
4. our afternoon of deep-sea fishing: highlight of the trip
5. terrible weather upsetting many of my sightseeing plans

Any one of these topics is narrow enough and specific enough to be the subject of a short essay. If you had written this list, you would now consider each narrowed topic and perhaps freewrite or brainstorm possible ways to support it.

Keeping your audience and purpose in mind may also help you narrow your topic. Your audience here might be your instructor and classmates; your purpose might be to inform (by giving tips about packing) or to entertain (by narrating a funny or a dramatic incident). Having considered your topic, audience, and purpose, you would then choose the topic that you could best develop into a good essay.

If you have difficulty with this step, reread Chapter 2, "Prewriting to Generate Ideas."

Writing the Thesis Statement

The thesis statement—like the topic sentence in a paragraph—further focuses the narrowed subject because it must clearly state, in sentence form, the writer's **controlling idea**—the main point, opinion, or angle that the rest of the essay will support and discuss.

Narrowed subject:	My job at the brewery
Controlling idea:	So bad it changed my life
Thesis statement:	That was the most boring and painful job I've ever had, but it motivated me to change my life.

■ This thesis statement has a clear controlling idea. From it, we expect the essay to discuss specific ways in which this job was boring and painful and how it motivated a change.

The thesis statement and its controlling idea should be as **specific** as possible. By writing a specific thesis statement, you focus the subject and give yourself and your readers a clear idea of what will follow. Here are three ways to make a vague thesis statement more specific.

1. As a general rule, replace vague words with more exact words* and replace vague ideas with more exact information:

Vague thesis statement:	My recent trip to Florida was really bad.
Revised thesis statement:	My recent trip to Florida was disappointing because the weather upset my sightseeing plans.

■ The first thesis statement above lacks a clear controlling idea. The inexact words *really bad* do not say specifically enough *why* the trip was bad or what the rest of the essay might discuss.

■ The second thesis statement is more specific. The words *really bad* are replaced by the more exact word *disappointing*. In addition, the writer has added more complete information about why the trip was disappointing. From this thesis statement, it is clear that the essay will discuss how the weather upset the writer's plans.

---

*For more practice in choosing exact language, see Chapter 21, "Revising for Language Awareness," Part A.

2. Sometimes you can make the thesis statement more specific by stating the natural divisions of the subject. If a subject naturally has two, three, or four divisions, stating these in the thesis can set up an outline for your entire essay:

Vague thesis statement:	The movie *Southern Smoke* seemed phony.
Revised thesis statement:	The costumes, the dialogue, and the plot of the movie *Southern Smoke* all seemed phony.

■ The first thesis statement above gives little specific direction to the writer or the reader.

■ The second thesis statement, however, actually sets up a plan for the whole essay. The writer has divided the subject into three parts—the costumes, the dialogue, and the plot—and he or she will probably devote one paragraph to discussing the phoniness of each one, following the order in the thesis statement.

3. Avoid a heavy-handed thesis statement that announces, "Now I will write about . . ." or "This essay will discuss. . . ." Don't state the obvious. Instead, craft a specific thesis statement that will capture the reader's interest and control what the rest of your essay will be about. Make every word count.

PRACTICE 2

Revise each vague thesis statement, making it more specific. Remember, a good thesis statement should have a clear controlling idea and indicate what the rest of the essay will be about.

EXAMPLE | Watching TV news programs has its good points.

Watching news programs on TV can make one a more informed and responsible

citizen.

1. The library at this college is bad.

_____

_____

2. A visit to the emergency room can be interesting.

_____

_____

3. There are many unusual people in my family.

_____

_____

4. School uniforms are a good idea.

_____

_____

5. I will write about my job, which is very cool.

_____

_____

6. Professors should teach better.

_____

_____

7. You can learn a lot by observing children.

_____

_____

8. Sketching caricatures is a great hobby.

_____

_____

PRACTICE 3

Eight possible essay topics follow. Pick three that interest you. For each one, **narrow** the topic, choose your **controlling idea,** and then compose a specific **thesis statement.**

an addictive habit	a problem on campus or at work
when parents work	a story or issue in the news now
a volunteer experience	handling anger (or other emotion)
the value of pets	a time when you surprised yourself

EXAMPLE Subject: handling anger

Narrowed subject: my angry adolescence

Controlling idea: channeling adolescent anger into art

Thesis statement: In a photography workshop for "at-risk" teenagers, I learned that anger can be channeled positively into art.

1. Subject: _____

   Narrowed subject: _____

Controlling idea: _____

Thesis statement: _____

_____

2. Subject: _____

Narrowed subject: _____

Controlling idea: _____

Thesis statement: _____

_____

3. Subject: _____

Narrowed subject: _____

Controlling idea: _____

Thesis statement: _____

_____

PART C   Generating Ideas for the Body

The thesis statement sets forth the main idea of the entire essay, but it is the **body** of the essay that must fully support and discuss that thesis statement. In composing the thesis statement, the writer should already have given some thought to what the body will contain. Now he or she should make a **plan** or an **outline** that includes the following:

1. Two to four main ideas to support the thesis statement

2. Two to four topic sentences stating these ideas

3. A plan for each paragraph in the body (developed in any of the ways explained earlier in this book)

4. A logical order in which to present these paragraphs

Different writers create such plans in different ways. Some writers brainstorm or freewrite ideas and then find paragraph groups. Others first write topic sentences and then plan paragraphs.

1. Brainstorm ideas and then find paragraph groups. Having written the thesis statement, some writers brainstorm on paper or on the computer—they jot down any ideas that develop the thesis statement, including main ideas, specific details, and examples, all jumbled together. Only after creating a long list do they go back over it, drop any ideas that do not support the thesis statement, and then look for "paragraph groups."

Suppose, for instance, that you have written this thesis statement: *Although people often react to stress in harmful ways, there are many positive ways to handle stress.* By brainstorming and then dropping ideas that do not relate, you might eventually produce a list like this:

work out

dig weeds or rake leaves

call a friend

talking out problems relieves stress

jogging

many sports ease tension

go to the beach

take a walk

taking breaks, long or short, relieves stress

talk to a shrink if the problem is really bad

escape into a hobby—photography, bird watching

go to a movie

talk to a counselor at the college

talk to a minister, priest, rabbi, etc.

many people harm themselves trying to relieve stress

they overeat or smoke

drinking too much, other addictions

do vigorous household chores—scrub a floor, beat the rugs, pound pillows

doing something physical relieves stress

some diseases are caused by stress

take a nap

some people blow up to help tension, but this hurts their relationships

Now read over the list, looking for groups of ideas that could become paragraphs. Some ideas might become topic sentences; others might be used to support a topic sentence. How many possible paragraphs can you find in this list?

PRACTICE 4

From the list, make a **plan** or an **outline** for an essay that supports the thesis statement *Although people often react to stress in harmful ways, there are many positive ways to handle stress.*

Plan four paragraphs for the body of the essay. Find four paragraph groups in the list and determine the main idea of each paragraph; then write a topic sentence stating this main idea.

Now arrange the topic sentences in an order that makes sense. Under each topic sentence, list supporting examples or details.

1. INTRODUCTION and   Although people often react to stress in harmful
   Thesis statement: ways, there are many positive ways to handle stress.

2. Topic sentence: _____

_____

(examples) _____

_____

3. Topic sentence: _____

_____

(examples) _____

_____

4. Topic sentence: _____

_____

(examples) _____

_____

5. Topic sentence: _____

_____

(examples) _____

_____

6. CONCLUSION: _____

_____

_____

_____

■ Does every topic sentence support the thesis statement?

■ Have you arranged the paragraphs in a logical order?

    2. **Write topic sentences and then plan paragraphs.** Sometimes a writer can compose topic sentences directly from the thesis statement without extensive jotting first. This is especially true if the thesis statement itself shows how the body will be divided or organized. Such a thesis statement makes the work of planning paragraphs easy because the writer has already broken down the subject into supporting ideas or parts:

Thesis statement:	Because the student cafeteria has many problems, the college should hire a new administrator to see that it is properly managed in the future.

■ This thesis statement contains two main ideas: (1) that the cafeteria has many problems and (2) that a new administrator should be hired. The first idea states the problem and the second offers a solution.

From this thesis statement, a writer could logically plan a two-paragraph body, with one paragraph explaining each idea in detail. He or she might compose two topic sentences as follows:

Thesis statement:	Because the student cafeteria has many problems, the college should hire a new administrator to see that it is properly managed in the future.
Topic sentence:	Foremost among the cafeteria's problems are unappetizing food, slow service, and high prices.
Topic sentence:	A new administrator could do much to improve these terrible conditions.

These topic sentences might need to be revised later, but they will serve as guides while the writer further develops each paragraph.

The writer might develop the first paragraph in the body by giving **examples*** of the unappetizing foods, slow service, and high prices.

He or she could develop the second paragraph through **process,**† by describing the **steps** that the new administrator could take to solve the cafeteria's problems. The completed essay **plan** might look like this:

1. INTRODUCTION and Thesis statement: Because the student cafeteria has many problems, the college should hire a new administrator to see that it is properly managed in the future.

2. Topic sentence: Foremost among the cafeteria's problems are unappetizing food, slow service, and high prices.

   Problem 1: Food is unappetizing

   —sandwiches with tough meat, stale bread
   —salads with wilted lettuce, tasteless tomatoes
   —hot meals often either overcooked or undercooked

   Problem 2: Service is slow

   —students wait 30 minutes for sandwiches
   —students wait 15 minutes just for a cup of coffee
   —have to gulp meals to get to class on time

   Problem 3: Prices too high

   —sandwiches overpriced
   —coffee or tea costs $1.50

3. Topic sentence: A new administrator could do much to improve these terrible conditions.

   Step 1. Set minimum quality standards

   —personally oversee purchase of healthful food
   —set and enforce rules about how long food can be left out

---

* For more work on developing paragraphs with examples, see Chapter 5, "Illustration."
† For more work on developing paragraphs by process, see Chapter 8, "Process."

—set cooking times for hot meals

Step 2. Reorganize service lines

—study which lines are busiest at different times of
  the day
—shift cooks and cashiers to those lines
—create a separate beverage line

Step 3. Lower prices

—better food and faster service would attract more
  student customers
—cafeteria could then lower prices

4. CONCLUSION

Note that the order of paragraphs logically follows the order in the thesis
statement, discussing first the problem and then the solution.

The writer now has a clear plan from which to write the first draft of the
essay.

PRACTICE 5

Write from two to four topic sentences to support *three* of the thesis statements
that follow. (First you may wish to brainstorm or freewrite on paper or on computer.) Make sure that every topic sentence really supports the thesis statement
and that every one could be developed into a good paragraph. Then arrange your
topic sentences in a **plan** in the space provided.

EXAMPLE   Before you buy a computer, do these three things.

Topic sentence: *Decide how much you can spend, and determine your price*

range.

Topic sentence: *Examine the models that are within your price range.*

Topic sentence: *Shop around; do not assume that all computer dealers are*

created equal.

1. I vividly recall the sights, smells, and tastes of _____

Topic sentence: _____

Topic sentence: _____

Topic sentence: _____

_____

Topic sentence: _____

_____

2. Living alone has both advantages and disadvantages.

Topic sentence: _____

_____

Topic sentence: _____

_____

Topic sentence: _____

_____

Topic sentence: _____

_____

3. Doing well at a job interview requires careful planning.

Topic sentence: _____

_____

Topic sentence: _____

_____

Topic sentence: _____

_____

Topic sentence: _____

_____

4. _____ is a fascinating and profitable hobby.

Topic sentence: _____

_____

Topic sentence: _____

_____

Topic sentence: _____

_____

Topic sentence: _____

_____

5. My three children have individual techniques for avoiding housework.

Topic sentence: _____

_____

Topic sentence: _____

_____

Topic sentence: _____

_____

Topic sentence: _____

_____

PRACTICE 6

Now choose *one* thesis statement you have written, or write one now, and develop a plan for an essay of your own. (For ideas, reread the thesis statements you wrote for Practice 3, p. 176.) Your plan should include your thesis statement, two to four topic sentences, and supporting details, facts, and examples. Brainstorm or freewrite every time you need ideas; revise the thesis statement and the topic sentences until they are sharp and clear.

PART D   Ordering and Linking Paragraphs in the Essay

An essay, like a paragraph, should have **coherence.** That is, the paragraphs in an essay should be arranged in a clear, logical order and should follow one another like links in a chain.

Ordering Paragraphs

It is important that the paragraphs in your plan, and later in your essay, follow a **logical order.** The rule for writers is this: Use your common sense and plan ahead. *Do not* leave the order of your paragraphs to chance.

The types of order often used in single paragraphs—**time order, space order,** and **order of importance***—can sometimes be used to arrange paragraphs within an essay. Essays about subjects that can be broken into stages or steps, with each step discussed in one paragraph, should be arranged according to *time. Space order* is used occasionally in descriptive essays. A writer who wishes to save the most important or convincing paragraph for last would use *order of importance.* Or he or she might wish to reverse this order and put the most important paragraph first.

Very often, however, the writer simply arranges paragraphs in whatever order makes sense in the particular essay. Suppose, for example, that you have written the thesis statement *Action heroes Jackie Chan and Michelle Yeow have much in common,* and you plan three paragraphs with these topic sentences:

Unlike other action heroes, they both do their own stunts.

Both were popular in Asia long before they were discovered by Western movie audiences.

By poking fun at themselves in their movies, both tweak the heroic image of the action star.

Because doing their own stunts and poking fun at themselves both deal with their style in the movies, it would seem logical to arrange these two paragraphs one after the other. Once the reader has read about who they are and how they approach action movies, it makes sense to end with their early popularity in Asia. A logical order of paragraphs, then, might be the following:

1. INTRODUCTION and Thesis statement: Action heroes Jackie Chan and Michelle Yeow have much in common.

2. Topic sentence: Unlike other action heroes, they both do their own stunts.

3. Topic sentence: By poking fun at themselves in their movies, both tweak the heroic image of the action star.

4. Topic sentence: Both were popular in Asia long before they were discovered by Western movie audiences.

5. CONCLUSION

Finally, if your thesis statement is divided into two, three, or four parts, the paragraphs in the body should follow the order in the thesis; otherwise, the reader will be confused. Assume, for instance, that you are planning three paragraphs to develop the thesis statement *Using a CD-ROM encyclopedia for the first time can be overwhelming, exciting, and educational.*

Paragraph 2 should discuss _____.

Paragraph 3 should discuss _____.

Paragraph 4 should discuss _____.

---

* For more work on time order, space order, and order of importance, see Chapter 4, "Achieving Coherence," Part A.

PRACTICE 7

Plans for three essays follow, each containing a thesis statement and several topic sentences in scrambled order. Number the topic sentences in each group according to an *order that makes sense.* Be prepared to explain your choices.

1. Thesis statement: The practice of tai chi can improve one's concentration, health, and peace of mind.

   Topic sentences: _____ In several ways, tai chi boosts physical health.

       _____ Peace of mind increases gradually as one becomes less reactive.

       _____ Concentrating on the movements of tai chi in practice promotes better concentration in other areas of life.

2. Thesis statement: The fastest-growing job markets through the year 2005 will be in the computer and medical fields.

   Topic sentences: _____ Numerous job openings also exist for home health aides, physical therapists, and occupational therapists.

       _____ The sources of these career opportunities are the rapid growth of the Internet and a generation of aging baby boomers needing more medical care.

       _____ Skilled computer engineers, systems analysts, and technical support personnel will find many job opportunities to choose from.

3. Thesis statement: The history of European contact with the Karaja Indians of Brazil is one of violence and exploitation.

   Topic sentences: _____ The Karaja, exposed to European diseases during the nineteenth century, were reduced in numbers by 90 percent.

       _____ During the eighteenth century, the *bandeirantes* led attacks on Karaja villages to get slaves.

       _____ Since the turn of the twentieth century, Brazilian pioneers have increasingly used Indian territory as grazing land.

PRACTICE 8

Now, go over the essay plan that you developed in Practice 6 and decide which paragraphs should come first, which second, and so forth. Does time order, space order, or order of importance seem appropriate to your subject? Number your paragraphs accordingly.

Linking Paragraphs

Just as the sentences within a paragraph should flow smoothly, so the paragraphs within an essay should be clearly **linked** one to the next. As you write your essay, do not make illogical jumps from one paragraph to another. Instead, guide your reader. Link the first sentence of each new paragraph to the thesis statement or to the paragraph before. Here are four ways to link paragraphs:

1. Repeat key words or ideas from the thesis statement.

2. Refer to words or ideas from the preceding paragraph.

3. Use transitional expressions.

4. Use transitional sentences.

1. Repeat key words or ideas from the thesis statement.* The topic sentences in the following essay plan repeat key words and ideas from the thesis statement.

Thesis statement:	Spending time in nature can promote inner peace and a new point of view.
Topic sentence:	A stroll in the woods or a picnic by the sea often brings feelings of inner peace and well-being.
Topic sentence:	Natural places can even give us a new point of view by putting our problems in perspective.

■ In the first topic sentence, the words *feelings of inner peace* repeat, in slightly altered form, words from the thesis statement. The words *a stroll in the woods or a picnic by the sea* refer to the idea of *spending time in nature.*

■ Which words in the second topic sentence repeat key words or ideas from the thesis statement?

2. Refer to words or ideas from the preceding paragraph. Link the first sentence of a new paragraph to the paragraph before, especially by referring to words or ideas near the end of the paragraph. Note how the two paragraphs are linked in the following passage:

(1) Would you rather take the risk of starting your own business than work for someone else? Would you prefer an insecure job with a large income over a secure job with an average income? Do you have a high energy level? If you answered yes to these questions, you might have some of the traits of what Dr. Frank Farley calls the "Type T" personality.

(2) According to Farley, Type T people ("T" stands for "Thrill") are creative risk takers. He believes that as much as 30 percent of the American public falls into this category. "They are the great experimenters of life," declares Farley. "They break the rules."

—Ira Peck and Larry F. Krieger, *Sociology: The Search for Social Patterns*

* For more work on repetition of key words, see Chapter 4, "Achieving Coherence," Part B. See also "Synonyms and Substitutions" in the same section.

■ What words and groups of words in paragraph 2 clearly refer to paragraph 1?

_____

3. Use transitional expressions.* Transitional expressions—words like *for example*, *therefore*, and *later on*—are used within a paragraph to show the relationship between sentences. Transitional expressions can also be used within an essay to show the relationships between paragraphs:

> (1) The house where I grew up was worn out and run-down. The yard was mostly mud, rock hard for nine months of the year but wet and swampy for the other three. Our nearest neighbors were forty miles away, so it got pretty lonely. Inside, the house was shabby. The living room furniture was covered in stiff, nubby material that had lost its color over the years and become a dirty brown. Upstairs in my bedroom, the wooden floor sagged a little further west every year.
>
> (2) *Nevertheless*, I love the place for what it taught me. There I learned to thrive in solitude. During the hours I spent alone, when school was over and the chores were done, I learned to play the guitar and sing. Wandering in the fields around the house or poking under stones in the creek bed, I grew to love the natural world. Most of all, I learned to see and to appreciate small wonders.

■ The first paragraph describes some of the negative details about the writer's early home. The second paragraph *contrasts* the writer's attitude, which is positive. The transitional expression *nevertheless* eases the reader from one paragraph to the next by pointing out the exact relationship between the paragraphs.

■ Transitional expressions can also highlight the *order* in which paragraphs are arranged.† Three paragraphs arranged in time order might begin: *First . . . , Next . . . , Finally. . . .* Three paragraphs arranged in order of importance might begin: *First . . . , More important . . . , Most important. . . .* Use transitional expressions alone or together with other linking devices.

4. Use transitional sentences. From time to time, you may need to write an entire sentence of transition to link one paragraph to the next, as shown in this passage:

> (1) Dee Kantner and Violet Palmer are hardly radicals, but they have helped bring about a revolution in sports. In 1995, both were experienced referees in women's college basketball and in the newly created Women's National Basketball Association, the WNBA. Although they were the top women in their profession, they wanted the prize all great referees want—to work in the NBA. In 1997, they won that prize, becoming the first women to referee regular-season games in the NBA and in professional football, hockey, and baseball.
>
> (2) *Achieving this goal, however, created a new challenge.* The two women now faced the criticism and even taunts of male players and coaches. Former Chicago Bulls coach Phil Jackson stated publicly that gender got them into NBA, not qualifications. Dennis Rodman shouted negative comments

_____

* For a complete list of transitional expressions, see Chapter 4, "Achieving Coherence," Part B. See also the chapters in Unit 3 for ways to use transitional expressions in each paragraph and essay pattern.

† For more work on transitional expressions of time, space, and importance, see Chapter 4, "Achieving Coherence," Part A.

on the court. Kenny Anderson responded to a foul call by telling Kantner to keep her eyes on the game and off his pants. Yet Kantner and Palmer have kept their cool, above all, focusing on the game. When asked how they can curb the behavior of quick-tempered players like Rodman, Charles Barkley, and Anthony Mason, Palmer told a reporter, "Confrontation is part of being a referee. If they cross a line, they get a technical foul."

■ In paragraph 1, Kantner and Palmer achieve their goal. In paragraph 2, they face the reaction of the all-male NBA. The topic sentence of paragraph 2 is the second sentence: *The two women now faced the criticism and even taunts of male players and coaches.*

■ The first sentence of paragraph 2 is actually a **sentence of transition** that eases the reader from success to a new challenge. (Note that it includes a transitional expression of contrast, *however.*)

Use all four methods of linking paragraphs as you write your essays.

PRACTICE 9

Read the essay that follows, noting the paragraph-to-paragraph *links*. Then answer the questions.

Skin Deep

(1) What do Johnny Depp, Lady Randolph Churchill, Whoopi Goldberg, and Charles Manson all have in common? Perhaps you guessed tattoos: body decorations made by piercing the skin and inserting colored pigments. In fact, tattoos have a long and nearly worldwide history, ranging from full-body art to a single heart, from tribal custom to pop-culture fad.

(2) The earliest known tattoo was found on the mummy of an Egyptian priestess dating back to 2200 B.C. Tattoos were also used in the ancient world to decorate Japanese noblemen, mark Greek spies, and hide expressions of fear on Maori tribesmen in New Zealand. Full-body tattooing was practiced for centuries in the South Seas; in fact, the word *tattoo* comes from the Tahitian word *tattaw*. In medieval times, small tattoos were common in Europe. For instance, in 1066, after the famous Battle of Hastings, the only way that the body of the Anglo Saxon King Harold could be identified was by the word *Edith* tattooed over his heart.

(3) For the next 600 years, however, Europeans lost interest in tattoos. Then, in the 1700s, explorers and sailors rekindled public excitement. Captain Cook, returning from a trip to Tahiti in 1761, described the wonders of tattoos. Cook enthusiastically paraded a heavily tattooed Tahitian prince named Omai through England's finest drawing rooms. People were intrigued by the colorful flowers, snakes, and geographical maps covering Omai's body. Although large tattoos were too much for the British, the idea of a pretty little bee or royal crest on the shoulder was very appealing. Tattooing remained popular with Europe's royalty and upper classes through the nineteenth century. The Prince of Wales, the Duke of York, Tsar Nicholas of Russia, and Winston Churchill's mother all had tattoos.

(4) When tattooing first reached America, on the other hand, its image was definitely not refined. American soldiers and sailors, feeling lonely and patriotic during World War II, visited tattoo parlors in South Pacific ports and came home with *Mother* or *Death Before Dishonor* inked into their arms. Soon motorcyclists started getting tattoos as part of their rebellious, macho image. The process was painful, with a high risk of infection, so the more elaborate a cyclist's bloody dagger or skull and crossbones, the better.

(5) Tattooing did not remain an outlaw rite of passage for long. Safer and less painful methods developed in the 1970s and 1980s brought tattooing into the American mainstream, especially among the young. Designs ranged from one butterfly to black-and-white patterns like Native American textiles to flowing, multicolored, stained-glass designs. With the media documenting the tattoos of the rich and famous, tattooing became a full-blown fad by the 1990s. Now the onetime symbols of daring have become so common that many rebels are having their tattoos removed. About one third of all the work performed by tattoo artists in the United States is "erasing" unwanted tattoos.

1. What transitional expressions does this writer use to link paragraphs? (Find

   at least two.) _____

   _____

2. How does the writer link paragraphs 1 and 2? _____

   _____

3. How does the writer link paragraphs 4 and 5? _____

   _____

PART E   Writing and Revising Essays

Writing the First Draft

Now you should have a clear plan or outline from which to write your first draft. This plan should include your thesis statement, two to four topic sentences that support it, details and facts to develop each paragraph, and a logical order. Write on every other line to leave room for later corrections, including all your ideas and paragraphs in the order you have chosen to present them. Explain your ideas fully, but avoid getting stuck on a particular word or sentence. When you have finished the draft, set it aside, if possible, for several hours or several days.

PRACTICE 10

Write a first draft of the essay you have been working on in Practices 6 and 8.

Revising and Proofreading

Revising is perhaps the most important step in the essay-writing process. Revising an essay involves the same principles as revising a paragraph.* Read your first draft slowly and carefully to yourself—aloud if possible. Imagine you are a reader who has never seen the paper before. As you read, underline trouble spots, draw arrows, and write in the margins, if necessary, to straighten out problems.

Here are some questions to keep in mind as you revise:

1. Is my thesis statement clear?

2. Does the body of the essay fully support my thesis statement?

3. Does the essay have unity; does every paragraph relate to the thesis statement?

4. Does the essay have coherence; do the paragraphs follow a logical order?

5. Are my topic sentences clear?

6. Does each paragraph provide good details, well-chosen examples, and so on?

7. Is the language exact, concise, and fresh?

8. Are my sentences varied in length and type?

9. Does the essay conclude, not just leave off?

If possible, ask a **peer reviewer**—a trusted classmate or friend—to read your paper and give you feedback. Of course, this person should not rewrite or correct the essay but should simply tell you which parts are clear and which parts are confusing.

To guide your peer reviewer, you might ask him or her to use the Peer Feedback Sheet on page 37 or to answer these questions in writing:

1. What do you like about this piece of writing?

2. What seems to be the main point?

3. Which parts could be improved (meaning unclear sentences, supporting points missing, order mixed up, writing not lively, and so forth)? Please be specific.

4. What one change would most improve this essay?

Proofreading and Writing the Final Draft

Next, carefully **proofread** the draft for grammar and spelling. Check especially for those errors you often make: verb errors, comma splices, and so forth.[†] If you are unsure about the spelling of a word, check a dictionary or use the spellcheck on your computer.

Finally, neatly recopy your essay or print out a final copy on 8½-by-11-inch paper. Write on one side only. When you finish, proofread the final copy.

The following sample essay by a student shows his first draft, the revisions he made, and the revised draft. Each revision has been numbered and explained to give you a clear idea of the thinking process involved.

---

*For more work on revising, see Chapter 3, "The Process of Writing Paragraphs," Part F, and Chapter 22, "Putting Your Revision Skills to Work."

[†] For practice proofreading for individual errors, see chapters in Unit 6; for mixed-error proofreading, see Chapter 36.

First Draft

Portrait of a Bike Fanatic

(1) I first realized how serious Diane was when I joined her on a long trip one Sunday afternoon. Her bike looked new, so I asked her if it was. When she told me she had bought it three years ago, I asked her how she kept it looking so good. She showed me how she took good care of it.

(2) Diane had just about every kind of equipment I've ever seen. She put on her white crash helmet and attached a tiny rearview mirror on it—the kind the dentist uses to check out the backs of your teeth. She put a warning light on her left leg. She carried a whole bag full of tools. When I looked into it, I couldn't believe how much stuff was in there (wrenches, inner tubes, etc.)—tools to meet every emergency. I was tempted to see if it had a false bottom.

(3) I had no idea she was such a bike nut. We rode thirty miles and I was exhausted. Her equipment was something else, but useful because she had a flat and was able to fix it, saving our trip.

(4) She doesn't look like a bike fanatic, just a normal person. You'd never guess that her bike has more than 10,000 miles on it.

(5) As we rode, Diane told me about her travels throughout the Northeast (Cape Cod, Vermont, Penn., New York). Riding to work saved her money, kept her in shape. Her goal for the next summer was a cross-country tour over the Rockies!

(6) Our trip was no big deal to her but to me it was something. I might consider biking to work because it keeps you in shape. But basically I'm lazy. I drive a car or take the bus. I do like to walk though.

Revisions

Portrait of a Bike Fanatic

① Add intro and thesis

② about bicycling

I first realized how serious Diane was ∧when I joined her on a ∧long trip one Sunday afternoon. Her

③ thirty-mile

bike looked new, so I asked her if it was. When she told me she had bought it three years ago, I asked her how she kept it looking so good. ~~She showed me how she took good care of it.~~

④ Describe in detail

Diane had just about every kind of equipment I've ever seen. ∧She put on her white crash helmet and attached a tiny rearview mirror on it—the kind the

⑤ For example,

⑥ examine

dentist uses to ~~check out~~ the backs of your teeth. She

⑦ strapped   to   , just below the knee

⑧ Mention trip location

~~put a warning light on~~ her leg.

> She carried a whole bag full of tools. When I looked into it, I couldn't believe how much stuff was in there (wrenches, inner tubes, etc.)—tools to meet every emergency. I was tempted to see if it had a false bottom.

⑨ New ¶ on tools, flat tire

⑩ ~~I had no idea she was such a bike nut. We rode thirty miles and I was exhausted.~~ Her equipment was something else, but useful because she had a flat and was able to fix it, saving our trip.

⑪ Combine into one ¶ on tools

⑫ Move to intro?

She doesn't look like a bike fanatic, just a normal person. You'd never guess that her bike has more than 10,000 miles on it.

⑬ Describe in detail. Make interesting!

As we rode, Diane told me about her travels throughout the Northeast (Cape Cod, Vermont, Penn., New York). Riding to work saved her money, kept her in shape. Her goal for the next summer was a cross-country tour over the Rockies!

⑭ Better conclusion needed

Our trip was no big deal to her, but to me it was something. ~~I might consider biking to work because it keeps you in shape. But basically I'm lazy. I drive a car or take the bus. I do like to walk though.~~

⑮ Drop. Irrelevant

Reasons for Revisions

1. No thesis statement. Add catchy introduction. (introduction and thesis statement)

2. Add *bicycling*. What she is serious *about* is not clear. (exact language)

3. Tell *how* long! (exact language)

4. Expand this; more details needed. (support, exact language)

5. Add transition. (transitional expression)

6. Wrong tone for college essay. (exact language)

7. Find more active verb; be more specific. (exact language)

8. Conclude paragraph; stress time order. (order)

9. This section is weak. Add one paragraph on tools. Tell story of flat tire? (paragraphs, support)

10. Drop! Repeats thesis. Not really a paragraph. (unity, paragraphs)

11. Put this in tools paragraph. Order is mixed up. (order)

12. Put this in introduction? (order)

13. Add details; make this interesting! (support, exact language)

14. Write a better conclusion. (conclusion)

15. Drop! Essay is about Diane and biking, not my bad exercise habits. (unity)

Final Draft

Portrait of a Bike Fanatic

(1) You'd never guess that the powder-blue ten-speed Raleigh had more than 10,000 miles on it. And you'd never guess that the tiny woman with the swept-back hair and the suntanned forearms had ridden those miles over the last two years, making trips through eleven states. But Diane is a bicycle fanatic.

(2) I first realized how serious Diane was about bicycling when I joined her on a thirty-mile trip one Sunday afternoon. Her bike looked new, so I asked her if it was. When she told me she had bought it three years ago, I asked her how she kept it looking so good. From her saddlebag she took the soft cloth that she wiped the bike down with after every long ride and the plastic drop cloth that she put over it every time she parked it outdoors overnight.

(3) Diane had just about every kind of bike equipment I've ever seen. For example, she put on her white crash helmet and attached a tiny rearview mirror to it—the kind the dentist uses to examine the backs of your teeth. She strapped a warning light to her left leg, just below the knee. Then we set off on our trip, starting at Walden Pond in Concord and planning to go to the Wayside Inn in Sudbury and back again before the sun set.

(4) We were still in Concord when Diane signaled me to stop. "I think I have a flat," she said. I cursed under my breath. I was sure that would mean the end of our trip; we'd have to walk her bike back to the car and she'd have to take it to the shop the next day. But she reached into her saddlebag again, and out came a wrench and a new tube. Before I knew it, she took the rear wheel off the bike, installed the new tube, and put the wheel back on. I began to wonder what else was in that saddlebag. When I asked, she showed me two sets of wrenches, another spare inner tube, two brake pads, a can of lubricating oil, two screwdrivers, a roll of reflective tape, extra bulbs for her headlight and taillight, and an extra chain. She had so much in the bag, I was tempted to see if it had a false bottom. Diane is one of those bicyclists who have tools to meet any emergency and know how to use them.

(5) As we rode along, Diane told me about her travels throughout the Northeast. She had taken her bike on summer vacations on Cape Cod and fall foliage tours in Vermont. She had ridden all over Pennsylvania and upstate New York, covering as much as seventy miles in a single day. She also rode to and from work every day, which she said saved money, kept her in shape, and helped her start each day feeling good. Her goal for the next summer, she said, was a cross-country tour. "All the way?" I asked. "What about the Rockies?" "I know," she said. "What a challenge!"

(6) Our trip took a little less than three hours, but I'm sure Diane was slowing down to let me keep up with her. When we got back to the parked car, I was breathing hard and had worked up quite a sweat. Diane was already there waiting for me, looking as if she did this every day—which she does. For Diane, riding a bike is as easy and natural as walking is for most people. Look out, Rockies.

PRACTICE 11

Now, carefully read over the first draft of your essay from Practice 10 and **revise** it, referring to the checklist of questions on page 190. You might wish to ask a peer reviewer for feedback before you revise. Ask specific questions or use the peer feedback sheet on page 37. Take your time and write the best essay you can. Once you are satisfied, **proofread** your essay for grammar and spelling errors. Neatly write the final draft or print a final copy.

WRITING ASSIGNMENTS

The assignments that follow will give you practice in writing essays. In each, concentrate on writing a clear thesis statement and a full, well-organized body. Because introductions and conclusions are not discussed until Chapter 16, you may wish to begin your essay with the thesis statement and conclude as simply as possible.

Before you write, make a plan or an outline that includes

■ a clear thesis statement

■ two to four topic sentences that support the thesis statement

■ details, facts, and examples to develop each paragraph

■ a logical order of paragraphs

1. Some college students cheat on their papers and exams; some people cheat on the job. Why do people cheat? What are the advantages and disadvantages of cheating? Does cheating pay off? Does it achieve the end that the cheater desires? Focus on cheating at college or at work, and choose one main idea to write about. You might wish to use examples to support your thesis. Plan your essay carefully on paper—before you write it.

2. Interview a classmate (or, if you do this assignment at home, someone with an unusual skill). As you talk to the person, look for a thesis: ask questions, take notes. What stands out about the person? Is there an overall impression or idea that can structure your essay? Use your descriptive powers. Notice the person's looks, clothes, typical expressions, and gestures. Later, formulate a thesis statement about the person, organize your ideas, and write.

3. Do you feel that certain television programs show stereotypical women, African Americans, Hispanics, or members of any other group instead of believable people? Examine and discuss just one such program and one group of people. What situations, words, and actions by the TV characters are stereotypical, not real? Focus your subject, make a plan, and write a well-organized essay.

You might wish to construct a thesis statement divided in this way: On the television program *(name show)*, *(name group)* are often portrayed as being *(name stereotype)*.

4. Give advice to the weary job hunter. Describe the most creative job-hunting strategies you have ever tried or heard about. Support your thesis statement with examples, or consider using time order to show a successful job-hunting day in the life of the expert, you.

5. For better or worse, sex education begins at home—whether or not parents speak about the subject, whether parents' words reinforce or contradict the message of their own behavior. How do you think a parent should handle this responsibility? Be as specific as possible, including details from your own and your friends' experiences to make your point.

6. Draw upon your romantic misfortunes to give dating advice to others. Think back to the two, three, or four most disastrous dates you ever had. Relive the unhappy details, the disappointment, the shock, and take notes; look for a pattern, a thesis, that can pull these isolated bad times together. Now write an excellent paper in which you tell what happened to you and share your hard-earned wisdom with those seeking love—or at least, a first-run movie and popcorn.

7. Have you ever had a close call with death? Describe the experience and its effect, if any, on your attitudes and actions since. If it has had little or no effect on you, try to explain why. Be sure to unify your essay with a clear thesis statement.

8. Many children have working parents; in fact, mothers of young children make up 45 percent of the American work force. How do you think children are affected when both parents work or when their single parent works? Focus your discussion on one aspect of this topic that you can discuss fully in a short essay—on the positive and/or negative emotional effects on children, on the way day care affects children, and so forth.

 CHECKLIST: The Process of Writing an Essay

—— 1. Narrow the topic in light of your audience and purpose. Be sure you can discuss this topic fully in a short essay.

—— 2. Write a clear thesis statement. If you have trouble, freewrite or brainstorm first; then narrow the topic and write the thesis statement.

—— 3. Freewrite or brainstorm, generating facts, details, and examples to support your thesis statement.

—— 4. Plan or outline your essay, choosing from two to four main ideas to support the thesis statement.

—— 5. Write a topic sentence that expresses each main idea.

—— 6. Decide on a logical order in which to present the paragraphs.

—— 7. Plan the body of each paragraph, using all you learned about paragraph development in Unit 2 of this book.

—— 8. Write the first draft of your essay.

—— 9. Revise as necessary, checking your essay for support, unity, and coherence. Refer to the list of revision questions on page 190.

—— 10. Proofread carefully for grammar, punctuation, sentence structure, spelling, and mechanics.

Suggested Topics for Essays

1. The career for which I am best suited

2. This college's worst problem (propose a solution)

3. A special or unusual person

4. A valuable discipline or practice (lifting weights, rock climbing, meditating, or other)

5. Why many Americans don't read the newspaper (vote, value education, or read poetry)

6. The best (or worst) teacher I ever had

7. Music videos (choose one performer or group, one type of music, or one TV show)

8. A lesson in diversity, race, or difference

9. The joys of homework (or housework or some other supposedly unpleasant task)

10. How to resolve a disagreement peacefully

11. An important film (book, magazine, or program)

12. The best gift I ever gave (or received)

13. Three ways that cigarette ads hook kids

14. Should courts require a one-year "cooling-off" period before a divorce?

15. Writer's choice: _____

Types of Essays

Because an essay is like an expanded paragraph, the methods for developing and organizing a paragraph that you learned in Unit 3—illustration, process, and so forth—can also be used to develop an entire essay. The rest of this chapter will show you how.

PART A   The Illustration Essay

The **illustration** essay is one of the most frequently used in college writing and in business. For papers and exams in history, psychology, health, English, and other subjects, you will often be asked to develop a main point with examples. In a letter of job application, you might wish to give examples of achievements that demonstrate your special skills.

Here is an illustration essay:

Libraries of the Future—Now

(1) When you think of the word *library*, do you picture an old-fashioned building, dusty books, and stern librarians? Think instead of an electronic theme park for readers, where people from tots to seniors can not only read books from the stacks around them, but explore cyberspace from one of many computer terminals. Imagine yourself calling up documents from libraries around the world or working with other students on multimedia projects. In fact, the future has arrived in a few pioneering libraries that are using technology to offer more resources to library users than ever before.

(2) For instance, the San Francisco Public Library is helping its diverse community enter the information age. At San Francisco's many branch libraries, visitors can now surf the Internet from public terminals, but the hub of the system is the $140 million San Francisco Main Public Library building, which opened in 1996. The seven-story building features 300 computer terminals where users can access catalogues, databases, and the World Wide Web. Another 1,100 users can plug their own laptops into the library's outlets. The huge children's book room has many more computers on child-sized tables. The San Francisco Library appears to be achieving its goal. In its first year, library visits jumped from 1.1 million to 2.1 million, and the number of library-card holders tripled.

(3) A second example of today's high-tech libraries is the private Vatican Library in Rome. The Vatican, headquarters of the Roman Catholic Church, has one of the finest collections of manuscripts and books in the world. The entire catalogue of this collection is now available on the Internet. Yet until recently, only about 2,000 scholars a year could come to Rome and examine such costly treasures as an ancient text handwritten on antelope skin or a perfect Gutenberg Bible. Now, with help from IBM, the Vatican is making digital images of these documents. In an underground, atom bomb–proof vault where the originals are kept, two technicians are scanning one page at a time with a special camera. Soon anyone will be able to see 20,000 rare, perfectly colored images and to enlarge the tiniest details on his or her computer screen.

(4) An even more futuristic library is the University of Michigan's new Media Union. Besides holding the University's art and architecture libraries, the 225,000-square-foot Media Union contains 500 computer workstations, computer training areas, four interactive multimedia classrooms, video and sound production facilities, a theater, a virtual reality and animation lab, a gallery, and, last but not least, books. Students can experience virtual worlds in dance, engineering, art, architecture, and computer science. Imagine two engineering students playing with 3-D designs of a century-old bridge to come up with a dynamic new form or a dance student moving with a virtual dance performance in real time. This exciting library lets people in many fields work together on new creations.

(5) These three unique libraries are helping to adapt the printed past to a digital future. However, they are still the exception, not the rule. Transforming our libraries requires millions of private and public dollars. As citizens, we can urge our elected officials to support the efforts of libraries as they help move all our citizens into the information age. When many of us were children, libraries opened the door to a world of dreams through books. The high-tech libraries of the future will open doors we cannot yet imagine.

■ The **thesis statement** of an illustration essay states the writer's central point—a general statement that the rest of the essay will develop with examples.

■ Which sentence in the introductory paragraph is the thesis statement?

_____

_____

■ How many examples does the writer use to develop the thesis statement? What are they?

_____

_____

■ Underline the topic sentence of each supporting paragraph.

■ The thesis statement and topic sentences setting forth the three examples create a **plan** for this essay. The writer no doubt made such a plan or an outline before she wrote the first draft.

Before writing an illustration essay, you may wish to reread Chapter 5, "Illustration." As you pick a topic and plan your illustration essay, make sure your thesis statement can be richly developed by examples. Then brainstorm or freewrite, jotting down as many possible examples as you can think of; choose the best two or three examples. If you devote one paragraph to each example, each topic sentence should introduce the example to be developed. As you revise, make sure you have fully discussed each example, including all necessary details and facts.

PRACTICE 1

Choose a topic from the following list or use a topic that you or your instructor has chosen. Write an illustration essay, referring to the essay checklist at the end of Chapter 14.

Suggested Topics: The Illustration Essay

1. Good deeds that backfired
2. Inventions that probably will shape the twenty-first century
3. Failure as the best teacher
4. TV talk show hosts who send a positive message (or who _____)
5. Small events that changed lives
6. Memorable neighbors (professors, friends, and so on)
7. Currently cool hairstyles or clothing styles
8. Unusual places to go on dates (or to study, de-stress, get married, and so on)
9. Successful (or unsuccessful) college students
10. Musicians or artists of a particular group (R&B, tropical Latin, surrealist, French impressionist, and so on)
11. Writer's choice: _____

PART B   The Narrative Essay

The narrative essay is used frequently in college writing. For instance, in a history course you might be assigned a paper on the major battles of World War I or be given an essay examination on the story of women's struggle to gain the right to vote. An English teacher may ask you to write a composition in which you retell a meaningful incident or personal experience. In all of these instances, your ability to organize facts and details in clear chronological, or time, order—to tell a story well—will be a crucial factor in the success of your paper.

Here is a narrative essay:

Maya Lin's Vietnam War Memorial

(1) The Vietnam War was the longest war in United States history, lasting from 1965 until 1975. Also our most controversial war, it left a deep wound in the nation's conscience. The creation of the Vietnam War Memorial helped heal this wound and put an unknown architecture student into the history books.

(2) In 1980, when the call went out for designs for a Vietnam War Memorial, no one could have predicted that as many as 14,000 entries would be submitted. The rules were clear. The memorial had to be contemplative, harmonize with its surroundings, list the names of those dead or missing, and—most important—make no political statement about the war. When the judges, all well-known architects and sculptors, met in April 1981, they unanimously chose entry number 1026. The winner was Maya Lin, a twenty-one-year-old Asian-American architecture student who, ironically, was too young to have had any direct experience of the war.

(3) Lin envisioned shining black granite slabs embedded in a long V-shaped trench, with one end pointing toward the Lincoln Memorial and the other toward the Washington Monument. She defined the trench as a cut in the earth, "an initial violence that in time would heal." Names would be carved into the granite in the order of the dates on which the soldiers had died or disappeared. Lin felt that finding a name on the memorial with the help of a directory would be like finding a body on a battlefield.

(4) Although her design satisfied all the contest criteria and was the judges' clear favorite, it aroused much controversy. Some critics called it a "black gash of shame and sorrow," labeling it unpatriotic, unheroic, and morbid. They were upset that the memorial contained no flags, no statues of soldiers, and no inscription other than the names. Privately, some complained that Lin was too young to win the contest—and that she was female besides. She fought back. She claimed that a flag would make the green area around the memorial look like a golf course and that a traditional statue on her modern structure would be like a mustache drawn on someone else's portrait. At last, a compromise was reached: A flag and a statue were added to the memorial, and the critics withdrew their complaints. On Veterans Day, November 11, 1982, the Vietnam War Memorial was finally dedicated.

(5) Since then, the memorial has become the most popular site in Washington, D.C. Some visit to see the monument and pay tribute to those who died in the war. Others come to locate and touch the names of loved ones. As they stand before the wall, they also learn the names of those who served and died with their relatives and friends. When the rain falls, all the names seem to disappear.

Visitors often leave memorials of their own—flowers, notes to the departed, bits of old uniforms. A place of national mourning and of love, Maya Lin's monument has helped heal the wounds of the Vietnam War.

- The **thesis statement** of a narrative essay gives the point of the essay.
- What is the thesis statement of the essay?

_____

_____

- Paragraphs 2, 4, and 5 of this essay tell in chronological order the incidents of the narrative.
- What are the incidents?

_____

_____

- What is the main idea of paragraph 3?

_____

- Paragraph 1 provides background information that helps the reader understand the narrative.
- What background material is given in this paragraph?

_____

_____

Before writing a narrative essay, you may wish to reread Chapter 6, "Narration." Make sure that your thesis statement clearly states the point of your narrative. Organize all the incidents and details in chronological, or time, order, in general beginning with the earliest event and ending with the latest. Be sure to supply any necessary background information. As you plan your essay, pay careful attention to paragraphing; if your narrative consists of just a few major incidents, you may wish to devote one paragraph to each one. Use transitional expressions that indicate time order to help your reader follow the narrative easily.

PRACTICE 2

Choose a topic from the following list or use a topic that you or your instructor has chosen. Write a narrative essay, referring to the essay checklist at the end of Chapter 14.

Suggested Topics: The Narrative Essay

1. A risk that paid off
2. How someone chose his or her career
3. The story behind a key scientific discovery or invention
4. An event that changed your view of yourself

5. An unforgettable incident you witnessed

6. An important historical event

7. A time someone acted with courage or cowardice

8. The plot line of a movie or TV show you would like to produce

9. Learning a new language (or other subject or skill)

10. Someone's battle with a serious illness

11. Writer's choice: _____

PART C   The Descriptive Essay

Although paragraphs of **description** are more common than whole essays, you will sometimes need to write a descriptive essay. In science labs, you may need to describe accurately cells under a microscope or a certain kind of rock. In business, you might have to describe a product or piece of equipment. Travel writers frequently use description, and personal letters often call on your descriptive powers.

Here is a descriptive essay:

The Day of the Dead

(1) The most important holiday in Mexico is the Day of the Dead, *El Día de Los Muertos.* Surprisingly, this holiday is anything but depressing. In the weeks before, Mexicans excitedly prepare to welcome the souls of the dead, who come back each year to visit the living. From October 31 through November 2 this year, I attended this fiesta with my roommate Manuel. By sharing Day of the Dead activities in his family's home, in the marketplace, and in a cemetery, I have observed that Mexicans, unlike other North Americans, accept and celebrate death as a part of life.

(2) For this holiday, the home altar, or *ofrenda,* lovingly celebrates the dead. In the Lopez home, a trail of marigold petals and the rich smell of incense led us from the front door to the altar. The bright orange marigold blooms, the flowers of the dead, also trimmed a card table overflowing with everything the dead would need to take up their lives again. For Manuel's Uncle Angel there was a fragrant bowl of mole,* a glass of tequila, cigars, playing cards, and two Miles Davis jazz CDs. For Manuel's cousin Lucia, who died at eighteen months, there was a worn stuffed puppy, a coral blanket, and a bowl of the rice pudding she loved. Heavy black and yellow beeswax candles threw a soft glow on photos of Angel and Lucia. It was as if the dead had never left and would always have a place of honor.

(3) While death is given an honored place in the home, it is celebrated with humor and mockery in the marketplace. Here the skeleton, or *calavera,* rules. Shops sell sugar skulls, humorous bone figures, and even skeletons made of flowers. At the candy store, Manuel's niece picked out a white chocolate skull decorated with blue icing and magenta sequins in the eye sockets. In many bakeries, skull-and-crossbones designs decorated the delicious "bread of the dead." Most impressive were the stalls filled with *calacas,* handmade wooden skeletons,

---

*mole: a spicy sauce made with unsweetened chocolate

some no bigger than my thumb. The shelves showed a lively afterlife where skeleton musicians played in a band; skeleton writers tapped bony fingers on tiny typewriters, and teenage skeletons hoisted boom boxes on their matchstick-sized shoulder bones.

(4) On the evening of November first, reverence and fun combined in an all-night vigil at the cemetery. On a path outside the cemetery gate, rows of vendors sold soft drinks and cotton candy as if it were a sporting event. Men drank a strong fermented cactus beverage called *pulque* and played cards at picnic tables. The loud music of a mariachi band serenaded the dead, who would come back to eat the food laid out for them on the graves. Old grandmothers wearing hand-woven shawls mourned and wept while children chased each other around the pink- and blue-painted graves. Nobody scolded the children. Life and death did not seem so separate.

(5) While I have always felt fearful in cemeteries at home, there I felt excited and hopeful. When a soft breeze made the rows of candles flicker, I wondered if the souls of the children, the *angelitos,* had come back, laughing and giggling. Or was it the real children I heard laughing? I really didn't know. But I felt more alive than ever, waiting for the dead to arrive in a dusty cemetery in Mexico.

—Jason Eady (Student)

◾ The **thesis statement** of a descriptive essay says what will be described and sometimes gives an overall impression of it or tells how the writer will approach the subject. Which sentence in the introductory paragraph is the thesis statement?

_____

_____

_____

◾ Each paragraph in the body of this essay describes one scene or aspect of the topic. How many scenes or aspects are described, and what are they?

_____

_____

◾ What kind of **order** does the writer follow in organizing paragraph 2?

_____

_____

◾ Paragraph 5 completes and **concludes** the essay. How effective is this student's conclusion?

_____

_____

_____

◾ Note that the thesis statement and topic sentences make a **plan** for the whole essay.

Before writing an essay of description, you may wish to reread Chapter 7, "Description." Make sure that your thesis statement clearly sets forth the precise subject your essay will describe. Use your senses—sight, smell, hearing, taste, and touch—as you jot down ideas for the body. As you plan, pay special attention to organizing details and observations; space order is often the best way to organize a description. As you revise, pay special attention to the richness and exactness of your language and details; these are what make good descriptions come alive.

<hr/>

PRACTICE 3

Choose a topic from the following list or use a topic that you or your instructor has chosen. Write an essay of description, referring to the essay checklist at the end of Chapter 14.

Suggested Topics: The Descriptive Essay

1. The decorations and rituals of a holiday you know

2. A person or animal you have closely observed

3. The scene of a historic event or battle as you imagine it

4. A school, church, prison, store, gym, or other public place

5. A tourist attraction or a place of natural beauty

6. College classrooms in the twenty-first century

7. A computer, motorcycle, or piece of equipment from your job

8. A place you know from travel or reading

9. Your family portrait

10. A scene you will never forget

11. Writer's choice: _____

PART D The Process Essay

The **process** essay is frequently used in college and business. In psychology, for example, you might describe the stages of personality development. In history, you might explain the process of electing a president or how a battle was won or lost, while in business, you might set forth the steps of an advertising campaign. In science labs, you will often have to record the stages of an experiment.

Here is a process essay:

How to Prepare for a Final Exam

(1) At the end of my first semester at college, I postponed thinking about final examinations, desperately crammed the night before, drank enough coffee to keep the city of Cincinnati awake, and then got C's and D's. I have since realized that the students who got A's on their finals weren't just lucky; they knew how to *prepare.* There are many different ways to prepare for a final examination, and each individual must perfect his or her own style, but over the years, I have developed a method that works for me.

(2) First, when your professor announces the date, time, and place of the final—usually at least two weeks before—ask questions and take careful notes on the answers. What chapters will be covered? What kinds of questions will the test contain? What materials and topics are most important? The information you gather will help you study more effectively.

(3) Next, survey all the textbook chapters the test will cover, using a high-lighter or colored pen to mark important ideas and sections to be studied later. Many textbooks emphasize key ideas with boldface titles or headlines; others are written so that key ideas appear in the topic sentences at the beginning of each paragraph. Pay attention to these guides as you read.

(4) Third, survey your class notes in the same fashion, marking important ideas. If your notes are messy or disorganized, you might want to rewrite them for easy reference later.

(5) Fourth, decide approximately how many hours you will need to study. Get a calendar and clearly mark off the hours each week that you will devote to in-depth studying. If possible, set aside specific times: Thursday from 1 to 2 p.m., Friday from 6 to 8 p.m., and so on. If you have trouble committing yourself, schedule study time with a friend; but pick someone as serious as you are about getting good grades.

(6) Fifth, begin studying systematically, choosing a quiet place free from dis-tractions in which to work—the library, a dorm room, whatever helps you con-centrate. One of my friends can study only in his attic; another, in her car. As you review the textbook and your notes, ask yourself questions based on your read-ing. From class discussions, try to spot the professor's priorities and to guess what questions might appear on the exam. Be creative; one friend of mine puts important study material on cassette tapes, which he plays walking to and from school.

(7) Finally, at least three days before the exam, start reviewing. At the least opportunity, refer to your notes, even if you are not prepared to digest all the mate-rial. Use the moments when you are drinking your orange juice or riding the bus; just looking at the material can promote learning. By the night before the exam, you should know everything you want to know—and allow for a good night's sleep!

(8) By following these simple procedures, you may find, as I do, that you are the most prepared person in the exam room, confident that you studied thor-oughly enough to do well on the exam.

—Mark Reyes (Student)

■ The **thesis statement** in a process essay tells the reader what process the rest of the essay will describe.

■ What is the thesis statement in this essay?

_____

_____

_____

■ What process will be described?

_____

■ How many steps make up this process, and what are they?

_____

_____

_____

■ What kind of order does the writer use to organize his essay?

_____

    Before writing a process essay, you may wish to reread Chapter 8, "Process." The thesis statement should clearly set forth the process you intend to describe. As you plan your essay, jot down all the necessary steps or stages and put them in logical order. As you revise, make sure you have fully and clearly explained each step so that a reader who may not be familiar with the subject matter can follow easily. Clear language and logical organization are the keys to good process writing. Pay special attention to paragraphing; if the process consists of just three or four steps, you may wish to devote one paragraph to each step. If the steps are short or numerous, you will probably wish to combine two or three steps in each paragraph.

PRACTICE 4

    Choose a topic from the list below or use a topic that you or your instructor has chosen. Write a process essay, referring to the essay checklist at the end of Chapter 14.

Suggested Topics: The Process Essay

1. How someone achieved success

2. How to prepare for a trip (backpacking, a weekend in Las Vegas, and so on)

3. How to get in shape

4. How a cell phone can ruin a date (or other social occasion)

5. How to get action on a community problem

6. How to teach a child a skill or value

7. The yearly cycle of a crop (corn, wheat, oranges, cocoa, and so on)

8. How to impress the boss

9. A process you learned in another course (stages of human moral development, how a lake becomes a meadow, and so on)

10. How to get an A in _____

11. Writer's choice: _____

PART E   The Definition Essay

    Although paragraphs of **definition** are more common in college writing than essays are, you may at some time have to write a definition essay. In a computer course, for example, you might be called on to define *Internet* and *intranet*. In psychology, you might need to define the *Oedipus complex,* or in biology, the terms *DNA* or *spontaneous remission.*

Here is a definition essay:

Winning

(1) The dictionary defines winning as "achieving victory over others in a competition, receiving a prize or reward for achievement." Yet some of the most meaningful wins of my life were victories over no other person, and I can remember winning when there was no prize for performance. To me, winning means overcoming obstacles.

(2) My first experience of winning occurred in elementary school gym. Nearly every day, after the preparatory pushups and squat-thrusts, we had to run relays. Although I had asthma as a child, I won many races. My chest would burn terribly for a few minutes, but it was worth it to feel so proud—not because I'd beaten others or won a prize, but because I'd overcome a handicap. (By the way, I "outgrew" my asthma by age eleven.)

(3) In high school, I had another experience of winning. Although I loved reading about biology, I could not bring myself to dissect a frog in lab. I hated the smell of the dead animals, and the idea of cutting them open disgusted me. Every time I tried, my hands would shake and my stomach would turn. Worst of all, my biology teacher reacted to my futile attempts with contempt. After an upsetting couple of weeks, I decided to get hold of myself. I realized that I was overreacting. "The animals are already dead," I told myself. With determination, I swept into my next lab period, walked up to the table, and with one swift stroke, slit open a frog. After that, I excelled in biology. I had won again.

(4) I consider the fact that I am now attending college winning. To get here, I had to surmount many obstacles, both outside and inside myself. College costs money, and I don't have much of it. College takes time, and I don't have much of that either with a little son to care for. But I overcame these obstacles and a bigger one still—lack of confidence in myself. I had to keep saying, "I won't give up." And here I am, winning!

(5) These examples should clarify what winning means to me. I don't trust anything that comes too easily. In fact, I expect the road to be rocky, and I appreciate a win more if I have to work, sacrifice, and overcome. This is a positive drive for me, the very spirit of winning.

—Audrey Holmes (Student)

■ The **thesis statement** of a definition essay tells the reader what term will be defined and usually defines it as well.

■ Which sentence in the introductory paragraph is the thesis statement?

_____

_____

■ What is the writer's definition of *winning?*

_____

_____

■ Underline the topic sentences of paragraphs 2, 3, and 4.

■ How do paragraphs 2, 3, and 4 develop the thesis statement?

_____

_____

■ What order does the writer follow in paragraphs 2, 3, and 4?

_____

_____

_____

Before writing a definition essay, you may wish to reread Chapter 9, "Definition." Choose a word or term that truly interests you, one about which you have something to say. Decide what type of definition you will use and write the thesis statement, which should state and define your term. Then brainstorm ideas to explain your definition. Consider using two or three examples to develop the term—the way the writer does in the preceding essay—devoting one paragraph to each example. As you revise, make sure your writing is very clear, so the reader knows exactly what you mean.

PRACTICE 5

Choose a topic from the following list or one that you or your instructor has chosen. Write a definition essay, referring to the essay checklist at the end of Chapter 14.

Suggested Topics: The Definition Essay

1. A special term from sports, music, art, science, or technology
2. Tolerance
3. A friend
4. An environmental term (_endangered species, wind chill, global warming,_ and so on)
5. A breed of dog or other animal
6. Sexual harassment
7. Maturity
8. A slang term in current use
9. A term from another language (_salsa, joi de vivre, machismo, zeitgeist,_ and so on)
10. A disease or medical condition
11. Writer's choice: _____

PART F The Comparison or Contrast Essay

Essays of **comparison** or **contrast** are frequently called for in college courses. In an English or a drama class, you might be asked to contrast two of Shakespeare's villains—perhaps Iago and Claudius. In psychology, you might have to contrast the training of the clinical psychologist and that of the psychiatrist, or in history, to compare ancient Greek and Roman religions.

Does the following essay compare or contrast?

Two Childhoods

(1) When I was young, my mother told me stories about her childhood. I loved her tales and still think of them. It was intriguing to hear about life thirty years before mine began. What fascinated me most, however, were the differences between her youth and mine.

(2) My mother grew up in the country. She spent most of her young years on a farm in South Carolina, surrounded by animals, orchards, cane fields, and agricultural machinery. By the time she was six, she was a walking agricultural textbook. Hers was a simple, serene, and comfortable life within a close-knit, neighborly environment. My mother's days were filled with swimming in nearby rivers and lakes, climbing and falling off trees, scooter riding down country lanes, playing marbles with siblings and friends, bird watching and mending of wings, and building fences and tree houses.

(3) My childhood, on the other hand, was spent in New York City, without animals, scenic surroundings, or close-knit neighbors. Mine was a lifestyle of fast activity crammed into a tight schedule. Nature was replaced by shops and businesses, trees by tall buildings. My knowledge was not based on the simple things at hand, but on expensive toys, the latest clothes, and the newest sneakers. Compared with my mother's country existence, my city childhood seems humdrum—a constant series of trips to the park or movies, visits to the grocery store or shopping center, picnics at the amusement park or beach, and a few birthday parties thrown in.

(4) Just as our lifestyles differed, so too did our personalities. Relatives say that my mother was a loving, caring child who was always willing to help. She was praised for being clever and vibrant, levelheaded and respectful to others. My mother was strong willed and spoke her mind when she saw fit, but she placed few demands on her parents for toys or fancy clothes. Somehow her environment, which had instilled in her an appreciation of nature and living things, was enough.

(5) I, on the other hand, was considered a bit too extroverted, selfish, and stubborn. I reveled in being petulant, pigheaded, demanding, and unstable. Although I could be loving, I cleverly used this trait to my advantage in an attempt to manipulate my parents and get the beautiful toys and clothes I wanted. After all, these gave me all the aesthetic appreciation I needed. In fact, I was a brazenfaced brat.

(6) Looking back, I think it would have been wonderful as a child to have fallen off a few trees or driven a scooter at maniacal speeds or even milked a cow or crushed some coffee beans in a mortar. Yes, that would have been wonderful. It really would have been.

—Cheryl Parris (Student)

■ The **thesis statement** of a comparison or contrast essay tells what two persons or things will be compared or contrasted.

■ What is the thesis statement of this essay?

_____

_____

■ Will this essay compare or contrast the two people? What word or words in the thesis indicate this?

_____

■ Does the writer discuss all points about A and then all points about B, or skip back and forth from A to B?

_____

■ Note that the thesis statement and topic sentences make a **plan** for this essay.

Before you plan or outline your essay, you may wish to reread Chapter 10, "Comparison and Contrast." Bear in mind, as you choose a subject, that the most interesting essays usually compare two things that are different or contrast two things that are similar. Otherwise, you run the risk of saying the obvious ("Cats and dogs are two different animals").

Here are a few tips to keep in mind as you write your thesis statement: Don't just say that A and B are similar or different; instead, say _in what way_ A and B are similar or different, as the writer does on page 209. You may wish to use this form for a contrast thesis: _Although A and B have this similarity, they are different in these ways._ And for a comparison: _Although A and B are unlike in this way, they are similar in these ways._

As you plan the body of your essay, you may wish to make a chart of all your points of comparison or contrast. In any case, if you discuss the food, service, price, and atmosphere of Restaurant A, you must discuss the food, service, price, and atmosphere of Restaurant B as well.

In your essay, you can first discuss A (one paragraph), then discuss B (one paragraph), or you can skip back and forth between A and B (one paragraph on point one, A and B, one paragraph on point two, A and B, and one paragraph on point three, A and B). Refer to the charts in Chapter 10, page 121.

PRACTICE 6

Choose a topic from the list below or use a topic that you or your instructor has chosen. Write either a comparison or a contrast essay, referring to the essay checklist at the end of Chapter 14.

Suggested Topics: The Comparison or Contrast Essay

1. Two entertainers, athletes, philosophers, politicians, or other public figures

2. Your mother's or father's childhood and your own

3. Two cultural attitudes about one subject

4. A neighborhood store and a chain store (bookstore, restaurant, music store, and so on)

5. Two cars, computers, or other machines

6. Two views on a controversial issue

7. Two houses or apartments that you know well

8. A traditional doctor and an alternative healer

9. A book and a movie made from that book

10. Two pets

11. Writer's choice: _____

PART G   The Classification Essay

The **classification** essay is useful in college and business. In music, for example, you might have to classify Mozart's compositions according to the musical periods of his life. A retail business might classify items in stock according to popularity—how frequently they must be reordered.

Although the classification essay is usually serious, the pattern can make a good humorous essay, as this essay shows:

The Potato Scale

(1) For years, television has been the great American pastime. Nearly every household has at least one TV, which means that people are spending time watching it, unless, of course, they bought it to serve as a plant stand. Television viewers can be grouped in many ways—by the type of shows they watch (but there is no accounting for taste) or by hours per week of watching (but that seems unfair since a working, twelve-hour-a-week viewer could conceivably become a fifty-hour-a-week viewer if he or she were out of a job). So I have developed the Potato Scale. The four major categories of the Potato Scale rank TV viewers on a combination of leisure time spent watching, intensity of watching, and the desire to watch versus the desire to engage in other activities.

(2) First, we have the True Couch Potatoes. They are diehard viewers who, when home, will be found in front of their televisions. They no longer eat in the dining room, and if you visit them, the television stays on. *TV Guide* is their Bible. They will plan other activities and chores around their viewing time, always hoping to accomplish these tasks in front of the tube. If a presidential address is on every channel but one, and they dislike the president, they will tune in that one channel, be it Bugs Bunny reruns or Polynesian barge cooking. These potatoes would never consider turning off the box.

(3) The second group consists of the Pseudo Couch Potatoes. These are scheduled potatoes. They have outside interests and actually eat at the table, but for a certain period of time (let's say from seven to eleven in the evening), they will take on the characteristics of True Couch Potatoes. Another difference between True and Pseudo Potatoes deserves note. The True Potato must be forced by someone else to shut off the television and do something different; however, if the Pseudo Potato has flipped through all the channels and found only garbage, he or she still has the capacity to think of other things to do.

(4) Third, we have the Selective Potatoes. These more discriminating potatoes enjoy many activities, and TV is just one of them. They might have a few shows they enjoy watching regularly, but missing one episode is not a world-class crisis. After all, the show will be on next week. They don't live by *TV Guide*, but use it to check for interesting specials. If they find themselves staring at an awful movie or show, they will gladly, and without a second thought, turn it off.

(5) The fourth group consists of Last Resort Potatoes. These people actually prefer reading, going to the theater, playing pickup basketball, walking in the woods, and many other activities to watching television. Only after they have exhausted all other possibilities or are dog tired or shivering with the flu, will they click on the tube. These potatoes are either excessively choosy or almost indifferent to what's on, hoping it will bore them to sleep.

(6) These are the principal categories of the Potato Scale, from the truly vegetable to the usually human. What type of potato are you?

—Helen Petruzzelli (Student)

■ The **thesis statement** in a classification essay tells the reader what group will be classified and on what basis.

■ This entire essay **classifies** people on the basis of their television viewing habits. Which sentence is the thesis statement?

_____

_____

■ Into how many categories are TV viewers divided?

_____

■ Each paragraph in the body of the essay discusses one of four categories, which the writer names. What are they?

1: _____

2: _____

3: _____

4: _____

■ The thesis statement and the topic sentences setting forth the four categories create a **plan** for the essay. The writer no doubt made the plan before she wrote the first draft.

■ Can you see the logic in the writer's *order* of paragraphs? That is, why does she present True Couch Potatoes first, Pseudo Potatoes second, Selective Potatoes third, and Last Resort Potatoes last?

_____

_____

Before writing your classification essay, you may wish to reread Chapter 11, "Classification." Choose a topic that lends itself to classification and carefully determine your basis of classification. Your thesis statement should state clearly the group you will classify and your basis of classification. As you plan, make sure that all your categories (three or four is a good number) reflect that basis of classification. Discuss one category per paragraph, including enough examples, details, and facts to let the reader completely understand your ideas.

PRACTICE 7

Choose a topic from the following list or use a topic that you or your instructor has chosen. Write a classification essay, referring to the essay checklist at the end of Chapter 14.

Suggested Topics: The Classification Essay

1. Members of your family

2. People studying in the library

3. Stories on the front page of the newspaper

4. Drivers

5. Soap operas

6. Teenagers whom you interview about their hopefulness or the lack of it (or their belief in education, thoughts about gangs, and so on)

7. Restaurants, music stores, or shoe stores in your neighborhood

8. Criminals

9. Your coworkers

10. People in a movie theater

11. Writer's choice: _____

PART H   The Cause and Effect Essay

Essays of **cause and effect** are among the most important kinds of essays to master because knowing how to analyze the causes and consequences of events will help you succeed in college, at work, and in your personal life. What *caused* a historic battle, an increase in homelessness since the 1980s, or two friends' breaking apart? How will a certain child be *affected* by owning a computer, spending time at Sunshine Day Care, or being teased because he loves to dance? In business, the success of every company and product relies on a grasp of cause and effect in the marketplace. Why does this brand of sneaker outsell all others? What causes employees to want to work hard? How will the Internet affect business in 2015?

Here is an essay of cause and effect. As you will see, this writer's eventual understanding of causes and effects might have saved her life.

Why I Stayed and Stayed

(1) It has been proven that about 1.8 million women are battered each year, making battery the single largest cause of injury to women in the United States. Domestic violence can be physical, emotional, verbal, financial, or sexual abuse from a partner you live with. I suffered from most of these abuses for almost ten years. I have had black eyes, busted lips, bruises, and scars on my face. He had affairs with other women, yet he claimed that he loved me. People ask, "Why did you wait so long to leave him?" I stayed for many reasons.

(2) First, I was born in a country that is male-dominated. Many of my people accept violence against women as a part of life. I grew up seeing hundreds of women staying in violent relationships for the sake of their children. They wanted their children to grow up with a father at home. Relatives convinced these women to try to make their marriages work. This was all I knew.

(3) Another reason I stayed was that I was afraid to make changes in my life. I had been with him so long that I thought I had nowhere to go. I depended on

him to provide me and my child with food and shelter. How could I manage on my own? Of course, the longer I believed these things, the more my self-confidence withered.

(4) Finally, I stayed because I was isolated. I felt ashamed to talk about the problem, believing it was somehow my fault. Fear was isolating, too. Living in a violent home is very frightening. Like many women, I was afraid to say anything to anyone, thinking he would get upset. If I just kept quiet, maybe he wouldn't hurt me. But nothing I did made any difference.

(5) When I finally realized that the abuse was not going to stop, I decided to do something about it. I was finally ready to end my pain. I began to talk to people and learn about ways to get help.

(6) On April 24 of this year, I fought back. When he punched me in the eye, I called 911. Thank God for changes in the way domestic violence cases are now being handled. The police responded quickly. He was arrested and taken to jail, where he waited for two days to go to court. The next day, I went to the court-house to press charges. I spoke to the district attorney in charge, asking for an order of protection. This order forbids him from having any verbal or physical contact with me.

(7) It is very hard to see someone you love being taken away in handcuffs, but I had to put my safety and my child's well-being first. Although he is now out of jail, I feel safe with my order of protection; however, I understand that court orders sometimes do not stop abusers. These are very difficult days for me, but I pray that time will heal my wounds. I cry often, which helps my pain. But an innocent life depends on me for guidance, and I cannot let her down.

(8) Every case is different, and you know your partner better than anyone, but help is out there if you reach for it. Most cities have a twenty-four-hour hot-line. There is help at this college at the PASS Center and the Department of Student Development. You can go to a shelter, to a friend, to your family. These people will not fail you. You too can break the chain.

—Fadima (Student, last name withheld by request)

■ The **thesis statement** in a cause and effect essay identifies the subject and tells whether causes or effects will be emphasized. What is this writer's thesis statement? Will she emphasize causes or effects?

_____

■ How many causes does the writer discuss, and what are they?

_____

■ Although some essays discuss either causes or effects, this one does both. Paragraph 5 marks a turning point, her decision to take action. What positive effects of this new decision does she discuss? Are there any negative effects?

_____

_____

_____

■ Before she wrote this essay, the writer probably made a plan like this:

Introduction and thesis statement

Reasons for staying with abusive partner — upbringing, fear of change, isolation

Decision to leave

Effects of leaving abusive partner — reached out for help, fought back (911, order of protection), acted for daughter, sadness, guilt

Advice for women in the same situation

■ What order does this essay follow?

_____

■ Do you think paragraph 8 makes an effective conclusion?

_____

Before writing an essay of cause or effect, reread Chapter 12, "Cause and Effect," especially the section called "Avoiding Problems in Cause and Effect Writing." Choose a subject that lends itself to analysis of causes or effects; see the topic lists in Chapter 12 and this chapter for ideas. Think on paper or on computer, listing many possible causes or effects; then choose the best three or four. Don't forget to consider short- and long-term effects, as well as positive and negative effects. Decide on a logical order—probably time order or order of importance.

PRACTICE 8

Choose a topic from the following list or one that your instructor has chosen. Write a cause and effect essay, referring to the checklist at the end of Chapter 14.

Suggested Topics: The Cause and Effect Essay

1. What are the reasons for the popularity of a product, musical group, or game?

2. What caused you to do something you are not proud of?

3. Analyze the main causes of a serious problem in society.

4. Analyze the effects of shyness on someone's life (or anger, pride, curiosity or the lack of it, and so on).

5. What are the effects of a tragedy?

6. What are the effects of a new experience (a trip, military service, living in another country, dorm life)?

7. What causes a hurricane, tornado, or other natural disaster?

8. Choose an event in history that interests you and analyze its causes.

9. What effects did an early failure or success (in public speaking, sports, and so on) have on someone you know?

10. How does being unusual looking affect one's daily life?

11. Writer's choice: _____

PART I   The Persuasive Essay

Persuasive essays are the essay type most frequently called for in college and business. That is, you will often be asked to take a stand on an issue—legalized abortion, capital punishment, whether a company should invest in on-site child care—and then try to persuade others to agree with you. Examination questions asking you to "agree or disagree" are really asking you to take a stand and make a persuasive case for that stand—for example, "World War II was basically a continuation of World War I. Agree or disagree." You are asked to muster factual evidence to support your stand.

Here is a persuasive essay:

Stopping Youth Violence: An Inside Job

(1) Every year, nearly a million twelve- to nineteen-year-olds are murdered, robbed, or assaulted—many by their peers—and teenagers are more than twice as likely as adults to become the victims of violence, according to the Children's Defense Fund. Although the problem is far too complex for any one solution, teaching young people conflict-resolution skills—that is, nonviolent techniques for resolving disputes—seems to help. To reduce youth violence, conflict-resolution skills should be taught to all children before they reach junior high school.

(2) First and most important, young people need to learn nonviolent ways of dealing with conflict. In a dangerous society where guns are readily available, many youngsters feel they have no choice but to respond to an insult or an argument with violence. If they have grown up seeing family members and neighbors react to stress with verbal or physical violence, they may not know that other choices exist. Robert Steinback, a *Miami Herald* columnist who works with at-risk youth in Miami, writes that behavior like carrying a weapon or refusing to back down gives young people "the illusion of control," but what they desperately need is to learn real control—for example, when provoked, to walk away from a fight.

(3) Next, conflict-resolution programs have been shown to reduce violent incidents and empower young people in a healthy way. Many programs and courses around the country are teaching teens and preteens to work through disagreements without violence. Tools include calmly telling one's own side of the story and listening to the other person without interrupting or blaming—skills that many adults don't have! Conflict Busters, a Los Angeles public school program, starts in the third grade; it trains students to be mediators, helping peers find their own solutions to conflicts ranging from "sandbox fights to interracial gang disputes," according to *Youthwatch: Statistics on Violence,* October 1999. Schools in Claremont, Connecticut, run a conflict-resolution course written by Dr. Luz Rivera, who said in a phone interview that fewer violent school incidents have been reported since the course began. Although conflict resolution is useful at any age, experts agree that students should first be exposed before they are hit by the double jolts of hormones and junior high school.

(4) Finally, although opponents claim that this is a "Band-Aid" solution that does not address the root causes of teen violence—poverty, troubled families, bad schools, and drugs, to name a few—in fact, conflict-resolution training saves lives now. The larger social issues must be addressed, but they will take years to solve, whereas teaching students new attitudes and "people skills" will empower them

immediately and serve them for a lifetime. For instance, fourteen-year-old Verna, who once called herself Vee Sinister, says that Ms. Rivera's course has changed her life: "I learned to stop and think before my big mouth gets me in trouble. I use the tools with my mother, and guess what? No more screaming at home."

(5) The violence devastating Verna's generation threatens everyone's future. One proven way to help youngsters protect themselves from violence is conflict-resolution training that begins early. Although it is just one solution among many, this solution taps into great power: the hearts, minds, and characters of young people.

■ The **thesis statement** in a persuasive essay clearly states the issue to be discussed and the writer's position on it. What is the thesis statement?

_____

_____

■ This introduction includes *facts*. What is the source of these facts and why does the writer include them here?

_____

_____

■ Sometimes a writer needs to define terms he or she is using. What term does the writer define?

_____

■ How many reasons does this writer give to back up the thesis statement?

_____

■ Notice that the writer presents one reason per paragraph.

■ Which reasons refer to an *authority*?

_____

■ Who are these authorities?

_____

_____

_____

■ How is the second reason supported?

_____

■ What is the source of information on Conflict Busters?

_____

■ Which reason is really an *answer to the opposition*?

_____

■ This reason also uses an *example*. What or who is the example?

_____

■ Note that the thesis statement and topic sentences make up a plan or an outline for the whole essay.

Before writing an essay of persuasion, reread Chapter 13, "Persuasion." Craft your thesis statement carefully. Devote one paragraph to each reason, developing each paragraph fully with facts and discussion. Use some of the methods of persuasion discussed in Chapter 13: *facts, referring to an authority, examples, predicting the consequence,* and *answering the opposition.* Revise for clarity and support, and remember, ample factual support is the key to successful persuasion. An excellent way to find interesting factual support is to do some basic research—for example, to find books or magazine articles by or about experts on your subject or even to conduct your own interviews, as does the author of "Stopping Youth Violence: An Inside Job."*

PRACTICE 9

In a group of four or five classmates, study this billboard. It is part of a campaign to persuade young people in Florida *not to smoke.*

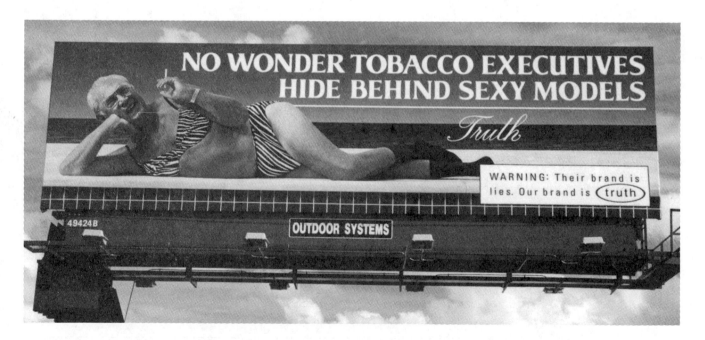

Now have someone record your group's answers to these questions:

1. How effective—how persuasive—is the antismoking message of this billboard? Why?

_____

* For information on summarizing and quoting outside sources, see Chapter 18, "Special College Skills: Summary and Quotation."

2. Do you think the intended audience of teens and young people will get the message? Why or why not?

3. The tobacco industry spends billions for ads that make smoking seem glamorous and grown-up. Does this picture successfully *oppose the tobacco industry's claim* that smoking is glamorous?

4. If your group were designing a billboard to persuade young people *not to smoke,* what would your message be?

PRACTICE 10

Choose a topic from the list below or one that your instructor has chosen. Make sure your thesis statement takes a clear stand. Write a persuasive essay, referring to the checklist at the end of Chapter 14.

Suggested Topics: The Persuasive Essay

1. Parents should routinely test their children's urine for evidence of drug use.

2. Computer and Internet classes should be given to every child in this state.

3. All animal testing of medicines should be banned, even if it will save human lives.

4. Every college student should be required to give three credit hours' worth of community service a year.

5. Only minority police should patrol minority neighborhoods.

6. A college education is (not) worth the time and money.

7. Gay couples should be allowed to adopt children.

8. Naturalized citizens should be allowed to run for president.

9. To better prepare students for the world of work, this college should do three things.

10. Illegal aliens in the United States should be entitled to receive basic health services.

11. Writer's choice: _____

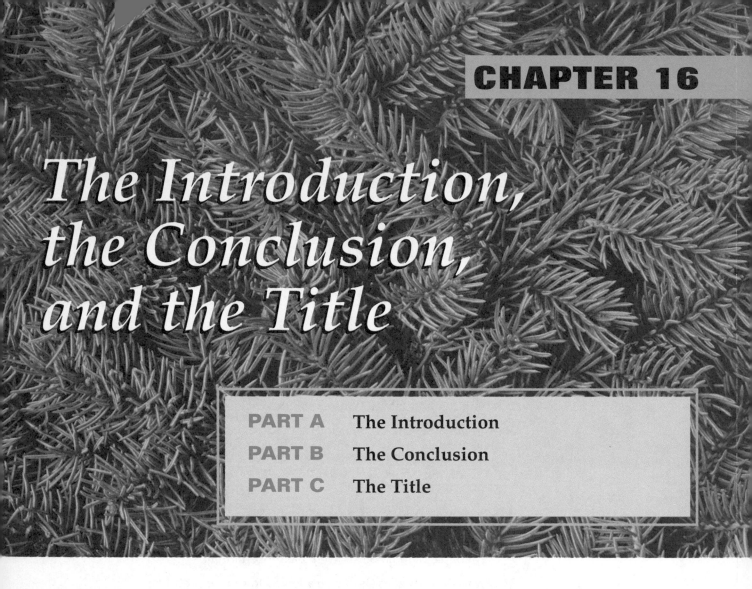

CHAPTER 16

The Introduction, the Conclusion, and the Title

PART A	**The Introduction**
PART B	**The Conclusion**
PART C	**The Title**

PART A   The Introduction

An **introduction** has two functions in an essay. First, it contains the **thesis statement** and, therefore, tells the reader what central idea will be developed in the rest of the paper. Since the reader should be able to spot the thesis statement easily, it should be given a prominent place—for example, the first or the last sentence in the introduction. Second, the introduction has to interest the reader enough that he or she will want to continue reading the paper.

Sometimes the process of writing the essay will help clarify your ideas about how best to introduce it. So once you have completed your essay, you may wish to revise and rewrite the introduction, making sure that it clearly introduces the essay's main idea.

There is no best way to introduce an essay, but you should certainly avoid beginning your work with "I'm going to discuss" or "This paper is about." You needn't tell the reader you are about to begin; just begin!

Here are six basic methods for beginning your composition effectively. In each example, the thesis statement is italicized.

1. **Begin with a single-sentence thesis statement.** A single-sentence thesis statement can be effective because it quickly and forcefully states the main idea of the essay:

> *Time management should be a required course at this college.*

■ Note how quickly and clearly a one-sentence thesis statement can inform the reader about what will follow in the rest of the essay.

2. **Begin with a general idea and then narrow to a specific thesis statement.** The general idea gives the reader background information or sets the scene. Then the topic narrows to one specific idea—the thesis statement. The effect is like a funnel, from wide to narrow.

> Few Americans stay put for a lifetime. We move from town to city to suburb, from high school to college in a different state, from a job in one region to a better job elsewhere, from the home where we raise our children to the home where we plan to live in retirement. *With each move we are forever making new friends, who become part of our new life at that time.*
>
> —Margaret Mead and Rhoda Metraux,
> "On Friendship," in *A Way of Seeing*

■ What general idea precedes the thesis statement and then leads the reader to focus on the specific main point of the essay?

_____

_____

3. **Begin with an illustration.** One or more brief illustrations in the introduction of an essay make the thesis statement more concrete and vivid:

> Lisette Flores-Nieves, a thirty-three-year-old consumer affairs representative for Colgate-Palmolive in New York City, was turned down when she first applied for a job at the company. But she was undaunted. "The original job was filled, but I believe in convincing people and letting them know where I stand." She decided to keep phoning the human resources staff, and as it turned out, a new position opened up and Flores-Nieves was hired. "This is all because I'm very assertive and persistent. After all, what can you lose?"
>
> *As job openings with America's top corporations continue to decrease in number and recruiters become more selective, entry-level job seekers need to be more creative and aggressive in their planning and hunting.*
>
> —Irene Middleman Thomas, "First Steps: Advice for Creating Your
> Own Opportunities," *Hispanic*

■ What example does the writer provide to make the thesis statement more concrete?

_____

_____

4. **Begin with a surprising fact or idea.** A surprising fact or idea arouses the reader's curiosity about how you will support this initial startling statement.

> *Millions of law-abiding Americans are physically addicted to caffeine—and most of them don't even know it.* Caffeine is a powerful central nervous system stimulant with substantial addiction potential. When deprived of their caffeine, addicts experience often severe withdrawal symptoms, which may include a throbbing headache, disorientation, constipation, nausea, sluggishness, depression, and irritability. As with other addictive drugs, heavy users develop a tolerance and require higher doses to obtain the expected effect.
>
> —Tom Ferguson and Joe Graedon, "Caffeine," *Medical Self-Care*

■ Why are the facts in this introduction likely to startle or surprise the reader?

_____

_____

5. **Begin with a contradiction.** In this type of introduction, your thesis statement contradicts what many or most people believe. In other words, your essay will contrast your opinion with the widely held view.

> Almost all of us have heard of the Amish, the religious sect that separates itself from the world and rejects modern conveniences and advanced technology. We imagine people wearing hand-sewn clothing and living in homes without refrigerators, dishwashers, televisions, and telephones. However, the Amish have been buying and using cell phones for years. They also use in-line skates, power-operated grass cutters, and gas grills for barbecuing. The Amish employ such conveniences when they do not interfere with family life. Cell phones, for example, are kept outside the home and are used for business purposes only. *The Amish people look at every modern-day convenience and accept it only if it works to bring together, not drive apart, members of the family and community.*
>
> —Adapted from Howard Rheingold, "Look Who's Talking," *Wired*

■ What widely held view does the author present?

_____

_____

■ How does he contradict this idea?

_____

_____

6. **Begin with a direct quotation.** A direct quotation is likely to catch your reader's attention and to show that you have explored what others have to say about the subject. You can then proceed to agree or to disagree with the direct quotation.

> "Speech is silver; silence is golden," according to an old Swiss saying. In a close relationship, however, silence often loses value. If we speak about certain issues, we may endanger the relationship; but if we do not speak, the relationship may become static and tense until the silence takes on a life of its own. Such silences are corrosive. They eat at the innards of intimacy until, often, *the silence itself causes the very rupture or break-up that we've tried to avoid by keeping silent.*
>
> —Adapted from Michael Ventura,
> "Don't Even Think About It," *Psychology Today*

■ Does the author agree or disagree with the Swiss saying?

_____

_____

Of course, definitions, comparisons, or any of the other kinds of devices you have already studied can also make good introductions. Just make sure that the reader knows exactly which sentence is your thesis statement.

WRITING ASSIGNMENT 1

Here are five statements. Pick three that you would like to write about and compose an introduction for each one. Use any of the methods for beginning compositions discussed in this chapter thus far.

1. Cell phones in cars can be dangerous.

2. Noise is definitely a form of pollution.

3. Serious illness—our own or a loved one's—sometimes can bring surprising blessings.

4. Studying with someone else can pay off in better grades.

5. My college should offer a three-day course in "How to _____."

PART B   The Conclusion

A conclusion signals the end of the essay and leaves the reader with a final thought. As with the introduction, you may wish to revise and rewrite the conclusion once you have completed your essay. Be certain your conclusion flows logically from the body of the essay.

Like introductions, conclusions can take many forms, and the right one for your essay depends on how you wish to complete your paper—with what thought you wish to leave the reader. However, never conclude your paper with "As I said in the beginning," and try to avoid the overused "In conclusion" or "In summary." Don't end by saying you are going to end; just end!

Here are three ways to conclude an essay.

1. **End with a call to action.** The call to action says that in view of the facts and ideas presented in this essay, the reader should *do something*.

> Thus, birdwatchers must work together to keep track of numbers and types of all birds—not just endangered species. Through BirdSource, a program that will revolutionize the monitoring of bird populations, you can join the growing number of volunteer birders across the country who report their sightings every day, online. Go to http://birdsource.cornell.edu. By sharing your observations, you can help assemble important data on the distribution, migratory pathways, and population trends of North American birds, almost instantly and on a scale that was impossible before the Internet.
>
> —Adapted from John Flicker, "Tracking Birds on the Net," *Audubon*

■ What does the writer want the reader to do?

_____

_____

2. **End with a final point.** The final point can tie together all the other ideas in the essay; it provides the reader with the sense that the entire essay has been leading up to this one final point.

> Students who follow their hearts in choosing majors will most likely end up laboring at what they love. They're the ones who will put in the long hours and intense effort that achievement requires. And they're the ones who will find the sense of purpose that underlies most human happiness.
>
> —Lynne V. Cheney, "Students of Success," *Newsweek*

■ With what final point does Cheney end her article?

_____

_____

3. **End with a question.** By ending with a question, you leave the reader with a final problem that you wish him or her to think about.

> Illness related to chemical dumping is increasing in Larkstown, yet only a handful of citizens have joined the campaign to clean up the chemical dump on the edge of town and to stop further dumping. Many people say that they don't want to get involved, but with their lives and their children's futures at stake, can they afford not to?

■ What problem does the writer's final question point to?

_____

WRITING ASSIGNMENT 2

Review two or three essays that you have written recently. Do the conclusions bring the essays to clear ends? Are those conclusions interesting? How could they be improved? Using one of the three strategies taught in this section, write a new conclusion for one of the essays.

PART C   The Title

If you are writing just one paragraph, chances are that you will not need to give it a title, but if you are writing a multiparagraph essay, a title is definitely in order.

The title is centered on the page above the body of the composition and separated from it by several blank lines (about 1 inch of space), as shown here.

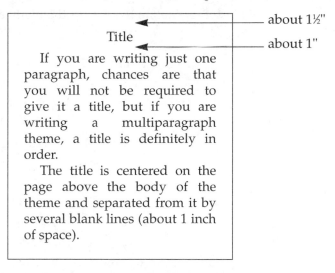

- *Do not* put quotation marks around the title of your own paper.

- *Do not* underline or italicize the title of your own paper.

- Remember, unlike the topic sentence, the title is not part of the first paragraph; in fact, it is usually only four to five words long and is rarely an entire sentence.

A good title has two functions: to suggest the subject of the essay and to spark the reader's interest. Although the title is the first part of your essay the reader sees, the most effective titles are usually written *after* the essay has been completed.

To create a title, reread your essay, paying special attention to the **thesis statement** and the **conclusion.** Try to come up with a few words that express the main point of your paper.

Here are some basic kinds of titles.

1. **The most common title used in college writing is the no-nonsense descriptive title.** In this title, stress key words and ideas developed in the essay:

The Search for Identity in Orwell's *1984*

Advantages and Disadvantages of Buying on Credit

The Role of Chlorophyll in Photosynthesis

2. **Two-part titles are also effective.** Write one or two words stating the general subject, and then add several words that narrow the topic:

> Legal Gambling: Pro and Con
>
> Tito Puente: King of Latin Music

3. **Write the title as a rhetorical question.** Then answer the question in your essay:

> What Can Be Done About the High Price of Higher Education?
>
> Are Athletes Setting Bad Examples?

4. **Relate the title to the method of development used in the essay** (see Unit 3 and Chapter 15):

Illustration:	Democracy in Action Three Roles I Play
Narration:	The Development of Jazz Sandra Cisneros: The Making of a Storyteller
Description:	Portrait of a Scientist A Waterfront Scene
Process:	How to Get Organized How to Get in Shape Fast
Definition:	What It Means to Be Unemployed A Definition of Love
Comparison:	Two Country Stars Who Crossed Over Strange Realities: *Star Wars* and *X Files*
Contrast:	Pleasures and Problems of Owning a Home Montreal: City of Contrasts
Classification:	Three Types of Soap Operas What Kind of Risk Taker Are You?
Cause and Effect:	What Causes Whales to Beach Themselves? The Effects of Divorce on Children
Persuasion:	Pornography Should Be Banned The Need for Metal Detectors in Our Schools

Use this list the next time you title a paper.

WRITING ASSIGNMENT 3

Review two or three essays that you have written recently. Are the titles clear and interesting? Applying what you've learned in this chapter, write a better title for at least one paper.

CHAPTER 17

Writing Under Pressure: The Essay Examination

PART A	Budgeting Your Time
PART B	Reading and Understanding the Essay Question
PART C	Choosing the Correct Paragraph or Essay Pattern
PART D	Writing the Topic Sentence or the Thesis Statement

Being able to write under pressure is a key skill both in college and in the workplace. Throughout your college career, you will be asked to write **timed papers** in class and to take **essay examinations.** In fact, many English programs base placement and passing on timed essay exams. Clearly, the ability to write under pressure is crucial.

An **essay question** requires the same writing skills that a student uses in composing a paragraph or an essay. Even in history and biology, how well you do on an essay test depends partly on how well you write; yet many students, under the pressure of a test, forget or fail to apply what they know about good writing. This chapter will improve your ability to write under pressure. Many of the sample exam questions on the following pages were taken from real college examinations.

PART A Budgeting Your Time

To do well on a timed essay or an essay test, it is not enough to know the material. You must also be able to call forth what you know, organize it, and present it in writing—all under pressure in a limited time.

Since most essay examinations are timed, it is important that you learn how to **budget** your time effectively so that you can devote adequate time to each question *and* finish the test. The following six tips will help you use your time well.

1. **Make sure you know exactly how long the examination lasts.** A one-hour examination may really be only fifty minutes; a two-hour examination may last only one hour and forty-five minutes.

2. **Note the point value of all questions and allot time accordingly to each question.** That is, allot the most time to questions that are worth the most points and less time to ones that are worth fewer.

3. **Decide on an order in which to answer the questions.** You do not have to begin with the first question on the examination and work, in order, to the last. Instead, you may start with the questions worth the most points. Some students prefer to begin with the questions they feel they can answer most easily, thereby guaranteeing points toward the final grade on the examination. Others combine the two methods. No matter which system you use, be sure to allot enough time to the questions that are worth the most points—whether you do them first or last.

4. **Make sure you understand exactly what each question asks you to do; then quickly prewrite and plan your answer.** It is all-important to take a breath, study the question, and make a quick scratch outline or plan of your answer *before you start to write.* Parts B through D of this chapter will guide you through these critical steps.

5. **Time yourself.** As you begin a particular question, calculate when you must be finished with that question in order to complete the examination, and note that time in the margin. As you write, check the clock every five minutes so that you remain on schedule.

6. **Finally, do not count on having enough time to recopy your work.** Skip lines and write carefully so that the instructor can easily read your writing as well as any neat corrections you might make.

PRACTICE 1

Imagine that you are about to take the two-hour history test shown below. Read the test carefully, noting the point value of each question, and then answer the questions that follow the examination.

> Part I   Answer both questions. 15 points each.
>
>   1. Do you think that the Versailles Peace Treaty was a "harsh" one? Be specific.
>
>   2. List the basic principles of Karl Marx. Analyze them in terms of Marx's claim that they are scientific.

Part II   Answer two of the following questions. 25 points each.

   3. Describe the origins of, the philosophies behind, and the chief policies of either Communist Russia or Fascist Italy. Be specific.

   4. What were the causes of Nelson Mandela's presidential victory in South Africa in 1994?

   5. European history of the nineteenth and twentieth centuries has been increasingly related to that of the rest of the world. Why? How? With what consequences for Europe?

Part III   Briefly identify ten of the following. 2 points each.

   a. John Locke   h. Jacobins
   b. Franco-Prussian War   i. The Opium Wars
   c. Stalingrad   j. Social Darwinism
   d. Cavour   k. The Reform Bill of 1832
   e. Manchuria, 1931   l. The most interesting
   f. Entente Cordiale   reading you have done
   g. Existentialism   this term (from the
                                   course list)

1. Which part would you do first and why? _____

   _____

   _____

   How much time would you allot to the questions in this part and why?

   _____

   _____

2. Which part would you do second and why? _____

   _____

   _____

   How much time would you allot to the questions in this part and why?

   _____

   _____

   _____

3. Which part would you do last and why? _____

   _____

   _____

   _____

How much time would you allot to the questions in this part and why?

_____

_____

_____

PART B Reading and Understanding the Essay Question

Before you begin writing, carefully examine each question to decide exactly what your purpose is: that is, what the instructor expects you to do.

> *Question:*   Using either Communist China or Nazi Germany as a model,
> (a) describe the characteristics of a totalitarian state, and
> (b) explain how such a state was created.

■ This question contains three sets of instructions.

■ First, you must use "either Communist China or Nazi Germany as a model." That is, you must **choose** *one or the other* as a model.

■ Second, you must **describe**, and third, you must **explain.**

■ Your answer should consist of two written parts, a **description** and an **explanation.**

   It is often helpful to underline the important words, as shown in the box above, to make sure you understand the entire question and have noted all its parts.

> *The student must*   (1) choose to write about either Communist China or
> Nazi Germany, not both; (2) describe the totalitarian
> state; (3) explain how such a state was created.

PRACTICE 2

Read each essay question and underline key words. Then, on the lines beneath the question, describe in your own words exactly what the question requires: (1) What directions does the student have to follow? (2) How many parts will the answer contain?

EXAMPLE | What were the causes of the Cold War? What were its chief episodes? Why has there not been a "hot" war?

Student must   (1) tell what caused the Cold War (two or more causes), (2) mention

main events of Cold War, (3) give reasons why we haven't had a full-scale war. The

essay will have three parts: causes, main events, and reasons.

1. State Newton's First Law and give examples from your own experience.

   Student must _____

   _____

   _____

   _____

2. Choose one of the following terms. Define it, give an example of it, and then show how it affects *your* life: (a) freedom of speech, (b) justice for all, (c) equal opportunity.

   Student must _____

   _____

   _____

   _____

3. Shiism and Sunni are the two great branches of Islam. Discuss the religious beliefs and the politics of each branch.

   Student must _____

   _____

   _____

   _____

4. Name and explain four types of savings institutions. What are three factors that influence one's choice of a savings institution?

   Student must _____

   _____

   _____

   _____

5. Steroids: the athlete's "unfair advantage." Discuss.

   Student must _____

   _____

   _____

   _____

6. Discuss the causes and consequences of the Broad Street cholera epidemic in mid–nineteenth-century London. What was the role of Dr. John Snow?

Student must _____

_____

_____

_____

7. Define the Monroe Doctrine of the early nineteenth century and weigh the arguments for and against it.

Student must _____

_____

_____

_____

8. The sixteenth century is known for the Renaissance, the Reformation, and the Commercial Revolution. Discuss each event, showing why it was important to the history of Western civilization.

Student must _____

_____

_____

_____

9. Erik Erikson has theorized that adult actions toward children may produce either (a) trust or mistrust, (b) autonomy or self-doubt, (c) initiative or guilt. Choose one of the pairs above and give examples of the kinds of adult behavior that might create these responses in a child.

Student must _____

_____

_____

_____

_____

10. Simón Bolívar may not have been as great a hero as he was believed to be. Agree or disagree.

Student must _____

_____

_____

_____

_____

_____

PART C   Choosing the Correct Paragraph or Essay Pattern

Throughout this book, you have learned how to write various types of para-graphs and compositions. Many examinations will require you simply to **illus-trate**, **define**, **compare**, and so forth. How well you answer questions may depend partly on how well you understand these terms.

> 1. _Illustrate_ "behavior modification."
>
> 2. _Define_ "greenhouse effect."
>
> 3. _Compare_ Agee and Nin as diarists.

■ The key words in these questions are _illustrate_, _define_, and _compare_—**instruction words** that tell you what you are supposed to do and what form your answer should take.

Here is a review list of some common instruction words used in college examinations.

1. **Classify:** Gather into categories, types, or kinds according to a single basis of division (see Chapter 11).

2. **Compare:** Point out similarities (see Chapter 10). Instructors often use _compare_ to mean point out both _similarities_ and _differences_.

3. **Contrast:** Point out differences (see Chapter 10).

4. **Define:** State clearly and exactly the meaning of a word or term (see Chapter 9). You may be required to write a single-sentence definition or a full paragraph. Instructors may use _identify_ as a synonym for _define_ when they want a short definition.

5. **Discuss:** (analyze, describe, or explain) Often an instructor uses these terms to mean "thoughtfully examine a subject, approaching it from different angles." These terms allow the writer more freedom of approach than many of the others.

6. **Discuss causes:** Analyze the reasons or causes for something; answer the question _Why?_ (see Chapter 12).

7. **Discuss effects:** Analyze the effects, consequences, or results of something (see Chapter 12).

8. **Evaluate:** Weigh the pros and cons, advantages and disadvantages (see Chapters 10 and 13).

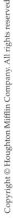

9. **Identify:**   Give a capsule who-what-when-where-why answer.
                          Sometimes *identify* is a synonym for *define*.

10. **Illustrate:**   Give one or more examples (see Chapter 5).

11. **Narrate:**   Follow the development of something through
    (trace)   time, event by event (see Chapters 6 and 8).

12. **Summarize:**   Write the substance of a longer work in condensed form
                          (see Chapter 18, Part B).

13. **Take a stand:**   Persuade; argue for a particular position (see Chapter 13).

PRACTICE 3

You should have no trouble deciding what kind of paragraph or composition to use if the question uses one of the terms just defined—*contrast, trace, classify,* and so on. However, questions are often worded in such a way that you have to discover what kind of paragraph or essay is required. What kind of paragraph or essay is required by each of the following questions?

EXAMPLE| What is *schizophrenia*? (*Write a paragraph to. . . .*)   _define_____

1. In one concise paragraph, give   _____
   the main ideas of Simone de
   Beauvoir's famous book *The
   Second Sex.*

2. What is the difference   _____
   between veins and arteries?

3. Follow the development of   _____
   Wynton Marsalis's musical style.

4. How do jet- and propeller-   _____
   driven planes differ?

5. Who or what is each of the   _____
   following: the Gang of Four,
   Ho Chi Minh, Tiananmen Square?

6. Explain the causes of the   _____
   American Civil War.

7. Explain what is meant by   _____
   "magical realism."

8. Take a stand for or against   _____
   legalizing marijuana in this country.
   Give reasons to support your stand.

9. Give two recent instances of military   _____
   hazing that you consider "out of control."

10. Divide into groups the   _____
    different kinds of web sites
    giving out medical information.

PART D   Writing the Topic Sentence or the Thesis Statement

A good way to ensure that your answer truly addresses itself to the question is to compose a topic sentence or a thesis statement that contains the key words of the question.

> *Question:* How do fixed-rate and adjustable-rate mortgages differ?

- The key words in this question are *fixed-rate* and *adjustable-rate mortgages*, and *differ.*
- What kind of paragraph or essay would be appropriate for this question?

_____

_____

> *Topic sentence* or *thesis statement of answer:* Fixed-rate and adjustable-rate mortgages differ in three basic ways.

- The answer repeats the key words of the question: *fixed-rate, adjustable-rate, mortgages,* and *differ.*

PRACTICE 4

Here are eight examination questions. Write a topic sentence or thesis statement for each question by using the question as part of the answer. Pretend that you know all the material. Even though you may not know anything about the subjects, you should be able to formulate a topic sentence or thesis statement based on the question.

1. Do you think the Dawes Allotment Act was fair to Native Americans?

   Topic sentence or thesis statement: _____

   _____

   _____

2. Contrast high school requirements in Jamaica with those in the United States.

   Topic sentence or thesis statement: _____

   _____

   _____

3. What steps can a busy person take to reduce the destructive impact of stress in his or her life?

Topic sentence or thesis statement: _____

_____

_____

4. Gay couples should be allowed to adopt children. Agree or disagree with this statement.

Topic sentence or thesis statement: _____

_____

_____

5. Assume that you manage a small shop that sells men's apparel. What activities would you undertake to promote the sale of sportswear?

Topic sentence or thesis statement: _____

_____

_____

6. The U.S. government should cover the medical costs of AIDS. Agree or disagree with this statement.

Topic sentence or thesis statement: _____

_____

_____

7. The state should subsidize students in medical school because the country needs more doctors. Agree or disagree with this statement.

Topic sentence or thesis statement: _____

_____

_____

8. Does religion play a more vital role in people's lives today than it did in your parents' generation?

Topic sentence or thesis statement: _____

_____

_____

✔ CHECKLIST: The Process of Writing the Essay Question

—— 1. Survey the test and note the point value for each question.

—— 2. Calculate how much time you need for each question. Then check the clock as you write so that you complete all the questions.

—— 3. Read each question carefully, underlining important words.

—— 4. Determine how many parts the answer should contain.

—— 5. Considering your audience (usually the teacher) and purpose, choose the paragraph or essay pattern that would best answer the question.

—— 6. Write a topic sentence or a thesis statement that repeats the key words of the question.

—— 7. Quickly freewrite or brainstorm ideas on scrap paper and arrange them in a logical order, making a scratch outline or plan.

—— 8. Write your paragraph or essay neatly, skipping lines so you will have enough room to make corrections.

CHAPTER 18

Special College Skills: Summary and Quotation

PART A	**Avoiding Plagiarism**
PART B	**Writing a Summary**
PART C	**Using Direct and Indirect Quotation**

In some college courses, you will write papers without using **outside sources**—that is, sources other than yourself that provide information on a subject (for example, books, articles, Internet sites, or people). However, many college courses and jobs require that you refer to outside sources as you write reports, essays, and research papers. In addition, information from outside sources can vastly enrich your writing with facts, statistics, experts' ideas, and more.

Two important skills that will help you use outside sources effectively are **writing summaries** and **quoting others. Summarizing** requires you to condense information and present it clearly in your own words. **Quotation** allows you to enliven your writing with other people's words and thoughts (giving credit, of course, to the original author).

PART A   Avoiding Plagiarism

Before we discuss summarizing and quoting, it is all-important that you understand—so you can avoid—**plagiarism.** Plagiarism means passing off someone else's words or ideas as your own. Whether intentional or careless, plagiarism is stealing. A college student who plagiarizes a paper may be expelled from the course or from college. Whatever your career may be, publishing material that you copied from someone else is a crime.

To avoid plagiarism, you must give proper credit to the original author, as this chapter shows. Meanwhile, keep this simple rule in mind: **Always tell your reader the source of any words and ideas not your own.**

PART B   Writing a Summary

A **summary** presents the main idea and supporting points of a longer work *in much shorter form.* It might be one sentence, one paragraph, or several paragraphs long, depending on the length of the original and the nature of your assignment.

Summarizing is important both in college and at work. In a persuasive essay, you might summarize the ideas of an expert whose views support one of your points. A professor might ask you to summarize a book, a market survey, or even the plot of a film—that is, to condense it in your own words, presenting only the highlights. Of course, many essay exams also call for written summaries.

Compare this short newspaper article—the *source*—with the *summary* that follows:

Source

Paul Recer, "Dogs Tamed 100,000 Years Ago," *The Miami Herald*, June 13, 1997, p. 9A.

Fido may be cute, cuddly, and harmless. But in his genes, he's a wolf.

Researchers tracing the genetic family tree of man's best friend have confirmed that domestic dogs, from petite poodles to huge elkhounds, descended from wolves that were tamed 100,000 years ago.

"Our data show that the origin of dogs seems to be much more ancient than indicated in the archaeological record," said Robert K. Wayne of UCLA, the leader of a team that tested the genes from 67 dog breeds and 62 wolves on four continents.

Wayne said the study showed so many DNA changes that dogs had to have diverged genetically from wolves 60,000 to more than 100,000 years ago.

The study suggests that primitive humans living in a hunting and gathering culture tamed wolves and then bred the animals to create the many different types of dogs that now exist.

Summary

Dogs began evolving from wolves between 60,000 and 100,000 years ago, reports Paul Recer in *The Miami Herald* ("Dogs Tamed 100,000 Years Ago," June 13, 1997, p. 9A). Apparently, humans tamed wolves far earlier than was previously thought. Researchers at UCLA, led by Robert K. Wayne, came to these conclusions after studying the genes of sixty-seven breeds of dogs and sixty-two wolves on four continents.

■ Notice that sentence 1 states the author, title, source, and date of the original article. Sentence 1 also states the main idea of the article. What is its main idea?

■ What evidence supports this idea?

■ The original is short, so the summary is very short—just three sentences long.

■ Note that the summary writer does not add her own opinions about dogs or evolution but simply states the main ideas of the source. Unlike many kinds of writing, a summary should not contain your personal opinions and feelings.

Preparing to Write a Summary

The secret of writing a good summary is clearly understanding the original. If you doubt this, try to summarize out loud Chapter 3 of your biology book. To summarize well, you have to know the subject matter.

Before you summarize a piece of writing, notice the title and subtitle, if there is one; these often state the main idea. Read quickly for meaning; then carefully read the work again, underlining or jotting down notes for yourself. What is the author's thesis or main point? What points does he or she offer in support? Be careful to distinguish between the most and least important points; your summary should include only the most important ones.

To help you understand *what the author thinks is important,* notice which ideas get the most coverage. Read with special care the topic sentence of each paragraph and the first and last paragraphs of the work. If you are summarizing a magazine article or a textbook chapter, the subheads (often in boldface type) point out important ideas.

Your written summary should include the following:

1. The author, title, and source of the original

2. The main idea or thesis of the original, in your own words

3. The most important supporting ideas or points of the original, in your own words

Try to present the ideas in your summary in proportion to those in the original. For instance, if the author devotes one paragraph to each of four ideas, you might give one sentence to each idea. When you finish, compare your summary with the original, to avoid plagiarism; that is, make sure you have not just copied the phrasing and sentences of the original.

A summary differs from much other writing in that it *should not* contain your feelings or opinions—just the facts. Your job is to capture the essence of the original, with nothing added.

Following are two summaries of the student essay in Chapter 15, Part F, of this book. Which do you think is the better summary, A or B? Be prepared to say specifically why.

Summary A

(1) In "Two Childhoods" (printed in *Evergreen,* 6th Edition, by Susan Fawcett and Alvin Sandberg, Houghton Mifflin Company, 2000), student Cheryl Parris contrasts her mother's childhood on a farm in South Carolina and her own childhood in New York City. (2) As a child, the author's mother enjoyed simple, slow-paced country activities like swimming in rivers and mending birds' wings whereas Ms. Parris's fast-paced youth was

crammed with such urban activities as movie-going, parties, and shopping. (3) Their personalities differed as much as—and perhaps because of—their lifestyles. (4) As a girl, the mother was known as caring, respectful, and content with nature and invented games. (5) Ms. Parris, however, describes herself as "petulant, pigheaded, demanding, and unstable"—very focused on material possessions. (6) Now she seems to have examined her values, however, and wishes her childhood had been more like her mother's.

Summary B

(1) This excellent essay is by Ms. Cheryl Parris, student. (2) I enjoyed reading about Cheryl's mother, who grew up on a farm in South Carolina. (3) When Cheryl was young, her mother told stories about her own childhood. (4) Cheryl loved those tales and still thinks of them. (5) It was intriguing to hear about life thirty years before her life began. (6) What fascinated her most, however, were the differences between the mother's youth and hers. (7) The mother's days were filled with swimming in nearby lakes and rivers, climbing and falling off trees. (8) Life in the country is definitely easier than life in the city. (9) Although the rural pace of life is slower, nature can teach you many things. (10) Cheryl lived in the city, so she missed out. (11) I liked the writer's honesty; she admits that she was not a nice child.

■ The test of a good summary is how well it captures the original. Does A or B better summarize Ms. Parris's essay? Why?

_____

_____

■ If you picked A, you are right. Sentence 1 states the author and title of the essay, as well as the title, authors, publisher, and date of the book in which it appears. Sentence 1 also states the main idea of the original, which _contrasts_ the mother's childhood with the writer's. Does any sentence in B state the main idea of the original essay?

_____

■ Compare the original with the two summaries. How many points of contrast does A include? B? _____

_____

■ Does each writer summarize the essay _in his or her own words?_ If not, which sentences might seem plagiarized? _____

■ Writer A once quotes Ms. Parris directly. How is this shown? Why do you think the summary writer chose this sentence to quote?

_____

_____

■ Do both summaries succeed in keeping personal opinion out? If not, which

sentences contain the summary writer's opinion? _____

_____

_____

_____

PRACTICE 1

Form a group with three or four other classmates, and choose just one of the following essays to summarize: "Libraries of the Future—Now" (Chapter 15, Part A); "The Day of the Dead" (Chapter 15, Part C); "Stopping Youth Violence: An Inside Job" (Chapter 15, Part I); or "Skin Deep" (Chapter 14, Part D). Read your chosen essay in the group, aloud if possible. Then each person should write a one-paragraph summary of it, referring to the following checklist (15–20 minutes).

Now read your finished summaries aloud to your group. How well does each writer briefly capture the meaning of the original? Has he or she kept out personal opinion? What suggestions for improvement can you offer? Your instructor may wish to have the best summary in each group read aloud to the whole class.

PRACTICE 2

Flip through a copy of a current magazine: *Newsweek, People, Essence, Wired,* or another. Pick one article that interests you, read it carefully, and write a one- to three-paragraph summary of the article, depending on how long the article is. The points you include in your summary should reflect the emphasis of the original writer. Try to capture the essence of the article. Remember to give your source at the beginning, to keep out personal opinion, and to check your summary for plagiarism. Refer to the checklist.

✔ CHECKLIST: The Process of Writing a Summary

—— 1. Notice the title and subtitle of the original; do these state its main idea?

—— 2. Read the original quickly for meaning; then carefully read it again, underlining important ideas and jotting down notes for yourself.

—— 3. Determine the author's thesis or main idea.

—— 4. Now find the main supporting points. Subheads (if any), topic sentences, and the first and last paragraphs of the original may help you find key points.

—— 5. Write your topic sentence or thesis statement, stating the author's thesis, title, source, and date of the original.

—— 6. In your own words, give the author's most important supporting points, in the same order in which the author gives them. Keep the same proportion of coverage as the original.

——— 7. Write your summary, skipping lines so you will have room to make corrections.

——— 8. Now revise, asking yourself, "Will my summary convey to someone who has never read the original the author's main idea and key supporting points?"

——— 9. Proofread, making neat corrections above the lines.

——— 10. Compare your final draft with the original to avoid plagiarism.

PART C   Using Direct and Indirect Quotation

Sometimes you will want to quote an outside source directly. A quotation might be part of a summary or part of a longer paper or report. Quoting the words of others can add richness and authority to your writing; in fact, that is why we include a Quotation Bank at the end of this book—a kind of minireader of great thoughts. Use short quotations in these ways:

■ Use a quotation to stress a key idea.

■ Use a quotation to lend expert opinion to your argument.

■ Use a quotation to provide a catchy introduction or conclusion.

■ Use a quotation about your topic that is wonderfully written and "quotable" to add interest.

However, avoid using very long quotations or too many quotations. Both send the message that you are filling up space because you don't have enough to say. Of course, to avoid plagiarism, you always must credit the original author or speaker.

Here are some methods for introducing quotations:

Ways to Introduce Quotations	
Ms. Taibi says, . . .	Ms. Taibi writes, . . .
One expert notes that . . .	. . . , one authority reports.
In a recent *Times* article, Russell Baker observes . . .	

Following are a passage from a well-known book and two ways that students quoted the author:

Source   Dr. Deborah Prothrow-Stith, *Deadly Consequences* (HarperPerennial 1991), p. 34.

On film or videotape, violence begins and ends in a moment. "Bang bang, you're dead." Then the death is over. This sense of action-without-consequences replicates and reinforces the dangerous "magical" way many children think. Do the twelve- and fourteen-year-olds who are shooting each other to death in Los Angeles, Chicago, or Washington, D.C., really understand that death is permanent, unalterable, final, tragic? Television certainly is not telling them so.

Two students who wrote about the effects of TV violence correctly quoted Dr. Prothrow-Stith as follows:

Direct Quotation

"This sense of action-without-consequences replicates and reinforces the dangerous 'magical' way many children think," writes Dr. Deborah Prothrow-Stith in *Deadly Consequences* (p. 34).

Indirect Quotation

In *Deadly Consequences*, Dr. Deborah Prothrow-Stith points out that TV and movie violence, which has no realistic consequences, harms children by reinforcing the magical way in which they think (p. 34).

- The first sentence gives Dr. Prothrow-Stith's exact words inside quotation marks. This is direct quotation. Note the punctuation.

- The second sentence uses the word *that* and gives the *meaning* of Prothrow-Stith's words without quotation marks. This is indirect quotation. Note the punctuation.

- Both correctly quote the writer and credit the source. (See Chapter 35, Parts B and C, for more on correctly writing titles and punctuating quotations.)

PRACTICE 3

Following are passages from three sources. Read each one, and then, as if you were writing a paper, quote two sentences from each, one directly quoting the author's words and one indirectly quoting the author's ideas. Review the boxed ways to introduce quotations and try several methods. Finally, write a brief summary of each passage. Check your work to avoid plagiarism.

Source 1

Institute of Noetic Sciences with William Poole, *The Heart of Healing* (Turner Publishing, Inc. 1993), p. 134.

In most cultures throughout history, music, dance, rhythmic drumming, and chanting have been essential parts of healing rituals. Modern research bears out the connection between music and healing. In one study, the heart rate and blood pressure of patients went down when quiet music was piped into their hospital coronary care units. At the same time, the patients showed greater tolerance for pain and less anxiety and depression. Similarly, listening to music before, during, or after surgery has been shown to promote various beneficial effects—from alleviating anxiety to reducing the need for sedation by half. When researchers played Brahms' "Lullaby" to premature infants, these babies gained weight faster and went home from the hospital sooner than babies who did not hear the music. Music may also affect immunity by altering the level of stress chemicals in the blood. An experiment at Rainbow Babies and Children's Hospital found that a single thirty-minute music therapy session could increase the level of salivary IgA, an immunoglobulin that protects against respiratory infections.

Direct quotation: _____

_____

Indirect quotation: _____

_____

Summary:

_____

_____

_____

_____

_____

_____

Source 2   Ira Peck and Larry F. Krieger, *Sociology: The Search for Social Patterns* (Scholastic 1989), p. 181.

Identical twins account for about one in every 250 births. In a recent project at the Minnesota Center for Twin and Adoption Research, scientists conducted an exhaustive study of 350 pairs of identical twins reared apart. Identical twins who are reared apart can provide important clues for understanding the factors that influence personality and behavior. Since they have the same genetic background yet live in different environments, these identical twins help clarify the influence of heredity and environment on a variety of character traits. Each pair of twins answered 15,000 items on a comprehensive multidimensional personality questionnaire. Investigators then compared these results with answers given by the general population.

The results suggest an important genetic influence on some personality traits. For example, on the basis of their tests, researchers estimate that 61 percent of extroversion is inherited. The data also indicated that the traits of conformity, optimism, and cautiousness were 50 to 60 percent inherited. Heredity played a less significant role in other traits. Aggressiveness, ambitiousness, orderliness, and social closeness were only 33 to 48 percent inherited.

Direct quotation: _____

_____

Indirect quotation: _____

_____

Summary:

_____

_____

_____

_____

_____

Source 3   Samantha Baldwin, "Sky Primer," *Boulder Views*, December 12, 1999, pp. 8–9.

Besides the nine known planets, our universe contains billions of other bodies. Among them are asteroids and comets. Both are of interest to scientists because they are thought to be unspoiled primal bodies that hold clues to the origin of the solar system. They are also responsible for nearly all of the many direct hits that Earth and its moon have sustained over millions of years. In 1997, news that a huge asteroid might hit Earth in 2028 (soon corrected) intensified people's curiosity about asteroids and comets.

Although their name means "starlike," asteroids are not stars. They are chunks of rock that orbit the sun. Upwards of 4,000 have been catalogued, most of them fairly small. The largest known asteroid, Ceres, is about 940 kilometers across. Most asteroids orbit in the asteroid belt between Mars and Jupiter, and astronomers think of them as moving in "families." Some do cross the Earth's orbit.

Comets are sometimes called "dirty snowballs" because they are chunks of ice that grow long, glowing tails as they approach the sun. Comets can be classified by their tails. Type I tails are made of ionized molecules, while Type II tails are made of dust particles that reflect sunlight. Although the core of a comet may be quite small—perhaps a few kilometers in diameter—their tails can be millions of miles long.

About once every 100,000 years, a huge asteroid or comet might hit the Earth, with devastating results. The chances of this happening are slim. Astronomers are currently watching about 200 large asteroids and about 12 comets. What worries some sky-watchers, however, are the 2,000 giant asteroids and countless comets that humans don't yet know about.

Direct quotation: _____

_____

Indirect quotation: _____

_____

Summary:

_____

_____

_____

_____

_____

_____

Analyze a Social Problem

Because essays are longer and more complex than paragraphs, organizing an essay can be a challenge, even for experienced writers. Techniques like having a clear *controlling idea,* a good *thesis statement,* and a *plan or an outline* all help an essay writer manage the task. Another useful approach is dividing the subject into three parts, as one student does here. In your group or class, read the essay, aloud if possible, underlining the parts you find most powerful and paying special attention to organization.

It's Great to Get Old

(1) I knock at the door and patiently await an answer. I listen and hear the thump of a cane on the hard wood floor, edging slowly toward the door. "It's great to get old," my grandmother says facetiously[1] as she opens the door, apologizing for making me wait. Through her I learn firsthand the problems of the aged. Loneliness, lack of money, and ailing health are just some of the problems old people must deal with.

(2) For one thing, loneliness seems endemic[2] among old people in America. With difficulty getting around, many spend most of their time confined to their apartments, awaiting visits from family or friends. Through my grandmother, I realize that as much as old people's families may care about them, the family members obviously have lives of their own and cannot visit as much as old persons would like. And when people are very old, most of their friends have already died, so they spend most of their time alone.

(3) Poor health is also a major problem. Any number of physical ailments create a problem. Cataracts, for example, are a common eye problem among old people. Health problems can make life very difficult for an old person.

(4) Last but not least is the financial burden old people must cope with. The rising costs of basic necessities such as food, housing, and health care are especially difficult for old people to meet. Sadly, most are forced to compromise what they need for what they can afford. Take, for example, an old person who buys pounds of inexpensive pasta for dinner every night. While the person may need other nutrients, the person forfeits this need for what the person can afford. Financial problems also make life very difficult for an old person.

(5) There is no easy way to ease the problems of the aged. Simply being aware of them is an important step in the right direction. If we turn our attention and compassion toward the elderly, we can begin to help them find solutions.

—Denise Nelley (Student)

---

[1]facetiously: humorously
[2]endemic: typical in a certain place or population

1. How effective is Ms. Nelley's essay?

   ____ Strong thesis statement?   ____ Good supporting details?

   ____ Logical organization?   ____ Effective conclusion?

2. Did the introductory paragraph catch your interest? Explain why or why not.

3. What is the controlling idea of the essay? What is the thesis statement?

4. This writer has skillfully organized her ideas. Her thesis names three problems facing the elderly. What are they? Does the body of the essay discuss these three problems in the same order that the thesis names them? If not, what changes would you suggest?

5. Are the three problems fully explained in paragraphs 2, 3, and 4? That is, does Ms. Nelley provide enough support for each problem? If not, what revision suggestions would you give the writer, especially for paragraph 3?

6. This student movingly presents some problems of the elderly. Do you think she should have included solutions? Why or why not?

7. Can you spot any error patterns (the same error two or more times) that this student should watch out for?

GROUP WORK

In your group or class, evaluate (or grade) Ms. Nelley's essay. Then, based on your evaluation, decide what changes or revisions would most improve the essay, and revise it accordingly, as if it were your own. If your group wishes to add any new ideas or support, brainstorm together and choose the strongest ideas. Rewrite as needed.

When you are done, evaluate the essay again, with your changes.

 ## WRITING AND REVISING IDEAS

1. Discuss the ways in which a loved one's experience has taught you about a problem (addiction, AIDS, disability, and so on).

2. Analyze a social problem (crowded classrooms or shoplifting, for example).

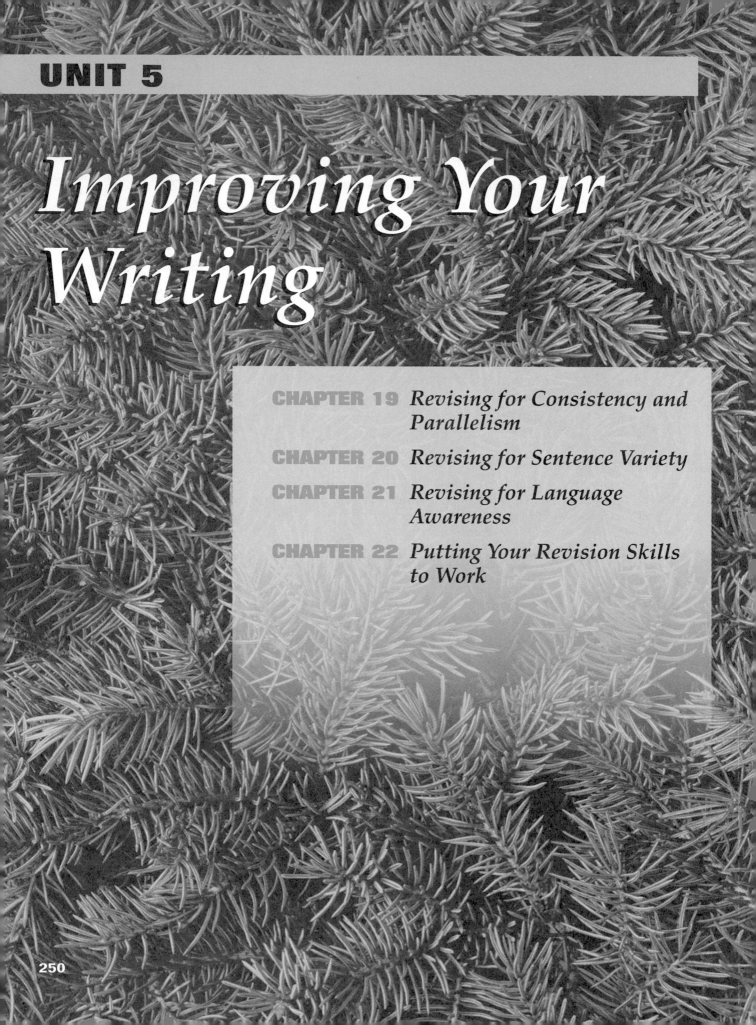

UNIT 5

Improving Your Writing

CHAPTER 19

Revising for Consistency and Parallelism

PART A	Consistent Tense
PART B	Consistent Number and Person
PART C	Parallelism

All good writing is **consistent.** That is, each sentence and paragraph in the final draft should move along smoothly without confusing shifts in **tense, number,** or **person.** In addition, good writing uses **parallel structure** to balance two or more similar words, phrases, or clauses.

Although you should be aware of consistency and parallelism as you write the first draft of your paragraph or essay, you might find it easier to **revise** for them—that is, to write your first draft and then, as you read it again later, check and rewrite for consistency and parallelism.

PART A   Consistent Tense

Consistency of tense means using the same verb tense whenever possible throughout a sentence or an entire paragraph. Do not shift from one verb tense to another—for example, from present to past or from past to present—unless you really mean to indicate different times.

> 1. Inconsistent tense: We *stroll* down Bourbon Street as the jazz bands *began* to play.
>
> 2. Consistent tense: We *strolled* down Bourbon Street as the jazz bands *began* to play.
>
> 3. Consistent tense: We *stroll* down Bourbon Street as the jazz bands *begin* to play.

■ Sentence 1 begins in the present tense with the verb *stroll* but then slips into the past tense with the verb *began.* The tenses are inconsistent since both actions (strolling and beginning) occur at the same time.

■ Sentence 2 is consistent. Both verbs, *strolled* and *began,* are now in the past tense.

■ Sentence 3 is also consistent, using the present tense forms of both verbs, *stroll* and *begin.* The present tense here gives a feeling of immediacy, as if the action is happening now.*

Of course, you should use different verb tenses in a sentence or paragraph if they convey the meaning that you wish to convey:

> 4. Last fall I *took* English 02; now I *am taking* English 13.

■ The verbs in this sentence accurately show the time relationship between the two classroom experiences.†

PRACTICE 1

Read the following sentences carefully for meaning. Then correct any inconsistencies of tense by changing the verbs that do not accurately show the time of events.

EXAMPLE

I took a deep breath and opened the door; there stands a well-dressed man with a large box.

                                   stood

Consistent: I took a deep breath and opened the door; there ~~stands~~ a well-dressed man with a large box.

or

         take   *open*

Consistent: I ~~took~~ a deep breath and ~~opened~~ the door; there stands a well-dressed man with a large box.

1. Two seconds before the buzzer sounded, Allan Houston sank a basket from

    midcourt, and the crowd goes wild.

---

* For more work on spotting verbs, see Chapter 23, "The Simple Sentence," Part C.

† For more work on particular verb tenses and forms, see Chapters 26, 27, and 28.

2. Nestlé introduced instant coffee in 1938; it takes eight years to develop this product.

3. We expand our sales budget, doubled our research, and soon saw positive results.

4. For twenty years, Dr. Dulfano observed animal behavior and seeks clues to explain the increasing violence among human beings.

5. I knew how the system works.

6. I was driving south on Interstate 90 when a truck approaches with its high beams on.

7. Two brown horses graze quietly in the field as the sun rose and the mist disappeared.

8. Lollie had a big grin on her face as she walks over and kicked the Coke machine.

9. Maynard stormed down the hallway, goes right into the boss's office, and shouts, "I want curtains in my office!"

10. The nurses quietly paced the halls, making sure their patients rest comfortably.

PRACTICE 2

Inconsistencies of tense are most likely to occur within paragraphs and longer pieces of writing. Therefore, it is important to revise your writing for tense consistency. Read this paragraph for meaning. Then revise, correcting inconsistencies of tense by changing incorrect verbs.

It was 1850. A poor German-born peddler named Levi Strauss came to San Francisco, trying to sell canvas cloth to tentmakers. By chance he met a miner who complained that sturdy work pants are hard to find. Strauss had an idea, measures the man, and makes him a pair of canvas pants. The miner loved his new breeches, and Levi Strauss goes into business. Although he ordered more canvas, what he gets is a brown French cloth called *serge de Nimes*, which Americans soon called "denim." Strauss liked the cloth but had the next batch dyed blue. He became successful selling work pants to such rugged men as cowboys and lumberjacks. In the 1870s, hearing about a tailor in Nevada adding copper rivets to a pair of the pants to make them stronger, Strauss patents the idea. When he died in 1902, Levi Strauss was famous in California, but the company keeps growing. In the 1930s, when Levi's jeans became popular in the East, both men and women wear them. By the 1990s, people all over the world were buying 85 million pairs of jeans a year.

PRACTICE 3

The following paragraph is written in the past tense. Rewrite it in consistent present tense; make sure all verbs agree with their subjects.*

The tension built as I got into my car. I sat down, breathed deeply, and went through the motions of changing gears, practicing for the race. The seconds crawled by. I heard my heart pound and felt my stomach churning. I stared ahead at the long stretch of road equivalent to a quarter mile. My opponent entered his car, looked at me with a smirk on his face, and gave me the thumbs-down signal. I paid no attention to his teasing but wiped my hands on my shirt. I flexed my fingers and gripped the wheel. The race was about to begin.

_____

_____

_____

_____

_____

_____

_____

_____

PRACTICE 4

The following paragraph is written in the present tense. Rewrite it in consistent past tense.†

On the night of December 2, 1777, in Philadelphia, a woman stands breathlessly at a closed door in her house. While she listens at the keyhole, the British soldiers inside plan a surprise attack on George Washington's army. On the

_____

* For more work on agreement, see Chapter 26, "Present Tense (Agreement)."

† For more work on the past tense, see Chapter 27, "Past Tense."

morning of December 4, carrying an empty flour sack, Lydia Darragh sets out. As she passes the British soldiers who occupy the town, she tells them she is on her way to buy flour. She walks five miles to the miller's, leaves her sack to be filled, and then heads toward the American camp. On the road, she meets American Colonel Thomas Craig and gives him her message. Craig gallops off to warn Washington of the danger—and Darragh goes back to pick up her flour. When British General Howe marches his army out of Philadelphia that night, the American troops are ready for the attack. Although Lydia Darragh's actions help the Americans win the Revolutionary War, she is never suspected.

_____

_____

_____

_____

_____

_____

_____

_____

_____

_____

_____

PRACTICE 5

Longer pieces of writing often use both the past tense and the present tense. However, switching correctly from one tense to the other requires care. Read the following essay carefully and note when a switch from one tense to another is logically necessary. Then revise verbs as needed.

A Quick History of Chocolate

Most of us now take solid chocolate—especially candy bars—so much for granted that we find it hard to imagine a time when chocolate didn't exist. However, this delicious food becomes an eating favorite only about one hundred and fifty years ago.

The ancient peoples of Central America began cultivating cacao beans almost three thousand years ago. A cold drink made from the beans is served to

Hernando Cortés, the Spanish conqueror, when he arrives at the Aztec court of Montezuma in 1519. The Spaniards took the beverage home to their king. He likes it so much that he kept the formula a secret. For the next one hundred years, hot chocolate was the private drink of the Spanish nobility. Slowly, it makes its way into the fashionable courts of France, England, and Austria. In 1657, a Frenchman living in London opened a shop where devices for making the beverage are sold at a high price. Soon chocolate houses appeared in cities throughout Europe. Wealthy clients met in them, sipped chocolate, conducted business, and gossip.

During the 1800s, chocolate became a chewable food. The breakthrough comes in 1828 when cocoa butter was extracted from the bean. Twenty years later, an English firm mixed the butter with chocolate liquor, which results in the first solid chocolate. Milton Hershey's first candy bar come on the scene in 1894, and Tootsie Rolls hit the market two years later. The popularity of chocolate bars soar during World War I when they are given to soldiers for fast energy. M&Ms gave the industry another boost during World War II; soldiers needed candy that wouldn't melt in their hands.

On the average, Americans today eat ten pounds of hard chocolate a year. Their number-one choice is Snickers, which sold more than a billion bars every year. However, Americans consume far less chocolate than many Western Europeans. The average Dutch person gobbled up more than fifteen pounds a year while a Swiss packed away almost twenty pounds. Chocolate is obviously an international favorite.

PART B Consistent Number and Person

Just as important as verb tense consistency is consistency of **number** and **person**.

Consistency of Number

Consistency of number means avoiding confusing shifts from singular to plural or from plural to singular within a sentence or paragraph. Choose *either* singular *or* plural; then be *consistent.*

> 1. Inconsistent number: *The wise jogger* chooses *their* running shoes with care.
>
> 2. Consistent number: *The wise jogger* chooses *his or her* running shoes with care.
>
> 3. Consistent number: *Wise joggers* choose *their* running shoes with care.

■ Since the subject of sentence 1, *the wise jogger,* is singular, use of the plural pronoun *their* is *inconsistent.*

■ Sentence 2 is *consistent.* The singular pronoun *his* (or *her*) now clearly refers to the singular *jogger.*

■ In sentence 3, the plural number is used *consistently. Their* clearly refers to the plural *joggers.*

If you begin a paragraph by referring to a small-business owner as *she,* continue to refer to *her* in the **third person singular** throughout the paragraph:

> The small-business owner . . . .; she . . . .
> . . . . The law may not protect *her* . . . .
> . . . . Therefore, *she* . . . .

Do not confuse the reader by shifting unnecessarily to *they* or *you.*

PRACTICE 6

Correct any inconsistencies of **number** in the following sentences.* Also make necessary changes in verb agreement.

EXAMPLE A singer must protect ~~their~~ voice.
                         his or her

1. An individual's self-esteem can affect their performance.

2. Jorge started drinking diet sodas only last November, but already he hates the taste of it.

3. The headlines encouraged us, but we feared that it wasn't accurate.

4. The defendant who wishes to do so may ask a higher court to overturn their conviction.

---

* For more practice in agreement of pronouns and antecedents, see Chapter 30, "Pronouns," Part B.

5. Dreams fascinate me; it is like another world.

6. If a person doesn't know how to write well, they will face limited job opportunities.

7. Oxford University boasts of the great number of ancient manuscripts they own.

8. Always buy corn and tomatoes when it is in season.

9. The average American takes their freedom for granted.

10. Women have more opportunities than ever before. She is freer to go to school, get a job, and choose the kind of life she wants.

Consistency of Person

Consistency of person—closely related to consistency of number—means using the same *person,* or indefinite pronoun form, throughout a sentence or paragraph whenever possible.

> *First person* is the most personal and informal in written work: (singular) *I,* (plural) *we*
>
> *Second person* speaks directly to the reader: (singular and plural) *you*
>
> *Third person* is the most formal and most frequently used in college writing: (singular) *he, she, it, one, a person, an individual, a student,* and so on; (plural) *they, people, individuals, students,* and so on

Avoid confusing shifts from one person to another. Choose one, and then be *consistent.* When using a noun in a general way—*a person, the individual, the parent*—be careful not to slip into the second person, *you,* but continue to use the third person, *he or she.*

> 4. Inconsistent person: A *player* collects $200 when *you* pass "Go."
>
> 5. Consistent person: A *player* collects $200 when *he or she* passes "Go."
>
> 6. Consistent person: *You* collect $200 when *you* pass "Go."

■ In sentence 4, the person shifts unnecessarily from the third person, *a player,* to the second person, *you.* The result is confusing.

■ Sentence 5 maintains consistent third person. *He or she* now clearly refers to the third person subject, *a player.*

■ Sentence 6 is also consistent, using the second person, *you,* throughout.

Of course, inconsistencies of person and number often occur together, as shown in the next box.

7. Inconsistent person and number:	Whether *one* enjoys or resents commercials, *we* are bombarded with them every hour of the day.
8. Consistent person and number:	Whether *we* enjoy or resent commercials, *we* are bombarded with them every hour of the day.
9. Consistent person and number:	Whether *one* enjoys or resents commercials, *he or she* (or *one*) is bombarded with them every hour of the day.

■ Sentence 7 shifts from the third person singular, *one,* to the first person plural, *we.*

■ Sentence 8 uses the first person plural consistently.

■ Sentence 9 uses the third person singular consistently.

PRACTICE 7

Correct the shifts in **person** in these sentences. If necessary, change the verbs to make them agree with any new subjects.

EXAMPLE| One should eliminate saturated fats from ~~your~~ *one's* diet.

1. Sooner or later, most addicts realize that you can't just quit when you want to.

2. One problem facing students on this campus is that a person doesn't know when the library will be open and when it will be closed.

3. One should rely on reason, not emotion, when they are forming opinions about such charged issues as abortion.

4. I have reached a time in my life when what others expect is less important than what one really wants to do.

5. Members of the orchestra should meet after the concert and bring your instruments and music.

6. The wise mother knows that she is asking for trouble if you let a small child watch violent television shows.

7. The student who participates in this program will spend six weeks in Spain and Morocco. You will study the art and architecture firsthand, working closely with an instructor.

8. You shouldn't judge a person by the way they dress.

9. If you have been working that hard, one needs a vacation.

10. People who visit the Caribbean for the first time are struck by the lushness of

the landscape. The sheer size of the flowers and fruit amazes you.

PRACTICE 8

The following paragraph consistently uses the third person singular—*the sales-person, he or she,* and so on. For practice in revising for consistency, rewrite the paragraph in **consistent third person plural.** Begin by changing *the salesperson* to *salespeople* or *salesclerks.* Then change verbs, nouns, or pronouns as necessary.

The salesperson is crucial to a customer's satisfaction or dissatisfaction with a particular store. In reality, the salesperson acts as the store's representative or ambassador; often he or she is the only contact a customer has with the store. Thousands of dollars may be spent in advertising to woo customers and build a favorable image, only to have this lost by the uncaring salesclerk.

—Robert F. Hartley, *Retailing: Challenge and Opportunity*

_____

_____

_____

_____

_____

_____

_____

_____

PRACTICE 9

Revise the following essay for inconsistencies of person and number. Correct any confusing shifts (changing words if necessary) to make the writing clear and *consistent* throughout.

Immortality in Wax

"Madame Tussaud's. Come and find out who's in. And who's out." That's

what English radios advertise to lure visitors to a most unusual show—a display

of the rich, the famous, and the infamous in the form of lifelike wax statues.

Nearly three million line up each year to rub shoulders with the images of historic and contemporary celebrities. You make Madame Tussaud's the most popular paid tourist attraction in England.

Visitors are treated to some of Madame Tussaud's original handiwork, as well as to other figures that have been added over the past two hundred years. All told, tourists can see and be photographed with more than four hundred eerily lifelike statues. In the Grand Hall, one can view British royalty standing with past and present leaders of other countries. The very popular Chamber of Horrors introduces you to the most notorious criminals of all time. The Conservatory houses entertainers, from Marilyn Monroe and Joan Collins to Madonna and Brad Pitt.

Each month, a committee decides who should be added to or taken out of the collection. A celebrity is chosen for your fame, recognizability, and publicity potential. You are invited to sit for moldings. Each image takes about six months to complete, at a cost of more than $32,000. The celebrity usually poses with their finished statue for the press. Then the figure is put on display. Entertainers who have sat for moldings recently include John Travolta and Cybill Shepherd, the first American television comic actress in Madame Tussaud's. Newly represented political figures include Nelson Mandela and the Dalai Lama.

PART C   Parallelism

Parallelism, or **parallel structure,** is an effective way to add smoothness and power to your writing. **Parallelism** is a balance of two or more similar words, phrases, or clauses.

Compare the two versions of each of these sentences:

1. She likes dancing, swimming, and to jog.
2. She likes *dancing, swimming,* and *jogging.*
3. The cable runs across the roof; the north wall is where it runs down.
4. The cable runs *across the roof* and *down the north wall.*
5. He admires people with strong convictions and who think for themselves.
6. He admires people *who have strong convictions* and *who think for themselves.*

■ Sentences 2, 4, and 6 use **parallelism** to express parallel ideas.

■ In sentence 2, *dancing, swimming,* and *jogging* are parallel; all three are the *-ing* forms of verbs, used here as nouns.

■ In sentence 4, *across the roof* and *down the north wall* are parallel prepositional phrases, each consisting of a preposition and its object.

■ In sentence 6, *who have strong convictions* and *who think for themselves* are parallel clauses beginning with the word *who.*

Sometimes two entire sentences can be parallel:

> In a democracy we are all equal before the law. In a dictatorship we are all equal before the police.
>
> —Millor Fernandes

■ In what way are these two sentences parallel? _____

_____

Certain special constructions require parallel structure:

> 7. The fruit is *both* tasty *and* fresh.
>
> 8. He *either* loves you *or* hates you.
>
> 9. Yvette *not only* plays golf *but also* swims like a pro.
>
> 10. I would *rather* sing in the chorus *than* perform a solo.

Each of these constructions has two parts:

both . . . and

(n)either . . . (n)or

not only . . . but also

rather . . . than

The words, phrases, or clauses following each part must be parallel:

tasty . . . fresh

loves you . . . hates you

plays golf . . . swims like a pro

sing in the chorus . . . perform a solo

PRACTICE 10

Rewrite each of the following sentences, using parallel structure to accent parallel ideas.

EXAMPLE The summer in Louisiana is very hot and has high humidity.

The summer in Louisiana is very hot and humid.

1. Teresa is a gifted woman—a chemist, does the carpentry, and she can cook.

_____

_____

2. The shape of the rock, how big it was, and its color reminded me of a small elephant.

_____

_____

3. He is an affectionate husband, a thoughtful son, and kind to his kids.

_____

_____

4. Marvin was happy to win the chess tournament and he also felt surprised.

_____

_____

5. Dr. Tien is the kindest physician I know; she has the most concern of any physician I know.

_____

_____

6. Joe would rather work on a farm than spending time in an office.

_____

_____

7. Every afternoon in the mountains, it either rains or there is hail.

_____

_____

8. _Sesame Street_ teaches children nursery rhymes, songs, how to be courteous, and being kind.

_____

_____

9. Alexis would rather give orders than taking them.

_____

_____

10. His writing reveals not only intelligence but also it is humorous.

_____

_____

PRACTICE 11

Write one sentence that is parallel to each sentence that follows, creating pairs of parallel sentences.

EXAMPLE   On Friday night, she dressed in silk and sipped champagne.

On Monday morning, she put on her jeans and crammed for a history test.

1. When he was twenty, he worked seven days a week in a fruit store.

_____

_____

2. The child in me wants to run away from problems.

_____

_____

3. The home team charged enthusiastically onto the field.

_____

_____

4. "Work hard and keep your mouth shut" is my mother's formula for success.

_____

_____

5. The men thought the movie was amusing.

_____

_____

PRACTICE 12

The following paragraph contains both correct and faulty parallel structures. Revise the faulty parallelism.

During World War II, United States Marines who fought in the Pacific

possessed a powerful weapon that was also unbeatable: Navaho Code Talkers.

Creating a secret code, Code Talkers sent and were translating vital military information. Four hundred twenty Navahos memorized the code, and it was used by them. It consisted of both common Navaho words and there were also about four hundred invented words. For example, Code Talkers used the Navaho words for *owl, chicken hawk,* and *swallow* to describe different kinds of aircraft. Because Navaho is a complex language that is also uncommon, the Japanese military could not break the code. Although Code Talkers helped the Allied Forces win the war, their efforts were not publicly recognized until the code was declassified in 1968. On August 14, 1982, the first Navaho Code Talkers Day honored these heroes, who not only had risked their lives but also been developing one of the few unbroken codes in history.

PRACTICE 13

The following essay contains both correct and faulty parallel structures. Revise the faulty parallelism.

Nellie Bly

As a writer for the *New York World* in the 1880s, Nellie Bly was one of the leading journalists of her time. With determination and courageously, she pioneered what we now call the "media event." Nellie's most renowned exploit was her famous trip that was daring around the world.

Nellie bet her publisher that she could beat the fictional record set by Phineas Fogg in Jules Verne's novel *Around the World in Eighty Days.* Moreover, her telegraphed reports of the trip would boost newspaper sales. Nellie left Jersey City on November 14, 1889, and to travel first to England, France, and the land of Italy. From there, she journeyed over the Mediterranean Sea and the Indian Ocean to Ceylon. After stops in Singapore, Hong Kong, and also in Tokyo, she set sail for San Francisco. During this leg of the journey, she almost lost her bet. First, low winds delayed the sailing; then powerful storms were striking at sea. Adopting the motto "We'll win or die for Nellie Bly," the crew managed to get the ship to America. An easy cross-country train trip that was fast returned Nellie Bly to New York on January 25, 1890. Her trip had lasted seventy-two days, six hours, and there were eleven minutes.

Nellie arrived home a great hero and to be a national figure. Cheering crowds greeted her, songs were dedicated to her, toys were named after her, and there were parades that were organized in her honor. She embarked on a national tour, making speeches about her travels and to fascinate crowds with her tales. Nellie had shown the world that a gutsy American woman could travel the world alone, quickly, and with safety.

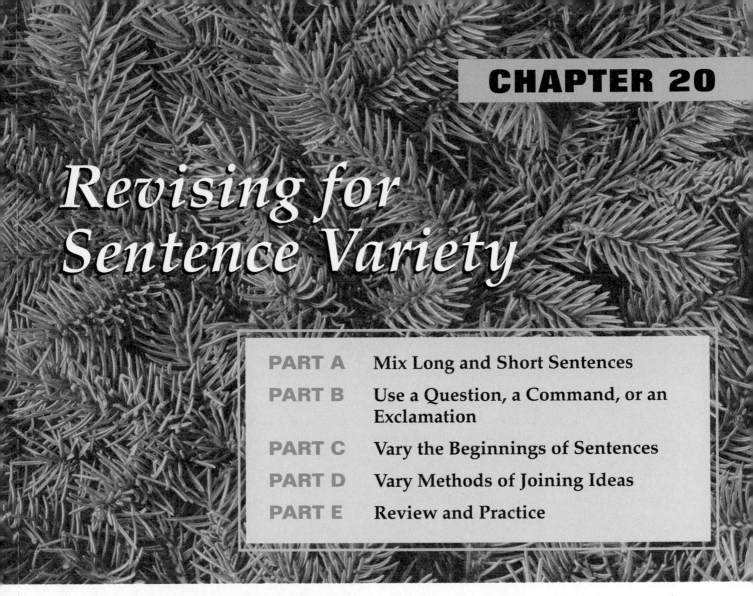

CHAPTER 20

Revising for Sentence Variety

PART A	Mix Long and Short Sentences
PART B	Use a Question, a Command, or an Exclamation
PART C	Vary the Beginnings of Sentences
PART D	Vary Methods of Joining Ideas
PART E	Review and Practice

Good writers pay attention to **sentence variety.** They notice how sentences work together within a paragraph, and they seek a mix of different sentence lengths and types. Experienced writers have a variety of sentence patterns from which to choose. They try not to overuse one pattern.

This chapter will present several techniques for varying your sentences and paragraphs. Some of them you may already know and use, perhaps unconsciously. The purpose of this chapter is to make you more conscious of the **choices** available to you as a writer.

Remember, you achieve sentence variety by practicing, by systematically **revising** your papers and by trying out new types of sentences or combinations of sentences.

PART A   Mix Long and Short Sentences

One of the basic ways to achieve sentence variety is to use both long and short sentences. Beginning writers tend to overuse short, simple sentences, which quickly become monotonous. Notice the length of the sentences in the following paragraph:

(1) There is one positive result of the rising crime rate. (2) This has been the growth of neighborhood crime prevention programs. (3) These programs really work. (4) They teach citizens to patrol their neighborhoods. (5) They teach citizens to work with the police. (6) They have dramatically reduced crime in cities and towns across the country. (7) The idea is catching on.

The sentences in the paragraph above are all nearly the same length, and the effect is choppy and almost childish. Now read this revised version, which contains a variety of sentence lengths.

(1) One cause of the falling crime rate in some cities is the growth of neighborhood crime prevention programs. (2) These programs really work. (3) By patrolling their neighborhoods and working with the police, citizens have shown that they can dramatically reduce crime. (4) The idea is catching on.

This paragraph is more effective because it mixes two short sentences, 2 and 4, and two longer sentences, 1 and 3. Although short sentences can be used effectively anywhere in a paragraph or an essay, they can be especially useful as introductions or conclusions, like sentence 4 above. Note the powerful effect of short sentences used between longer ones in the paragraph that follows. Underline the short sentences.

(1) I recall being told, when I first moved to Los Angeles and was living on an isolated beach, that the Indians would throw themselves into the sea when the bad wind blew. (2) I could see why. (3) The Pacific turned ominously glossy during a Santa Ana period, and one woke in the night troubled not only by the peacocks screaming in the olive trees but by the eerie absence of surf. (4) The heat was surreal. (5) The sky had a yellow cast, the kind of light sometimes called "earthquake weather." (6) My only neighbor would not come out of her house for days, and there were no lights at night, and her husband roamed the place with a machete. (7) One day he would tell me that he had heard a trespasser, the next a rattlesnake.

—Joan Didion, *Slouching Towards Bethlehem*

PRACTICE 1

Revise and rewrite the following paragraph in a variety of sentence lengths. Recombine sentences in any way you wish. You may add connecting words or drop words, but do not alter the meaning of the paragraph. Compare your work with a fellow student's.

The park is alive with motion today. Joggers pound up and down the boardwalk. Old folks watch them from the benches. Couples row boats across the lake. The boats are green and wooden. Two teenagers hurl a Frisbee back and forth. They yell and leap. A shaggy white dog dashes in from nowhere. He snatches the red disk in his mouth. He bounds away. The teenagers run after him.

_____

_____

_____

_____

_____

_____

PART B　Use a Question, a Command, or an Exclamation

The most commonly used sentence is the **declarative sentence,** which is a statement. However, an occasional carefully placed **question, command,** or **exclamation** is an effective way to achieve sentence variety.

The Question

> *Why did I become a cab driver?* First, I truly enjoy driving a car and exploring different parts of the city, the classy avenues and the hidden back streets. In addition, I like meeting all kinds of people, from bookmakers to governors, each with a unique story and many willing to talk to the back of my head. Of course, the pay isn't bad and the hours are flexible, but it's the places and the people that I love.

This paragraph begins with a question. The writer does not really expect the reader to answer it. Rather, it is a **rhetorical question,** one that will be answered by the writer in the course of the paragraph. A rhetorical question used as a topic sentence can provide a colorful change from the usual declarative sentences: *Is America really the best-fed nation in the world? What is courage? Why do more young people take drugs today than ever before?*

The Command and the Exclamation

> (1) Try to imagine using failure as a description of an animal's behavior. (2) Consider a dog barking for fifteen minutes, and someone saying, "He really isn't very good at barking, I'd give him a C." (3) How absurd! (4) It is impossible for an animal to fail because there is no provision for evaluating natural behavior. (5) Spiders construct webs, not successful or unsuccessful webs. (6) Cats hunt mice; if they aren't successful in one attempt, they simply go after another. (7) They don't lie there and whine, complaining about the one that got away, or have a nervous breakdown because they failed. (8) Natural behavior simply is! (9) So apply the same logic to your own behavior and rid yourself of the fear of failure.
>
> —Dr. Wayne W. Dyer, *Your Erroneous Zones*

The previous paragraph begins and ends with **commands, or imperative sentences.** Sentences 1, 2, and 9 address the reader directly and have as their implied subject *you.* They tell the reader to do something: *(You) try to imagine . . . , (you) consider . . . , (you) apply. . . .* Commands are most frequently used in giving directions,* but they can be used occasionally, as in the previous paragraph, for sentence variety.

Sentences 3 and 8 in the Dyer paragraph are **exclamations,** sentences that express strong emotion and end with an exclamation point. These should be used very sparingly. In fact, some writers avoid them altogether, striving for words that convey strong emotion instead.

Be careful with the question, the command, and the exclamation as options in your writing. Try them out, but use them—especially the exclamation—sparingly.

WRITING ASSIGNMENT 1

On a separate piece of paper, write a paragraph that begins with a rhetorical question. Choose one of the questions below or compose your own. Be sure that the body of the paragraph really does answer the question.

1. How has college (or anything else) changed me?

2. Is marriage worth the risks?

3. Do some MTV videos encourage the mistreatment of women?

4. Why do we do things that we know are bad for us?

5. Should people pamper their pets?

PART C Vary the Beginnings of Sentences

Begin with an Adverb

Since the first word of many sentences is the subject, one way to achieve sentence variety is by occasionally starting a sentence with a word or words other than the subject.

For instance, you can begin with an **adverb:**†

1. He *laboriously* dragged the large crate up the stairs.

2. *Laboriously,* he dragged the large crate up the stairs.

3. The contents of the beaker *suddenly* began to foam.

4. *Suddenly,* the contents of the beaker began to foam.

■ In sentences 2 and 4, the adverbs *laboriously* and *suddenly* are shifted to the first position. Notice the difference in rhythm that this creates, as well as the slight change in meaning: Sentence 2 emphasizes *how* he dragged the crate—*laboriously;* sentence 4 emphasizes the *suddenness* of what happened.

---

* For more work on giving directions, see Chapter 8, "Process."

† For more work on adverbs, see Chapter 32, "Adjectives and Adverbs."

■ A comma usually follows an adverb that introduces a sentence; however, adverbs of time—*often, now, always*—do not always require a comma. As a general rule, use a comma if you want the reader to pause briefly.

PRACTICE 2

Rewrite the following sentences by shifting the adverbs to the beginning. Punctuate correctly.

EXAMPLE | He skillfully prepared the engine for the race.

Skillfully, he prepared the engine for the race.

1. Two deer moved silently across the clearing.

   _____

2. The chief of the research division occasionally visits the lab.

   _____

3. Proofread your writing always.

   _____

4. Children of alcoholics often marry alcoholics.

   _____

5. Jake foolishly lied to his supervisor.

   _____

PRACTICE 3

Begin each of the following sentences with an appropriate adverb. Punctuate correctly.

1. _____ the detective approached the ticking suitcase.

2. _____ Martina Hingis powered a forehand past her opponent.

3. _____ she received her check for $25,000 from the state lottery.

4. _____ he left the beach.

5. _____ the submarine sank out of sight.

Write five sentences of your own that begin with adverbs. Use different adverbs from those in Practices 2 and 3; if you wish, use *graciously, absent-mindedly, cheerfully, furiously, sometimes.* Punctuate correctly.

1. _____

2. _____

3. _____

4. _____

5. _____

Begin with a Prepositional Phrase

A **prepositional phrase** is a group of words containing a **preposition** and its **object** (a noun or pronoun). *To you, in the evening,* and *under the old bridge* are prepositional phrases.*

Preposition	Object
to	you
in	the evening
under	the old bridge

Here is a partial list of prepositions:

Common Prepositions			
about	beneath	into	throughout
above	beside	near	to
across	between	of	toward
against	by	on	under
among	except	onto	up
at	for	out	upon
behind	from	over	with
below	in	through	without

For variety in your writing, begin an occasional sentence with a prepositional phrase:

---

* For work on spotting prepositional phrases, see Chapter 31, "Prepositions."

5. Charles left the room *without a word.*

6. *Without a word,* Charles left the room.

7. A fat yellow cat lay sleeping *on the narrow sill.*

8. *On the narrow sill,* a fat yellow cat lay sleeping.

■ In sentences 6 and 8, the prepositional phrases have been shifted to the beginning. Note the slight shift in emphasis that results. Sentence 6 stresses that Charles left the room *without a word,* and 8 stresses the location of the cat, *on the narrow sill.*

■ Prepositional phrases that begin sentences are usually followed by commas. However, short prepositional phrases need not be.

Prepositional phrases are not always movable; rely on the meaning of the sentence to determine whether they are movable:

9. The dress *in the picture* is the one I want.

10. Joelle bought a bottle *of white wine for dinner.*

■ *In the picture* in sentence 9 is a part of the subject and cannot be moved. *In the picture the dress is the one I want* makes no sense.

■ Sentence 10 has two prepositional phrases. Which one *cannot* be moved to the beginning of the sentence? Why?

_____

_____

PRACTICE 5

Underline the prepositional phrases in each sentence. Some sentences contain more than one prepositional phrase. Rewrite each sentence by shifting a prepositional phrase to the beginning. Punctuate correctly.

EXAMPLE | A large owl with gray feathers watched us from the oak tree.

From the oak tree, a large owl with gray feathers watched us.

1. The coffee maker turned itself on at seven o'clock sharp.

_____

_____

2. A growling Doberman paced behind the chainlink fence.

_____

_____

3. A man and a woman held hands under the street lamp.

_____

_____

4. They have sold nothing except athletic shoes for years.

_____

_____

5. A group of men played checkers and drank iced tea beside the small shop.

_____

_____

PRACTICE 6

Begin each of the following sentences with a different prepositional phrase. Refer to the list and be creative. Punctuate correctly.

1. _____ we ordered potato skins, salad, and beer.

2. _____ a woman in horn-rimmed glasses balanced her checkbook.

3. _____ everyone congratulated Jim on his promotion.

4. _____ one can see huge sculptures in wood, metal, and stone.

5. _____ three large helium-filled balloons drifted.

PRACTICE 7

Write five sentences of your own that begin with prepositional phrases. Use these phrases if you wish: _in the dentist's office, between them, at my wedding, under that stack of books, behind his friendly smile._ Punctuate correctly.

1. _____

2. _____

3. _____

4. _____

5. _____

PART D   Vary Methods of Joining Ideas*

Join Ideas with a Compound Predicate

A sentence with a **compound predicate** contains more than one verb, but the subject is *not* repeated before the second verb. Such a sentence is really composed of two simple sentences with the same subject:

> 1. The nurse entered.
>
> 2. The nurse quickly closed the door.
>
> 3. The nurse *entered* and quickly *closed* the door.

- *The nurse* is the subject of sentence 1, and *entered* is the verb; *the nurse* is also the subject of sentence 2, and *closed* is the verb.

- When these sentences are combined with a compound predicate in sentence 3, *the nurse* is the subject of both *entered* and *closed* but is not repeated before the second verb.

- No comma is necessary when the conjunctions *and, but, or,* and *yet* join the verbs in a compound predicate.

A compound predicate is useful in combining short, choppy sentences:

> 4. He serves elaborate meals.
>
> 5. He never uses a recipe.
>
> 6. He serves elaborate meals yet never uses a recipe.
>
> 7. Aviators rarely get nosebleeds.
>
> 8. They often suffer from backaches.
>
> 9. Aviators rarely get nosebleeds but often suffer from backaches.

- Sentences 4 and 5 are joined by *yet;* no comma precedes *yet.*

- Sentences 7 and 8 are joined by *but;* no comma precedes *but.*

---

* For work on joining ideas with coordination and subordination, see Chapter 24, "Coordination and Subordination."

PRACTICE 8

Combine each pair of short sentences into one sentence with a compound predicate. Use *and, but, or,* and *yet*. Punctuate correctly.

EXAMPLE Toby smeared peanut butter on a thick slice of white bread.
He devoured the treat in thirty seconds.

Toby smeared peanut butter on a thick slice of white bread and devoured the treat

in thirty seconds.

1. Americans eat more than 800 million pounds of peanut butter.
   They spend more than $1 billion on the product each year.

   _____

   _____

2. Peanut butter was first concocted in the 1890s.
   It did not become the food we know for thirty years.

   _____

   _____

3. George Washington Carver did not discover peanut butter.
   He published many recipes for pastes much like it.

   _____

   _____

   _____

4. The average American becomes a peanut butter lover in childhood.
   He or she loses enthusiasm for it later on.

   _____

   _____

   _____

5. Older adults regain their passion for peanut butter.
   They consume great quantities of the delicious stuff.

   _____

   _____

   _____

PRACTICE 9

Complete the following compound predicates. *Do not repeat* the subjects.

1. Three Korean writers visited the campus and _____

   _____ .

2. The singer breathed heavily into the microphone but _____

   _____ .

3. Take these cans to the recycling center or _____

   _____ .

4. The newspaper printed the story yet _____

   _____ .

5. Three men burst into the back room and _____

   _____ .

PRACTICE 10

Write five sentences with compound predicates. Be careful to punctuate correctly.

1. _____

2. _____

3. _____

4. _____

5. _____

Join Ideas with an *-ing* Modifier

An excellent way to achieve sentence variety is by occasionally combining two sentences with an *-ing* modifier.

10. He peered through the microscope.
11. He discovered a squiggly creature.
12. *Peering through the microscope,* he discovered a squiggly creature.

■ Sentence 10 has been converted to an *-ing* modifier by changing the verb *peered* to *peering* and dropping the subject *he*. *Peering through the microscope* now introduces the main clause, *he discovered a squiggly creature.*

■ A comma sets off the *-ing* modifier from the word it refers to, *he*. To avoid confusion, the word referred to must appear in the immediately following clause.

An *-ing* modifier indicates that two actions are occurring at the same time. The main idea of the sentence should be contained in the main clause, not in the *-ing* modifier. In the preceding example, the discovery of the creature is the main idea, not the fact that someone peered through a microscope.

Be careful; misplaced *-ing* modifiers can result in confusing sentences: *He discovered a squiggly creature peering through the microscope.* (Was the creature looking through the microscope?)

Convert sentence 13 into an *-ing* modifier and write it in the blank:

13. We drove down Tompkins Road.

14. We were surprised by the number of "for sale" signs.

15. _____, we were surprised by the number of "for sale" signs.

■ The new *-ing* modifier is followed directly by the word to which it refers, *we.*

PRACTICE 11

Combine the following pairs of sentences by converting the first sentence into an *-ing* modifier. Make sure the subject of the main clause directly follows the *-ing* modifier. Punctuate correctly.

EXAMPLE Jake searched for his needle-nose pliers.
He completely emptied the tool chest.

Searching for his needle-nose pliers, Jake completely emptied the tool chest.

1. She installed the air conditioner.
She saved herself $50 in labor.

_____

_____

2. The surgeons raced against time.
The surgeons performed a liver transplant on the child.

_____

_____

3. They conducted a survey of Jackson Heights residents.
   They found that most opposed construction of the airport.

   _____

   _____

4. Three flares spiraled upward from the little boat.
   They exploded against the night sky.

   _____

   _____

5. Virgil danced in the Pennsylvania Ballet.
   Virgil learned discipline and self-control.

   _____

   _____

6. The hen squawked loudly.
   The hen fluttered out of our path.

   _____

   _____

7. The engineer made a routine check of the blueprints.
   He discovered a flaw in the design.

   _____

   _____

8. Dr. Jackson opened commencement exercises with a humorous story.
   He put everyone at ease.

   _____

   _____

PRACTICE 12

Add either an introductory -*ing* modifier *or* a main clause to each sentence. Make sure that each -*ing* modifier refers clearly to the subject of the main clause.

EXAMPLE | _Reading a book a week_____, Jeff increased his vocabulary.

Exercising every day, _I lost five pounds_____.

1. _____, she felt a sense of accomplishment.

2. Growing up in Hollywood, _____

_____.

3. _____, the father and son
were reconciled.

4. Interviewing his relatives, _____

_____.

5. _____, the wrecking ball
swung through the air and smashed into the brick wall.

Write five sentences of your own that begin with *-ing* modifiers. Make sure that
the subject of the sentence follows the modifier and be careful of the punctuation.

1. _____

_____

2. _____

_____

3. _____

_____

4. _____

_____

5. _____

_____

Join Ideas with a Past Participial Modifier

Some sentences can be joined with a **past participial modifier.** A sentence that
contains a *to be* verb and a **past participle*** can be changed into a past participial
modifier:

————————————

* For more work on past participles, see Chapter 28, "The Past Participle."

16. Judith *is trapped* in a dead-end job.

17. Judith decided to enroll at the local community college.

18. *Trapped in a dead-end job,* Judith decided to enroll at the local community college.

■ Sentence 16 has been made into a past participial modifier by dropping the helping verb *is* and the subject *Judith*. The past participle *trapped* now introduces the new sentence.

■ A comma sets off the past participial modifier from the word it modifies, *Judith*. To avoid confusion, the word referred to must directly follow the modifier.

Be careful; misplaced past participial modifiers can result in confusing sentences: *Packed in dry ice, Steve brought us some ice cream.* (Was Steve packed in dry ice?)

Sometimes two or more past participles can be used to introduce a sentence:

19. The term paper *was revised* and *rewritten*.

20. It received an A.

21. *Revised and rewritten,* the term paper received an A.

■ The past participles *revised* and *rewritten* become a modifier that introduces sentence 21. What word(s) do they refer to?

_____

PRACTICE 14

Combine each pair of sentences into one sentence that begins with a past participial modifier. Convert the sentence containing a form of *to be* plus a past participle into a past participial modifier that introduces the new sentence.

EXAMPLE   Duffy was surprised by the interruption.
He lost his train of thought.

Surprised by the interruption, Duffy lost his train of thought.

1. My mother was married at the age of sixteen.
   My mother never finished high school.

   _____

   _____

2. The 2:30 flight was delayed by an electrical storm.
   It arrived in Lexington three hours late.

   _____

   _____

3. The old car was waxed and polished.
   It shone in the sun.

   _____

   _____

4. The house was built by Frank Lloyd Wright.
   It has become famous.

   _____

   _____

5. The Nineteenth Amendment was ratified in 1920.
   It gave women the right to vote.

   _____

   _____

6. The manuscript seems impossible to decipher.
   It is written in code.

   _____

   _____

7. Dr. Bentley will address the premed students.
   He has been recognized for his contributions in the field of immunology.

   _____

   _____

8. Mrs. Witherspoon was exhausted by night classes.
   She declined the chance to work overtime.

   _____

   _____

PRACTICE 15

Complete each sentence by filling in *either* the past participial modifier *or* the main clause. Remember, the past participial modifier must clearly refer to the subject of the main clause.

EXAMPLE   Wrapped in blue paper and tied with string, _the gift arrived_____.

Chosen to represent the team, Phil proudly accepted the trophy.

1. Made of gold and set with precious stones, _____

   _____.

2. Overwhelmed by the response to her ad in *The Star*, _____

_____ .

3. _____ , Tom left no
forwarding address.

4. _____ , we found a
huge basket of fresh fruit on the steps.

5. Astonished by the scene before her, _____

_____ .

PRACTICE 16

Write five sentences of your own that begin with past participial modifiers. If you wish, use participles from this list:

thrilled	moved	seen	honored
shocked	dressed	hidden	bent
awakened	lost	stuffed	examined
annoyed	found	pinched	rewired

Make sure that the subject of the sentence clearly follows the modifier.

1. _____

_____

2. _____

_____

3. _____

_____

4. _____

_____

5. _____

_____

Join Ideas with an Appositive

A fine way to add variety to your writing is to combine two choppy sentences with an appositive. An **appositive** is a word or group of words that renames or describes a noun or pronoun:

22. Carlos is the new wrestling champion.

23. He is a native of Argentina.

24. Carlos, *a native of Argentina,* is the new wrestling champion.

■ *A native of Argentina* in sentence 24 is an appositive. It renames the noun *Carlos.*

■ An appositive must be placed either directly *after* the word it refers to, as in sentence 24, or directly *before* it, as follows:

25. *A native of Argentina,* Carlos is the new wrestling champion.

■ Note that an appositive is set off by commas.

Appositives can add versatility to your writing because they can be placed at the beginning, in the middle, or at the end of a sentence. When you join two ideas with an appositive, place the idea you wish to stress in the main clause and make the less important idea the appositive:

26. Naomi wants to become a fashion model.

27. She is the daughter of an actress.

28. *The daughter of an actress,* Naomi wants to become a fashion model.

29. FACT made headlines for the first time only a few years ago.

30. FACT is now a powerful consumer group.

31. FACT, *now a powerful consumer group,* made headlines for the first time only a few years ago.

32. Watch out for Smithers.

33. He is a dangerous man.

34. Watch out for Smithers, *a dangerous man.*

Using an appositive to combine sentences eliminates unimportant words and creates longer, more fact-filled sentences.

PRACTICE 17

Combine the following pairs of sentences by making the *second sentence* an appositive. Punctuate correctly.

These appositives should occur at the *beginning* of the sentences.

EXAMPLE | My uncle taught me to use watercolors.
He is a well-known artist.

A well-known artist, my uncle taught me to use watercolors.

1. Dan has saved many lives.
   He is a dedicated fire fighter.

   _____

   _____

2. Acupuncture is becoming popular in the United States.
   It is an ancient Chinese healing system.

   _____

   _____

   _____

3. The Cromwell Hotel was built in 1806.
   It is an elegant example of Mexican architecture.

   _____

   _____

These appositives should occur in the *middle* of the sentences. Punctuate correctly.

EXAMPLE His American history course is always popular with students.
It is an introductory survey.

His American history course, an introductory survey, is always popular with

students.

4. The Korean Ping-Pong champion won ten games in a row.
   She is a small and wiry athlete.

   _____

   _____

5. The pituitary is located below the brain.
   It is the body's master gland.

   _____

   _____

6. The elevator shudders violently and begins to rise.
   It is an ancient box of wood and hope.

   _____

   _____

These appositives should occur at the *end* of the sentences. Punctuate correctly.

EXAMPLE | I hate fried asparagus.
It is a vile dish.

I hate fried asparagus, a vile dish.

7. Jennifer flaunted her new camera.
It was a Nikon with a telephoto lens.

_____

_____

8. At the intersection stood a hitchhiker.
He was a young man dressed in a tuxedo.

_____

_____

9. We met for pancakes at the Cosmic Cafe.
It was a greasy diner on the corner of 10th and Vine.

_____

_____

PRACTICE 18

Write six sentences using appositives. In two sentences, place the appositive at the *beginning;* in two sentences, place the appositive in the *middle;* and in two sentences, place it at the *end.*

1. _____

   _____

2. _____

   _____

3. _____

   _____

4. _____

   _____

5. _____

   _____

6. _____

   _____

Join Ideas with a Relative Clause

Relative clauses can add sophistication to your writing. A **relative clause** begins with *who, which,* or *that* and describes a noun or pronoun. It can join two simple sentences in a longer, more complex sentence:

35. Jack just won a scholarship from the Arts Council.

36. He makes wire sculpture.

37. Jack, *who makes wire sculpture,* just won a scholarship from the Arts Council.

■ In sentence 37, *who makes wire sculpture* is a relative clause, created by replacing the subject *he* of sentence 36 with the relative pronoun *who.*

■ *Who* now introduces the subordinate relative clause and connects it to the rest of the sentence. Note that *who* directly follows the word it refers to, *Jack.*

The idea that the writer wishes to stress is placed in the main clause, and the subordinate idea is placed in the relative clause. Study the combinations in sentences 38 through 40 and 41 through 43.

38. Carrots grow in cool climates.

39. They are high in vitamin A.

40. Carrots, *which* are high in vitamin A, grow in cool climates.

41. He finally submitted the term paper.

42. It was due six months ago.

43. He finally submitted the term paper *that* was due six months ago.

■ In sentence 40, *which are high in vitamin A* is a relative clause, created by replacing *they* with *which.* Which word in sentence 40 does *which* refer to?

_____

■ What is the relative clause in sentence 43?

_____

■ Which word does *that* refer to?

_____

Punctuating relative clauses can be tricky; therefore, you will have to be careful:*

44. Claude, *who grew up in Haiti,* speaks fluent French.

_____

* For more practice in punctuating relative clauses, see Chapter 34, "The Comma," Part D.

■ *Who grew up in Haiti* is set off by commas because it adds information about Claude that is not essential to the meaning of the sentence. In other words, the sentence would make sense without it: *Claude speaks fluent French.*

■ *Who grew up in Haiti* is called a **nonrestrictive clause.** It does not restrict or provide vital information about the word it modifies.

---

45. People *who crackle paper in theaters* annoy me.

■ *Who crackle paper in theaters* is not set off by commas because it is vital to the meaning of the sentence. Without it, the sentence would read, *People annoy me;* yet the point of the sentence is that people *who crackle paper in theaters* annoy me, not all people.

■ *Who crackle paper in theaters* is called a **restrictive clause** because it restricts the meaning of the word it refers to, *people.*

Note that *which* usually begins a nonrestrictive clause and *that* usually begins a restrictive clause.

PRACTICE 19

Combine each pair of sentences by changing the second sentence into a relative clause introduced by *who, which,* or *that.* Remember, *who* refers to persons, *that* refers to persons or things, and *which* refers to things.

These sentences require **nonrestrictive relative clauses.** Punctuate correctly.

EXAMPLE | My cousin will spend the summer hiking in the Rockies.
She lives in Indiana.

My cousin, who lives in Indiana, will spend the summer hiking in the Rockies.

1. Scrabble has greatly increased my vocabulary.
   It is my favorite game.

   _____

   _____

2. Contestants on game shows often make fools of themselves.
   They may travel thousands of miles to play.

   _____

   _____

3. Arabic is a difficult language to learn.
   It has a complicated verb system.

   _____

   _____

The next sentences require **restrictive relative clauses.** Punctuate correctly.

EXAMPLE | He described a state of mind.
I have experienced it.

He described a state of mind that I have experienced.

4. The house is for sale.
   I was born in it.

   _____

   _____

5. My boss likes reports.
   They are clear and to the point.

   _____

   _____

6. People know how intelligent birds are.
   They have owned a bird.

   _____

   _____

PRACTICE 20

Combine each pair of sentences by changing one into a relative clause introduced by *who, which,* or *that.* Remember, *who* refers to persons, *that* refers to persons or things, and *which* refers to things.

Be careful of the punctuation. (Hint: *Which* clauses are usually set off by commas and *that* clauses are usually not.)

1. Her grandfather enjoys scuba diving.
   He is seventy-seven years old.

   _____

   _____

2. You just dropped an antique pitcher.
   It was worth two thousand dollars.

   _____

   _____

3. Parenthood has taught me acceptance, forgiveness, and love.
   It used to terrify me.

   _____

   _____

4. James Fenimore Cooper was expelled from college.
   He later became a famous American novelist.

   _____

   _____

5. The verb *to hector* means "to bully someone."
   It derives from a character in Greek literature.

   _____

   _____

PART E   Review and Practice

Before practicing some of the techniques of sentence variety discussed in this chapter, review them briefly:

1. Mix long and short sentences.

2. Add an occasional question, command, or exclamation.

3. Begin with an adverb: *Unfortunately,* the outfielder dropped the fly ball.

4. Begin with a prepositional phrase: *With great style,* the pitcher delivered a curve.

5. Join ideas with a compound predicate: The fans *roared and banged* their seats.

6. Join ideas with an *-ing* modifier: *Diving chin first onto the grass,* Johnson caught the ball.

7. Join ideas with a past participial modifier: *Frustrated by the call,* the batter kicked dirt onto home plate.

8. Join ideas with an appositive: Beer, *the cause of much rowdiness,* should not be sold at games.

9. Join ideas with a relative clause: Box seats, *which are hard to get for important games,* are frequently bought up by corporations.

Of course, the secret of achieving sentence variety is practice. Choose one, two, or three of these techniques to focus on and try them out in your writing. Revise your paragraphs and essays with an eye to sentence variety.

PRACTICE 21

Revise and then rewrite this essay, aiming for sentence variety. Vary the length and pattern of the sentences. Vary the beginnings of some sentences. Join two sentences in any way you wish, adding appropriate connecting words or dropping unnecessary words. Punctuate correctly.

Little Richard, the King of Rock 'n' Roll

With "A-Wop-Bop-A-Loo-Bop-A-Lop-Bam-Boom," Little Richard hit the U.S. music scene on September 14, 1955. It has never been the same since. He had almost insane energy. He wore flamboyant clothes. He defined the rebellious behavior at the heart of rock 'n' roll. He has influenced countless performers. These performers include the Beatles, Mick Jagger and the Rolling Stones, David Bowie, and the artist formerly known as Prince.

Richard Wayne Penniman was born on December 5, 1932, in Macon, Georgia. He was the third of thirteen children. He sang gospel music with his siblings. They were called the Penniman Singers. Richard was a wild and independent child. He left home at fourteen. During his teens, he traveled throughout Georgia with musical shows of all kinds. These included "Dr. Hudson's Medicine Show" and the "Tidy Jolly Steppers." He appeared in "Sugarfoot Sam from Alabam." Here he played "Princess Lavonne" and wore a dress. He sang with B. Brown and his orchestra. He was called "Little Richard" for the first time.

By 1955, Richard had developed his own musical style. It combined gospel with rhythm and blues. At its center was a wild scream of pure joy. He had developed a stage style as well. It combined outrageous costumes, a mile-high pompadour, thick mascara, manic piano-playing, and uninhibited hip-swinging. "Tutti Frutti" made him an overnight sensation. Over the next two years, he produced one hit after another. Fans will never forget such classics as "Long Tall Sally," "Slippin' and Slidin'," "Rip It Up," "Lucille," and "Good Golly Miss Molly."

Richard had a five-year lull. He resurfaced in 1962. He became a cult figure for the next thirteen years. He was called "The Prince of Clowns" and "The King of Rock 'n' Roll." His behavior on and off the stage became more and more outrageous. In one show, he would dress as Queen Elizabeth. In the next show, he would dress as the pope. He once wore a suit covered with small mirrors. It prevented him from sitting in a car. His followers treated him royally. He was seated on a throne and crowned with jewels. He was carried into restaurants like a king.

Between 1957 and 1962, and then again in 1975, Little Richard had a spiritual awakening. The demon of rock 'n' roll dropped alcohol, drugs, and sexual promiscuity. He took on a devout lifestyle. He became an evangelist. He went to work for a Bible company. During these times, he returned to singing the gospel music of his youth.

Little Richard is still going strong. In 1992, he released an album for children, *Shake It All About.* It featured extremely lively remakes of children's classics. It has sold more than 250,000 copies. It introduced Little Richard's musical style to a new generation. In 1993, he performed at the presidential inaugural celebration. In 1997, he received the Award of Merit at the American Music Awards. At that time, he proclaimed, "I never burned out. Rock still lifts my spirit and gives me joy and an energy force."

Little Richard, the King of Rock 'n' Roll

Little Richard, the King of Rock 'n' Roll

_____

_____

_____

_____

_____

_____

_____

_____

_____

_____

_____

_____

WRITING ASSIGNMENT

Study this photograph of a wedding; then write a paragraph explaining how this scene came about. Invent a story of how the couple met, their courtship, and their decision to marry.

In your topic sentence, state the general feeling or mood of the photograph. Then tell the story behind the picture. Revise your paragraph, paying special attention to sentence variety. Try to vary sentence types and lengths.

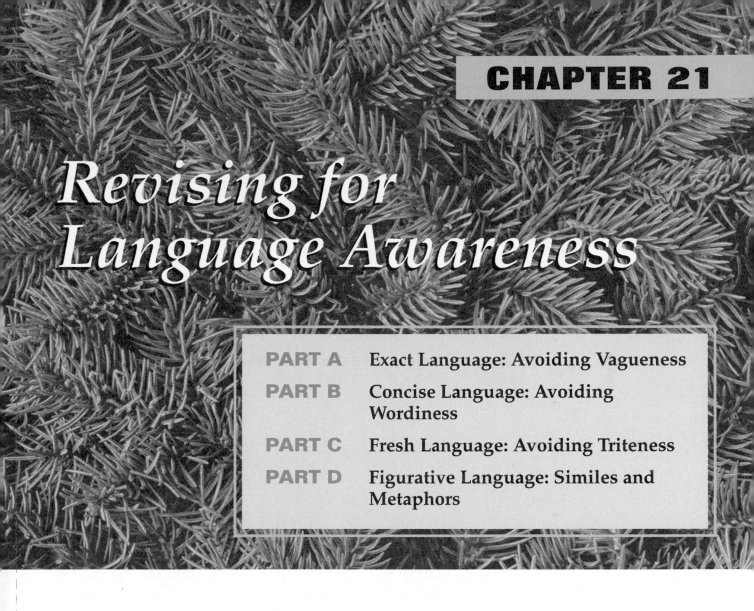

Revising for Language Awareness

Although it is important to write grammatically correct English, good writing is more than just correct writing. Good writing has life, excitement, and power. It captures the attention of the reader and compels him or her to read further.

The purpose of this chapter is to increase your awareness of the power of words and your skill at making them work for you. The secret of effective writing is **revision.** *Do not settle* for the first words that come to you, but go back over what you have written, replacing dull or confusing language with exact, concise, fresh, and sometimes figurative language.

PART A   Exact Language: Avoiding Vagueness

Good writers express their ideas as *exactly* as possible, choosing *specific, concrete,* and *vivid* words and phrases. They do not settle for vague terms and confusing generalities.

Which sentence in each of the following pairs gives the more *exact* information? That is, which uses specific and precise language? Which words in these sentences make them sharper and more vivid?

1. A car went around the corner.

2. A battered blue Mustang careened around the corner.

3. Janet quickly ate the main course.

4. Janet devoured the plate of ribs in two and a half minutes.

5. The president did things that caused problems.

6. The president's military spending increased the budget deficit.

■ Sentences 2, 4, and 6 contain language that is *exact*.

■ Sentence 2 is more exact than sentence 1 because *battered blue Mustang* gives more specific information than the general term *car*. The verb *careened* describes precisely how the car went around the corner, fast and recklessly.

■ What specific words does sentence 4 substitute for the more general words *ate, main course,* and *quickly* in sentence 3?

■ _____ , _____ , and

_____

Why are these terms more exact than those in sentence 3?

_____

_____

■ What words in sentence 6 make it clearer and more exact than sentence 5?

_____

_____

Concrete and detailed writing is usually exciting as well and makes us want to read on, as does this passage by Toni Morrison, who won the Nobel Prize for literature:

It is called the suburbs now, but when black people lived there it was called the Bottom. One road, shaded by beeches, oaks, maples, and chestnuts, connected it to the valley. The beeches are gone now, and so are the pear trees where children sat and yelled down through the blossoms at passersby. Generous funds have been allotted to level the stripped and faded buildings that clutter the road from Medallion up to the golf course. They are going to raze the Time and a Half Pool Hall, where feet in long tan shoes once pointed down from chair rungs. A steel ball will knock to dust Irene's Palace of Cosmetology, where women used to lean their heads back on sink trays and doze while Irene lathered Nu Nile into their hair. Men in khaki work clothes will pry loose the slats of Reba's Grill, where the owner cooked in her hat because she couldn't remember the ingredients without it.

—Toni Morrison, *Sula*

Now compare a similar account written in general and inexact language:

> It is called the suburbs now, but when black people lived there it was called the Bottom. One road, shaded by big trees, connected it to the valley. Many of the trees are gone now. Generous funds have been allotted to level the buildings on the road from Medallion up to the golf course. They are going to knock down the pool hall, the beauty parlor, and the restaurant.

You do not need a large vocabulary to write exactly and well, but you do need to work at finding the right words to fit each sentence. As you revise, cross out vague or dull words and phrases and replace them with more exact terms. When you are tempted to write *I feel good*, ask yourself exactly what *good* means in that sentence: *relaxed? proud? thin? in love?* When people walk by, do they *flounce, stride, lurch, wiggle,* or *sneak*? When they speak to you, do people *stammer, announce, babble, murmur,* or *coo*? Question yourself as you revise; then choose the right words to fit that particular sentence.

PRACTICE 1

Lively verbs are a great asset to any writer. The following sentences contain four overused general verbs—*to walk, to see, to eat,* and *to be*. In each case, replace the general verb in parentheses with a more exact verb *chosen to fit the context of the sentence.* Use a different verb in every sentence. Consult a dictionary or thesaurus* if you wish.

EXAMPLES   In no particular hurry, we __strolled__ (walked) through the botanical gardens.

Jane __fidgets__ (is) at her desk and watches the clock.

1. With guns drawn, three police officers _____ (walked) toward the door of the warehouse.

2. As we stared in fascination, an orange lizard _____ (walked) up the wall.

3. The four-year-old _____ (walked) onto the patio in her mother's high-heeled shoes.

4. A furious customer _____ (walked) into the manager's office.

5. Two people who _____ (saw) the accident must testify in court.

6. We crouched for hours in the underbrush just to _____ (see) a rare white fox.

7. Three makeshift wooden rafts were _____ (seen) off the coast this morning.

8. For two years, the zoologist _____ (saw) the behavior of bears in the wild.

---

* A thesaurus is a book of *synonyms*—words that have the same or similar meanings.

9. There was the cat, delicately _____ (eating) my fern!

10. Senator Gorman astounded the guests by loudly _____ (eating) his soup.

11. All through the movie, she _____ (ate) hard candies in the back row.

12. Within seconds, Dan had bought two tacos from a street vendor and _____ (eaten) them both.

13. During rush hour, the temperature hit 98 degrees, and dozens of cars _____ (were) on the highway.

14. A young man _____ (is) on a stretcher in the emergency room.

15. Workers who _____ (are) at desks all day should make special efforts to exercise.

16. Professor Nuzzo _____ (was) in front of the blackboard, excited about this new solution to the math problem.

PRACTICE 2

The following sentences contain dull, vague language. Revise them using vivid verbs, specific nouns, and colorful adjectives. As the examples show, you may add and delete words.

EXAMPLES   A dog lies down in the shade.

A mangy collie flops down in the shade of a parked car.

My head hurts.

My head throbs.

I have shooting pains in the left side of my head.

1. Everything about the man looked mean.

_____

_____

2. I feel good today for several reasons.

_____

_____

3. A woman in unusual clothes went down the street.

_____

_____

4. The sunlight made the yard look pretty.

_____

_____

5. What the company did bothered the townspeople.

_____

_____

6. The pediatrician's waiting room was crowded.

_____

_____

7. As soon as he gets home from work, he hears the voice of his pet asking for dinner.

_____

_____

8. The noises of construction filled the street.

_____

_____

9. When I was sick, you were helpful.

_____

_____

10. This college does things that make the students feel bad.

_____

_____

PRACTICE 3

A word that works effectively in one sentence might not work in another sentence. In searching for the right word, always consider the **context** of the sentence into which the word must fit. Read each of the following sentences for meaning. Then circle the word in parentheses that *most exactly fits* the context of the sentence.

EXAMPLE | The alchemist cautiously (threw, (dripped,) held) the liquid mercury onto copper in order to make it look like gold.

1. Alchemy, an early form of chemistry, was a (course, way, science) that flourished from ancient times until around 1700.

2. It was based on the (knowledge, belief, fact) that a metal could be converted into another element.

3. Alchemists considered gold the (perfect, nicest, shiniest) metal.

4. Therefore, their goal was to (transform, redo, make) base metals, like lead, into gold.

5. They searched (eagerly, high and low, lots) for the "philosopher's stone," the formula that would make this change possible.

6. All "philosopher's stones" consisted of sulphur and mercury; the trick was to discover the proper way to (combine, destroy, mix up) the two.

7. Over time, alchemy incorporated various (aspects, things, stuff) of astrology and magic.

8. For example, certain metals were (the same as, equated with, sort of like) specific heavenly bodies—gold with the sun or silver with the moon.

9. One famous alchemist proudly (said, muttered, boasted) that he could magically transform winter into summer.

10. Many alchemists went to work for greedy princes and kings, who always (liked, lusted for, thought about) more gold.

11. It was dangerous work though; more than one alchemist was (done away with, executed, knocked off) because he could not produce gold.

12. In their search for gold, however, some alchemists (foolishly, hopefully, accidentally) made valid scientific discoveries that led to the development of modern chemistry.

PRACTICE 4

The following paragraph begins a mystery story. Using specific and vivid language, revise the paragraph to make it as exciting as possible. Then finish the story; be careful to avoid vague language.

The weather was bad. I was in the house alone, with a funny feeling that something was going to happen. Someone knocked at the door. I got up to answer it and found someone outside. She looked familiar, but I didn't know from where or when. Then I recognized her as a person from my past. I let her in although I was not sure I had done the right thing.

_____

_____

_____

_____

_____

_____

_____

_____

_____

_____

_____

PART B   Concise Language: Avoiding Wordiness

Concise writing comes quickly to the point. It avoids **wordiness**—unnecessary and repetitious words that add nothing to the meaning.

Which sentence in each of the following pairs is more _concise?_ That is, which does _not_ contain unnecessary words?

1. Because of the fact that the watch was inexpensive in price, he bought it.

2. Because the watch was inexpensive, he bought it.

3. In my opinion I think that the financial aid system at Ellensville Junior College is in need of reform.

4. The financial aid system at Ellensville Junior College needs reform.

5. On October 10, in the fall of 1999, we learned the true facts about the robbery.

6. On October 10, 1999, we learned the facts about the robbery.

■ Sentences 2, 4, and 6 are _concise_ whereas sentences 1, 3, and 5 are _wordy._

■ In sentence 1, _because of the fact that_ is really a _wordy_ way of saying _because. In price_ simply repeats information already given by the word _inexpensive._

■ The writer of sentence 3 undercuts the point with the wordy apology of _in my opinion I think._ As a general rule, leave out such qualifiers and simply state the opinion; but if you do use them, use either _in my opinion_ or _I think_, not both! Sentence 4 replaces _is in need of_ with one direct verb, _needs._

■ _In the fall of_ in sentence 5 is _redundant;_ it repeats information already given by which word?

■ Why is the word *true* also eliminated in sentence 6?

_____

Concise writing avoids wordiness, unnecessary repetition, and padding. Of course, conciseness *does not mean* writing short, bare sentences, but simply cutting out all deadwood and never using fifteen words when ten will do.

PRACTICE 5

The following sentences are *wordy*. Make them more *concise* by crossing out or replacing unnecessary words or by combining two sentences into one concise sentence. Rewrite each new sentence on the lines beneath, capitalizing and punctuating correctly.

EXAMPLES

The U.S. Census uncovers many interesting facts that have a lot of truth to them.

The U.S. Census uncovers many interesting facts.

In the year 1810, Philadelphia was called the cigar capital of the United States. The reason why was because the census reported that the city produced sixteen million cigars each year.

In 1810, Philadelphia was called the cigar capital of the United States because the

census reported that the city produced sixteen million cigars each year.

1. The Constitution requires and says that the federal government of the United States must take a national census every ten years.

_____

_____

2. At first, the original function of the census was to ensure fair taxation and representation.

_____

_____

3. Since the first count in 1790, however, the census has been controversial. There have been several reasons why it has been controversial.

_____

_____

4. One reason why is because there are always some people who aren't included.

_____

_____

5. The 1990 census, for example, missed almost five million people, many of whom were homeless with no place to live.

_____

_____

6. For the 2000 census, the Census Bureau considered using statistical methods. The statistical methods would have been used instead of the traditional direct head count.

_____

_____

7. The Bureau would have directly counted about 90 percent of U.S. residents who live in the United States and then estimated the number and characteristics of the remainder of the rest of the people.

_____

_____

8. Those who opposed the idea believed that in their opinion statistical methods would have introduced new errors that were mistaken into the count.

_____

_____

9. The distribution of $100 billion in money, as well as the balance of power in the House of Representatives, depended on how and in which manner the census was conducted.

_____

_____

10. Despite controversy, the U.S. census still continues to serve a beneficial purpose that is for the good of the United States.

_____

_____

PRACTICE 6

Rewrite this essay _concisely,_ cutting out all unnecessary words. Reword or combine sentences if you wish, but do not alter the meaning.

Dr. Alice Hamilton, Medical Pioneer

At the age of forty years old, Dr. Alice Hamilton became a pioneer in the field

of industrial medicine. In 1910, the governor of Illinois appointed her to investigate rumors that people who were doing the work in Chicago's paint factories were dying from lead poisoning. The result of her investigation was the first state law that was passed to protect workers.

The following year, the U.S. Department of Labor hired this woman, Dr. Hamilton to study industrial illness throughout the country of the United States. In the next decade, she researched and studied many occupational diseases, including tuberculosis among quarry workers and silicosis—clogged lungs—among sandblasters. To gather information, Dr. Hamilton went to the workplace—deep in mines, quarries, and underwater tunnels. She also spoke to the workers in their homes where they lived.

With great zeal, Dr. Hamilton spread her message about poor health conditions on the job. What happened with her reports is that they led to new safety regulations, workmen's compensation insurance, and improved working conditions in many industries. She wrote many popular articles and spoke to groups of interested citizens. In the year of 1919, she became the first woman to hold courses and teach at Harvard University. Her textbook which she wrote, *Industrial Poisons in the U.S.,* became the standard book on the subject. By the time she died in 1970—she was 101—she had done much to improve the plight of many working people. The reason why she is remembered today is because she cared at a time when many others seemed not to care at all.

PART C   Fresh Language: Avoiding Triteness

Fresh writing uses original and lively words. It avoids **clichés,** those tired and trite expressions that have lost their power from overuse.

Which sentence in each pair that follows contains fewer expressions that you have heard or read many times before?

1. Some people can relate to the hustle and bustle of city life.
2. Some people thrive on the energy and motion of city life.

3. This book is worth its weight in gold to the car owner.
4. This book can save the car owner hundreds of dollars a year in repairs.

■ You probably found that sentences 2 and 4 contained fresher language. Which words and phrases in sentences 1 and 3 have you heard or seen before, in conversation, on TV, or in magazines and newspapers? List them:

_____

_____

Clichés and trite expressions like the following have become so familiar that they have almost no impact on the reader. Avoid them. Say what you mean in your own words:

Cliché: She is pretty as a picture.

Fresh: Her amber eyes and wild red hair mesmerize me.

Or occasionally, play with a cliché and turn it into fresh language:

Cliché: . . . as American as apple pie.

Fresh: . . . as American as a Big Mac.

Cliché: The grass is always greener on the other side of the fence.

Fresh: "The grass is always greener over the septic tank."—Erma Bombeck

The following is a partial list of trite expressions to avoid. Add to it any others that you overuse in your writing.

Trite Expressions	
at a loss for words	in this day and age
at this point in time	last but not least
better late than never	living hand to mouth
break the ice	one in a million
cold cruel world	out of this world
cool, hot, awesome	sad but true
cry your eyes out	tried and true
easier said than done	under the weather
free as a bird	work like a dog
hustle and bustle	green with envy

PRACTICE 7

Cross out clichés and trite expressions in the following sentences and replace them with fresh and exact language of your own.

1. In 1929, toy dealer Edwin S. Lowe came across people having more fun than

a barrel of monkeys while playing a game at a carnival in rural Georgia.

2. A leader called out each and every number, and the players used beans to cover the matching numbers on their cards.

3. The winners yelled "Beano!" at the top of their lungs when they had filled in a row of numbers.

4. According to the carnival owner, a stranger had brought the game from Europe, so it went without saying that no one owned the game.

5. Quick as a wink, Lowe saw the game was a winner.

6. As soon as he returned home, the businessman, who was as sharp as a tack, began testing beano out on friends.

7. One night, instead of "Beano!" a guest who was beside himself with excitement shouted out, "Bingo!"

8. Lowe went on to market the game as Bingo, and it sold like crazy.

9. Soon many nonprofit organizations were holding bingo tournaments as a tried and true method of raising funds.

10. Because Lowe had produced only twenty-four different cards, too many people were cleaning up.

11. Therefore, Lowe paid a mathematics professor an awesome amount to develop six thousand cards, each with a different combination of numbers.

12. By 1934, hundreds of thousands of Americans were playing bingo like there was no tomorrow.

PART D Figurative Language: Similes and Metaphors

One way to add sparkle and exactness to your writing is to use an occasional simile or metaphor. A **simile** is a comparison of two things using the word *like* or *as:*

> "He was *as ugly as* a wart." —Anne Sexton
>
> "The frozen twigs of the huge tulip poplar next to the hill clack in the cold *like* tinsnips." —Annie Dillard

A **metaphor** is a similar comparison without the word *like* or *as:*

> "My soul is a dark forest." —D. H. Lawrence
>
> Love is a virus.

■ The power of similes and metaphors comes partly from the surprise of comparing two apparently unlike things. A well-chosen simile or metaphor can convey a lot of information in very few words.

■ To compare a person to a wart, as Sexton does, lets us know quickly just how ugly that person is. And to say that *twigs clack like tinsnips* describes the sound so precisely that we can almost hear it.

■ What do you think D. H. Lawrence means by his metaphor? In what ways is a person's soul like a *dark forest?*

_____

_____

■ The statement *love is a virus* tells us something about the writer's attitude toward love. What is it? In what ways is love like a virus?

_____

_____

_____

Similes and metaphors should not be overused; however, once in a while, they can be a delightful addition to a paper that is also exact, concise, and fresh.

PRACTICE 8

The author of the following paragraph contrasts a fat priest and his thin parishioners. He uses at least one simile and two metaphors in his description. Underline the simile and circle the metaphors.

He was a large, juicy man, soft and sappy as a melon, and this sweet roundness made him appear spoiled and self-indulgent, especially when contrasted with the small, spare, sticklike peons* who comprised his parish. . . . Everything about them, the peons, was withered and bone-dry. Everything about him was full and fleshy and wet. They were mummies. He was a whale, beached upon the desert sands, draped in black to mourn his predicament.

—Bill Porterfield, *Texas Rhapsody*

_____

* peons: farm workers or laborers of the southwest United States or Latin America

PRACTICE 9

Think of several similes to complete each sentence that follows. Be creative! Then underline your favorite simile, the one that best completes each sentence.

EXAMPLE   My English class is like   an orchestra.
                                      the Everglades.
                                      an action movie.
                                      a vegetable garden.

1. Job hunting is like _____   3. Writing well is like _____

    _____   _____

    _____   _____

    _____   _____

2. My room looks like _____   4. Marriage is like _____

    _____   _____

    _____   _____

    _____   _____

PRACTICE 10

Think of several metaphors to complete each sentence that follows. Jot down three or four ideas, and then underline the metaphor that best completes each sentence.

EXAMPLE   Love is   a blood transfusion.
                      a sunrise.
                      a magic mirror.
                      a roller coaster ride.

1. Television is _____   3. My car is _____

    _____   _____

    _____   _____

    _____   _____

2. Registration is _____   4. Courage is _____

    _____   _____

    _____   _____

    _____   _____

WRITING ASSIGNMENTS

1. Good writing can be done on almost any subject if the writer approaches the subject with openness and with "new eyes." Take a piece of fruit or a vegetable—a lemon, a green pepper, a cherry tomato. Examine it as if for the first time. Feel its texture and parts, smell it, weigh it in your palm.

   Now capture your experience of the fruit or vegetable in words. First jot down words and ideas, or freewrite, aiming for the most *exact* description possible. Don't settle for the first words you think of. Keep writing. Then go back over what you have written, underlining the most exact and powerful writing. Compose a topic sentence and draft a paragraph that conveys your unique experience of the fruit or vegetable.

2. In the paragraph that follows, Don DeLillo describes a "small" experience in such rich, exact detail that it becomes alive and intriguing to the reader. Read his paragraph, underlining language that strikes you as especially *exact* and *fresh.* Can you spot the two similes? Can you find any especially vivid adjectives or unusual verbs?

   You have to know the feel of a baseball in your hand, going back awhile, connecting many things, before you can understand why a man would sit in a chair at four in the morning holding such an object, clutching it—how it fits the palm so reassuringly, the corked center making it buoyant in the hand, and the rough spots on an old ball, the marked skin, how an idle thumb likes to worry the scuffed horsehide. You squeeze a baseball. You kind of juice it or milk it. The resistance of the packed material makes you want to press harder. There's an equilibrium, an agreeable animal tension between the hard leather object and the sort of clawed hand, veins stretching with the effort. And the feel of raised seams across the fingertips, cloth contours like road bumps under the knuckle joints—how the whorled cotton can be seen as a magnified thumbprint. . . . The ball was smudged green near the Spalding trademark; it was still wearing a small green bruise where it had struck a pillar, according to the history that came with it—flaked paint from a bolted column in the left-field stands embedded in the surface of the ball.

   —Don DeLillo, *Underworld*

   Write a paragraph or essay in which you also describe a brief but interesting experience (or event), perhaps a time you observed, admired, or truly studied an object or person. As you freewrite or brainstorm, try to capture the most precise and minute details of what you experienced or what happened. Now revise your piece of writing, making the language as *exact*, *concise*, and *fresh* as you can.

3. The photo above shows a painting by Milan Kunc called "Crocodile Village." Look closely at this painting, noting the small huts on the crocodile's back, the man in the boat, and the unusual position of the moon. What overall impression or mood does the painting communicate to you? Is it peaceful, threatening, magical?

Now write a two-paragraph composition discussing the painting. In the first paragraph, describe the painting, very specifically pointing out important details. In the second paragraph, explain what you think the painter is trying to convey by creating this picture. As you revise, make your writing as *exact*, *concise*, and *fresh* as possible so that a reader who has not seen the painting has a clear sense of it.

CHAPTER 22

Putting Your Revision Skills to Work

In Units 2 and 3, you learned to **revise** basic paragraphs, and in Unit 4, you learned to revise essays. All revising requires that you rethink and rewrite with such questions as these in mind:

Can a reader understand and follow my ideas?

Is my topic sentence or thesis statement clear?

Does the body of my paragraph or essay fully support the topic or thesis statement?

Does my paragraph or essay have unity? That is, does every sentence relate to the main idea?

Does my paragraph or essay have coherence? That is, does it follow a logical order and guide the reader from point to point?

Does my writing conclude, not just leave off?

Of course, the more writing techniques you learn, the more options you have as you revise. Unit 5 has moved beyond the basics to matters of style: consistency and parallelism, sentence variety, and clear, exact language. This chapter will guide you again through the revision process, adding questions like the following to your list:

Are my verb tenses and pronouns consistent?

Have I used parallel structure to highlight parallel ideas?

Have I varied the length and type of my sentences?

Is my language exact, concise, and fresh?

Many writers first revise and rewrite with questions like these in mind. They do *not* worry about grammar and minor errors at this stage. Then in a separate, final process, they **proofread*** for spelling and grammatical errors.

---

* For practice in proofreading for particular errors, see individual chapters in Units 6 and 7. For practice in proofreading for mixed errors, see Chapter 36, "Putting Your Proofreading Skills to Work."

Here are two sample paragraphs by students, showing the first draft, the revisions made by the student, and the revised draft of each. Each revision has been numbered and explained to give you a clear idea of the thinking process involved.

Writing Sample 1

First Draft

I like to give my best performance. I must relax completely before a show. I often know ahead of time what choreography I will use and what I'll sing, so I can concentrate on relaxing completely. I usually do this by reading, etc. I always know my parts perfectly. Occasionally I look through the curtain to watch the people come in. This can make you feel faint, but I reassure myself and say I know everything will be okay.

Revisions

① In order
~~I like~~ to give my best performance, I must relax completely before a

② and vocals
show. I often know ahead of time what choreography I will use, and ~~what~~

③ during that long, last hour before curtain,   ④
~~I'll sing;~~ so I can concentrate on relaxing ~~completely.~~ I usually do this by

⑤ an action-packed mystery, but sometimes I joke with the
other performers or just walk around backstage.   ⑦ peek
reading, ~~etc.~~ (I always know my parts perfectly,) Occasionally I ~~look~~

⑥   audience file   ⑧ me
through the curtain to watch the ~~people come~~ in. This can make ~~you~~ feel

⑨ "Vickie," I say, "the minute you're out there
singing to the people, everything will be okay."
faint, but I reassure myself ~~and say I know everything will be okay.~~

Reasons for Revisions

1. Combine two short sentences. (sentence variety)

2. Make *choreography* and *vocals* parallel and omit unnecessary words. (parallelism)

3. Make time order clear: First discuss what I've done during the days before the performance, and then discuss the hour before performance. (time order)

4. Drop *completely*, which repeats the word used in the first sentence. (avoid wordiness)

5. This is important! Drop *etc.*, add more details, and give examples. (add examples)

6. This idea belongs earlier in the paragraph—with what I've done during the days before the performance. (order)

7. Use more specific and interesting language in this sentence. (exact language)

8. Use the first person singular pronouns *I* and *me* consistently throughout the paragraph. (consistent person)

9. Dull—use a direct quotation, the actual words I say to myself. (exact language, sentence variety)

Revised Draft

In order to give my best performance, I must relax completely before a show. I often know ahead of time what choreography and vocals I will use, and I always know my parts perfectly, so during that long, last hour before curtain, I can concentrate on relaxing. I usually do this by reading an action-packed mystery, but sometimes I joke with the other performers or just walk around backstage. Occasionally I peek through the curtain to watch the audience file in. This can make me feel faint, but I reassure myself. "Vickie," I say, "the minute you're out there singing to the people, everything will be okay."

—Victoria DeWindt (Student)

Writing Sample 2

First Draft

My grandparents' house contained whole rooms that my parents' house did not (pantry, a parlor, a den where Grandpa kept his loot). The furniture and things always fascinated me. Best of all was the lake behind the house. Grandpa said that Evergreen Lake had grown old just like Grandma and him, that the game fish are gone and only a few bluegills remained. But one day he let me fish. No one thought I'd catch anything, but I caught a foot-long goldfish! Grandpa said it was a goddam carp, but it was a goldfish to me and I nearly fainted with ecstasy.

Revisions

(1) Visiting my grandparents at Evergreen Lake was always an exotic adventure.

(2) Their cavernous (3)

My grandparents' house contained whole rooms that my parents' house

(4) —a pantry,   with a big black grand piano, and   (5) The rooms

did not (pantry, a parlor, a den where Grandpa kept his loot). The furniture

were furnished with musty deer heads, hand-painted candlesticks, and velvet drapes.

and things always fascinated me. Best of all was the lake behind the house.

Grandpa said that Evergreen Lake had grown old just like Grandma and

(6) were

him, that the game fish are gone and only a few bluegills remained. But one

(7) Add new section below*

day he let me fish. No one thought I'd catch anything, but I caught a foot-

B

long goldfish. Grandpa said it was a goddam carp, but it was a goldfish to me,

(8)

and I nearly fainted with ecstasy.

*Add: But one day he rigged up a pole for me and tossed my line into the water. I sat motionless for several hours, waiting for a miracle. Suddenly I felt a tug on my line. I screeched and yanked upward. By the time Grandpa arrived on the dock, there on the surface lazily moving its fins was the biggest goldfish I had ever seen, nearly a foot long! Grandpa reached down with the net and scooped the huge orange fish out of the water. "Bring down the pail," he shouted. "It's a goddam carp."

Reasons for Revisions

1. No topic sentence; add one. (topic sentence)

2. Now *grandparents'* repeats the first sentence; use *their.* (pronoun substitution)

3. Add a good descriptive word to give the feeling of the house. (exact language)

4. Expand this; add more details. (details, exact language)

5. More details and examples needed for support! Try to capture the "exotic" feeling of the house. (details, exact language)

6. Verb shifts to present tense; use past tense consistently. (consistent tense)

7. This section is weak. Tell the story of the goldfish; try to create the sense of adventure this had for me as a kid. Quote Grandpa? (details, exact language, direct quotation)

8. Revised paragraph is getting long. Consider breaking into two paragraphs, one on the house and one on the lake.

Revised Draft

Visiting my grandparents at Evergreen Lake was always an exotic adventure. Their cavernous house contained whole rooms that my parents' house did not—a pantry, a parlor with a big black grand piano, and a den where Grandpa kept his loot. The rooms were furnished with musty deer heads, hand-painted candlesticks, and velvet drapes.

Best of all was the lake behind the house. Grandpa said that Evergreen Lake had grown old just like Grandma and him, that the game fish were gone and only a few bluegills remained. But one day he rigged up a pole for me and tossed my line into the water. I sat motionless for several hours, waiting for a miracle. Suddenly I felt a tug on my line. I screeched and yanked upward. By the time Grandpa arrived on the dock, there on the surface lazily moving its fins was the biggest goldfish I had ever seen, nearly a foot long! Grandpa reached down with the net and scooped the huge orange fish out of the water. "Bring down the pail," he shouted. "It's a goddam carp." But it was a goldfish to me, and I nearly fainted with ecstasy.

PRACTICE

Because revising, like writing, is a personal process, the best practice is to revise your own paragraphs and essays. Nevertheless, here are two first drafts that need revising.

Revise each one *as if you had written it.* Mark your revisions on the first draft, using and building on the good parts, crossing out unnecessary words, rewriting unclear or awkward sentences, adding details, and perhaps reordering parts. Then, recopy your final draft on the lines. Especially, ask yourself these questions:

Are my verb tenses and pronouns consistent?

Have I used parallel structure?

Have I varied the length and type of my sentences?

Is my language exact, concise, and fresh?

First Draft A

Home

In the South, the redbird is considered a good omen. It is not surprising to see a pair of redbirds nesting in the highest corner of the porch at 1314 Rally Road Lane. They are just two of the many visitors who found comfort under that roof. Some are drawn by the freshly baked bread that is offered to every guest. Its smell seemed to fill the house with fruity bakery scents. Others were drawn by the warmth of the owner. Her name is Louise. She stood five feet six inches. She weighs 150 pounds. She had skin of bronze and her heart was made gold. She has prominent frown lines around her nose and on her forehead. These might suggest to a stranger that she is not to be messed with. But looks can be deceiving. Louise is a friendly woman. Humor is another quality she has, and she is accepting of everyone. She teaches her children to be the same. She is careful to guide them with a gentle but steady hand. Louise's love is contagious. The little green house with pretty colored shutters welcomes a constant stream of friends, neighbors, and even nesting birds. Family members come too.

—Based on work by Linda Lupe, Student

Revised Draft A

Home

_____

_____

_____

_____

_____

_____

_____

_____

_____

_____

_____

First Draft B

Breaking the Yo-Yo Syndrome

For years, I was a yo-yo dieter. I bounced from fad diets to eating binges when I ate a lot. This leaves you tired and with depression. Along the way, though, I learned a few things. As a result, I personally will never go on a diet again for the rest of my life.

First of all, diets are unhealthy. Some of the low carbohydrate diets are high in fat. Accumulating fat through meat, eggs, and the eating of cheese can raise blood levels of cholesterol and led to artery and heart disease. Other diets are too high in protein and can cause kidney ailments, and other things can go wrong with your body, too. Most diets also leave you deficient in essential vitamins and minerals that are necessary to health, such as calcium and iron.

In addition, diets are short-term. I lose about ten pounds. I wind up gaining more weight than I originally lost. I also get sick and tired of the restricted diet. On one diet, I ate cabbage soup for breakfast, lunch, and dinner. You are allowed to eat some fruit on day one, some vegetables on day two, and so on, but mostly you are supposed to eat cabbage soup. After a week, I never want to see a bowl of cabbage soup again. Because the diet was nutritionally unbalanced, I ended up craving bread, meat, and all the other foods I am not supposed to eat. Moreover, in the short-term, all one loses is water. You cannot lose body fat unless you reduce regularly and at a steady rate over a long period of time.

The last diet I try was a fat-free diet. On this diet I actually gained weight while dieting. I am surprised to discover that you can gain weight on a fat-free diet snacking on fat-free cookies, ice cream, and cheese and crackers. I also learn that the body needs fat—in particular, the unsaturated fat in foods like olive oil, nuts, avocados, and salad dressings. If a dieter takes in too little fat, you are constantly hungry. Furthermore, the body thinks it is starving, so it makes every effort to try to conserve fat, which makes it much harder for one to lose weight.

In place of fad diets, I now follow a long-range plan. It is sensible and improved my health. I eat three well-balanced meals, exercise daily, and am meeting regularly with my support group for weight control. I am much happier and don't weigh as much than I used to be.

Revised Draft B

Breaking the Yo-Yo Syndrome

_____

_____

_____

_____

_____

_____

_____

_____

_____

_____

_____

_____

_____

_____

_____

_____

_____

_____

_____

_____

_____

_____

_____

_____

Revised Draft B

Examine the Bright (or Dark) Side of Family Life

Revising is the key to all good writing—taking the time to sit down, reread, and rethink what you have written. In this unit, you have practiced revising for consistent verb tense, consistent person, parallelism, sentence variety, and language awareness.

In your group or class, read this student's essay, aloud if possible. Underline the parts that strike you as especially effective, and put a check by anything that might need revising.

Family Secrets: Don't You Go Talking

(1) Most families have secrets, but in some families, the secrets become too important. They shape the way people think about themselves and his or her relatives. What people are not supposed to talk about can seem more real than official family history. This was true in my family. Yet when I think about some of our secrets now, they don't seem much like secrets anymore.

(2) Psychologists say that "most secrets arise out of shame." The fact that my father drank excessively brought about a certain family shame. Quiet comments were made protesting his behavior, but no one dared discuss his drinking freely. In fact, I can remember "that look" my mother would give me, meaning "Don't you go talking about nothing that goes on in this house." I couldn't understand that. It was not as if he drank at home where no one but the family could see the staggering or hear the loud profanities. Yet because he was a member of the family, we were expected to turn a blind side.

(3) Secrets help create family history, and since history is said to repeat itself, I feel it safe to say that behavior kept hidden in family secrets may be hereditary. For instance, I have heard talk among family members of an aunt who loved to gamble. As the story goes, Aunt Sally loved to gamble so much that in her ninth month of pregnancy she left her home in California and traveled to Las Vegas by bus. She wanted to play the slot machines. Aunt Sally went into labor. She refused to stop gambling. The contractions were six minutes apart. She was heavily involved in a poker game. Still she refused to leave. The labor pains were four minutes apart. Aunt Sally continued to play. She was enjoying a winning streak. She intended to see it out.

(4) Four hours and $63,000 later, Aunt Sally gives birth to a baby boy. He weighs eight pounds, eight ounces. As luck would have it, her winning hand holds a pair of eights. Aunt Sally's left palm supposedly grips one particular chip so tightly during each contraction that the imprint drew blood. Today that baby born in Vegas is said to be a gambler among gamblers. In the palm of his left hand is a birthmark, red in color and perfectly round in shape just like a poker chip. His name,

by the way, is Chip. I don't see how that story can be a family secret, yet after years of not being able to talk freely about certain things, a discomfort remains when these things are in fact discussed.

(5) Shame over a particular event is defined by the values of the era in which the event takes place. Although it was an earlier generation that insisted years ago that certain things need not be openly discussed in my family, the shame lives on, outliving the people. The shame is inherited, if you will. Almost 115 years ago, my great grandfather supposedly stole a handful of rice. Because of shame, I was never supposed to know about it. The story is a family secret. I guess I understand why. After all, we don't want great grand-dad's picture showing up on "America's Most Wanted" anytime now.

—Jo-Ann Jenkins (Student)

1. How effective is Ms. Jenkins's essay?

_____ Strong thesis statement?   _____ Good supporting details?

_____ Logical organization?   _____ Effective conclusion?

2. What do you like best about this essay? What details or sections most command your attention or make you think?

3. Although this student writes about her personal family history, she is also *thinking about the meaning* of that experience and making sense of it for herself and the reader. What ideas about family secrets does this essay include? Do you agree or disagree?

4. Does your family have secrets? What effect does this have on you or other family members?

5. Do you spot any instance of inconsistent person (paragraph 1) or wordiness (paragraph 4)?

6. Are all the verb tenses correct, or do you notice any inconsistent tense?

7. Are there any places, especially in paragraph 3, where choppy sentences detracted from the excellent content?

8. Can you spot any error patterns (the same error two or more times) that this student should watch out for?

GROUP WORK

In your group, revise Ms. Jenkins's essay as if it were your own. First, decide what problems need attention. Then rewrite those parts, sentence by sentence, aiming for a truly fine paper. Share your revision with the class, explaining why you made the changes you did.

 WRITING AND REVISING IDEAS

1. Examine the bright (or dark) side of family life.

2. Discuss the effects of living with a secret or a lie.

UNIT 6

Reviewing the Basics

CHAPTER 23

The Simple Sentence

PART A	Defining and Spotting Subjects
PART B	Spotting Prepositional Phrases
PART C	Defining and Spotting Verbs

PART A — Defining and Spotting Subjects

Every sentence must contain two basic elements: a **subject** and a **verb.**

A subject is the *who* or *what* word that performs the action or the *who* or *what* word about which a statement is made:

> 1. Three *hunters* tramped through the woods.
>
> 2. The blue *truck* belongs to Ralph.

■ In sentence 1, *hunters,* the *who* word, performs the action—"tramped through the woods."

■ In sentence 2, *truck* is the *what* word about which a statement is made— "belongs to Ralph."

■ Some sentences have more than one subject, joined by *and:*

> 3. Her *aunt and uncle* love country music.

■ In sentence 3, *aunt and uncle,* the *who* words, perform the action—they "love country music."

■ *Aunt and uncle* is called a **compound subject.**

Sometimes an *-ing* word can be the subject of a sentence:

> 4. *Reading* strains my eyes.

■ *Reading* is the *what* word that performs the action—"strains my eyes."

PRACTICE 1

Circle the subjects in these sentences.

1. Do you know the origin and customs of Kwanzaa?

2. This African-American holiday celebrates black heritage and lasts for seven days—from December 26 through January 1.

3. Maulana Karenga introduced Kwanzaa to America in 1966.

4. In Swahili, Kwanzaa means "first fruits of the harvest."

5. During the holiday, families share simple meals of foods from the Caribbean, Africa, South America, and the American South.

6. Specific foods have special meanings.

7. For instance, certain fruits and vegetables represent the products of group effort.

8. Another important symbol is corn, which stands for children.

9. At each dinner, celebrants light a black, red, or green candle and discuss one of the seven principles of Kwanzaa.

10. These seven principles are unity, self-determination, collective work and responsibility, cooperative economics, purpose, creativity, and faith.

PART B   Spotting Prepositional Phrases

One group of words that may confuse you as you look for subjects is the prepositional phrase. A **prepositional phrase** contains a **preposition** (a word like *at, in, of, from,* and so forth) and its **object.**

Preposition	Object
at	the beach
on	time
of	the students

The object of a preposition *cannot be* the subject of a sentence. Therefore, spotting and crossing out the prepositional phrases will help you find the subject.

> 1. The sweaters in the window look handmade.
>
> 2. The sweaters ~~in the window~~ look handmade.
>
> 3. ~~On Tuesday,~~ a carton ~~of oranges~~ was left ~~on the porch.~~

■ In sentence 1, you might have trouble finding the subject. But once the prepositional phrase is crossed out in sentence 2, the subject, *sweaters*, is easy to spot.

■ In sentence 3, once the prepositional phrases are crossed out, the subject, *carton,* is easy to spot.

Here are some common prepositions that you should know:

Common Prepositions			
about	before	in	through
above	behind	into	to
across	between	like	toward
after	by	near	under
along	during	of	until
among	for	on	up
at	from	over	with

PRACTICE 2

Cross out the prepositional phrases in each sentence. Then circle the subject of the sentence.

1. From 6 A.M. until 10 A.M., Angel works out.

2. Local buses for Newark leave every hour.

3. Three of my friends take singing lessons.

4. That man between Ralph and Cynthia is the famous actor Hank the Hunk.

5. Near the door, a pile of laundry sits in a basket.

6. Toward evening, the houses across the river disappear in the thick fog.

7. Before class, Helena and I meet for coffee.

8. In one corner of the lab, beakers of colored liquid bubbled and boiled.

PART C   Defining and Spotting Verbs

Action Verbs

In order to be complete, every sentence must contain a **verb.** One kind of verb, called an **action verb,** expresses the action that the subject is performing:

> 1. The star quarterback *fumbled.*
> 2. The carpenters *worked* all day, but the bricklayers *went* home early.

■ In sentence 1, the action verb is *fumbled.*

■ In sentence 2, the action verbs are *worked* and *went.**

Linking Verbs

Another kind of verb, called a **linking verb,** links the subject to words that describe or identify it:

> 3. Don *is* a fine mathematician.
> 4. This fabric *feels* rough and scratchy.

■ In sentence 3, the verb *is* links the subject *Don* with the noun *mathematician.*

■ In sentence 4, the verb *feels* links the subject *fabric* with the adjectives *rough* and *scratchy.*

Here are some common linking verbs:

Common Linking Verbs	
appear	feel
be (am, is, are, was, were, has been, have been, had been . . .)	look
become	seem

Verbs of More Than One Word—Helping Verbs

So far you have dealt with verbs of only one word—*fumbled, worked, is, feels,* and so on. But many verbs consist of more than one word:

---

* For work on compound predicates, see Chapter 20, "Revising for Sentence Variety," Part D.

5. He *should have taken* the train home.

6. *Are* Tanya and Joe *practicing* the piano?

7. The lounge *was painted* last week.

■ In sentence 5, *taken* is the main verb; *should* and *have* are the **helping verbs.**

■ In sentence 6, *practicing* is the main verb; *are* is the helping verb.

■ In sentence 7, *painted* is the main verb; *was* is the helping verb.*

PRACTICE 3

Underline the verbs in these sentences.

1. The ten-year-old stared at the cockpit of the Boeing 747.

2. Her thoughts raced.

3. She would have loved a runway takeoff or a landing.

4. However, she was only at the Museum of Science and Industry in Tampa, Florida, not in a real plane.

5. Science centers like this one will be attracting record crowds of parents and children.

6. Many of these centers emphasize local industry.

7. For example, the Tech Museum in California introduces visitors to computer technology.

8. The Louisville Science Center, on the other hand, features automotive games.

9. The beauty of these centers lies in their interactive exhibits.

10. Visitors can experience the latest technology firsthand and can learn about careers of the present and future.

PRACTICE 4

Circle the subjects and underline the verbs in the following sentences. First, cross out any prepositional phrases.

1. Do you think of baseball as America's oldest team sport?

---

* For more work on verbs in the passive voice, see Chapter 28, "The Past Participle," Part E.

2. In fact, lacrosse takes that honor.

3. Native Americans were playing the sport long before the arrival of Europeans.

4. A team scores by throwing a ball into the opposing team's goal.

5. The goal is ferociously guarded by a goalie.

6. Each player uses a curved racket with a mesh basket at its end.

7. Algonquin tribes in the valley of the St. Lawrence River invented the game.

8. The Hurons and Iroquois soon learned this demanding sport.

9. By 1500, the rough-and-tumble game was played by dozens of tribes in Canada and the United States.

10. Sometimes matches would require hundreds of players and might last for days.

11. Playing lacrosse trained young warriors for battle.

12. With this in mind, the Cherokees named lacrosse "little brother of war."

13. However, tribes often settled their differences peaceably with a lacrosse match.

14. French missionaries saw a resemblance between the racket and a bishop's cross.

15. They changed the name of the game from *boggotaway*, the native word, to *lacrosse*, French for *the cross*.

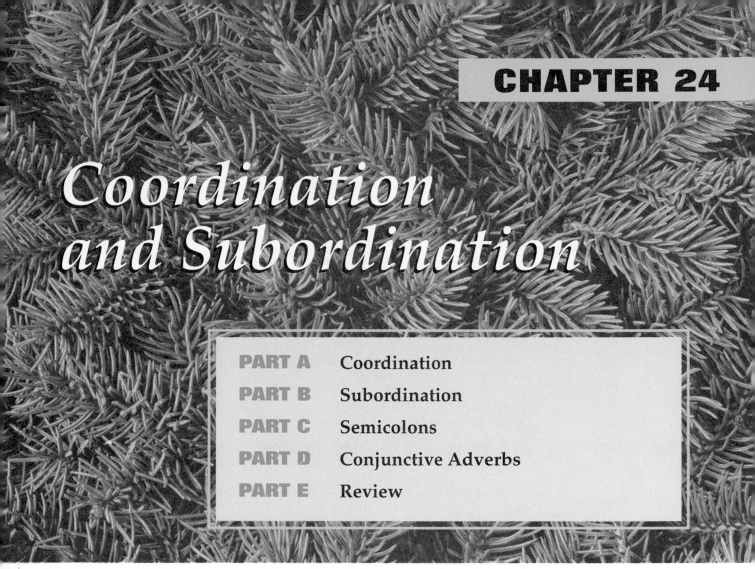

CHAPTER 24

Coordination and Subordination

PART A	Coordination
PART B	Subordination
PART C	Semicolons
PART D	Conjunctive Adverbs
PART E	Review

PART A   Coordination

A **clause** is a group of words that includes a subject and a verb. If a clause can stand alone as a complete idea, it is an **independent clause** and can be written as a **simple sentence.***

Here are two independent clauses written as simple sentences:

1. The dog barked all night.
2. The neighbors didn't complain.

You can join two clauses together by placing a comma and a **coordinating conjunction** between them:

---

* For more work on simple sentences, see Chapter 23, "The Simple Sentence."

3. The dog barked all night, *but* the neighbors didn't complain.

4. Let's go to the beach today, *for* it is too hot to do anything else.

■ The coordinating conjunctions *but* and *for* join together two clauses.

■ Note that *a comma precedes each coordinating conjunction.*

Here is a list of the most common coordinating conjunctions:

Coordinating Conjunctions			
and	for	or	yet
but	nor	so	

Be sure to choose the coordinating conjunction that best expresses the *relationship* between the two clauses in a sentence:

5. It was late, *so* I decided to take a bus home.

6. It was late, *yet* I decided to take a bus home.

■ The *so* in sentence 5 means that the lateness of the hour caused me to take the bus. (The trains don't run after midnight.)

■ The *yet* in sentence 6 means that despite the late hour I still decided to take a bus home. (I knew I might have to wait two hours at the bus stop.)

■ Note that a comma precedes the coordinating conjunction.

PRACTICE 1

Read the following sentences for meaning. Then fill in the coordinating conjunction that *best* expresses the relationship between the two clauses. Don't forget to add the comma.

1. Diners still dot the highways of the United States _____ they are not as popular as they once were.

2. In 1872, Walter Scott of Providence, Rhode Island, decided to make prepared and cooked food easier to buy _____ he started selling sandwiches and pies from a large horse-drawn wagon.

3. Customers flocked to this first "diner" _____ the food was delicious, plentiful, and inexpensive.

4. Many did not like standing outside to eat _____ another businessman, Sam Jones, redecorated the wagon and invited customers inside to dine.

5. In order to widen the appeal of their diners, some owners installed stained-glass windows _____ other proprietors added elegant decorations.

6. In the 1920s, narrow booths began to replace stools _____ diners were fixed permanently on the ground.

7. Stainless steel, efficient-looking diners were everywhere by the 1940s

   _____ even this style gave way to the fancy colonial and Mediterranean designs of the 1960s.

8. Diners are not as common as they were twenty years ago _____ can they compete with fast-food take-out chains like McDonald's and Wendy's.

9. Nonetheless, customers do have a choice; they can stand in line and wait for

   a quick hamburger _____ they can sit and be waited on in a diner.

10. Most choose fast food _____ some find that the more leisurely diner still has its charm.

PRACTICE 2

Combine these simple sentences with a coordinating conjunction. Punctuate correctly.

1. My daughter wants to be a mechanic. She spends every spare minute at the garage.

   _____

   _____

2. Ron dared not look over the edge. Heights made him dizzy.

   _____

   _____

3. Tasha's living room is cozy. Her guests always gather in the kitchen.

   _____

   _____

4. Meet me by the bicycle rack. Meet me at Lulu's Nut Shop.

   _____

   _____

5. In 1969, the first astronauts landed on the moon. Most Americans felt proud.

   _____

   _____

PART B　Subordination

Two clauses can also be joined with a **subordinating conjunction**. The clause following a subordinating conjunction is called a **subordinate** or **dependent clause** because it depends on an independent clause to complete its meaning:

> 1. We will light the candles *when Flora arrives*.

■ *When Flora arrives* is a subordinate or dependent clause introduced by the subordinating conjunction *when*.

■ By itself, *when Flora arrives* is incomplete; it depends on the independent clause to complete its meaning.*

Note that sentence 1 can also be written this way:

> 2. *When Flora arrives*, we will light the candles.

■ The meaning of sentences 1 and 2 is the same, but the punctuation is different.

■ In sentence 1, because the subordinate clause *follows* the independent clause, *no comma* is needed.

■ In sentence 2, however, because the subordinate clause *begins* the sentence, it is followed by a *comma*.

Here is a partial list of subordinating conjunctions:

Subordinating Conjunctions			
after	because	since	when(ever)
although	before	unless	whereas
as (if)	if	until	while

Be sure to choose the subordinating conjunction that *best expresses the relationship* between the two clauses in a sentence:

> 3. This course was excellent *because* Professor Green taught it.
> 4. This course was excellent *although* Professor Green taught it.

■ Sentence 3 says that the course was excellent *because* Professor Green, a great teacher, taught it.

■ Sentence 4 says that the course was excellent *despite the fact that* Professor Green, apparently a bad teacher, taught it.

---

* For more work on incomplete sentences, or fragments, see Chapter 25, "Avoiding Sentence Errors," Part B.

PRACTICE 3

Read the following sentences for meaning. Then fill in the subordinating conjunction that *best* expresses the relationship between the two clauses.

1. We could see very clearly last night _____ the moon was so bright.

2. Violet read *Sports Illustrated* _____ Daisy walked in the woods.

3. _____ it is cold outside, our new wood-burning Franklin stove keeps us warm.

4. The students buzzed with excitement _____ Professor Hargrave announced that classes would be held at the zoo.

5. _____ his shoulder loosens up a bit, Ron will stay on the bench.

PRACTICE 4

Punctuate the following sentences by adding a comma where necessary. Put a C after any correct sentences.

1. More than 2,000 unfortunate infants have had a good home because Clara Hale and her daughter, Lorraine, took care of them.

2. After she left her mother's apartment one day in 1969 Lorraine saw a woman sleeping on the street beside a baby in a crate.

3. Hale sent the woman to her mother's home because Clara had been caring for foster children for years.

4. When Clara welcomed the baby the seed of a new idea was planted.

5. Although many children were in need of special care no centers existed at the time for babies born addicted to drugs and alcohol.

6. Because Clara and Lorraine established Hale House the first such nonprofit nursery in the United States came into being.

7. Hale House became nationally known for its loving care of addicted and HIV-positive children after President Reagan praised it in 1985.

8. Since Clara "Mother" Hale died in 1992 Dr. Lorraine Hale and her staff have continued to provide that same loving care at Hale House.

Combine each pair of ideas below by using a subordinating conjunction. Write each combination twice, once with the subordinating conjunction at the beginning of the sentence and once with the subordinating conjunction in the middle of the sentence. Punctuate correctly.

EXAMPLE   We stayed on the beach.

The sun went down.

We stayed on the beach until the sun went down.

Until the sun went down, we stayed on the beach.

1. This cactus has flourished.
2. I talk to it every day.

_____

_____

3. Ralph takes the train to Philadelphia.
4. He likes to sit by the window.

_____

_____

5. I had known you were coming.
6. I would have vacuumed the guest room.

_____

_____

_____

7. He was the first person to eat a slice of meat between two pieces of bread.
8. The sandwich was named after the Earl of Sandwich.

_____

_____

_____

_____

_____

9. Akila was about to answer the final question.
10. The buzzer sounded.

_____

_____

_____

_____

11. Few soap operas remain on the radio.
12. Daytime television is filled with them.

_____

_____

_____

_____

13. She connected the speakers.
14. The room filled with glorious sound.

_____

_____

_____

15. The chimney spewed black smoke and soot.
16. Nobody complained to the local environmental agency.

_____

_____

_____

_____

_____

PART C   Semicolons

You can join two independent clauses by placing a **semicolon** between them. The semicolon takes the place of a conjunction:

1. She hopes to receive good grades this semester; her scholarship depends on her maintaining a 3.5 average.

2. Tony is a careless driver; he has had three minor accidents this year alone.

■ Each of the sentences above could also be made into two *separate sentences* by replacing the semicolon with a period.

■ Note that the first word after a semicolon is *not* capitalized (unless, of course, it is a word that is normally capitalized, like someone's name).

PRACTICE 6

Combine each pair of independent clauses by placing a semicolon between them.

1. Rush-hour traffic was worse than usual no one seemed to mind.

2. The senator appeared ill at ease at the news conference he seemed afraid of saying the wrong thing.

3. The new seed catalogue, a fifteen-hundred-page volume, was misplaced the volume weighed ten pounds.

4. On Thursday evening, Stuart decided to go camping on Friday morning, he packed his bags and left.

5. In the early 1960s, the Beatles burst on the rock scene rock music has never been the same.

6. Ron Jackson has been promoted he will be an effective manager.

7. This stream is full of trout every spring men and women with waders and fly rods arrive on its banks.

8. Not a single store was open at that hour not a soul walked the streets.

PRACTICE 7

Each independent clause that follows is the first half of a sentence. Add a semicolon and a second independent clause. Make sure your second thought is also independent and can stand alone.

1. At 2 A.M. I stumbled toward the ringing telephone _____

_____

2. *People* magazine published my letter to the editor _____

   _____

3. The officer pulled over the speeding pickup truck _____

   _____

4. Faulkner's stories often depict life in the South _____

   _____

5. None of my friends can polka _____

   _____

6. During the Great Depression, millions of workers were unemployed _____

   _____

7. Cameras are not permitted in the museum _____

   _____

8. Bill's waiter recommended the vegetable soup _____

   _____

PART D   Conjunctive Adverbs

A **conjunctive adverb** placed after the semicolon can help clarify the relationship between two clauses:

> 1. I like the sound of that stereo; *however*, the price is too high.
> 2. They have not seen that film; *moreover*, they have not been to a theater for three years.

■ Note that a comma follows the conjunctive adverb.

Here is a partial list of conjunctive adverbs.

Conjunctive Adverbs		
consequently	in fact	nevertheless
furthermore	indeed	then
however	moreover	therefore

PRACTICE 8

Punctuate each sentence correctly by adding a semicolon, a comma, or both, where necessary. Put a *C* after any correct sentences.

1. I hate to wash my car windows nevertheless it's a job that must be done.

2. Sonia doesn't know how to play chess however she would like to learn.

3. Dean Fader is very funny in fact he could be a professional comedian.

4. Deep water makes Maurice nervous therefore he does not want to row to the middle of the lake.

5. I like this painting; the soft colors remind me of tropical sunsets.

6. The faculty approved of the new trimester system; furthermore, the students liked it too.

7. Bill has a cassette player plugged into his ear all day consequently he misses a lot of good conversations.

8. We toured the darkroom then we watched an actual photo shoot.

PRACTICE 9

Combine each pair of independent clauses by placing a semicolon and a conjunctive adverb between them. Punctuate correctly.

1. The lake is quite long we rowed from one end of it to the other.

2. I can still see the streaks under the fresh white paint we will have to give the room another coat.

3. Mr. Farrington loves bluegrass music he plays in a local bluegrass band.

4. Jay, a tall boy, has poor eyesight he was turned down for the basketball team.

5. Yesterday, hikers from the Nature-Walkers' Club made real progress in blazing a trail they managed to get as far as the foot of Mt. Lookout.

6. By midnight Tien had finished tuning his engine he still had enough time for a short nap before the race.

7. An arthroscope helps doctors examine the inside of an injured knee the use of this instrument can prevent unnecessary surgery.

8. Rhinoceroses live in protected animal preserves poachers still manage to kill a few of these magnificent beasts each year.

PART E   Review

In this chapter, you have combined simple sentences by means of a **coordinating conjunction,** a **subordinating conjunction,** a **semicolon,** and a **semicolon** and **conjunctive adverb.** Here is a review chart of the sentence patterns discussed in this chapter.*

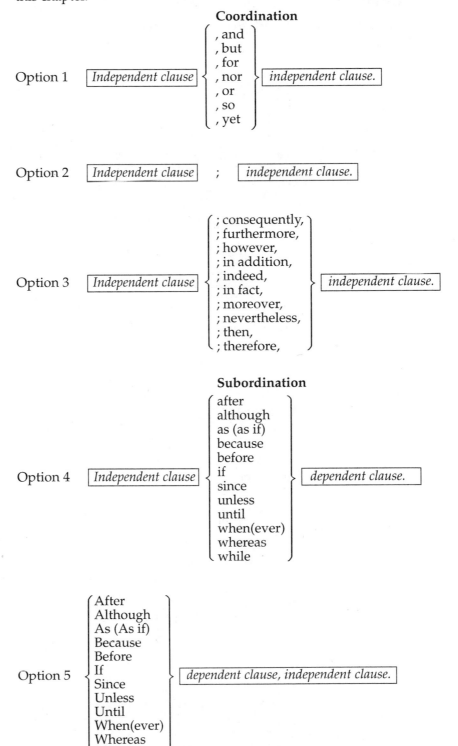

Coordination

Option 1   *Independent clause* { , and / , but / , for / , nor / , or / , so / , yet }   *independent clause.*

Option 2   *Independent clause*   ;   *independent clause.*

Option 3   *Independent clause* { ; consequently, / ; furthermore, / ; however, / ; in addition, / ; indeed, / ; in fact, / ; moreover, / ; nevertheless, / ; then, / ; therefore, }   *independent clause.*

Subordination

Option 4   *Independent clause* { after / although / as (as if) / because / before / if / since / unless / until / when(ever) / whereas / while }   *dependent clause.*

Option 5   { After / Although / As (As if) / Because / Before / If / Since / Unless / Until / When(ever) / Whereas / While }   *dependent clause, independent clause.*

* For more ways to combine sentences, see Chapter 20, "Revising for Sentence Variety," Part D.

PRACTICE 10

Read each pair of simple sentences to determine the relationship between them. Then join each pair in three different ways, using the conjunctions or conjunctive adverbs in parentheses at the left. Punctuate correctly.

EXAMPLE | The company picnic was canceled.

Rain started to fall in torrents.

(for) _The company picnic was canceled, for the rain started to fall in torrents._

(because) _Because the rain started to fall in torrents, the company picnic was_

canceled.

(therefore) _The rain started to fall in torrents; therefore, the company picnic was_

canceled.

1. My grandmother is in great shape.

   She eats right and exercises regularly.

   (for) _____

   _____

   (because) _____

   _____

   (therefore) _____

   _____

2. We just put in four hours paving the driveway.

   We need a long break and a cold drink.

   (since) _____

   _____

   (because) _____

   _____

   (consequently) _____

   _____

3. The bus schedule was difficult to read.

   Penny found the right bus.

   (but) _____

   _____

   (although) _____

   _____

   (however) _____

   _____

4. Don is an expert mechanic.

   He intends to open a service center.

   (and) _____

   _____

   (since) _____

   _____

   (furthermore) _____

   _____

5. We haven't heard from her.

   We haven't given up hope.

   (but) _____

   _____

   (although) _____

   _____

   (nevertheless) _____

   _____

PRACTICE 11

In your writing, aim for variety by mixing coordination, subordination, and simple sentences.* Rewrite the following paragraphs to eliminate monotonous simple sentences. First, read the paragraph to determine the relationships between

_____

* For more work on sentence variety, see Chapter 20, "Revising for Sentence Variety."

ideas; then choose the conjunctions that best express these relationships. Punctuate correctly.

Paragraph a   In 1996, Franck Goddio made the greatest discovery of his life. He found the sunken royal city of Cleopatra under the Mediterranean Sea. Almost 2000 years earlier, the fabled queen had ruled Egypt from her island palace near Alexandria. During the fourth and fifth centuries, the island gradually sank into the sea. Goddio and his high-tech team searched the sea bottom near Alexandria for two years. They found roads, temples, and palaces in a murky corner of the harbor. The silt of centuries covered the sunken treasures. They are being cleaned and left in place underwater. Goddio hopes that the Egyptian government will create an underwater museum. Cleopatra's glorious city will be preserved for generations to come.

_____

_____

_____

_____

_____

_____

_____

Paragraph b   Languages are disappearing all over the world. North America has two hundred Native American languages. Only about fifty have more than a thousand speakers. Europe's Celtic languages have been declining for generations. Language decline is most noticeable in tiny communities in Asia and Australia. Each isolated community speaks a different language. The population shrinks. The language begins to die out. In addition, a small community may make contact with a large one. The native language may start to fade. People use the "more important" language. It gives them better access to education, jobs, and new technology. A "powerful language" will almost always prevail over a native mother tongue.

_____

_____

_____

_____

_____

_____

_____

_____

_____

Paragraph c   A great star blazed in the sky. Paiea was born in Hawaii in 1758. Seers had foretold that this son of a chieftain would defeat his enemies and govern a united Hawaii. A jealous former ruler ordered the baby killed. Sympathetic courtiers hid the noble infant in a cave. There he was renamed Kamehameha. This name means "The Lonely One" or "The One Set Apart." In time, it was safe for young Kamehameha to leave the cave. He was very strong and agile. He excelled in war games. James Cook, an English sea captain, landed in Hawaii in 1778. Kamehameha had already become the most important chieftain. He gained even more power by conquering one independent island after another. With the help of English sailors, he successfully invaded Maui. Eventually, the rest of the Hawaiian islands came under his control. By 1810, this shrewd and powerful king ruled a united country. A lover of his native culture, he continued many ancient traditions of his homeland. He also borrowed many ideas from the Europeans. The prophecies at his birth had come true. He had defeated his enemies and become the sole ruler of a united Hawaii.

_____

_____

_____

_____

_____

_____

_____

_____

_____

_____

_____

CHAPTER 25

Avoiding Sentence Errors

PART A	Avoiding Run-Ons and Comma Splices
PART B	Avoiding Fragments

PART A Avoiding Run-Ons and Comma Splices

Be careful to avoid **run-ons** and **comma splices.**

A **run-on sentence** incorrectly runs together two independent clauses without a conjunction or punctuation. This error confuses the reader, who cannot tell where one thought stops and the next begins:

> 1. Run-on: My neighbor Mr. Hoffman is seventy-five years old he plays tennis every Saturday afternoon.

A **comma splice** incorrectly joins two independent clauses with a comma but no conjunction:

> 2. Comma splice: My neighbor Mr. Hoffman is seventy-five years old, he plays tennis every Saturday afternoon.

The run-on and the comma splice can be corrected in five ways:

Use two separate sentences.	My neighbor Mr. Hoffman is seventy-five years old. He plays tennis every Saturday afternoon.
Use a coordinating conjunction. (See Chapter 24, Part A.)	My neighbor Mr. Hoffman is seventy-five years old, but he plays tennis every Saturday afternoon.
Use a subordinating conjunction. (See Chapter 24, Part B.)	Although my neighbor Mr. Hoffman is seventy-five years old, he plays tennis every Saturday afternoon.
Use a semicolon. (See Chapter 24, Part C.)	My neighbor Mr. Hoffman is seventy-five years old; he plays tennis every Saturday afternoon.
Use a semicolon and a conjunctive adverb. (See Chapter 24, Part D.)	My neighbor Mr. Hoffman is seventy-five years old; however, he plays tennis every Saturday afternoon.

PRACTICE 1

Some of these sentences contain run-ons or comma splices; others are correct. Put a *C* next to the correct sentences. Revise the run-ons and comma splices in any way you choose. Be careful of the punctuation.

1. It was an astonishing exhibit, the Guggenheim Museum's recent show was called "The Art of the Motorcycle."

   Revised: _____

   _____

2. Museumgoers sported leather vests and ponytails, their motorcycles jammed New York City streets.

   Revised: _____

   _____

3. Displayed were motorcycles through the years, including the earliest-known cycle.

   Revised: _____

   _____

4. That was the 1868 French velocipede, it looked more like a bicycle with a steam engine under the seat than a motorcycle.

   Revised: _____

   _____

5. The Italian MV Agusta F4 was the latest model on display this one looked like a fantastic space machine.

   Revised: _____

   _____

6. A 1993 Harley-Davidson stole the show it was a replica of Dennis Hopper's *Easy Rider* cycle.

   Revised: _____

   _____

7. The show attracted more visitors than any other Guggenheim exhibit museum attendance was 45 percent higher than usual.

   Revised: _____

   _____

8. Tickets and gift-shop sales brought in more than $1 million the exhibit catalog alone sold for $85.

   Revised: _____

   _____

9. Although Ducati leather jumpsuits cost $1,595, museumgoers could buy their kids red plastic BMW motorcycles for $120 each.

   Revised: _____

   _____

10. Whether motorcycles are art or not, "The Art of the Motorcycle" certainly brought many new visitors to the Guggenheim, the show was considered a huge success.

Revised: _____

_____

_____

PRACTICE 2

Proofread the following paragraph for run-ons and comma splices. Correct them in any way you choose.

(1) Many couples today live together before they marry. (2) Marriage is a serious step, they want to get to know each other as well as possible. (3) However, research shows that living together is not good preparation for marriage. (4) In fact, living together usually does not lead to marriage it leads to breakups. (5) Even happy couples are less likely to get married as time goes on. (6) If they do marry, they tend to divorce eventually researchers cannot explain these outcomes. (7) Perhaps couples who live together are not really committed to the relationship, perhaps they find it easier to break up a household than a marriage. (8) Regardless of the reasons, statistics don't lie living together rarely leads to a happy marriage.

PRACTICE 3

Proofread the following essay for run-ons and comma splices. Correct them in any way you choose, writing your revised essay on a separate sheet of paper. Be careful of the punctuation.

Will K. Kellogg, Least Likely to Succeed

(1) Will Kellogg was an unlikely candidate for fame and fortune, he became one of America's great successes.

(2) The two Kellogg boys could not have been more different. (3) Will was a slow learner with few friends and interests. (4) His father pulled him from school at the age of thirteen he made Will a traveling broom salesman for the family company. (5) Eight years older than Will, John Harvey Kellogg was the family genius. (6) He became a noted surgeon and head of an exclusive health resort.

(7) He treated his patients with exercise and a strict vegetarian diet, he wrote best-selling books about healthful living.

(8) In 1880, Will was twenty years old, Dr. John hired him to work at the resort. (9) For the next twenty-five years, Will served as his brother's flunky. (10) According to rumor, he shaved Dr. John every day and shined his shoes. (11) John bicycled to work, Will jogged alongside getting his daily work orders. (12) Dr. John was a wealthy man, he never paid Will more than eighty-seven dollars a month.

(13) One of the special foods at the resort was pressed wheat. (14) The brothers boiled wheat dough then they pressed it through rollers into thin sheets. (15) One night, they left the boiled dough out. (16) When they pressed it, it turned into flakes instead of forming sheets. (17) Will suggested that they toast the flakes. (18) Resort guests loved the new cereal, former guests ordered it from their homes. (19) To meet the demand, the brothers opened a mail-order business, however, the snobbish Dr. John refused to sell the flakes to grocery stores.

(20) In 1906, Will finally bought out John's share of the cereal patents, struck out on his own. (21) Will turned out to be a business genius. (22) He invented advertising techniques that made his new product, Kellogg's Corn Flakes, a household word. (23) Will K. Kellogg quickly became one of the richest persons in America.

(24) Sadly, the two brothers never reconciled. (25) In 1943, ninety-one-year-old Dr. John wrote Will an apology John died before the letter reached his younger brother.

PART B   Avoiding Fragments

Another error to avoid is the **sentence fragment.** A **sentence** must contain a subject and a verb and must be able to stand alone as a complete idea. A **sentence**

fragment, therefore, can be defined in terms of what it lacks: either a subject or a verb, or both—it cannot stand alone as a complete idea.

Here are common kinds of sentence fragments and ways to correct them.

Fragments with Dependent Clauses

Complete sentence:	1. Kirk decided to major in psychology.
Fragment:	2. Because human behavior had always fascinated him.

■ Example 1 is a complete simple sentence.

■ Example 2 is a fragment because it is a dependent clause beginning with the subordinating conjunction *because.* Furthermore, it is not a complete idea.

This fragment can be corrected in two ways:

Corrected:	3. Kirk decided to major in psychology because human behavior had always fascinated him.
	4. Kirk decided to major in psychology. Human behavior had always fascinated him.

■ In sentence 3, the fragment is combined with the sentence before it.

■ In sentence 4, the fragment is changed into a complete sentence.

Fragments with Relative Clauses

Complete sentence:	5. Mrs. Costa is a chemistry teacher who never runs out of creative ideas.
Fragment:	6. Who has the ability to keep her classes involved throughout the lesson.

■ Example 5 is a complete sentence.

■ Example 6 is a fragment because it is a relative clause beginning with *who.**

The fragment in example 6 can be corrected in two ways, as shown below:

Corrected:	7. Mrs. Costa is a chemistry teacher who never runs out of creative ideas and who has the ability to keep her classes involved throughout the lesson.
	8. Mrs. Costa is a chemistry teacher who never runs out of creative ideas. She has the ability to keep her classes involved throughout the lesson.

---

* For more work on relative clauses, see Chapter 20, "Revising for Sentence Variety," Part D, and Chapter 26, "Present Tense (Agreement)," Part G.

- In sentence 7, the fragment is combined with the sentence before it.
- In sentence 8, the fragment is changed into a complete sentence.

Fragments with *-ing* Modifiers

Complete sentence:	9. Daniel can always be seen on the track in the morning.
Fragment:	10. Running a mile or two before breakfast.

- Example 9 is a complete sentence.
- Example 10 is a fragment because it lacks a subject and because an *-ing* verb form cannot stand alone without a helping verb.*

   This fragment can be corrected in two ways:

Corrected:	11. Daniel can always be seen on the track in the morning, running a mile or two before breakfast.
	12. Daniel can always be seen on the track in the morning. He runs a mile or two before breakfast.

- In sentence 11, the fragment is combined with the sentence before it.
- In sentence 12, the fragment is changed into a complete sentence.

Fragments with Phrases

Fragment:	13. A fine pianist.
Complete sentence:	14. Marsha won a scholarship to Juilliard.

- Example 13 is a fragment because it lacks a verb and is not a complete idea.
- Example 14 is a complete sentence.

   This fragment can be corrected in two ways:

Corrected:	15. A fine pianist, Marsha won a scholarship to Juilliard.
	16. Marsha is a fine pianist. She won a scholarship to Juilliard. *or* Marsha won a scholarship to Juilliard. She is a fine pianist.

- In sentence 15, the fragment is combined with the sentence after it.
- In sentence 16, the fragment is changed into a complete sentence by the addition of a verb, *is,* and a subject, *Marsha* in the first option and *she* in the second option.

---

* For more work on joining ideas with an *-ing* modifier, see Chapter 20, "Revising for Sentence Variety," Part D

Fragments with Infinitives

Complete sentence:	17. Laura has always wanted to become a travel agent.
Fragment:	18. To tell people about exotic countries that they might visit.

■ Example 17 is a complete sentence.

■ Example 18 is a fragment because it lacks a subject and contains only the infinitive form of the verb—*to* plus the simple form of the verb *tell*.

This fragment can be corrected in two ways:

Corrected:	19. Laura has always wanted to become a travel agent and to tell people about exotic countries that they might visit.
	20. Laura has always wanted to become a travel agent. She would find it exciting to tell people about exotic countries that they might visit.

■ In sentence 19, the fragment is combined with the sentence before it.

■ In sentence 20, the fragment is changed into a complete sentence.

Quick Review Chart: Types of Fragments

Type of Fragment	Example	How to Correct Them
dependent clause	Because it gets dark early.	All fragments can be fixed in one of two ways:
relative clause	Who loves computer games.	
-ing modifier	Skating across the pond.	1. Add the missing subject and/or verb.
phrase	In the attic.	2. Connect the fragment to a neighboring sentence.
infinitive	To go to the movies tonight.	

PRACTICE 4

Some of these examples are fragments; others are complete sentences. Put a C next to the complete sentences. Revise the fragments in any way you choose.

EXAMPLE | Leaping into the air.

Revised: <u>Leaping into the air, she shouted, "I won, I won!"</u>

1. Interviewing divorced people for her research project.

   Revised: _____

   _____

2. Since we live near the Colorado River.

   Revised: _____

   _____

3. Couldn't find the group's new album.

   Revised: _____

   _____

4. A tall, thin man with bushy eyebrows.

   Revised: _____

   _____

5. To earn money for college.

   Revised: _____

   _____

6. Ten minutes after they won the Super Bowl.

   Revised: _____

   _____

7. She has patented three of her inventions.

   Revised: _____

   _____

8. Frantically flipping through the pages of the dictionary.

   Revised: _____

   _____

9. Someone who loves to take risks.

   Revised: _____

   _____

10. Although I usually ask my friends for advice.

Revised: _____

_____

PRACTICE 5

Proofread this paragraph for fragments. Correct them in any way you choose, either adding the fragments to other sentences or making them into complete sentences.

(1) The sinking of the *Titanic* in 1912 has inspired fifteen motion pictures over the years. (2) All of them requiring special effects. (3) What set James Cameron's *Titanic* apart, however, was his attention to detail. (4) Following the blueprints and plans for the original ship. (5) Cameron's team created scaled sets and models accurate down to the rivets. (6) Scenes of the ship in the water were made possible through the brilliant use of computer technology and a small model. (7) A larger model of the liner's huge cargo hold was needed. (8) To show the ocean rushing into the ship. (9) Although the model was only a quarter as large as the original. (10) It still had enough room for period luggage and a brand-new Renault. (11) The largest model was a 775-foot replica of the luxury ship. (12) Which reproduced every detail, from the ship's name lettered on the façade to the chairs on the deck. (13) That set took almost a year to build. (14) And a good chunk of the $287 million that Cameron spent on the most expensive movie ever made.

PRACTICE 6

Proofread this essay for fragments. Correct them in any way you choose, either adding the fragments to other sentences or making them into complete sentences. Be careful of the punctuation.

The Regent Diamond

(1) Throughout its exciting history. (2) The Regent diamond has been one of the world's most desired jewels.

(3) In 1701, the 410-carat gem was discovered in an Indian mine by a slave. (4) Who risked his life to smuggle it out. (5) Slashing his leg. (6) He stuffed the huge diamond into the wound and headed for the seacoast. (7) A shifty sea captain offered to sail him to freedom for half the value of the jewel. (8) When at sea, the captain stole the stone. (9) And threw the slave overboard. (10) He then sold the precious rock to a powerful diamond merchant.

(11) The merchant had difficulty unloading the diamond. (12) Because it was so large and because it was stolen. (13) He finally sold it to Robert Pitt, a young Englishman. (14) Who had come to India seeking his fortune. (15) By the time this shrewd adventurer returned home. (16) The English had nicknamed him "Diamond" Pitt and christened the stone "the Pitt."

(17) Few people believed Pitt had come by the diamond honestly. (18) So he also had trouble selling it. (19) Pitt was terrified of being robbed and murdered. (20) Whenever he carried the stone. (21) He disguised himself and would not sleep in the same place for more than two nights. (22) If someone recognized him. (23) He would deny that he carried the stone with him. (24) It took years. (25) But he finally sold his diamond in 1717 for an enormous sum to the Duke of Orleans. (26) The Regent of France.

(27) Now called the Regent diamond. (28) The fabulous stone was the most valuable French crown jewel. (29) In 1792, during the French Revolution. (30) It disappeared, only to be found in a ditch in the middle of Paris. (31) Upon becoming emperor. (32) Napoleon had the diamond set into the hilt of his ceremonial sword. (33) In 1887 when the last French monarchy fell and the jewel collection was auctioned. (34) The Regent diamond was placed in the Louvre, the famous museum in Paris. (35) Where it still glitters today.

PRACTICE 7   Review

Proofread these paragraphs for run-ons, comma splices, and fragments. Correct the errors in any way you choose.

Paragraph a   (1) Many experts believe that before the year 2020. (2) The moon will be a popular tourist destination. (3) Adventure travelers now might climb Mount Everest or take a canoe trip down the Amazon, soon they will be paying large sums for the adventure of a lifetime, in space. (4) After careful training and space suit drills, they will rocket out of Earth's orbit and spend a day at a fuel depot. (5) Circling Earth and playing in zero gravity. (6) Then they will board the space ship for the two-day flight to the moon. (7) Once they land near the hotel's main airlock and check in, guests will stare at Mother Earth in the black vastness of the sky, take tours in special buses through the dusty lunar landscape, and experience the thrill of moving at one-sixth the gravity of Earth. (8) This means they will jump six times higher and feel six times lighter. (9) The week will fly by. (10) As they pack for the return trip. (11) Many travelers will trade ten pounds of their baggage allowance for the moon rocks they've been collecting. (12) After an unforgettable final flight and decontamination, the space visitors will re-enter their lives on Earth, changed.

—Adapted from Gregory Bennett, "Your Vacation on the Moon"

Paragraph b   (1) Some teenagers seem to start the day tired, they are worn out even before they leave for school. (2) Once in class, they might doze off, even in the middle of an exciting lesson. (3) Are these students lazy, have they stayed out too late partying? (4) Medical research provides a different explanation for the exhaustion of these teens. (5) As children become adolescents, they develop an increased need for sleep, especially in the morning. (6) Unfortunately, most American high schools start around 7:30 A.M. many students have to get up as early as 5:00 A.M. (7) Scientists suggest that if students could start school later in the day. (8) They might get the extra sleep they need. (9) To test this theory, many schools have begun to experiment with later hours. (10) Congress is even paying the extra operating costs for schools that start after 9:00 A.M. (11) The hope is that teens will be less tired, furthermore, because schools that start later will end later, students will be off the streets and out of trouble during the late afternoon. (12) Which is prime mischief time.

Proofread these two essays for run-ons, comma splices, and fragments. Correct the errors in any way you choose, writing the revised draft on a separate piece of paper.

Words for the Wise

(1) Everyone knows that Scrabble is America's favorite word game. (2) It was invented by Alfred Butts. (3) An architect who wanted to create a word game that required both luck and skill. (4) In 1938, Butts produced a board with 225 squares and 100 tiles with letters on them. (5) Each letter was worth a certain number of points, depending on how easy it was to use that letter in a word.

(6) Butts made fifty Scrabble sets by hand he gave them to his friends. (7) Who loved playing Scrabble. (8) Strangely enough, Butts could not interest a manufacturer in the game. (9) A friend of his, James Brunot, asked Butts for permission to manufacture and sell the game. (10) However, Brunot also had little success. (11) Selling only a few sets a year. (12) Then suddenly, in 1953, Scrabble caught on a million sets were sold that year.

(13) Butts and Brunot couldn't keep up with the demand, they sold the rights to a game manufacturer. (14) The rest is history today Scrabble is produced in half a dozen foreign languages it is also used as a learning tool. (15) To teach children spelling and vocabulary.

Dance Craze

(1) Do you remember the Macarena? (2) Which became the hottest dance craze since the Twist? (3) After Los del Rio recorded a song in 1993 about a heartbroken seductress named Macarena. (4) The tune sold more than four million

copies worldwide. (5) A duo of male musicians from Seville, Spain. (6) Los del Rio created the dance on the spot one night. (7) The audience imitated the singers, what happened next is dance-fad history. (8) Dancers bought Macarena albums they danced at Macarena marathons.

(9) Like the Macarena, country line dancing also spread very quickly across the United States. (10) The music is country western the line goes back to the conga line and the Harlem Hustle. (11) Country line dancing invites any dancer to join long lines of folks. (12) Who are all doing the same steps at the same time. (13) The trend was already under way Billy Ray Cyrus's 1992 hit "Achy Breaky Heart" led to a line dance called the Achy Breaky. (14) From then on, dances like the Electric Slide, Tush Push, and Boot Scootin' Boogie sprang up on the heels of one another.

(15) Recent years have seen a revival of the big bands and the swing dancing of the 1920s and '30s. (16) Dances like the jitterbug, the Lindy Hop, and the Carolina Shag make demands on couples. (17) To learn complicated steps. (18) A high-energy dance form. (19) Swing requires partners to flip, slide, and dip. (20) The clothing of the period also has been revived, dancers often wear wide-brim fedora hats, double-breasted zoot suits, suspenders, and wing-tip shoes. (21) Swing clubs have sprung up practically overnight dance studios can't keep up with the demand for lessons.

(22) Swing dancing seems to have come into the mainstream; ironically, some of its original fans are now looking for the next step. (23) Will the newest dance craze be an invention like the Macarena, will it be a revival of an older dance, perhaps the waltz or the two-step? (24) Nobody is predicting yet what will next ignite our soles—and our souls!

CHAPTER 26

Present Tense (Agreement)

PART A   Defining Subject-Verb Agreement

Subjects and verbs in the present tense must **agree** in number; that is, singular subjects take verbs with singular endings, and plural subjects take verbs with plural endings.

Verbs in the Present Tense
Sample Verb: *To Leap*

	Singular		Plural	
	If the subject is	**the verb is**	**If the subject is**	**the verb is**
1st person:	I	leap	we	leap
2nd person:	you	leap	you	leap
3rd person:	he she it	leaps	they	leap

■ Use an *-s* or *-es* ending on the verb only when the subject is *he, she,* or *it* or the equivalent of *he, she,* or *it*.

   The subjects and verbs in the following sentences agree:

1. He *bicycles* to the steel mills every morning.

2. They *bicycle* to the steel mills every morning.

3. This student *hopes* to go to social work school.

4. The planets *revolve* around the sun.

■ In sentence 1, the singular subject, *he,* takes the singular form of the verb, *bicycles. Bicycles* agrees with *he.*

■ In sentence 2, the plural subject, *they,* takes the plural form of the verb, *bicycle. Bicycle* agrees with *they.*

■ In sentence 3, the subject, *student,* is equivalent to *he* or *she* and takes the singular form of the verb, *hopes.*

■ In sentence 4, the subject, *planets,* is equivalent to *they* and takes the plural form of the verb, *revolve.*

   Subjects joined by the conjunction *and* usually take a plural verb:

5. Kirk and Quincy *attend* a pottery class at the Y.

■ The subject, *Kirk and Quincy,* is plural, the equivalent of *they.*

■ *Attend* agrees with the plural subject.*

---

* For work on consistent verb tense, see Chapter 19, "Revising for Consistency and Parallelism," Part A.

PRACTICE 1

Underline the subject and circle the correct present tense verb.

1. A signed Green Bay Packers' helmet (brings, bring) in $2,000.

2. Bill Gates (pays, pay) $30.8 million for a notebook handwritten by Leonardo da Vinci.

3. Obviously, autographs (sells, sell)!

4. They (falls, fall) into three major categories—history, sports, and entertainment.

5. To a historian, an autograph (means, mean) a signed document, like a letter signed by President Lincoln.

6. For a sports fan, it (includes, include) anything signed, like a baseball or a cap.

7. In the entertainment field, collectors (associates, associate) an autograph with a signed photograph, like an eight-by-ten glossy of Jimmy Smits.

8. Some people (collects, collect) only specific items—for example, autographs of the signers of the Declaration of Independence or signed photographs of Bruce Willis.

9. Autograph shops (flourishes, flourish) in malls and airports.

10. However, technology and business (complicates, complicate) collecting.

11. For example, more and more public figures (uses, use) computers instead of pen and paper.

12. To make the situation even more complicated, an autopen sometimes (confuses, confuse) the unsuspecting buyer.

13. That pen, a perfect counterfeiter, automatically (writes, write) signatures for some celebrities.

14. Also, unlike their predecessors, athletes and movie stars sometimes (asks, ask) to be paid for their signatures.

15. Even with such problems, however, autograph hounds (continues, continue) to raise collecting to new heights.

PART B   Three Troublesome Verbs in the Present Tense:
To Be, To Have, To Do

Choosing the correct verb form of *to be, to have,* and *to do* can be tricky. Study these charts:

Reference Chart—*To Be*
Present Tense

	Singular		Plural	
	If the subject is	the verb is	If the subject is	the verb is
1st person:	I	am	we	are
2nd person:	you	are	you	are
3rd person:	he she it	is	they	are

Reference Chart—*To Have*
Present Tense

	Singular		Plural	
	If the subject is	the verb is	If the subject is	the verb is
1st person:	I	have	we	have
2nd person:	you	have	you	have
3rd person:	he she it	has	they	have

Reference Chart—*To Do*
Present Tense

	Singular		Plural	
	If the subject is	the verb is	If the subject is	the verb is
1st person:	I	do	we	do
2nd person:	you	do	you	do
3rd person:	he she it	does	they	do

PRACTICE 2

Write the correct present tense form of the verb in the space at the right of the pronoun.

To be   *To have*   *To do*

I _____   we _____   it _____

we _____   she _____   they _____

he _____   he _____   she _____

you _____   they _____   you _____

it _____   I _____   he _____

they _____   it _____   we _____

she _____   you _____   I _____

PRACTICE 3

Fill in the correct present tense form of the verb in parentheses.

1. Rock climbing _____ (to be) an extreme sport that _____ (to have) become very popular.

2. Some beginners _____ (to have) a terrific fear of heights, and they

   _____ (to be) better off "bouldering," or climbing big rocks on or near the ground.

3. These inexperienced climbers also _____ (to do) what is called "top roping."

4. In top roping, the beginner and an experienced climber _____ (to have) one rope between them.

5. The experienced climber _____ (to have) the job of taking up the slack on

   the ground while the beginner, or top roper, _____ (to do) the climbing.

6. If the climber _____ (to do) slip and fall, top roping _____ (to do) not allow serious injury.

7. Strangely enough, even the non-outdoorsperson now _____ (to have) a way to rock climb—indoor rock climbing.

8. Indoor climbing clubs _____ (to have) more than tripled since 1994, and

   climbing walls _____ (to be) now standard equipment in gyms around the country.

9. Some enthusiasts even _____ (to have) climbing walls in their homes.

10. If their walls _____ (to be) not high enough, a rolling rock wall _____ (to do) the trick.

11. By going down as the climber _____ (to be) going up, the rolling wall

   _____ (to be) a combination of treadmill and climbing wall.

12. Indoor climbing _____ (to have) all the benefits of outdoor rock climbing—overall body toning, stress relief, improved balance and coordination, and fun—without the danger.

PART C   Special Singular Constructions

Each of these constructions takes a **singular** verb:

Special Singular Constructions		
either (of) . . .	each (of) . . .	every one (of) . . .
neither (of) . . .	one (of) . . .	which one (of) . . .

1. *Neither* of the birds *has* feathers yet.
2. *Each* of the solutions *presents* difficulties.

■ In sentence 1, *neither* means *neither one. Neither* is a singular subject and requires the singular verb *has.*

■ In sentence 2, *each* means *each one. Each* is a singular subject and requires the singular verb *presents.*

However, an exception to this general rule is the case in which two subjects are joined by *(n)either . . . (n)or. . . .* Here, the verb agrees with the subject closer to it:

3. Neither the teacher nor the *pupils want* the semester shortened.
4. Either the graphs or the *map has* to be changed.

■ In sentence 3, *pupils* is the subject closer to the verb. The plural subject *pupils* takes the verb *want.*

■ In sentence 4, *map* is the subject closer to the verb. The singular subject *map* takes the verb *has.*

PRACTICE 4

Underline the subject and circle the correct verb in each sentence.

1. Each of these ferns (needs, need) special care.

2. One of the customers always (forget, forgets) his or her umbrella.

3. Which one of the flights (goes, go) nonstop to Dallas?

4. Every one of those cameras (costs, cost) more than I can afford.

5. Either you or Doris (is, are) correct.

6. Either of these computer diskettes (contain, contains) the information you need.

7. Do you really believe that one of these oysters (holds, hold) a pearl?

8. Neither of the twins (resembles, resemble) his parents.

9. One of the scientists (believes, believe) he can cure baldness.

10. Each of these inventions (has, have) an effect on how we spend our leisure time.

PART D   Separation of Subject and Verb

Sometimes a phrase or a clause separates the subject from the verb. First, look for the subject; then make sure that the verb agrees with the subject.

> 1. The economist's *ideas* on this matter *seem* well thought out.
> 2. *Radios* that were made in the 1930s *are* now collectors' items.

■ In sentence 1, the *ideas* are well thought out. The prepositional phrase *on this matter* separates the subject *ideas* from the verb *seem*.*

■ In sentence 2, *radios* are now collectors' items. The relative clause *that were made in the 1930s* separates the subject *radios* from the verb *are*.

PRACTICE 5

Read each sentence carefully for meaning. Cross out any phrase or clause that separates the subject from the verb. Underline the subject and circle the correct verb.

---

* For more work on prepositional phrases, see Chapter 23, "The Simple Sentence," Part B.

1. The plums in that bowl (tastes, taste) sweet.

2. The instructions on the package (is, are) in French and Japanese.

3. Our new community center, which has a swimming pool and tennis courts, (keeps, keep) everyone happy.

4. The lampshades that are made of stained glass (looks, look) beautiful at night.

5. All the CD players on that shelf (comes, come) with a remote control.

6. A movie that lasts more than three hours usually (puts, put) me to sleep.

7. The man with the dark sunglasses (looks, look) like a typical movie villain.

8. The two nurses who check blood pressure (enjoys, enjoy) chatting with the patients.

9. The function of these metal racks (remains, remain) a mystery to me.

10. The lizard on the wall (has, have) only three legs.

PART E Sentences Beginning with *There* and *Here*

In sentences that begin with **there** or **here,** the subject usually follows the verb:

> 1. There *seem* to be two *flies* in my soup.
> 2. Here *is* my *prediction* for the coming year.

- In sentence 1, the plural subject *flies* takes the plural verb *seem.*
- In sentence 2, the singular subject *prediction* takes the singular verb *is.*

You can often determine what the verb should be by reversing the word order: *two flies seem . . .* or *my prediction is. . . .*

PRACTICE 6

Underline the subject and circle the correct verb in each sentence.

1. There (goes, go) Tom Hanks.

2. There (is, are) only a few seconds left in the game.

3. Here (is, are) a terrific way to save money—make a budget and stick to it!

4. There (has, have) been robberies in the neighborhood lately.

5. Here (is, are) the plantains you ordered.

6. Here (comes, come) Johnny, the television talk-show host.

7. There (is, are) no direct route to Black Creek from here.

8. There (seems, seem) to be something wrong with the doorbell.

9. Here (is, are) the teapot and sugar bowl I've been looking for.

10. There (is, are) six reporters in the hall waiting for an interview.

PART F   Agreement in Questions

In questions, the subject usually follows the verb:

> 1. What *is* the *secret* of your success?
> 2. Where *are* the *copies* of the review?

■ In sentence 1, the subject *secret* takes the singular verb *is*.

■ In sentence 2, the subject *copies* takes the plural verb *are*.

You can often determine what the verb should be by reversing the word order: *the secret of your success is . . .* or *the copies are. . . .*

PRACTICE 7

Underline the subject and circle the correct verb in each sentence.

1. How (does, do) the combustion engine actually work?

2. Why (is, are) Robert and Charity so suspicious?

3. Where (is, are) the new suitcases?

4. Which tour guide (have, has) a pair of binoculars?

5. (Are, Is) Dianne and Bill starting a mail-order business?

6. What (seems, seem) to be the problem here?

7. Why (is, are) those boxes stacked in the corner?

8. (Is, Are) the mattress factory really going to close in June?

9. How (does, do) you explain that strange footprint?

10. Who (is, are) those people on the fire escape?

PART G Agreement in Relative Clauses

A **relative clause** is a subordinate clause that begins with *who, which,* or *that.* The verb in the relative clause must agree with the antecedent of the *who, which,* or *that.**

---

1. People *who have a good sense of humor* make good neighbors.

2. Be careful of a scheme *that promises you a lot of money fast.*

■ In sentence 1, the antecedent of *who* is *people. People* should take the plural verb *have.*

■ In sentence 2, the antecedent of *that* is *scheme. Scheme* takes the singular verb *promises.*

PRACTICE 8

Underline the antecedent of the *who, which,* or *that.* Then circle the correct verb.

1. Most patients prefer doctors who (spends, spend) time talking with them.

2. The gnarled oak that (shades, shade) the garden is my favorite tree.

3. Laptop computers, which (has, have) become very popular recently, are still fairly expensive.

4. My neighbor, who (swims, swim) at least one hour a day, is seventy years old.

5. Planning ahead, which (saves, save) hours of wasted time, is a good way to manage time effectively.

6. Employers often appreciate employees who (asks, ask) intelligent questions.

7. This air conditioner, which now (costs, cost) eight hundred dollars, rarely breaks down.

8. Everyone admires her because she is someone who always (sees, see) the bright side of a bad situation.

9. He is the man who (creates, create) furniture from scraps of walnut, cherry, and birch.

10. Foods that (contains, contain) artificial sweeteners may be hazardous to your health.

---

* For more work on relative clauses, see Chapter 20, "Revising for Sentence Variety," Part D.

PRACTICE 9   Review

Proofread the following essay for verb agreement errors. Correct any errors by writing above the lines.

Chimp Smarts

(1) Chimpanzees sometimes seem uncannily human, especially in their use of tools and language. (2) Neither the gorilla nor the orangutan, both close relatives of the chimp, exhibit such behavior.

(3) Chimps employs a number of tools in their everyday lives. (4) They dine by inserting sticks into insect nests and then licking their utensils clean. (5) Each of these intelligent animals also crack fruit and nuts with stones. (6) What's more, chimpanzees creates their own tools. (7) They make their eating sticks by cleaning leaves from branches. (8) They even attaches small sticks together to make longer rods for getting at hard-to-reach insects. (9) Some of the other tools chimps make is fly-whisks, sponges of chewed bark, and leaf-rags to clean themselves with. (10) Scientists on safari has observed infant chimps imitating their parents' use of these tools.

(11) Recent experiments indicate that chimpanzees probably also understands language though they lack the physical ability to speak. (12) There are little doubt that they can comprehend individual words. (13) Using sign language and keyboards, some chimps in captivity use nearly two hundred words. (14) This vocabulary include nouns, verbs, and prepositions. (15) Hunger and affection is needs that they have expressed by punching keyboard symbols. (16) Do chimps has the ability to string words into sentences? (17) Intriguingly, one chimp named Lucy has shown that she understand the difference between such statements as "Roger tickles Lucy" and "Lucy tickles Roger."

(18) Scientists still argue about just how much language a chimpanzee truly comprehend. (19) However, no one who have watched them closely doubt the intelligence of these remarkable beings.

CHAPTER 27

Past Tense

PART A	Regular Verbs in the Past Tense
PART B	Irregular Verbs in the Past Tense
PART C	A Troublesome Verb in the Past Tense: *To Be*
PART D	Troublesome Pairs in the Past Tense: *Can/Could, Will/Would*

PART A   Regular Verbs in the Past Tense

Regular verbs in the past tense take an *-ed* or *-d* ending:

1. The captain *hoisted* the flag.
2. They *purchased* lawn furniture yesterday.
3. We *deposited* a quarter in the meter.

■ *Hoisted, purchased,* and *deposited* are regular verbs in the past tense.

■ Each verb ends in *-ed* or *-d.*

PRACTICE 1

Fill in the past tense of the regular verbs in parentheses.*

1. I _____ (raise) my arms in a move called "embrace the tiger."

_____

* If you have questions about spelling, see Chapter 37, "Spelling," Parts D, E, and F.

2. Then I _____ (shift) my weight and _____ (walk) forward on my right foot to start the next move, "stroke the peacock's tail."

3. After stepping forward with my left foot, I _____ (reach) out my

   left hand and _____ (pull) back my right arm.

4. Unfortunately, my muscles _____ (clench), which _____ (result) in an awkward movement.

5. Talking calmly to myself, I _____ (relax) and _____ (start) again.

6. Then I _____ (move) fluidly to a new position.

7. These positions, which connect and flow into each other, _____ (evolve) over the centuries into what we now call tai chi.

8. Though tai chi _____ (develop) from the martial arts, today it emphasizes relaxation and stress reduction in addition to flexibility and fitness.

9. I chose to practice tai chi because it _____ (require) no special

   equipment, _____ (challenge) me physically, and _____ (promise) many benefits.

10. Tai chi is excellent exercise for all ages; a recent study _____

    (show) that when older people _____ (perform) it regularly, they

    _____ (reduce) the likelihood of falling—and thus breaking bones—by almost 25 percent.

PART B   Irregular Verbs in the Past Tense

Irregular verbs do not take an -ed or -d ending in the past but change internally:

1. I *wrote* that letter in ten minutes.
2. Although the orange cat *fell* from a high branch, she escaped unharmed.
3. The play *began* on time but ended fairly late.

■ *Wrote* is the past tense of *write*.

■ *Fell* is the past tense of *fall*.

■ *Began* is the past tense of *begin*.

Here is a partial list of irregular verbs:

Reference Chart
Irregular Verbs in the Past Tense

Simple Form	Past Tense	Simple Form	Past Tense
be	was, were	leave	left
become	became	let	let
begin	began	lie	lay
blow	blew	lose	lost
break	broke	make	made
bring	brought	mean	meant
build	built	meet	met
buy	bought	pay	paid
catch	caught	put	put
choose	chose	quit	quit
come	came	read	read
cut	cut	ride	rode
deal	dealt	rise	rose
dig	dug	run	ran
dive	dove (dived)	say	said
do	did	see	saw
draw	drew	seek	sought
drink	drank	sell	sold
drive	drove	send	sent
eat	ate	shake	shook
fall	fell	shine	shone (shined)
feed	fed	sing	sang
feel	felt	sit	sat
fight	fought	sleep	slept
find	found	speak	spoke
fly	flew	spend	spent
forbid	forbade	split	split
forget	forgot	spring	sprang
forgive	forgave	stand	stood
freeze	froze	steal	stole
get	got	stink	stank
give	gave	swim	swam
go	went	take	took
grow	grew	teach	taught
have	had	tear	tore
hear	heard	tell	told
hide	hid	think	thought
hold	held	throw	threw
hurt	hurt	understand	understood
keep	kept	wake	woke (waked)
know	knew	wear	wore
lay	laid	win	won
lead	led	write	wrote

Fill in the past tense of the regular and irregular verbs in parentheses. If you are not sure of the past tense, use the chart. Do not guess.

Entrepreneurs Did It Their Way

(1) Beth Cross and Pam Parker _____ (work) in the same company. (2) After they _____ (become) friends, they _____ (discover) that they both _____ (love) to ride horses. (3) Both women also _____ (think) that their riding boots were extremely uncomfortable. (4) Eventually, they _____ (leave) their jobs, _____ (design) a new boot, and _____ (begin) their own company. (5) The boots _____ (catch) on, sales _____ (double) every year for the first four years, and they now sell boots in more than two thousand outlets in the United States, Canada, Great Britain, and Australia.

(6) Cross and Parker _____ (go) from being employees to being entrepreneurs, individuals who start their own business. (7) These risk takers _____ (choose) to leave their job security so that they could try their hand at producing a new product.

(8) Duyen Le is a different type of entrepreneur, one who _____ (follow) his dream without ever joining a big company. (9) Le _____ (immigrate) to the United States from Vietnam. (10) Although he _____ (expect) to go into computer science, instead he _____ (open) a tiny Vietnamese restaurant in his neighborhood. (11) For years, he _____ (get) up at five each morning to search for the spices and vegetables he couldn't afford to have delivered.

(12) When customers almost _____ (pour) in, a rival _____ (challenge) him by opening a new Vietnamese restaurant around the corner. (13) Le simply _____ (buy) out his competitor. (14) Encouraged by his large number of non-Vietnamese customers, he very successfully _____

(start) many restaurants, first in local Boston neighborhoods and then in upscale areas of the city.

(15) Not every entrepreneur _____ (want) to become one. (16) However, when companies _____ (downsize) in recent years, thousands of employees _____ (lose) their jobs. (17) They _____ (have) to find new positions—or become entrepreneurs. (18) As it _____ (happen), thousands upon thousands of ordinary workers _____ (find) greater satisfaction—and sometimes _____ (make) far more money—when they _____ (do) it their way!

PART C A Troublesome Verb in the Past Tense: *To Be*

To be is the only verb that in the past tense has different forms for different persons. Be careful of subject-verb agreement:

	Reference Chart—*To Be* **Past Tense**			
	Singular		**Plural**	
	If the subject is	**the verb is**	**If the subject is**	**the verb is**
1st person:	I	was	we	were
2nd person:	you	were	you	were
3rd person:	he she it	was	they	were

■ Note that the first person singular form and the third person singular form are the same—*was*.

Be especially careful of agreement when adding *not* to *was* or *were* to make a contraction:

> was + not = wasn't
> were + not = weren't

PRACTICE 3

Circle the correct form of the verb *to be* in the past tense. Do not guess. If you are not sure of the correct form, use the chart on page 371.

1. Oprah Winfrey (was, were) always an avid reader.

2. In fact, books (was, were) sometimes her only comfort during her difficult childhood and painful adolescence.

3. When her producers (was, were) considering a television book club, Winfrey (was, were) understandably enthusiastic.

4. With a daily audience of more than twenty million, the world's most popular talk show host (was, were) sure she could get the whole country reading.

5. Her first book club selection (was, were) *The Deep End of the Ocean* by Jacquelyn Mitchard, the story of a kidnapped child.

6. The public's rush to buy books (wasn't, weren't) anticipated.

7. Mitchard's publishers (was, were) astonished to have to reprint the book nearly twenty times; all in all, 900,000 hardcovers and over 2 million paperbacks eventually (was, were) sold.

8. Winfrey's next book club choice (was, were) *Song of Solomon* by Nobel Prize winner Toni Morrison, a classic novel that (was, were) almost twenty years old.

9. About 300,000 copies (was, were) in print, but after Winfrey chose it, that figure (was, were) over 1,400,000.

10. Every book club pick (was, were) an enormous success, and even people who didn't read much found they (was, were) eagerly waiting for Winfrey's next selection.

PART D   Troublesome Pairs in the Past Tense: *Can/Could, Will/Would*

Use **could** as the past tense of **can.**

1. Maria is extraordinary because she *can* remember what happened to her when she was three years old.

2. When I was in high school, I *could* do two sit-ups in an hour.

■ In sentence 1, *can* shows the action is in the present.

■ In sentence 2, *could* shows the action occurred in the past.

PRACTICE 4

Fill in either the present tense *can* or the past tense *could*.

1. Tom is so talented that he _____ play most music on the piano by ear.

2. He _____ leave the hospital as soon as he feels stronger.

3. Last week we _____ not find fresh strawberries.

4. When we were in Spain last summer, we _____ see all of Madrid from our hotel balcony.

5. As a child, I _____ perform easily in public, but I _____ no longer do it.

6. Anything you _____ do, he _____ do better.

7. Nobody _____ find the guard after the robbery yesterday.

8. These days, Fred _____ usually predict the weather from the condition of his bunions.

Use **would** as the past tense of **will.**

> 3. Roberta says that she *will* arrive with her camera in ten minutes.
> 4. Roberta said that she *would* arrive with her camera in ten minutes.

- In sentence 3, *will* points to the future from the present.
- In sentence 4, *would* points to the future from the past.

PRACTICE 5

Fill in either the present tense *will* or the past tense *would*.

1. Sean expected that he _____ arrive at midnight.

2. Sean expects that he _____ arrive at midnight.

3. I hope the sale at the used car lot _____ continue for another week.

4. I hoped the sale at the used car lot _____ continue for another week.

5. When Benny had time, he _____ color-code his computer disks.

6. When Benny has time, he _____ color-code his computer disks.

7. The chefs assure us that the wedding cake _____ be spectacular.

8. The chefs assured us that the wedding cake _____ be spectacular.

PRACTICE 6 **Review**

Proofread the following essay for past tense errors. Then write the correct past tense form above the line.

The Warrior Queen of Jhansi

(1) The British cursed her as a devil; the people of India revered her almost as a god. (2) All agreed, however, that the Indian queen, Lakshmi Bai, were a powerful and daring woman.

(3) Before the ruler of Jhansi died in 1853, he willed his land and title to his five-year-old son. (4) He told his young wife, Lakshmi Bai, to rule until their child come of age. (5) Despite the young queen's ability and popularity, the British declared the will illegal and seize the kingdom. (6) Lakshmi Bai swallowed the insult and remained loyal to the British.

(7) However, throughout India, discontent against the British grew until rebellion broken out in 1857. (8) In Jhansi, rebels taked the British fort and then massacred the British women and children living in the city. (9) Though the queen do not support this bloodshed, the British held her responsible. (10) For a while in late 1857, in the absence of the British, the queen gotten her chance to rule. (11) Rising at 3:00 A.M., she spended her days first attending to matters of state, then riding and training with arms, and later meditating and praying.

(12) Finally, in early 1858, the British maked the queen an outlaw and lay siege to Jhansi for more than two weeks. (13) The queen heroically fighted for her city from a high tower where her people and the enemy can clearly see her. (14) As the city prepared for defeat, the queen, an expert horsewoman, fleed. (15) After riding for four days, she at last formally join the rebelling forces.

(16) The queen lead the defense at Gwalior, the last rebel stronghold. (17) Leading her men in hand-to-hand combat, she wore trousers, a silk blouse, and a red silk cap with a loose turban around it. (18) A pearl necklace that were one of the treasures of India hang around her neck. (19) Mortally wounded in this battle, she immediately become a beloved hero of the Indian nationalist movement.

CHAPTER 28

The Past Participle

PART A	Past Participles of Regular Verbs
PART B	Past Participles of Irregular Verbs
PART C	Using the Present Perfect Tense
PART D	Using the Past Perfect Tense
PART E	Using the Passive Voice (*To Be* and the Past Participle)
PART F	Using the Past Participle as an Adjective

PART A   Past Participles of Regular Verbs

The **past participle** is the form of the verb that can be combined with helping verbs like *have* and *has* to make verbs of more than one word:

Present Tense	Past Tense	Helping Verb plus Past Participle
1. They *skate*.	1. They *skated*.	1. They *have skated*.
2. Beth *dances*.	2. Beth *danced*.	2. Beth *has danced*.
3. Frank *worries*.	3. Frank *worried*.	3. Frank *has worried*.

■ *Skated, danced,* and *worried* are all past participles of regular verbs.

■ Note that both the *past tense* and the *past participle* of regular verbs end in *-ed* or *-d.*

PRACTICE 1

The first sentence of each pair that follows contains a regular verb in the past tense. Fill in *have* or *has* plus the past participle of the same verb to complete the second sentence.

1. Vance locked his keys in the car.

   Vance _____ _____ his keys in the car.

2. The carpenters gathered their tools from the littered floor.

   The carpenters _____ _____ their tools from the littered floor.

3. Clearly, you planned your vacation with care.

   Clearly, you _____ _____ your vacation with care.

4. Twice, Dianne and Carol visited the Dominican Republic.

   Twice, Dianne and Carol _____ _____ the Dominican Republic.

5. Detectives discovered the love letters in the garage.

   Detectives _____ _____ the love letters in the garage.

6. Mr. Yosufu carved this chess set out of wood.

   Mr. Yosufu _____ _____ this chess set out of wood.

7. My boss impressed everyone with her ability to read Chinese.

   My boss _____ _____ everyone with her ability to read Chinese.

8. Illness interrupted his work on the film.

   Illness _____ _____ his work on the film.

9. The windshields reflected the glow of the streetlights.

   The windshields _____ _____ the glow of the streetlights.

10. These three women studied with Madame Tebaldi.

    These three women _____ _____ with Madame Tebaldi.

PART B   Past Participles of Irregular Verbs

Most verbs that are irregular in the past tense are also irregular in the past participle, as shown in the box below.

Present Tense	Past Tense	Helping Verb plus Past Participle
1. We *sing*.	1. We *sang*.	1. We *have sung*.
2. Bill *writes*.	2. Bill *wrote*.	2. Bill *has written*.
3. I *think*.	3. I *thought*.	3. I *have thought*.

■ Irregular verbs change from present to past to past participle in unusual ways.

■ *Sung, written,* and *thought* are all past participles of irregular verbs.

■ Note that the past tense and past participle of *think* are the same—*thought*.

Reference Chart
Irregular Verbs, Past and Past Participle

Simple Form	Past Tense	Past Participle
be	was, were	been
become	became	become
begin	began	begun
blow	blew	blown
break	broke	broken
bring	brought	brought
build	built	built
buy	bought	bought
catch	caught	caught
choose	chose	chosen
come	came	come
cut	cut	cut
deal	dealt	dealt
dig	dug	dug
dive	dove (dived)	dived
do	did	done
draw	drew	drawn
drink	drank	drunk
drive	drove	driven
eat	ate	eaten
fall	fell	fallen
feed	fed	fed
feel	felt	felt
fight	fought	fought
find	found	found
fly	flew	flown
forbid	forbade	forbidden
forget	forgot	forgotten
forgive	forgave	forgiven

(continued)

Reference Chart
Irregular Verbs, Past and Past Participle

(continued)

Simple Form	Past Tense	Past Participle
freeze	froze	frozen
get	got	got (gotten)
give	gave	given
go	went	gone
grow	grew	grown
have	had	had
hear	heard	heard
hide	hid	hidden
hold	held	held
hurt	hurt	hurt
keep	kept	kept
know	knew	known
lay	laid	laid
lead	led	led
leave	left	left
let	let	let
lie	lay	lain
lose	lost	lost
make	made	made
mean	meant	meant
meet	met	met
pay	paid	paid
put	put	put
quit	quit	quit
read	read	read
ride	rode	ridden
rise	rose	risen
run	ran	run
say	said	said
see	saw	seen
seek	sought	sought
sell	sold	sold
send	sent	sent
shake	shook	shaken
shine	shone (shined)	shone (shined)
sing	sang	sung
sit	sat	sat
sleep	slept	slept
speak	spoke	spoken
spend	spent	spent
split	split	split
spring	sprang	sprung
stand	stood	stood
steal	stole	stolen
stink	stank	stunk
swim	swam	swum
take	took	taken
teach	taught	taught
tear	tore	torn

(continued)

Reference Chart
Irregular Verbs, Past and Past Participle

(continued)

Simple Form	Past Tense	Past Participle
tell	told	told
think	thought	thought
throw	threw	thrown
understand	understood	understood
wake	woke (waked)	woken (waked)
wear	wore	worn
win	won	won
write	wrote	written

PRACTICE 2

The first sentence of each pair that follows contains an irregular verb in the past tense. Fill in *have* or *has* plus the past participle of the same verb to complete the second sentence.

1. Sean took plenty of time buying the groceries.

   Sean _____ _____ plenty of time buying the groceries.

2. We sent our latest budget to the mayor.

   We _____ _____ our latest budget to the mayor.

3. My daughter hid her diary.

   My daughter _____ _____ her diary.

4. The jockey rode all day in the hot sun.

   The jockey _____ _____ all day in the hot sun.

5. Hershey, Pennsylvania, became a great tourist attraction.

   Hershey, Pennsylvania, _____ _____ a great tourist attraction.

6. The company's managers knew about these hazards for two years.

   The company's managers _____ _____ about these hazards for two years.

7. Carrie floated down the river on an inner tube.

   Carrie _____ _____ down the river on an inner tube.

8. At last, our team won the bowling tournament.

   At last, our team _____ _____ the bowling tournament.

9. Larry and Marsha broke their long silence.

   Larry and Marsha _____ _____ their long silence.

10. Science fiction films were very popular this past year.

   Science fiction films _____ _____ very popular this past year.

PRACTICE 3

Complete each sentence by filling in *have* or *has* plus the past participle of the verb in parentheses. Some verbs are regular, some irregular.

1. Recently, soccer _____ _____ (gain) in popularity in the United States.

2. Traditionally, most North Americans _____ _____ (consider) soccer much less exciting than basketball, football, or hockey.

3. Moreover, many North American players _____ _____ (find) it very difficult to compete at the highest levels of the game.

4. In the 1990 World Cup, for example, the United States lost all three of its games; that defeat _____ _____ (haunt) many soccer fans.

5. However, Canadian and U.S. interest in soccer _____ _____ (grow) ever since the 1994 World Cup, which was held in the United States.

6. Sports fans _____ _____ (see) the enormous enthusiasm and passionate emotion that soccer arouses in such countries as Brazil, Argentina, Italy, and Portugal.

7. The United States also _____ _____ (demonstrate) that it is able to win games in the biggest soccer competition in the world.

8. Unexpected victories _____ _____ (add) even more excitement to the game, like France's defeat of Brazil in the 1998 World Cup.

9. Attention _____ _____ (turn) to the 2002 World Cup, which Japan and Korea will co-host.

10. So far, every host team _____ _____ (win) at least one of the World Cup games played in the host country; the world will be watching to see if Japan, Korea, or both can rise to that traditional soccer feat.

PRACTICE 4

Proofread the following paragraph for past participle errors. Correct the errors by writing above the lines.

(1) Chattanooga, Tennessee, has went from being one of the dirtiest cities in the United States to one of the cleanest. (2) Local businesses and neighborhoods have chose to join government agencies in the rehabilitation effort. (3) For example, a nonprofit organization called Chattanooga Venture has brung together more than a thousand residents, who have addressed problems of air pollution, downtown deterioration, and a poor economy. (4) The group has attracted "clean industry" to Chattanooga and has holded on to environmentally sound businesses. (5) The Chattanooga Neighborhood Enterprise has builded or renovate thousands of units of inner-city housing. (6) The Tennessee River, once nothing but a source of filthy water because of the industrial sites on its banks, has maked a complete comeback. (7) Riverwalk has reclaimed miles of waterfront, creating parks, playgrounds, and walkways. (8) In recent years, people have even ate fish from the river, something many thought would never be possible again. (9) The Tennessee Aquarium—the world's largest freshwater aquarium—has opened, surrounded by art galleries, restaurants, and modern stores and residences. (10) With its free electric shuttle bus service, Chattanooga also has became the electric bus capital of the world. (11) The city has did such outstanding work that it has winned an international reputation for being a leader in "sustainable development programs."

PART C   Using the Present Perfect Tense

The **present perfect tense** is composed of the present tense of *to have* plus the past participle. The present perfect tense shows that an action has begun in the past and is continuing into the present.

1. Past tense:	Beatrice *taught* English for ten years.
2. Present perfect tense:	Beatrice *has taught* English for ten years.

■ In sentence 1, Beatrice *taught* English in the past, but she no longer teaches it. Note the use of the simple past tense, *taught*.

■ In sentence 2, Beatrice *has taught* for ten years and is still teaching English *now*. *Has taught* implies that the action is continuing.

PRACTICE 5

Read these sentences carefully for meaning. Then circle the correct verb—either the **past tense** or the **present perfect tense.**

1. He (directed, has directed) traffic for many years now.

2. Emilio lifted the rug and (has swept, swept) the dust under it.

3. Kelly (worked, has worked) in the computer industry for ten years; she now owns her own software company.

4. She (went, has gone) to the library last night.

5. The coffee maker gurgled so loudly that the noise (awakened, has awakened) me at 6:00 A.M.

6. For the past four years, I (enrolled, have enrolled) in summer school every summer.

7. We (talked, have talked) about the problem of your lateness for three days; it's time for you to do something about it.

8. While I was in Japan, I (took, have taken) many photographs of shrines.

9. She (won, has won) that contest ten years ago.

10. The boxers (fought, have fought) for an hour, and they look very tired.

11. He (applied, has applied) to three colleges and attended the one with the best engineering department.

12. Raymond looked at the revised plans for his new house and (decided, has decided) he could afford to build.

13. These useless tools (have been, were) here for quite a while, but no one wants to throw them out.

14. The most exciting moment of the game (occurred, has occurred) during the sudden death overtime.

15. The coauthors (worked, have worked) together for eight years and are now planning a new book.

PART D   Using the Past Perfect Tense

The **past perfect tense** is composed of the past tense of *to have* plus the past participle. The past perfect tense shows that an action occurred further back in the past than other past action.

1. Past tense:	Rhonda *left* for the movies.
2. Past perfect tense:	Rhonda *had* already *left* for the movies by the time we *arrived*.

■ In sentence 1, *left* is the simple past.

■ In sentence 2, the past perfect *had left* shows that this action occurred even before another action in the past, *arrived*.

PRACTICE 6

Read these sentences carefully for meaning. Then circle the correct verb—either the **past tense** or the **past perfect tense.**

1. Tony came to the office with a cane last week because he (sprained, had sprained) his ankle a month ago.

2. As Janice (piled, had piled) the apples into a pyramid, she thought, "I should become an architect."

3. Celia (finished, had finished) her gardening by the time I (drove, had driven) up in my new convertible.

4. Bonnie (operated, had operated) a drill press for years before she became a welder.

5. The man nervously (looked, had looked) at his watch and then walked a bit faster.

6. Last year Ming bought a compact disc player; he (wanted, had wanted) one for years.

7. Roberto told us that he (decided, had decided) to enlist in the Marines.

8. I (worked, had worked) on that essay for a week before I handed it in.

9. The caller asked whether we (received, had received) our free toaster yet.

10. Dianne (completed, had completed) college before her younger brother was old enough for the first grade.

11. Last week he told me that he (forgot, had forgotten) to mail the rent check.

12. As the curtain came down, everyone (rose, had risen) and applauded the Brazilian dance troupe.

13. Scott (closed, had closed) his books and went to the movies.

14. Brad missed the rehearsal on Saturday because no one (notified, had notified) him earlier in the week.

15. The prosecutor proved that the defendant was lying; until then I (believed, had believed) he was innocent.

PART E   Using the Passive Voice
(*To Be* and the Past Participle)

The **passive voice** is composed of the past participle with some form of *to be* (*am, is, are, was, were, has been, have been,* or *had been*). In the passive voice, the subject does not act but is *acted upon.*

Compare the passive voice with the active voice in the following pairs of sentences.

1.	Passive voice:	This newspaper *is written* by journalism students.
2.	Active voice:	Journalism students *write* this newspaper.
3.	Passive voice:	My garden *was devoured* by rabbits.
4.	Active voice:	Rabbits *devoured* my garden.

■ In sentence 1, the subject, *this newspaper,* is passive; it is acted upon. In sentence 2, the subject, *students,* is active; it performs the action.

■ Note the difference between the passive verb *is written* and the active verb *write.*

■ However, both verbs (*is written* and *write*) are in the *present tense.*

■ The verbs in sentences 3 and 4 are both in the *past tense: was devoured* (passive) and *devoured* (active).

   Use the passive voice sparingly. Write in the passive voice when you want to emphasize the receiver of the action rather than the doer.

PRACTICE 7

Fill in the correct **past participle** form of the verb in parentheses. If you are not sure, check the chart on pages 378–380.

1. The barn was _____ (build) by friends of the family.

2. Who was _____ (choose) to represent us at the union meeting?

3. These ruby slippers were _____ (give) to me by my grandmother.

4. These jeans are _____ (sell) in three sizes.

5. On their weekend camping trip, Sheila and Una were constantly

   _____ (bite) by mosquitoes and gnats.

6. It was _____ (decide) that Bill would work the night shift.

7. The getaway car is always _____ (drive) by a man in a gray fedora.

8. Her articles have been _____ (publish) in the *Texas Monthly*.

9. Harold was _____ (see) sneaking out the back door.

10. A faint inscription is _____ (etch) on the back of the old gold watch.

PRACTICE 8

Rewrite each sentence, changing the verb into the **passive** voice. Make all necessary verb and subject changes. Be sure to keep the sentence in the original tense.

EXAMPLE My father wore this silk hat.

This silk hat was worn by my father. _____

1. The goalie blocked the shot.

   _____

2. The lifeguard taught us to swim.

   _____

3. The usher warned the noisy group.

   _____

4. Her rudeness hurt her reputation.

   _____

5. The campers folded up the tent.

_____

6. The judges declared the match a draw.

_____

7. The conductor punched my ticket full of holes.

_____

8. The interviewer asked too many personal questions.

_____

PART F   Using the Past Participle as an Adjective

The **past participle** form of the verb can be used as an **adjective** after a linking verb:

> 1. The window is _broken_.

■ The adjective _broken_ describes the subject _window_.

The **past participle** form of the verb can sometimes be used as an adjective before a noun or a pronoun.

> 2. This _fried_ chicken tastes wonderful.

■ The adjective _fried_ describes the noun _chicken_.

PRACTICE 9

Use the past participle form of the verb in parentheses as an adjective in each sentence.

1. My _____ (use) car was a great bargain at only $700.

2. Bob is highly _____ (qualify) to install a water heater.

3. The _____ (air-condition) room was making everyone shiver.

4. The newly _____ (rise) cinnamon bread smelled wonderful.

5. Were you _____ (surprise) to hear about my raise?

6. He feels _____ (depress) on rainy days.

7. She knows the power of the _____ (write) word.

8. My gym teacher seems _____ (prejudice) against short people.

9. The _____ (embarrass) child pulled her jacket over her head.

10. We ordered _____ (toss) salad, _____ (broil) salmon, _____ (mash) potatoes, and _____ (bake) apple rings.

PRACTICE 10

Proofread the following paragraph for errors in past participles used as adjectives. Correct the errors by writing above the lines.

(1) Ice palaces, magical buildings made entirely from ice, have a long history. (2) These exquisitely built castles first appeared in Russia. (3) The most famous one was Empress Anna's palace, constructed in 1739 on the froze Neva River during one of the coldest winters ever recorded. (4) Cutted blocks of ice were set in place with cranes; water, which froze in the cold air, joined the blocks so smoothly that they appeared to be all one piece. (5) Considered the most magnificently craft ice palace ever, Anna's fairy-tale castle had finely furnish rooms and surroundings, including sculpted trees and birds painted in natural colors. (6) Although the Russians created other celebrate ice palaces, it took more than a hundred years for this almost losed art form to come to North America. (7) Now, beautifully carve and design ice palaces are a major attraction of winter festivals all over the world.

PRACTICE 11   Review

Proofread the following essay for past participle errors. Correct the errors by writing above the lines.

The Man of a Thousand Faces

(1) Lon Chaney, who was knowed as "the man of a thousand faces," was born in Colorado in 1883. (2) Both his parents were unable to hear or speak, and as a child, Chaney communicated with them through gestures and facial

expressions. (3) Later, his astonishing ability to express himself in pantomime was often credit to his childhood experiences with his parents.

(4) In the most famous of his many silent-film roles, Chaney played repulsive-appearing characters who made the audience feel both disgust and pity. (5) In *The Hunchback of Notre Dame,* which was maked in 1923, Chaney played Quasimodo, a grotesquely deformed man who nevertheless aroused compassion. (6) In *The Phantom of the Opera,* which was bringed out two years later, Chaney played a hideous-looking composer who haunted the sewers under the Paris Opera; again he was able to make people see the man behind the ugliness.

(7) Chaney is also celebrate for his use of makeup and extraordinary disguises. (8) In *The Hunchback of Notre Dame,* for example, he wore a forty-pound rubber hump, which was attach to a thirty-pound breastplate. (9) A hairy rubber skin was then stretch over everything. (10) His crooked nose and mismatch eyes were molded onto his face with wax.

(11) Chaney's great talents as an actor, as well as his use of those creative, if sometimes painful, disguises, have gave him a distinguish place in the history of film. (12) Ironically, Chaney died of throat cancer when he was only forty-seven; in his last days he was force once again to pantomime what he wanted to communicate.

Nouns

PART A	Defining Singular and Plural
PART B	Signal Words: Singular and Plural
PART C	Signal Words with *Of*

PART A   Defining Singular and Plural

Nouns are words that refer to people, places, or things. They can be either singular or plural. **Singular** means one. **Plural** means more than one.

Singular	Plural
the glass	glasses
a lamp	lamps
a lesson	lessons

■ As you can see, nouns usually add -*s* or -*es* to form the plural.

Some nouns form their plurals in other ways. Here are a few examples:

Singular	Plural	
child	children	
crisis	crises	
criterion	criteria	
foot	feet	*(continued)*

Copyright © Houghton Mifflin Company. All rights reserved.

	Singular	Plural
(continued)	goose	geese
	man	men
	medium	media
	memorandum	memoranda (memorandums)
	phenomenon	phenomena
	tooth	teeth
	woman	women

These nouns ending in *-f* or *-fe* change endings to *-ves* in the plural:

Singular	Plural
half	halves
knife	knives
life	lives
scarf	scarves
shelf	shelves
wife	wives
wolf	wolves

Hyphenated nouns form plurals by adding *-s* or *-es* to the main word:

Singular	Plural
brother-in-law	brothers-in-law
maid-of-honor	maids-of-honor
passer-by	passers-by

Other nouns do not change at all to form the plural; here are a few examples:

Singular	Plural
deer	deer
fish	fish
moose	moose
sheep	sheep

If you are unsure about the plural of a noun, check a dictionary. For example, if you look up the noun *woman* in the dictionary, you may see an entry like this:

woman, women

The first word listed, *woman*, is the singular form of the noun; the second word, *women*, is the plural.

Some dictionaries list the plural form of a noun only if the plural is unusual. If no plural is listed, that noun probably adds *-s* or *-es*.* *Remember:* Do not add an *-s* to words that form plurals by changing an internal letter. For example, the plural of *man* is *men*, not *mens*; the plural of *woman* is *women*, not *womens*; the plural of *foot* is *feet*, not *feets*.

PRACTICE 1

Make these singular nouns plural.

1. man _____   11. passer-by _____

2. half _____   12. criterion _____

3. foot _____   13. shelf _____

4. son-in-law _____   14. mouse _____

5. moose _____   15. child _____

6. life _____   16. father-in-law _____

7. tooth _____   17. knife _____

8. medium _____   18. deer _____

9. woman _____   19. secretary _____

10. crisis _____   20. goose _____

PART B Signal Words: Singular and Plural

A **signal word** tells you whether a singular or a plural noun usually follows.

■ These signal words tell you that a singular noun usually follows:

Signal Words
a(n)
a single
another
each } house
every
one

---

* For more work on spelling plurals, see Chapter 37, "Spelling," Part H.

■ These signal words tell you that a plural noun usually follows:

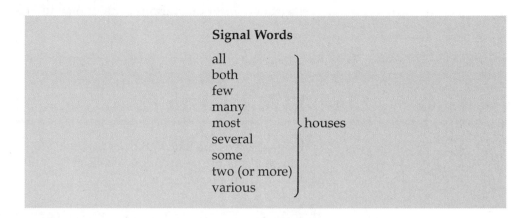

Signal Words

all
both
few
many
most   } houses
several
some
two (or more)
various

PRACTICE 2

Some of the following sentences contain incorrect singulars and plurals. Correct the errors. Put a C after correct sentences.

1. Following the lead of celebrities like Naomi Campbell and Demi Moore,

   many woman are experimenting with the body painting known as *mehndi.*

2. Although some American think mehndi is a new trend, it actually dates back

   thousands of years in India, Africa, and the Middle East.

3. Today, every traditional Hindu brides still is painted to celebrate her wed-

   ding, and in Morocco, mehndi is used to ward off evil.

4. In the United States, however, mehndi customers typically have their

   hands, necks, foots, legs, or even backs painted only for the beautiful

   effects.

5. Most mehndi painter use the ancient traditional patterns in their detailed

   designs.

6. The paint is made by mixing crushed henna leafs with tea, lemon juice, and

   several different oils.

7. This henna paste stays on for about twelve hours; then it cracks off and

   leaves a brown-orange stain that lasts about a month.

8. Few mehndi artist can use just their fingers to create the intricate decorations.

9. Instead, they use a fine-tipped funnels to paint the elaborate patterns.

10. Besides the gorgeous designs, there is another bonuses for customers; they can explore mehndi's various connection with meditation, spirituality, good fortune, and love.

PART C   Signal Words with *Of*

Many signal words are followed by *of . . .* or *of the. . . .* Usually, these signal words are followed by a **plural** noun (or a collective noun) because they really refer to one or more from a larger group.

> one of the
> each of the } pictures is . . .
>
> many of the
> a few of the } pictures are . . .
> lots of the

■ *Be careful:* The signal words *one of the* and *each of the* are followed by a **plural** noun, but the verb is **singular** because only the signal word (*one* or *each*) is the real subject.*

> *One* of the coats *is* on sale.
>
> *Each* of the flowers *smells* sweet.

PRACTICE 3

Fill in your own nouns in the following sentences. Use a different noun in each sentence.

1. Since Jacob wrote each of his _____ with care, the A's came as no surprise.

2. You are one of the few _____ I know who can listen to the radio and watch television at the same time.

3. Naomi liked several of the new _____ but remained faithful to her long-time favorites.

4. Many of the _____ wore Walkmans.

5. Determined to win the Salesperson of the Year award, Clyde called on all his _____ two or three times a month.

---

* For more work on this type of construction, see Chapter 26, "Present Tense (Agreement)," Part C.

6. One of the _____ was wearing a down jacket.

7. Before spring, each of these old _____ will have to be demolished.

Proofread the following essay for errors in singular and plural nouns. Correct the errors above the lines.

Hot off the Press

(1) Although it was certainly not the *New York Times* or the *Washington Post,* the first newspaper was a media not all that different from the papers we read today.

(2) In 59 B.C., the Roman government began to publish *Action Journal,* which carried many story of social events and political activities. (3) Roman men and woman could read about the births of childrens, as well as the marriages and deaths of other citizen. (4) The trials of thiefs and other lawless persons—and their executions—were also described. (5) In addition, this early newspaper reviewed the many spectacular show presented at the Colosseum.

(6) Several century later, on another continents, the Chinese government began publishing a news sheet. (7) Each government officials could read about social and political occurrences, as well as about court intrigues and gossip. (8) Many diplomat also found out about natural phenomenons—like eclipses and meteors—which they believed were good or bad omens. (9) This court chronicle was the first printed newspaper. (10) It lasted for almost 1,200 year until the Chinese Empire fell in 1911.

(11) The main difference between both of these newspaper and today's U.S. press is that they were state-run and state-controlled. (12) Roman and Chinese authoritys applied strict criterions of censorship to every articles. (13) In contrast, the modern press, freely written and circulated, was begun by Dutch merchants in the two city of Antwerp and Venice during the seventeenth century.

CHAPTER 30

Pronouns

PART A   Defining Pronouns and Antecedents

Pronouns take the place of or refer to nouns, other pronouns, or phrases. The word that the pronoun refers to is called the **antecedent** of the pronoun.

> 1. *Eric* ordered *baked chicken* because *it* is *his* favorite dish.
>
> 2. *Simone and Lee* painted *their* room.
>
> 3. *I* like *camping in the woods* because *it* gives *me* a chance to be alone with *my* thoughts.

- In sentence 1, *it* refers to the antecedent *baked chicken,* and *his* refers to the antecedent *Eric.*

- In sentence 2, *their* refers to the plural antecedent *Simone and Lee.*

- In sentence 3, *it* refers to the antecedent *camping in the woods.* This antecedent is a whole phrase. *Me* and *my* refer to the pronoun antecedent *I.*

In each sentence, a pronoun is circled. Write the pronoun first and then its antecedent, as shown in the example.

EXAMPLE | Have you ever wondered why we exchange rings in (our) wedding ceremonies?

our _____ *we* _____

1. When a man buys a wedding ring, (he) follows an age-old tradition.

   _____

2. Rich Egyptian grooms gave (their) brides gold rings five thousand years ago.

   _____

3. To Egyptian couples, the ring represented eternal love; (it) was a circle without beginning or end.

   _____

4. By Roman times, gold rings had become more affordable, so ordinary people could also buy (them).

   _____

5. Still, many a Roman youth had to scrimp to buy (his) bride a ring.

   _____

6. The first bride to slip a diamond ring on (her) finger lived in Venice about five hundred years ago.

   _____

7. The Venetians knew that setting a diamond in a ring was an excellent way of displaying (its) beauty.

   _____

8. Nowadays, a man and a woman exchange rings to symbolize the equality of (their) relationship.

   _____

PART B   Making Pronouns and Antecedents Agree

A pronoun must *agree* with its antecedent in number and person.*

1. When *Tom* couldn't find *his* pen, *he* asked to borrow mine.
2. The three *sisters* wanted to start *their* own business.

---

* For more work on pronoun agreement, see Chapter 19, "Revising for Consistency and Parallelism," Part B.

■ In sentence 1, *Tom* is the antecedent of *his* and *he*. Since *Tom* is singular and masculine, the pronouns referring to *Tom* are also singular and masculine.

■ In sentence 2, *sisters* is the antecedent of *their*. Since *sisters* is plural, the pronoun referring to *sisters* must also be plural.

As you can see from these examples, making pronouns agree with their antecedents is usually easy. However, three special cases can be tricky.

1. Indefinite Pronouns

anybody
anyone
everybody
everyone
nobody
no one
one
somebody
someone

Each of these words is **singular**. Any pronoun that refers to one of them must also be singular: *he, him, his, she,* or *her*.

3. *Anyone* can quit smoking if *he* or *she* wants to.

4. *Everybody* should do *his* or *her* best to keep the reception area uncluttered.

■ *Anyone* and *everybody* require the singular pronouns *he, she, his,* and *her*.

In the past, writers used *he* or *him* to refer to both men and women. Now, however, many writers use *he or she, his or her,* or *him or her*. Of course, if *everyone* or *someone* is a woman, use *she* or *her*; if *everyone* or *someone* is a man, use *he* or *him*. For example:

5. *Someone* left *her* new dress in a bag on the sofa.

6. *Everyone* is wearing *his* new tie.

PRACTICE 2

Fill in the correct pronoun and circle its antecedent. Make sure each pronoun agrees in number and person with its antecedent.

1. Anyone can become a good cook if _____ tries.

2. Someone dropped _____ lipstick behind the bookcase.

3. No one in the mixed doubles let _____ guard down for a minute.

4. Everybody wants _____ career to be rewarding.

5. Everyone is entitled to _____ full pension.

6. Mr. Hernow will soon be here, so please get _____ contract ready.

7. One should wear a necktie that doesn't clash with _____ suit.

8. The movie theater was so cold that nobody took off _____ coat.

2. Special Singular Antecedents

each (of) . . .	
either (of) . . .	Each of these constructions is **singular.** Any
neither (of) . . .	pronoun that refers to one of them must also be
every one (of) . . .	singular.*
one (of) . . .	

7. *Neither* of the two men paid for *his* ticket to the wrestling match.

8. *Each* of the houses has *its* own special charm.

■ The subject of sentence 7 is the singular *neither,* not *men*; therefore, the singular masculine pronoun *his* is required.

■ The subject of sentence 8 is the singular *each,* not the plural *houses*; therefore, the singular pronoun *its* is required.

PRACTICE 3

Fill in the correct pronoun and circle its antecedent. Make sure each pronoun agrees in number and person with its antecedent.

1. Each of the men wanted to be _____ own boss.

2. One of the saleswomen left _____ sample case on the counter.

3. Every one of the colts has a white star on _____ forehead.

4. Neither of the actors knew _____ lines by heart.

5. Neither of the dentists had _____ office remodeled.

6. Each of these arguments has _____ flaws and _____ strengths.

7. Every one of the jazz bands had _____ own distinctive style.

8. Either of these telephone answering machines will work very well if

   _____ is properly cared for.

---

* For more work on prepositional phrases, see Chapter 23, "The Simple Sentence," Part B.

3. Collective Nouns

Collective nouns represent a group of people but are usually considered **singular.** They usually take singular pronouns.

> 9. The *jury* reached *its* decision in three hours.
> 10. The debating *team* is well known for *its* fighting spirit.

■ In sentence 9, *jury* is a collective noun. Although it has several members, the jury acts as a unit—as one. Therefore, the antecedent *jury* takes the singular pronoun *its.*

■ In sentence 10, why does the collective noun *team* take the singular pronoun *its*?

Here is a partial list of collective nouns:

Common Collective Nouns		
class	family	panel
college	flock	school
committee	government	society
company	group	team
faculty	jury	tribe

PRACTICE 4

Read each sentence carefully for meaning. Circle the antecedent and then fill in the correct pronoun.

1. My family gave me all _____ support when I went back to school.

2. The government should reexamine _____ domestic policy.

3. The college honored _____ oldest graduate with a reception.

4. Eco-Wise has just begun to market a new pollution-free detergent that

   _____ is proud of.

5. The panel will soon announce _____ recommendations to the hospital.

6. The two teams gave _____ fans a real show.

7. The jury deliberated for six days before _____ reached a verdict.

8. After touring the Great Pyramid, the class headed back to Cairo in

_____ air-conditioned bus.

PART C   Referring to Antecedents Clearly

A pronoun must refer *clearly* to its antecedent. Avoid vague, repetitious, or ambiguous pronoun reference.

1. Vague pronoun:		At the box office, *they* said that tickets were no longer available.
2. Revised:	⎧	The cashier at the box office said. . . .
		or
3. Revised:	⎩	At the box office, I was told. . . .

■ In sentence 1, who is *they*? *They* does not clearly refer to an antecedent.

■ In sentence 2, *they* is replaced by *the cashier.*

■ In sentence 3, the problem is avoided by a change of language.*

4. Repetitious pronoun:		In the article, *it* says that Tyrone was a boxer.
5. Revised:	⎧	The article says that. . . .
		or
6. Revised:	⎩	It says that. . . .

■ In sentence 4, *it* merely repeats *article,* the antecedent preceding it.

■ Use either the pronoun or its antecedent, but not both.

7. Ambiguous pronoun:	Mr. Tedesco told his son that *his* car had a flat tire.
8. Revised:	Mr. Tedesco told his son that the younger man's car had a flat tire.
9. Revised:	Mr. Tedesco told his son Paul that Paul's car had a flat tire.

■ In sentence 7, *his* could refer either to Mr. Tedesco or to his son.

_____

*For more work on using exact language, see Chapter 21, "Revising for Language Awareness," Part A.

PRACTICE 5

Revise the following sentences, removing vague, repetitious, or ambiguous pronoun references. Make the pronoun references clear and specific.

1. In this book it says that most ducks and geese travel between forty and sixty miles per hour.

   Revised: _____

   _____

2. On the radio they warned drivers that the Interstate Bridge was closed.

   Revised: _____

   _____

3. Sandra told her friend that she shouldn't have turned down the promotion.

   Revised: _____

   _____

4. In North Carolina they raise tobacco.

   Revised: _____

   _____

5. The moving van struck a lamppost; luckily, no one was injured, but it was badly damaged.

   Revised: _____

   _____

6. In this college, they require every entering student to take a hearing test.

   Revised: _____

   _____

7. Professor Grazel told his parrot that he had to stop chewing telephone cords.

   Revised: _____

   _____

8. Vandalism was so out of control at the local high school that they stole sinks and lighting fixtures.

   Revised: _____

   _____

9. On the news, it said that the president hopes to present his new tax bill to Congress in the next two weeks.

   Revised: _____

   _____

10. Mr. Highwater informed his cousin that his wholesale rug business was a success.

    Revised: _____

    _____

11. The saleswoman at Wigged Out, she said I look like a rock star in this wig.

    Revised: _____

    _____

12. I don't watch Sunday night wrestling because they show ten commercials an hour.

    Revised: _____

    _____

13. Keiko is an excellent singer, yet she has never taken a lesson in it.

    Revised: _____

    _____

14. Rosalie's mother said she was glad she had decided to become a nurse.

    Revised: _____

    _____

15. At my church, they run a soup kitchen for people who need a hot meal.

    Revised: _____

    _____

PART D   Special Problems of Case

Personal pronouns take different forms depending on how they are used in a sentence. Pronouns can be **subjects, objects,** or **possessives.**

Pronouns used as **subjects** are in the **subjective case:**

1. *He* and *I* go backpacking together.
2. The peaches were so ripe that *they* fell from the trees.

■ *He, I,* and *they* are in the subjective case.

Pronouns that are **objects of verbs** or **prepositions** are in the **objective case.** Pronouns that are **subjects of infinitives** are also in the **objective case:**

3. A sudden downpour soaked *her.* (object of verb)
4. Please give this card to *him.* (object of preposition)
5. We want *them* to leave right now. (subject of infinitive)

■ *Her, him,* and *them* are in the objective case.

Pronouns that **show ownership** are in the **possessive case:**

6. The carpenters left *their* tools on the windowsill.
7. This flower has lost *its* brilliant color.

■ *Their* and *its* are in the possessive case.

Pronoun Case Chart			
Singular	**Subjective**	**Objective**	**Possessive**
1st person	I	me	my (mine)
2nd person	you	you	your (yours)
3rd person	he	him	his (his)
	she	her	her (hers)
	it	it	its (its)
	who	whom	whose
	whoever	whomever	
Plural			
1st person	we	us	our (ours)
2nd person	you	you	your (yours)
3rd person	they	them	their (theirs)

Using the correct case is usually fairly simple, but three problems require special care.

1. Case in Compound Constructions

A **compound construction** consists of two nouns, two pronouns, or a noun and a pronoun joined by *and*. Make sure that the pronouns in a compound construction are in the correct case.

> 8. *Serge* and *I* went to the pool together.
>
> 9. Between *you* and *me,* this party is a bore.

- In sentence 8, *Serge* and *I* are subjects.
- In sentence 9, *you* and *me* are objects of the preposition *between.*

Never use *myself* as a substitute for either *I* or *me* in compound constructions.

PRACTICE 6

Determine the case required by each sentence, and circle the correct pronoun.

1. (He, Him) and Harriet plan to enroll in the police academy.

2. A snowdrift stood between (I, me) and the subway entrance.

3. Tony used the software and then returned it to Barbara and (I, me, myself).

4. The reporter's questions caught June and (we, us) off guard.

5. By noon, Julio and (he, him) had already cleaned the garage and mowed the lawn.

6. These charts helped (she, her) and (I, me) with our statistics homework.

7. Professor Woo gave Diane and (she, her) extra time to finish the geology final.

8. Between you and (I, me), I have always preferred country music.

2. Case in Comparisons

Pronouns that complete **comparisons** may be in the **subjective, objective,** or **possessive** case:

> 10. His son is as stubborn as *he.* (subjective)
>
> 11. The cutbacks will affect you more than *her.* (objective)
>
> 12. This essay is better organized than *mine.* (possessive)

To decide on the correct pronoun, simply complete the comparison mentally and then choose the pronoun that naturally follows:

13. She trusts him more than I . . . (trust him).

14. She trusts him more than . . . (she trusts) . . . me.

■ Note that in sentences 13 and 14, the case of the pronoun in the comparison can change the meaning of the entire sentence.

PRACTICE 7

Circle the correct pronoun.

1. Your hair is much shorter than (she, her, hers).

2. We tend to assume that others are more self-confident than (we, us).

3. She is just as funny as (he, him).

4. Is Hanna as trustworthy as (he, her)?

5. Although they were both research scientists, he received a higher salary than (she, her).

6. I am not as involved in this project as (they, them).

7. Sometimes we become impatient with people who are not as quick to learn as (we, us).

8. Michael's route involved more overnight stops than (us, our, ours).

3. *Use of* Who *(or* Whoever*) and* Whom *(or* Whomever*)*

Who and **whoever** are in the **subjective** case. **Whom** and **whomever** are in the **objective** case.

15. *Who* is at the door?

16. For *whom* is that gift?

17. *Whom* is that gift for?

■ In sentence 15, *who* is the subject.

■ The same question is written two ways in sentences 16 and 17. In both, *whom* is the object of the preposition *for*.

■ Sometimes, deciding on *who* or *whom* can be tricky:

18. I will give the raise to *whoever* deserves it.

19. Give it to *whomever* you like.

■ In sentence 18, *whoever* is the subject in the clause *whoever deserves it.*

■ In sentence 19, *whomever* is the object in the clause *whomever you like.*

If you have trouble deciding on *who* or *whom,* change the sentence to eliminate the problem.

20. I prefer working with people *whom* I don't know as friends.
    or
    I prefer working with people I don't know as friends.

PRACTICE 8

Circle the correct pronoun.

1. (Who, Whom) will deliver the layouts to the ad agency?

2. To (who, whom) are you speaking?

3. (Who, Whom) prefers hiking to skiing?

4. For (who, whom) are those boxes piled in the corner?

5. The committee will award the scholarship to (whoever, whomever) it chooses.

6. (Who, Whom) do you wish to invite to the open house?

7. At (who, whom) did the governor fling the cream pie?

8. I will hire (whoever, whomever) can use a computer and speak Korean.

PART E   Using Pronouns with *-Self* and *-Selves*

Pronouns with *-self* or *-selves* can be used in two ways—as reflexives or as intensives.

A reflexive pronoun indicates that someone did something to himself or herself:

1. My daughter Miriam felt very grown up when she learned to dress *herself.*

■ In sentence 1, Miriam did something to *herself;* she *dressed herself.*

An intensive pronoun emphasizes the noun or pronoun it refers to:

> 2. Anthony *himself* was surprised at how relaxed he felt during the interview.

■ In sentence 2, *himself* emphasizes that Anthony—much to his surprise—was not nervous at the interview.

The following chart will help you choose the correct reflexive or intensive pronoun.

	Antecedent	Reflexive or Intensive Pronoun
Singular	I	myself
	you	yourself
	he	himself
	she	herself
	it	itself
Plural	we	ourselves
	you	yourselves
	they	themselves

Note that in the plural *-self* is changed to *-selves.*

■ *Be careful:* Do not use reflexives or intensives as substitutes for the subject of a sentence.

> Incorrect: Harry and *myself* will be there on time.
>
> Correct: Harry and *I* will be there on time.

PRACTICE 9

Fill in the correct reflexive or intensive pronoun. Be careful to make pronouns and antecedents agree.

1. Though he hates to cook, André _____ sautéed the mushrooms.

2. Rhoda found _____ in a strange city with only the phone number of a cousin whom she had not seen for years.

3. Her coffee machine automatically turns _____ on in the morning and off in the evening.

4. The librarian and I rearranged the children's section _____.

5. When it comes to horror films, I know that you consider _____ an expert.

6. They _____ didn't care if they arrived on time or not.

7. After completing a term paper, I always buy _____ a little gift to celebrate.

8. Larry _____ was surprised at how quickly he grew to like ancient history.

PRACTICE 10   Review

Proofread the following essay for pronoun errors. Then write the correct pronoun above the line.

The Many Lives of Jackie Chan

(1) Few movie stars can claim a career as unusual as him. (2) For one thing, Jackie Chan usually performs his death-defying stunts hisself. (3) Although he was a huge star in Asia for more than twenty years, fame eluded him in the United States until recently.

(4) Chan was born on April 7, 1954, in Hong Kong, but him and his parents soon moved to Canberra, Australia. (5) When he was only seven, he was sent back to Hong Kong to attend the Chinese Opera Research Institute. (6) At the school, they trained him in singing, acting, dancing, sword fighting, acrobatics, and kung fu. (7) When the Chinese Opera Research Institute closed in 1971, their training paid off for Chan, but not in the way his parents expected.

(8) Chan worked as a stuntman and fight choreographer and landed acting roles in several films, including Bruce Lee's *Enter the Dragon*. (9) Lee, he died in 1973, and Chan was the natural choice to fill Lee's shoes. (10) In several films, Chan tried to imitate Lee, but the films were unsuccessful. (11) In 1978, however, Chan came up with the idea of turning Lee's tough style into comedy. (12) *Snake in the Eagle's Shadow* and *Drunken Master* were hilarious hits; it established "kung fu comedy." (13) Jackie Chan became one of Hong Kong's most popular stars. (14) However, Hollywood directors did not appreciate Chan as a stuntman,

comedian, director, or scriptwriter when he first came to the United States in 1980. (15) Chan understood his own strengths better than them, but he couldn't gain much filmmaking control, and every film flopped. (16) Chan returned to Hong Kong, but him and his fans always believed he could make a U.S. comeback.

(17) When *Rumble in the Bronx,* China's most popular film ever, was dubbed in English, Chan finally began to attract attention in the United States. (18) Each of his English-dubbed films that followed worked their way up the charts. (19) *Rush Hour,* Chan's first U.S. movie in more than thirteen years, was released in 1998. (20) Now Jackie Chan's U.S. films are being received almost as well as its Hong Kong counterparts.

Prepositions

PART A	Working with Prepositional Phrases
PART B	Prepositions in Common Expressions

PART A   Working with Prepositional Phrases

Prepositions are words like *about, at, behind, into, of, on,* and *with.** They are followed by a noun or a pronoun, which is called the **object** of the preposition. The preposition and its object are called a **prepositional phrase.**

> 1. Ms. Fairworth remained *in the reading room.*
>
> 2. Students *with a 3.5 grade average* will receive a special award.
>
> 3. Traffic *at this corner* is dangerously heavy.

■ In sentence 1, the prepositional phrase *in the reading room* explains where Ms. Fairworth remained.

■ In sentence 2, the prepositional phrase *with a 3.5 grade average* describes which students will receive a special award.

■ Which is the prepositional phrase in sentence 3?

_____

■ What word does it describe?

_____

---

* For more work on prepositions, see Chapter 23, "The Simple Sentence," Part B.

In/On *for Time*

Two prepositions often confused are *in* and *on*. Use *in* before months not followed by a specific date, before seasons, and before years that do not include specific dates.

1. *In March,* the skating rink will finally open for business.
2. *In the summer,* I earn extra money as a lifeguard.
3. Rona expects to pay off her car *in 2005.*

Use *on* before days of the week, before holidays, and before months if a date follows.

4. *On Sunday,* the Kingston family spent the day at the beach.
5. Everyone is looking forward to the fireworks *on July Fourth.*
6. *On January 6,* Bernard left for a month of mountain climbing.

PRACTICE 1

Write either *in* or *on* in the following sentences.

1. _____ Labor Day _____ 1998, Mark McGwire hit his sixty-first home run of the season.

2. He thus tied the record set _____ 1961 by Roger Maris, a record that had stood for thirty-seven years.

3. McGwire proceeded to hit his sixty-second home run the following day,

   breaking Maris's record set _____ September 8, 1998.

4. _____ the following Sunday, Sammy Sosa hit *his* sixty-first home run; McGwire and Sosa continued to bat homers in an unusually supportive

   competition until the season ended _____ September 28.

5. Although McGwire set the official record at seventy home runs, the rivalry generated a level of excitement and appreciation not seen since baseball

   players went on strike _____ 1994.

In/On *for Place*

In means *inside* a place.

> 1. Tonia put her CD player *in the bedroom.*
> 2. Many country groups got their start *in Nashville.*

On means *on top of* or *at a particular place.*

> 3. That mess *on your desk* needs to be cleared off.
> 4. Pizza Parlor will be opening a new parlor *on Highland Avenue.*

PRACTICE 2

Write either *in* or *on* in the following sentences.

1. No official records were kept of black baseball played _____ the segregated United States of the 1930s and 1940s, but Josh Gibson is credited with season home runs of sixty-nine, seventy-five, and even eighty-four.

2. An incredibly powerful hitter, he once sent a home run so far out _____ some railroad tracks that the mayor of the town had the homer measured—at 512 feet.

3. Gibson once hit a home run _____ York, Pennsylvania, that landed _____ the roof of a truck _____ the Pennsylvania Turnpike.

4. _____ winter league games _____ Puerto Rico, he hit so many balls over the fences that fans hung signs _____ the trunks of palm trees to show where the balls had landed.

5. A plaque _____ the Baseball Hall of Fame _____ Cooperstown, New York, estimates that Gibson hit a total of "almost 800" home runs, but other estimates say he topped 950.

PART B Prepositions in Common Expressions

Prepositions are often combined with other words to form fixed expressions. Determining the correct preposition in these expressions can sometimes be confusing. Following is a list of some troublesome expressions with prepositions. Consult a dictionary if you need help with others.

Expressions with Prepositions

Expression	Example
according to	*According to* the directions, this flap fits here.
acquainted with	Tom became *acquainted with* his classmates.
addicted to	He is *addicted to* soap operas.
afraid of	Tanya is *afraid of* flying.
agree on (a plan)	Can we *agree on* our next step?
agree to (something or another's proposal)	Roberta *agreed to* her secretary's request for a raise.
angry about or at (a thing)	Jake seemed *angry about* his meager bonus.
angry with (a person)	Sonia couldn't stay *angry with* Felipe.
apply for (a position)	By accident, the twins *applied for* the same job.
approve of	Do you *approve of* bilingual education?
argue about (an issue)	I hate *arguing about* money.
argue with (a person)	Edna *argues with* everyone about everything.
capable of	Mario is *capable of* accomplishing anything he attempts.
complain about (a situation)	Patients *complained about* the long wait to see the dentist.
complain to (a person)	Knee-deep in snow, Jed vowed to *complain to* a maintenance person.
comply with	Each contestant must *comply with* contest regulations.
consist of	This article *consists of* nothing but false accusations and half-truths.
contrast with	The light blue shirt *contrasts* sharply *with* the dark brown tie.
correspond with (write)	We *corresponded with* her for two months before we met.
deal with	Ron *deals* well *with* temporary setbacks.
depend on	Miriam can be *depended on* to say the embarrassing thing.
differ from (something)	A typewriter *differs from* a computer in many ways.
differ with (a person)	Kathleen *differs with* you on the gun control issue.
different from	Children are often *different from* their parents.
displeased with	Ms. Withers was *displeased with* her doctor's advice to eat less fat.
fond of	Ed is *fond of* his pet tarantula.
grateful for	Be *grateful for* having so many good friends.
grateful to (someone)	The team was *grateful to* the coach for his inspiration and confidence.

Expressions with Prepositions

(continued)

Expression	Example
identical with	Scott's ideas are often *identical with* mine.
inferior to	Saturday's performance was *inferior to* the one I saw last week.
in search of	I hate to go *in search of* change at the last moment before the toll.
interested in	Willa is *interested in* results, not excuses.
interfere with	That dripping faucet *interferes with* my concentration.
object to	Martin *objected to* the judge's comment.
protect against	This heavy wool scarf will *protect* your throat *against* the cold.
reason with	It's hard to *reason with* an angry person.
rely on	If Toni made that promise, you can *rely on* it.
reply to	He wrote twice, but the president did not *reply to* his letters.
responsible for	Kit is *responsible for* making two copies of each document.
sensitive to	Professor Godfried is *sensitive to* his students' concerns.
shocked at	We were *shocked at* the graphic violence in that PG-rated film.
similar to	Some poisonous mushrooms appear quite *similar to* the harmless kind.
speak with (someone)	Geraldine will *speak with* her supervisor about a raise.
specialize in	This disc jockey *specializes in* jazz of the 1920s and the 1930s.
succeed in	Oscar *succeeded in* painting the roof in less than five hours.
superior to	It's clear that the remake is *superior to* the original.
take advantage of	Celia *took advantage of* the snow day to visit the science museum.
worry about	Never *worry about* more than one problem at a time.

PRACTICE 3

Fill in the preposition that correctly completes each of the following expressions.

1. According _____ his own account, Howard Schultz discovered the allure of coffee bars while on a trip to Italy.

2. When his company objected _____ his idea of expanding its retail coffee business, Schultz left his employer and started his own coffee bar.

3. Customers obviously approved _____ Schultz's decision; within six months, he was serving more than a thousand coffee lovers a day in a tiny coffee bar in Seattle.

4. _____ search _____ ways to expand his business, Schultz opened another store in Seattle and one in Vancouver.

5. When his former employers decided to sell their stores, Schultz immediately

   took advantage _____ the opportunity to buy them out.

6. That is how Howard Schultz acquired Starbucks and became responsible

   _____ turning four stores that sold coffee beans into more than 1,500 coffee bars.

7. Now, of course, Schultz's enterprise specializes _____ all kinds of novelty coffee drinks.

8. While many people are grateful _____ the ever-increasing variety,

   others complain that it interferes _____ the magic of that strong brewed cup of "real" coffee.

PRACTICE 4   **Review**

Proofread this essay for preposition errors. Cross out the errors and write corrections above the lines.

Dr. Daniel Hale Williams, Pioneer Surgeon

(1) On a lifetime of many successes, Dr. Daniel Hale Williams's greatest achievement was to pioneer open-heart surgery.

(2) Young Williams, an African American who grew up in the mid-1800s, knew poverty. (3) He relied to his wits to get by, becoming in turn a shoemaker, musician, and barber. (4) At the age of twenty-two, he met Dr. Henry Palmer, who soon saw he was capable on becoming a physician. (5) Williams's medical education, the usual one at the time, consisted in a two-year apprenticeship with Dr. Palmer, followed by three years at the Chicago Medical College, where he specialized on surgery.

(6) It was an exciting time in medicine, for surgeons had just started using antiseptics to protect patients for infection. (7) "Dr. Dan," as he was now called, became an expert on the new surgical techniques and a leader in Chicago's med-

ical and African-American communities. (8) In 1891, he succeeded with opening Provident Hospital, the first interracial hospital in the United States. (9) There, African Americans were assured first-rate medical care; moreover, black interns and nurses received thorough professional training.

(10) It was to Provident Hospital that frightened friends brought James Cornish in July 9, 1893. (11) Near death, the young man had received a deep knife gash near his heart during a fight. (12) Sensitive to the dangerous situation, Dr. Williams decided to operate immediately. (13) According with eyewitnesses, he first made a six-inch incision and removed Cornish's fifth rib. (14) Then he repaired a torn artery and stitched up the punctured sac surrounding the heart. (15) Fifty-one days later, Cornish left the hospital, recovered and deeply grateful for Dr. Williams to his life. (16) The age of open-heart surgery had begun.

(17) Much lay ahead for Dr. Williams. (18) He was responsible to reorganizing the Freedmen's Hospital at Howard University from 1894 to 1898; on 1913, he accepted an invitation from the American College of Surgeons and succeeded on becoming its only African-American charter member. (19) The high point of his life, however, remained that night in 1893.

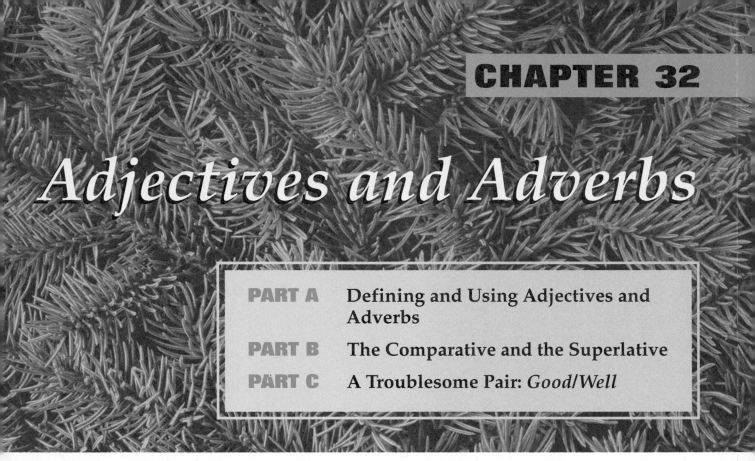

CHAPTER 32

Adjectives and Adverbs

PART A	Defining and Using Adjectives and Adverbs
PART B	The Comparative and the Superlative
PART C	A Troublesome Pair: *Good/Well*

PART A Defining and Using Adjectives and Adverbs

Adjectives and **adverbs** are two kinds of descriptive words. **Adjectives** describe or modify nouns or pronouns. They explain what kind, which one, or how many.

> 1. A *black* cat slept on the piano.
>
> 2. We felt *cheerful*.
>
> 3. *Three* windows in the basement need to be replaced.

- The adjective *black* describes the noun *cat*. It tells what kind of cat, a *black* one.

- The adjective *cheerful* describes the pronoun *we*. It tells what kind of mood we were in, *cheerful*.

- The adjective *three* describes the noun *windows*. It tells how many windows, *three*.

  Adverbs describe or modify verbs, adjectives, and other adverbs. They tell how, in what manner, when, where, and to what extent.

4. Joe dances *gracefully.*

5. *Yesterday* Robert left for a weekend of camping.

6. Brigit is *extremely* tall.

7. He travels *very* rapidly on that skateboard.

■ The adverb *gracefully* describes the verb *dances.* It tells how Joe dances, *gracefully.*

■ The adverb *yesterday* describes the verb *left.* It tells when Robert left, *yesterday.*

■ The adverb *extremely* describes the adjective *tall.* It tells how tall (to what extent), *extremely* tall.

■ The adverb *very* describes the adverb *rapidly,* which describes the verb *travels.* It tells how rapidly he travels, *very* rapidly.

Many adjectives can be changed into adverbs by adding an *-ly* ending. For example, *glad* becomes *gladly, hopeful* becomes *hopefully, awkward* becomes *awkwardly.*

Note the pairs on this list; they are easily confused:

Adjectives	Adverbs
awful	awfully
bad	badly
poor	poorly
quick	quickly
quiet	quietly
real	really
sure	surely

8. The fish tastes *bad.*

9. It was *badly* prepared.

■ In sentence 8, the adjective *bad* describes the noun *fish.*

■ In sentence 9, the adverb *badly* describes the verb *was prepared.*

PRACTICE 1

Circle the correct adjective or adverb in parentheses. Remember that adjectives modify nouns or pronouns; adverbs modify verbs, adjectives, or adverbs.

1. Have you ever seen (real, really) emeralds?

2. Try to do your work in the library (quiet, quietly).

3. We will (glad, gladly) take you on a tour of the Crunchier Cracker factory.

4. Lee, a (high, highly) skilled electrician, rewired his entire house last year.

5. She made a (quick, quickly) stop at the photocopy machine.

6. It was (awful, awfully) cold today; the weather was terrible.

7. The fans from Cleveland (enthusiastic, enthusiastically) clapped for the Browns.

8. Are you (sure, surely) this bus stops in Dusty Gulch?

9. He (hasty, hastily) wrote the essay, leaving out several important ideas.

10. It was a funny joke, but the comedian told it (bad, badly).

11. Tina walked (careful, carefully) down the icy road.

12. Sam swims (poor, poorly) even though he spends as much time as he can posing on the beach.

13. Sasha the crow is an (unusual, unusually) pet and a (humorous, humorously) companion.

14. The painting is not (actual, actually) a Picasso; in fact, it is a (real, really) bad imitation.

15. It is an (extreme, extremely) hot day, and I (sure, surely) could go for some (real, really) orange juice.

PART B   The Comparative and the Superlative

The **comparative** of an adjective or adverb compares two persons or things:

> 1. Ben is *more creative* than Robert.
> 2. Marcia runs *faster* than the coach.

■ In sentence 1, Ben is being compared with Robert.

■ In sentence 2, Marcia is being compared with the coach.

The **superlative** of an adjective or adverb compares three or more persons or things:

> 3. Sancho is the *tallest* of the three brothers.
> 4. Marion is the *most intelligent* student in the class.

■ In sentence 3, Sancho is being compared with the other two brothers.

■ In sentence 4, Marion is being compared with all the other students in the class.

Adjectives and adverbs of one syllable usually form the **comparative** by adding *-er*. They form the **superlative** by adding *-est*.

Adjective	Comparative	Superlative
fast	fast*er*	fast*est*
smart	smart*er*	smart*est*
tall	tall*er*	tall*est*

Adjectives and adverbs of more than one syllable usually form the **comparative** by using *more*. They form the **superlative** by using *most*.

Adjective	Comparative	Superlative
beautiful	*more* beautiful	*most* beautiful
brittle	*more* brittle	*most* brittle
serious	*more* serious	*most* serious

Note, however, that adjectives that end in *-y* (like *happy, lazy,* and *sunny*) change the *-y* to *-i* and add *-er* and *-est*.

Adjective	Comparative	Superlative
happy	happ*ier*	happ*iest*
lazy	laz*ier*	laz*iest*
sunny	sunn*ier*	sunn*iest*

PRACTICE 2

Write the comparative or the superlative of the words in parentheses. Remember: Use the comparative to compare two items; use the superlative to compare more than two. Use *-er* or *-est* for one-syllable words; use *more* or *most* for words of more than one syllable.*

1. The ocean is _____ (cold) than we thought it would be.

2. Please read your lines again, _____ (slowly) this time.

3. Which of these two roads is the _____ (short) route?

4. Which of these three highways is the _____ (short) route?

5. Belkys is the _____ (busy) person I know.

* If you have questions about spelling, see Chapter 37, "Spelling," Part G.

6. That red felt hat with feathers is the _____ (outlandish) one I've seen.

7. Today is _____ (warm) than yesterday, but Thursday was the

_____ (warm) day of the month.

8. The down coat you have selected is the _____ (expensive) one in the store.

9. Each one of Woody's stories is _____ (funny) than the last.

10. As a rule, mornings in Los Angeles are _____ (hazy) than afternoons.

11. Is Pete _____ (tall) than Louie? Is Pete the _____ (tall) player on the team?

12. If you don't do these experiments _____ (carefully), you will blow up the chemistry lab.

13. This farmland is much _____ (rocky) than the farmland in Iowa.

14. Therese says that Physics 201 is the _____ (challenging) course she has ever taken.

15. Mr. Wells is the _____ (wise) and _____

(experienced) leader in the community.

PRACTICE 3

Proofread the following paragraph for comparative and superlative errors. Cross out unnecessary words and write your corrections above the lines.

(1) With the hope of making counterfeiting more harder than it used to be, the federal government has started to issue new currency. (2) The new $100 bill appeared in 1996, the $50 bill in 1997, and the $20 bill in 1998. (3) The currency has been designed more carefuler than it was in the past. (4) The more recent of the three bills, the $20, features a larger portrait of President Andrew Jackson than the one that appeared on the older twenty. (5) The picture is off center, and the numerals are bigger and more darker than they were. (6) All the new bills have a portrait-shaped watermark, which can be seen only when a bill is held to the light. (7) One of the unsualest features is an embedded plastic thread that glows under ultraviolet light—red for the $100 bill, yellow for the $50, and green

for the $20. (8) Finally, the numeral in the lower right corner is printed in ink that looks green when seen straight on and black when seen from an angle. (9) Although the United States never recalls its currency, the old bills should be replaced naturally in about two years. (10) By then, everyone should be able to spot counterfeit currency more easier than before.

PART C   A Troublesome Pair: *Good/Well*

Adjective	Comparative	Superlative
good	better	best
bad	worse	worst

Adverb	Comparative	Superlative
well	better	best
badly	worse	worst

Be especially careful not to confuse the adjective **good** with the adverb **well:**

1. Jessie is a *good* writer.
2. She writes *well*.

■ *Good* is an **adjective** modifying *writer.*
■ *Well* is an **adverb** modifying *writes.*

PRACTICE 4

Fill in either the adjective *good* or the adverb *well* in each blank.

1. Corned beef definitely goes _____ with cabbage.

2. How _____ do you understand Spanish?

3. He may not take phone messages very _____, but he is

   _____ when it comes to handling e-mail.

4. Exercise is a _____ way to stay in shape; eating _____

   will help you maintain _____ health.

5. Tony looks _____ in his new beard and ponytail.

6. This is a _____ arrangement: I wash, you dry.

7. On a rainy night, Sheila loves to curl up with a _____ book.

8. The old Persian carpet and oak desk are a _____ match; they go _____ together.

9. At the finals, both teams played _____; it was a _____ game.

10. They are _____ neighbors and are _____ liked in the community.

PRACTICE 5

Fill in the correct comparative or superlative of the word in parentheses.

1. Lucinda is a _____ (good) chemist than she is mathematician.

2. Bascomb was the _____ (bad) governor this state has ever had.

3. When it comes to breaking appointments, you are _____ (bad) than I.

4. September is the _____ (good) month of the year for bird watching.

5. Jason used to be the _____ (good) mechanic on the lot; now he is the _____ (bad).

6. Of the two sisters, Leah is the _____ (good) markswoman.

7. You can carry cash when you travel, but using a credit card is _____ (good).

8. Our goalie is the _____ (good) in the league; yours is the _____ (bad).

9. When it comes to bad taste, movies are _____ (bad) than television.

10. The _____ part of going to a dentist is first sitting in that chair; I always feel _____ (good) when I have said good-bye.

11. Your cold seems _____ (bad) than it was yesterday.

12. Gina likes rock climbing _____ (good) than fishing; she prefers camping _____ (good) of all.

13. A parka is the _____ (good) protection against a cold wind; it is

   certainly _____ (good) than a hat.

14. I don't think teenagers are any _____ (bad) now than they were in
   my generation.

15. Note taking is one of the _____ (good) skills to acquire before you
   enter college.

PRACTICE 6   Review

Proofread the following essay for adjective and adverb errors. Correct errors by
writing above the lines.

Julia Morgan, Architect

   (1) Julia Morgan was one of San Francisco's most finest architects, as well as

the first woman licensed as an architect in California. (2) In 1902, Morgan became

the first woman to finish successful the program in architecture at the School of

Fine Arts in Paris. (3) Returning to San Francisco, she opened her own office and

hired and trained a very talented staff that eventual grew to thirty-five full-time

architects. (4) Her first major commission was to reconstruct the Fairmont Hotel,

one of the city's bestest-known sites, which had been damaged bad in the 1906

earthquake. (5) Morgan earned her reputation by designing elegant homes and

public buildings out of inexpensively and available materials and by treating her

clients real good. (6) She went on to design more than eight hundred residences,

stores, churches, offices, and educational buildings, most of them in California.

   (7) Her bestest customer was William Randolph Hearst, one of the country's

most rich newspaper publishers. (8) Morgan designed newspaper buildings and

more than twenty pleasure palaces for Hearst in California and Mexico. (9) She

maintained a private plane and pilot to keep her moving from project to project.

(10) The most big and famousest of her undertakings was sure San Simeon.

(11) Morgan worked on it steady for twenty years. (12) She converted a large

ranch overlooking the Pacific into a hilltop Mediterranean village composed of three of the beautifullest guest houses in the world. (13) The larger of the three was designed to look like a cathedral and incorporated Hearst's fabulous art treasures from around the world. (14) The finished masterpiece had 144 rooms and was larger than a football field. (15) San Simeon is now one of the most visited tourist attractions in California and seems to grow popularer each year.

CHAPTER 33

The Apostrophe

PART A	The Apostrophe for Contractions
PART B	The Apostrophe for Ownership
PART C	Special Uses of the Apostrophe

PART A   The Apostrophe for Contractions

Use the **apostrophe** in a **contraction** to show that letters have been omitted.

1. *I'll* buy that coat if it goes on sale.
2. At nine *o'clock* sharp, the store opens.

■ *I'll*, a contraction, is a combination of *I* and *will. Wi* is omitted.

■ The contraction *o'clock* is the shortened form of *of the clock.*

Be especially careful in writing contractions that contain pronouns:

Common Contractions

I + am = I'm	it + is or has = it's
I + have = I've	we + are = we're
I + will or shall = I'll	let + us = let's
you + have = you've	you + are = you're
you + will or shall = you'll	they + are = they're
he + will or shall = he'll	they + have = they've
she + is or has = she's	who + is or has = who's

Proofread these sentences and above the lines, supply any apostrophes missing from the contractions.

1. Ansel Adams wasnt only a great photographer; he was also a conservationist who helped save wildlife areas and establish national parks.

2. Hes best known for his dramatic scenes of the wilderness, but he also made huge technical contributions to the field of photography.

3. Because of Adams, theres now a film-exposure system that controls light and dark contrasts in every part of a photograph.

4. Adams was a talented musician who had planned to become a concert pianist; he hadnt expected a career in photography at all.

5. Its a well-known fact that the fourteen-year-old Adams took his first photo while on a family vacation trip to Yosemite National Park in 1916.

6. His decision didnt happen overnight, but he eventually realized that music wouldnt be as satisfying a field for him to work in as photography.

7. People werent surprised when he transferred the great attention to detail that he had given his piano technique to developing sharp, clear prints.

8. Whats most unusual is how Adams worked with light, space, and mood when he photographed storms, mountains, and other natural scenes.

9. Before Adams, many people couldnt believe that photography would become an art form.

10. Theyve been proven wrong: Adams published books about photography as well as books of his own photographs, and he established photography departments in museums and universities throughout the United States.

A photograph by Ansel Adams of Half-Dome and Merced River in Yosemite National Park appears on page 429.

PART B The Apostrophe for Ownership

Use the apostrophe to show ownership: Add an *'s* if a noun or an indefinite pronoun (like *someone, anybody,* and so on) does not already end in *-s:*

> 1. I cannot find my *friend's* book bag.
>
> 2. *Everyone's* right to privacy should be respected.
>
> 3. *John and Julio's* apartment has striped wallpaper.
>
> 4. The *children's* clothes are covered with mud.

- The *friend* owns the book bag.

- *Everyone* owns the right to privacy.

- Both John and Julio own one apartment. The apostrophe follows the compound subject *John and Julio.*

- The *children* own the clothes.

Add only an apostrophe to show ownership if the word already ends in *-s:**

> 5. My *aunts'* houses are filled with antiques.
>
> 6. The *knights'* table was round.
>
> 7. *Mr. Jonas'* company manufactures sporting goods and uniforms.

■ My *aunts* (at least two of them) own the houses.

■ The *knights* (at least two) own the table.

■ *Aunts* and *knights* already end in *-s,* so only an apostrophe is added.

■ *Mr. Jonas* owns the company. *Mr. Jonas* already ends in *-s,* so only an apostrophe is added.

Note that *possessive pronouns never take an apostrophe: his, hers, theirs, ours, yours, its:*

> 8. *His* car gets twenty miles to the gallon, but *hers* gets only ten.
>
> 9. That computer is *theirs; ours* is coming soon.

PRACTICE 2

Proofread the following sentences and add apostrophes where necessary to show ownership. In each case, ask yourself if the word already ends in -s. Put a C after any correct sentences.

1. Bills bed is a four-poster.

2. Martha and Davids house is a log cabin made entirely by hand.

3. Somebodys wedding ring was left on the sink.

4. During the eighteenth century, ladies dresses were heavy and uncomfortable.

5. Have you seen the childrens watercolor set?

6. Mr. James fried chicken and rice dish was crispy and delicious.

7. The class loved reading about Ulysses travels.

8. The Surgeon Generals latest report was just released.

9. Our citys water supply must be protected.

10. He found his ticket, but she cannot find hers.

* Some writers add an *'s* to one-syllable proper names that end in -s: *James's* bike.

11. Every spring, my grandmothers porch is completely covered with old furniture for sale.

12. Jacks Health Club just opened at Locust and Broad.

13. Celias final, a brilliant study of pest control on tobacco farms, received a high grade.

14. The mens locker room is on the right; the womens is on the left.

15. It seems that your orders have been lost in transit.

PART C   Special Uses of the Apostrophe

Use an apostrophe in certain expressions of time:

> 1. I desperately need a *week's* vacation.

■ Although the week does not own a vacation, it is a vacation of a week—*a week's vacation.*

Use an apostrophe to pluralize letters, numbers, and words that normally do not have plurals:

> 2. Be careful to cross your *t*'s.
>
> 3. Your *8*'s look like *F*'s.
>
> 4. Don't use so many *but*'s in your writing.

Use an apostrophe to show omitted numbers:

> 5. The class of '72 held its annual reunion last week.

PRACTICE 3

Proofread these sentences and add an apostrophe wherever necessary.

1. Cross your *t*s and dot your *i*s.

2. I would love a months vacation on a dude ranch.

3. Too many *and*s make this paragraph dull.

4. Those *9*s look crooked.

5. You certainly put in a hard days work!

PRACTICE 4 **Review**

Proofread the following essay for apostrophe errors. Correct the errors by adding apostrophes above the lines where needed and crossing out those that do not belong.

The True Story of Superman

(1) Sometimes, things just dont work out right. (2) That's how the creators of Superman felt for a long time.

(3) Supermans first home wasnt the planet Krypton, but Cleveland. (4) There, in 1933, Superman was born. (5) Jerry Siegels story, "Reign of Superman," accompanied by Joe Shuster's illustrations, appeared in the boys own magazine, *Science Fiction*. (6) Later, the teenagers continued to develop their idea. (7) Superman would come to Earth from a distant planet to defend freedom and justice for ordinary people. (8) He would conceal his identity by living as an ordinary person himself. (9) Siegel and Shuster hoped their characters strength and morality would boost peoples spirits' during the Great Depression.

(10) At first, the creators werent able to sell their concept; then, Action Comics' Henry Donnenfield bought it. (11) In June of 1938, the first *Superman* comic hit the stands. (12) Superman's success was immediate and overwhelming. (13) Finally, Americans had a hero who wouldnt let them down! (14) Radio and TV shows, movie serials, feature films, and generations of superheros' followed.

(15) While others made millions from their idea, Siegel and Shuster didnt profit from its' success. (16) They produced Superman for Action Comics for a mere fifteen dollars a page until they were fired a few years later when Joe Shusters eyes began to fail. (17) They sued, but they lost the case. (18) For a long time, both lived in poverty, but they continued to fight. (19) In 1975, Siegel and Shuster finally took their story to the press; the publicity won them lifelong pensions. (20) The two mens long struggle had ended with success.

The Comma

PART A   Commas for Items in a Series

Use commas to separate the items in a series:*

1. You need *bolts, nuts,* and *screws.*

2. I will be happy to *read your poem, comment on it,* and *return it to you.*

3. *Mary paints pictures, Robert plays the trumpet,* but *Sam just sits and dreams.*

Do not use commas when all three items are joined by *and* or *or*:

4. I enjoy *biking* and *skating* and *swimming.*

---

* For work on parallelism, see Chapter 19, "Revising for Consistency and Parallelism," Part C.

Punctuate the following sentences:

1. At the banquet, Ed served a salad of juicy red tomatoes crunchy green lettuce and stringless snap beans.

2. As a nursing assistant, Reva dispensed medication disinfected wounds and took blood samples.

3. Ali visited Santa Barbara Concord and Berkeley.

4. Hiking rafting, and snowboarding are her favorite sports.

5. The police found TV sets blenders and blow dryers stacked to the ceiling in the abandoned house.

6. I forgot to pack some important items for the trip to the tropics: insect repellent sunscreen and antihistamine tablets.

7. Don't eat strange mushrooms walk near the water or feed the squirrels.

8. Everyone in class had to present an oral report write a term paper and take a final.

9. We brought a Ouija board a Scrabble set and a Boggle game to the party.

10. To earn a decent wage make a comfortable home and educate my children—those are my hopes.

PART B   Commas with Introductory Phrases, Transitional Expressions, and Parentheticals

Use a comma after most introductory phrases of more than two words:*

1. *By four in the afternoon,* everybody wanted to go home.
2. *After the game on Saturday,* we all went dancing.

_____

* For more work on introductory phrases, see Chapter 20, "Revising for Sentence Variety," Part C.

Use commas to set off transitional expressions:

> 3. Ferns, *for example*, need less sunlight than flowering plants.
>
> 4. Instructors, *on the other hand*, receive a lower salary than assistant professors.

Use commas to set off parenthetical elements:

> 5. *By the way*, where is the judge's umbrella?
>
> 6. Nobody, *it seems*, wants to eat the three-bean salad.

■ *By the way* and *it seems* are called parenthetical expressions because they appear to be asides, words not really crucial to the meaning of the sentence. They could almost appear in parentheses: *(By the way) where is the judge's umbrella?*

Other common parenthetical expressions are *after all, actually, as a matter of fact,* and *to tell the truth.*

PRACTICE 2

Punctuate the following sentences:

1. Frankly I always suspected that you were a born saleswoman.

2. General Marsh it seems to me trusted only one or two of his advisers.

3. At two o'clock in the morning we were awakened by garbage cans clanging.

4. All twelve jurors by the way felt that the defendant was innocent.

5. On every April Fools' Day he tries out a new, dumb practical joke.

6. In fact Lucinda should never have written that poison-pen letter.

7. Close to the top of Mount Everest the climbers paused for a tea break.

8. To tell the truth that usher needs a lesson in courtesy.

9. My CD player I'm sorry to say gives me a shock every time I touch it.

10. These apples to tell the truth were organically grown in his back yard.

11. During the power blackout people tried to help one another.

12. Near the end of the driveway a large lilac bush bloomed and brightened the yard.

13. He prefers as a rule serious news programs to the lighter sitcoms.

14. To sum up Mr. Choi will handle all the details.

15. During my three years in Minnesota I learned how to deal with snow.

PART C   Commas for Appositives

Use commas to set off appositives:*

1. Yoko, *our new classmate,* is our best fielder.
2. *A humorous and charming man,* he was a great hit with my parents.
3. This is her favorite food, *ketchup sandwiches.*

■ Appositive phrases like *our new classmate, a humorous and charming man,* and *ketchup sandwiches* rename or describe nouns and pronouns—*Yoko, he, food.*

4. The poet *Shelley* wrote "Ode to the West Wind."
5. Shelley's wife, *Mary,* wrote *Frankenstein.*

■ A one-word appositive is not set off by commas when it is essential to the meaning of the sentence. Without the appositive *Shelley,* we do not know which poet wrote the ode.

■ A one-word appositive is set off by commas when it is not essential to the meaning of the sentence. The name *Mary* does not affect the meaning of the sentence.

PRACTICE 3

Punctuate the following sentences.

1. Hulk Hogan the popular wrestler and actor advises his fans to drink milk and say their prayers.

2. Long novels especially ones with complicated plots force me to read slowly.

3. David a resident nurse hopes to become a pediatrician.

4. I don't trust that tire the one with the yellow patch on the side.

_____

* For more work on appositives, see Chapter 20, "Revising for Sentence Variety," Part D.

5. Tanzania a small African nation exports cashew nuts.

6. Watch out for Phil a man whose ambition rules him.

7. Sheila a well-known nutritionist lectures at public schools.

8. A real flying ace Helen will teach a course in sky diving.

9. We support the Center for Science in the Public Interest a consumer education and protection group.

10. My husband Bill owns two stereos.

PART D Commas with Nonrestrictive and Restrictive Clauses

A **relative clause** is a clause that begins with *who, which,* or *that* and modifies a noun or pronoun. There are two kinds of relative clauses: **nonrestrictive** and **restrictive.***

A **nonrestrictive relative clause** is not essential to the meaning of the sentence:

> 1. Raj, *who is a part-time aviator,* loves to tinker with machines of all kinds.

■ *Who is a part-time aviator* is a relative clause describing *Raj.* It is a nonrestrictive relative clause because it is not essential to the meaning of the sentence. The point is that *Raj loves to tinker with machines of all kinds.*

■ **Commas** set off the nonrestrictive relative clause.

A **restrictive relative clause** is essential to the meaning of the sentence:

> 2. People *who do their work efficiently* make good students.

■ *Who do their work efficiently* is a relative clause describing *people.* It is a restrictive relative clause because it is *essential* to the meaning of the sentence. Without it, sentence 2 would read, *People make good students.* But the point is that certain people make good students—*those who do their work efficiently.*

■ Restrictive relative clauses *do not* require commas.

PRACTICE 4

Set off the nonrestrictive relative clauses in the following sentences with commas. Note that *which* usually begins a nonrestrictive relative clause and *that* usually

---

* For more work on nonrestrictive and restrictive clauses, see Chapter 20, "Revising for Sentence Variety," Part D.

begins a restrictive clause. Remember: Restrictive relative clauses are *not* set off by commas. Write a C after each correct sentence.

1. Olive who always wanted to go into law enforcement is a detective in the Eighth Precinct.

2. Employees who learn to use the new computers may soon qualify for a merit raise.

3. Polo which is not played much in the United States is very popular in England.

4. A person who always insists upon telling you the truth is sometimes a pain in the neck.

5. Statistics 101 which is required for the business curriculum demands concentration and perseverance.

6. Robin who is usually shy at large parties spent the evening dancing with Arsenio who is everybody's favorite dance partner.

7. This small shop sells furniture that is locally handcrafted.

8. His uncle who rarely eats meat consumes enormous quantities of vegetables, fruits, and grains.

9. Pens that slowly leak ink can be very messy.

10. Valley Forge which is the site of Washington's winter quarters draws many tourists every spring and summer.

PART E   Commas for Dates and Addresses

Use commas to separate the elements of an address. Note, however, that no punctuation is required between the state and ZIP code if the ZIP code is included.

1. Please send the books to *300 West Road, Stamford, CT 06860.*

2. We moved from *1015 Allen Circle, Morristown, New Jersey,* to *Farland Lane, Dubuque, Iowa.*

Use commas to separate the elements of a date:

3. The sociologists arrived in Tibet on *Monday, January 18, 1992,* and planned to stay for two years.

4. By *June 20, 2003,* I expect to have completed my B.A. in physical education.

Do not use a comma with a single-word address or date preceded by a preposition:

5. John DeLeon arrived *from Baltimore in January* and will be our new short-stop this season.

PRACTICE 5

Punctuate the following sentences. Write a C after each correct sentence.

1. The last few decades have seen the growth of an ancient Native American custom—the *powwow,* a gathering where tribal members dance to celebrate the circle of life.

2. At hundreds of powwows across the United States and Canada families and friends reaffirm their heritage, socialize, and compete for prize money.

3. Ten powwows were held in September 1999 alone, for example, each one with singing, chanting, drumming, and dancing.

4. On Wednesday September 1 1999 the Permian Basin Intertribal Powwow began in Odessa Texas.

5. On the weekend of September 4 to September 6 1999 Native Americans and visitors could choose between the Ottawa Celebration in Miami Oklahoma or the Traditions in the Making Powwow in Delta Utah.

6. The twenty-fourth Annual Fall Powwow took place on September 11 and 12 1999 at Jefferson Barracks Park St. Louis Missouri.

7. The Nause Waiwash Band of Indians Native American Festival was held in Sailwinds Park Cambridge Maryland on September 19 and 20 1999.

8. Some families even spend June to September going from powwow to pow-wow or traveling "the Red Road."

9. The Red Road is a path of commitment to living without alcohol and drugs and embracing a healthier lifestyle.

10. Each year, thousands attend the powwows to dance, admire the spectacular traditional costumes, meet interesting people, or just feel part of the circle of life.

11. For more information on powwows, you can contact the American Indian Heritage Foundation 6051 Arlington Blvd. Falls Church VA 22044.

12. Another resource is the National Native American Co-Op; the address is the Native American Trade and Information Center P.O. Box 1000 San Carlos AZ 85550-0301.

PART F   Minor Uses of the Comma

Use a comma after answering a question with *yes* or *no:*

1. *No,* I'm not sure about that answer.

Use a comma when addressing someone directly and specifically naming the person spoken to:

2. *Alicia,* where did you put my law books?

Use a comma after interjections like *ah, oh,* and so on:

3. *Ah,* these coconuts are delicious.

Use a comma to contrast:

4. Harold, *not Roy,* is my scuba-diving partner.

PRACTICE 6

Punctuate the following sentences.

1. Yes I do think you will be famous one day.

2. Well did you call a taxi?

3. The defendant ladies and gentlemen of the jury does not even own a red plaid jacket.

4. Cynthia have you ever camped in the Pacific Northwest?

5. No I most certainly will not marry you.

6. Oh I love the way they play everything to a salsa beat.

7. The class feels Professor Molinor that your grades are unrealistically high.

8. He said "March" not "Swagger."

9. Perhaps but I still don't think that the carburetor fits there.

10. We all agree Ms. Crawford that you are the best jazz bassist around.

PRACTICE 7   Review

Proofread the following essay for comma errors—either missing commas or commas used incorrectly. Correct the errors above the lines.

The Pyramids of Giza

(1) The pyramids of Giza, Egypt a wonder of the ancient world still inspire awe. (2) Built nearly five thousand years ago the largest of these tombs, was ordered by Khu-fu, a powerful pharaoh of ancient Egypt. (3) The two smaller pyramids nearby belonged to his successors his son Khafre and his grandson Menkaure. (4) The three pyramids—together with the Sphinx many temples and causeways—comprised a ceremonial complex for the dead not far from the Nile River.

(5) We marvel today at the ability of this ancient people to build such colossal structures without the benefit of work animals or machinery not even the wheel.

(6) The Great Pyramid for instance is 750 square feet and 480 feet high, roughly the size of Shea Stadium filled in with solid rock to a height of forty stories. (7) More than 100,000 workers, who were probably peasants forced into service cut two-and-a-half-ton limestone blocks from quarries on the other side of the Nile ferried them across the river, and then dragged them up ramps to be fitted exactly in place. (8) Experts estimate that 2.3 million blocks had to be moved over a period of more than twenty years, to complete the project.

(9) Perhaps the greatest wonder, however is that these structures have lasted. (10) Countless other buildings statues, and monuments have been constructed and admired, yet they have fallen into ruin while these magnificent structures remain. (11) The pyramids are considered all but indestructible. (12) It has been said, in fact that they could withstand a direct hit by an atomic bomb.

CHAPTER 35

Mechanics

PART A	Capitalization
PART B	Titles
PART C	Direct Quotations
PART D	Minor Marks of Punctuation

PART A   Capitalization

Always capitalize the following: *names, nationalities, religions, races, languages, countries, cities, months, days of the week, documents, organizations,* and *holidays.*

> 1. The *Protestant* church on the corner will offer *Spanish* and *English* courses starting *Thursday, June* 3.

Capitalize the following *only* when they are used as part of a proper noun: *streets, buildings, historical events, titles,* and *family relationships.*

> 2. We saw *Professor Rodriguez* at *Silver Hall,* where he was delivering a talk on the *Spanish Civil War.*

Do not capitalize these same words when they are used as common nouns:

> 3. We saw the professor at the lecture hall, where he was delivering a talk on a civil war.

Capitalize geographic locations but not directions:

4. The tourists went to the *South* for their winter vacation.
5. Go south on this boulevard for three miles.

Capitalize academic subjects only if they refer to a specific named and numbered course:

6. Have you ever studied psychology?
7. Last semester, I took *Psychology* 101.

PRACTICE 1

Capitalize wherever necessary in the following sentences. Put a C after each correct sentence.

1. Barbara Kingsolver, a well-known novelist, nonfiction writer, and poet, was born on april 8, 1955, in annapolis, maryland.

2. She grew up in rural kentucky and then went to college in indiana; after graduating, she worked in europe and since then has lived in and around tucson, arizona.

3. In college, Kingsolver majored first in music and then in biology; she later withdrew from a graduate program in biology and ecology at the university of arizona to work in its office of arid land studies.

4. Kingsolver's first novel, *The Bean Trees,* has become a classic; it is taught in english classes and has been translated into more than sixty-five languages.

5. The main character, named taylor greer, is considered one of the most memorable women in modern american literature.

6. In a later novel, *The Poisonwood Bible,* Kingsolver follows the family of a baptist minister in its move to the congo.

7. The fanaticism of reverend price brings misery to his family and destruction to the villagers he tries to convert to christianity.

8. Kingsolver's writing always deals with powerful political and social issues, but her novels don't sound preachy because she is a wonderful storyteller.

9. She has won awards and prizes from the american library association and many other organizations; she also has earned special recognition from the united nations national council of women.

10. This gifted writer, who plays drums and piano, performs with a band called rock bottom remainders; other band members are also notable writers—stephen king, amy tan, and dave barry.

PART B   Titles

Capitalize all the words of a title except short prepositions, short conjunctions, and the articles *the, an,* and *a.* Always capitalize the first and last words of the title, no matter what they are:

> 1. I liked *The Color Purple* but found *The House on the River* slow reading.

Underline the titles of long works: *books,** newspapers and magazines, television shows, plays, record albums, operas,* and *films.*
Put quotation marks around shorter works or parts of longer ones: *articles, short stories, poems, songs, paintings, scenes from plays,* and *chapters from full-length books.*

> 2. Have you read Hemingway's "The Killers" yet?
> 3. We are assigned "The Money Market" in *Essentials of Economics* for homework in my marketing course.

■ "The Killers" is a short story.
■ "The Money Market" is a chapter in the full-length book *Essentials of Economics.*

Do not underline or use quotation marks around the titles of your own papers.

---

* The titles and parts of sacred books are not underlined and are not set off by quotation marks: Job 5:6, Koran 1:14, and so on.

PRACTICE 2

Capitalize these titles correctly. Do not underline or use quotation marks in this practice.

1. the first immigrants

2. a trip through the Netherlands

3. making jams and jellies

4. a dangerous game

5. why every american should vote

6. nuclear power: safe or sorry?

7. you can build a sailboat

8. the quark theory

9. starting over

10. the millionaire next door

11. parents without partners

12. the value of friendship

13. what I would do with $50,000

14. three causes of world war II

15. the fate of the earth

PRACTICE 3

Wherever necessary, underline or place quotation marks around each title in the sentences below so that the reader will know at a glance what type of work the title refers to. Put a *C* after any correct sentence.

EXAMPLE Two of the best short stories in that volume are "Rope" and "The New Dress."

1. African-American writer Langston Hughes produced his first novel, Not Without Laughter, when he was a student at Lincoln University in Pennsylvania.

2. By that time, he had already been a farmer, a cook, a waiter, and a doorman at a Paris nightclub; he had also won a prize for his poem The Weary Blues, which was published in 1925 in the magazine Opportunity.

3. In 1926 Hughes wrote his famous essay The Negro Artist and the Racial Mountain, which appeared in the Nation magazine; he wanted young black writers to write without shame or fear about the subject of race.

4. Because he spoke Spanish, Hughes was asked in 1937 by the newspaper the Baltimore Afro-American to cover the activities of blacks in the International Brigades in Spain during the Spanish Civil War.

5. For the rest of his life, he wrote articles in newspapers such as the San Francisco Chronicle, the New York Times, and the Chicago Defender.

6. In fact, for more than twenty years he wrote a weekly column for the Chicago Defender, in which he introduced a character named Simple, who became popular because of his witty observations on life.

7. The stories about Simple were eventually collected and published in five books; two of those books are Simple Speaks His Mind and Simple Takes a Wife.

8. In 1938, Hughes established the Harlem Suitcase Theater in Manhattan, where his play Don't You Want to Be Free? was performed.

9. Because Hughes's poetry was based on the rhythms of African-American speech and music, many of his poems have been set to music, including Love Can Hurt You, Dorothy's Name Is Mud, and Five O'Clock Blues.

10. Few modern writers can rival Hughes's enormous output of fine poems, newspaper articles, columns, sketches, and novels.

PART C   Direct Quotations

Use quotation marks to enclose the exact words of the speaker:

1. He said, "These are the best seats in the house."

- The direct quotation is preceded by a comma or a colon.
- The first letter of the direct quotation is capitalized.
- Periods always go *inside* the quotation marks.

2. He asked, "Where is my laptop?"

3. Stewart yelled, "I don't like beans!"

■ Question marks and exclamation points go inside the quotation marks if they are part of the direct words of the speaker.

4. "That was meant for the company," he said, "but if you wish, you may have it."

5. "The trees look magnificent!" she exclaimed. "It would be fun to climb them all."

■ In sentence 4, the quotation is one single sentence interrupted by *he said.* Therefore, a comma is used after *he said,* and *but* is not capitalized.

■ In sentence 5, the quotation consists of two different sentences. Thus a period follows *exclaimed,* and the second sentence of the quotation begins with a capital letter.

PRACTICE 4

Insert quotation marks where necessary in each sentence. Capitalize and punctuate correctly.

1. The sign reads don't even think about parking here.

2. Can you direct me to the central bus stop he asked.

3. Alexander Pope wrote to err is human, to forgive divine.

4. Jim wondered why have I been having such good luck lately

5. Well, it takes all kinds she sighed

6. The report stated no one responded to the crisis in time.

7. He exclaimed you look terrific in those jeweled sandals

8. The article said Most American children do poorly in geography.

9. These books on ancient Egypt look interesting he replied but I don't have time to read them now.

10. Although the rain is heavy she said we will continue harvesting the corn.

11. Give up caffeine and get lots of rest the doctor advised.

12. This final is easy he whispered to himself it is a guaranteed A.

13. We haven't gone fishing for a month he complained and we really miss it

14. The label warns this product should not be taken by those allergic to aspirin.

15. Red, white, and blue Hillary said are my favorite colors

PART D Minor Marks of Punctuation

1. The Colon

Use a colon to show that a direct quotation will follow or to introduce a list:*

1. This is the opening line of his essay: "The airplane is humanity's greatest invention."
2. There are four things I can't resist in warm weather: fresh mangoes, a sandy beach, cold drinks, and a hammock.

Use a colon to separate the chapter and verse in a reference to the Bible or to separate the hour and minute:

3. This quotation comes from Genesis 1:1.
4. It is now exactly 4:15 P.M.

2. Parentheses

Use parentheses to enclose a phrase or word that is not essential to the meaning of the sentence:

5. Herpetology (the study of snakes) is a fascinating area of zoology.
6. She left her hometown (Plunkville) to go to the big city (Fairmount) in search of success.

3. The Dash

Use a dash to emphasize a portion of a sentence or to interrupt the sentence with an added element:

7. This is the right method—the only one—so we are stuck with it.

The colon, parentheses, and the dash should be used sparingly.

---

* Avoid using a colon after any form of the verb *to be* or after a preposition.

PRACTICE 5

Punctuate these sentences with colons, dashes, or parentheses.

1. Calvin asked for the following two light bulbs, a pack of matches, a lead pencil, and a pound of grapes.

2. They should leave by 1130 P.M.

3. The designer's newest fashions magnificent leather creations were generally too expensive for the small chain of clothing stores.

4. Harvey the only Missourian in the group remains unconvinced.

5. She replied, "This rock group The Woogies sounds like all the others I've heard this year."

6. If you eat a heavy lunch as you always do remember not to go swimming immediately afterward.

7. By 9:30 P.M., the zoo veterinarian a Dr. Smittens had operated on the elephant.

8. Note these three tips for hammering in a nail hold the hammer at the end of the handle, position the nail carefully, and watch your thumb.

9. Whenever Harold Garvey does his birdcalls at parties as he is sure to do everyone begins to yawn.

10. Please purchase these things at the hardware store masking tape, thumbtacks, a small hammer, and some sandpaper.

PRACTICE 6   Review

Proofread the following essay for errors in capitalization, quotation marks, colons, parentheses, and dashes. Correct the errors by writing above the lines.

The Passion of Thomas Gilcrease

(1) Thomas Gilcrease, a descendent of creek indians, became an instant Millionaire when oil was discovered on his homestead in 1907. (2) He spent most of his fortune collecting objects that tell the story of the american frontier, particularly of the Native American experience. (3) The Thomas Gilcrease institute of american history and arts in Tulsa, oklahoma, is the result of his lifelong passion.

(4) This huge collection more than 10,000 works of art, 90,000 historical documents, and 250,000 native american artifacts, spans the centuries from 10,000 B.C. to the 1950s. (5) Awed visitors can view nearly two hundred George Catlin paintings of Native American life. (6) They can walk among paintings and bronze sculptures by Frederic Remington with names like The Coming And Going Of The Pony Express that call up images of the West. (7) Museumgoers can admire Thomas Moran's watercolors that helped persuade congress to create yellowstone, the first national park. (8) In addition, visitors are treated to works by modern Native Americans, such as the display of wood sculptures by the cherokee Willard Stone.

(9) The museum also houses many priceless documents an original copy of the declaration of independence, the oldest known letter written from the new world, and the papers of Hernando Cortés. (10) A new glass storage area even allows visitors to view the 80 percent of the holdings that are not on display. (11) Thousands of beaded moccasins and buckskin dresses line the shelves, and a collection of magnificent war bonnets hangs from brackets.

(12) When the Gilcrease Institute opened its doors on May 2, 1949, *Life* declared "it is the best collection of art and literature ever assembled on the American frontier and the Indian. (13) Thousands of visitors agree.

CHAPTER 36

Putting Your Proofreading Skills to Work

After you have written a paragraph or an essay—once you have prewritten, drafted, and revised—you are ready for the next step—**proofreading.**

Proofreading, which takes place at the sentence level, means applying what you have learned in Unit 6. When you proofread, carefully check each sentence for correct grammar, punctuation, and capitalization. Is every sentence complete? Do all verbs agree with their subjects? Are there any comma errors? Do all proper nouns begin with a capital letter?

This chapter gives you the opportunity to put your proofreading skills to work in real-world situations. As you proofread the paragraphs and essays that follow, you must look for any—and every—kind of error, just as you would in the real world of college or work. The paragraph practices tell you what kinds of errors to look for; if you have trouble, go back to those chapters and review. The essay practices, however, contain a random mix of errors and give you no clues at all.

PROOFREADING PRACTICE 1

Proofread this paragraph, correcting any errors above the lines. To review, see these chapters:

Chapter 25	run-ons, comma splices, fragments
Chapter 26	present tense problems, subject-verb agreement
Chapter 27	past tense problems
Chapter 28	past participle problems

(1) Don't sit in a draft or you'll get a chill. (2) And catch a cold. (3) If you walks around with wet socks and shoes in winter or don't wear a hat, you'll catch a cold. (4) Sitting in a frosty air-conditioned room is sure to give you a cold. (5) If you haven't gave this advice, you've probably received it at some

time. (6) However, the fact is that the only way to catch a cold is by coming in direct contact with a cold virus when you are susceptible. (7) Cold viruses are called *Rhinoviruses* (*rhin* is Greek for *nose*). (8) Because they have entered the body through the nose. (9) Colds usually spread when people sneeze or cough, get the virus on their hands or a tissue, and then touches other people who touch their noses. (10) You can, therefore, sit in a draft or in a too-cold air-conditioned room and not catch a cold. (11) A chill actually be the first symptom of a cold, not the cause. (12) Similarly, you can be outdoors on a freezing day in wet shoes and socks—and without a hat—and not catch a cold if there is no cold germs present. (13) (You would probably be very uncomfortable, though.) (14) What should you do if you have catched a cold? (15) Unfortunately, there is no magic cure, the best advice is to stay indoors, keep warm, and drink lots of fluids.

PROOFREADING PRACTICE 2

Proofread this paragraph, correcting any errors above the lines. To review, see these chapters:

Chapter 25	run-ons, comma splices, fragments
Chapter 26	subject-verb agreement
Chapter 29	noun errors
Chapter 30	pronoun errors
Chapter 35	capitalization

(1) Since ancient times, the Zunis of New Mexico have used *fetishes*. (2) Small objects carved from stone or wood that are believed to have magical powers. (3) The Zuni religion have a complex tradition of fetishes based on the six directions. (4) North, south, east, west, above, and below. (5) Each of the directions are associated with special forces and a guardian animal. (6) The East, for example, where the sun rises, is the source of all life, truth, and new ideas it is represented by a white wolf. (7) Because wolfs are highly intelligent, social, and loving as parents, they are good to adopt as a personal fetish if you feel you share these qualities. (8) Likewise, someone facing a big decision or a family problem might seek

the help of their wolf fetish. (9) The other five guardian animals are the mountain lion, black bear, badger, eagle, and mole. (10) Additional fetish animals include coyotes, owls, snakes, deers, and rabbits. (11) The Zunis still holds fetishes sacred in its religion and continues to carve them. (12) In fact, some Zunis are famous for their distinctive carving, their fetishes sell all over the world as works of art.

PROOFREADING PRACTICE 3

Proofread this paragraph, correcting any errors above the lines. To review, see these chapters:

Chapter 25   run ons, comma splices, fragments
Chapter 31   preposition errors
Chapter 32   adjective and adverb errors

(1) Florence Griffith Joyner, the fastest woman in track and field history and one of the interestingest. (2) Flo-Jo, as she was known, was a sprinter, at the 1984 Olympics, she won a silver medal running the 200-meter sprint. (3) In the U.S. trials for the 1988 Olympics, she set a world record of 10.49 seconds. (4) For the 100-meter sprint. (5) At the Olympics, she won three gold medals and set a world record of 21.23 seconds for the 200. (6) No other female sprinter has ever run as swift; her records are unbroken. (7) Neither has any track star come close in style at the starting line, all eyes were on Flo-Jo. (8) Flo-Jo's hair was always the most beautiful styled, her makeup was applied perfect, and her nails were long and bright polished. (9) Her running gear was the more flamboyant imaginable. (10) At first, spectators were shocked with Flo-Jo's lacey spandex suits and neon-colored unitards. (11) Off the field, Flo-Jo was a business woman who did extremely good marketing her own line of athletic wear. (12) When she died at age 38 on 1998, she was serving on the President's Council on Physical Fitness and Sports. (13) She was a superb athlete and a model for women everywhere.

PROOFREADING PRACTICE 4

Proofread this paragraph, correcting any errors above the lines. To review, see these chapters:

(1) If you want to eat well and do our planet a favor become a Vegetarian. (2) Most vegetarian's eat eggs, milk, dairy products and fish. (3) All youre giving up are leathery steak's and overcooked chicken. (4) A vegetarian dinner might begin with a greek salad of, crisp cucumbers, sweet red onion black olives, and a sprinkling of feta cheese. (5) Youll think you're sitting in a little cafe overlooking the mediterranean sea. (6) For the main course, head to mexico for tamale pie. (7) A rich, flavorful dish made of pinto beans's, brown rice, green peppers and tomatoes. (8) On the table of course is a loaf of warm bread. (9) Do you have room for dessert how about some ben and jerrys ice cream, made in vermont? (10) As you linger over a cup of french espresso coffee think how your vegetarian meal was delicious, nutritious, and a help to our planet. (11) If more people ate vegetarian the land given to raising cattle and crops to feed cattle could be used for raising grain, many of the worlds hungry people could be fed. (12) To read about vegetarianism, get the best-known guide *laurels kitchen: a handbook for vegetarian cookery and nutrition.*

PROOFREADING PRACTICE 5

This essay contains many of the errors you learned to avoid in Unit 6. Proofread each sentence carefully, and then correct each error above the line.

Gators and Crocs

(1) With their scaly bodies slit eyes and long tails, alligators and crocodiles look a lot like dinosaurs. (2) In fact alligators and crocodiles descended from the same family as dinosaurs. (3) While its true that alligators and crocodiles look a lot alike, they differ in three ways.

(4) First alligators and crocodiles are found in different parts of the world. (5) Alligators be found in china, central america, and south america. (6) On the other

hand, crocodiles are found in africa (especially around the nile river), australia, southeast asia, india, cuba, and the west indies. (7) Only in the southern united states is both alligators and crocodiles found. (8) In all cases however alligator's and crocodile's live in hot, tropical regions. (9) Reptiles are cold-blooded, so at temperatures below 65 degrees, alligators and crocodiles gets sluggish and cannot hunt.

(10) Alligators and crocodiles also differ in appearance. (11) Alligators has broader flatter snouts that are rounded at the end. (12) Crocodiles has narrower almost triangular snouts. (13) The best way to tell the difference is to view both from the side when they have their mouths closed, you can see only upper teeth on an alligator, but you can also see four lower teeth on a croc. (14) If you get really close you can see that alligators have a space between they're nostrils while the nostrils of crocs are very close together.

(15) Finally alligators and crocodiles are temperamentally different. (16) Alligators are not aggressive they are even a bit shy. (17) They will lie in wait along a river bank for prey when on land, they move slow and uneven. (18) Crocodiles, however, are much more aggressive. (19) They are fast, mean, and often stalk they're prey. (20) The australian freshwater crocodile and the nile crocodile can even run on land, with their front and back legs working together like a dog. (21) Nile crocodiles kill hundred's of people every year.

(22) Alligators and crocodiles have outlived the dinosaurs, but they might not survive hunters who want to turn them into shoes wallets briefcases and belts. (23) In 1967, the u.s. government declared alligators an endangered species. (24) Fortunately american alligators have repopulated and are now reclassified as threatened. (25) Importing crocodile and alligator skins are banned worldwide, but some species is still threatened. (26) These frightening and fascinating ancient creatures need help worldwide if they are to survive.

This essay contains many of the errors you learned to avoid in Unit 6. Proofread each sentence carefully, and then correct each error above the line.

In the Market for a Used Car?

(1) For several year's now, used car sales have exceeded new car sales. (2) Good used cars can be founded at dealers. (3) And through newspaper ads. (4) You might also let your friends know your in the market for a used car, they might know of someone who wants to sell their car. (5) Wherever you look for a used car keep the following tips in mind.

(6) First shop before you need the car. (7) This way you can decide exactly what type of car suit you most best. (8) Do you want a compact. (9) Or a midsize car? (10) What features are important to you? (11) Should you get an american-made car or a japanese, german, or other import? (12) If you shop when you are'nt desperate, you are more likely to make a good choice and negotiate good.

(13) Second narrow your choices to three or four cars, and do some research. (14) Start with the *kelley blue book used car price manual*. (15) The blue book as its called for short gives the current value by model year and features. (16) Its also a good idea to check *consumer reports* magazine. (17) Every april issue lists good used car buys and cars to avoid. (18) Based on what you learn go back and test-drive the cars that interest you the mostest. (19) Drive each for at least an hour, drive in stop-and-go traffic in the highway, in winding roads, and in hills.

(20) When you do decide on a car ask your mechanic to look at it. (21) Be sure to get a written report that include an estimate of what repair's will cost. (22) Money spent at this point is money spent wise, if the seller wont allow an inspection take your business elsewhere.

(23) When you buy a used car you want dependability and value. (24) Follow these tip's youll be able to tell a good buy when you see it.

Adopt a New Point of View

No matter how excellent the content of an essay, report, or business letter, grammatical errors will diminish its impact. Ironically, errors call attention to themselves. Learning to proofread your writing might not seem terribly exciting, but it is an all-important skill.

When this student received the interesting assignment to *write as if you are someone or something else,* he decided to see what it's like to be a roach. His audience: humans. His tone: wacky. In your group or class, read his essay, aloud if possible. Underline details or sentences that are especially effective or humorous, and **proofread** as you go. If you spot any errors, correct them.

It's Not Easy Being a Roach

(1) It's not easy being a roach. My life consist of the constant struggle to survive. We have existed for millions of years, yet we still do not get the respect that we deserve. We have witnessed the dawn of the dinosaur and the coming of Jesus. We have experienced two world wars, enjoyed the benefits of cable television, and feasted our eyes on many women taking showers. Being small has its advantages, and it doesn't hurt to be quick either. Because we have live so long. You would think that respect would be ours, but that is not the case.

(2) We are looked upon as pests rather than pets, we are quieter than household pets. We don't eat much, and contrary to popular belief, we are very clean. Sure, some of us prefers the wild life of booze, drugs, and unprotected sex with other insects, but that doesn't mean that most of us are not seeking a happy life that includes love and affection from you humans. I think it's high time that you appreciated our value as insects, pets, and potential lifelong companions.

(3) I might have six legs, but that doesn't mean I can handle all the burdens that come with being a roach. My wife is pregnant again, which means 10,000 more mouths to feed. It's bad enough that I have to find a meal fit for thousands, I also live in fear of becoming a Roach McNugget. For some strange reason, rodents consider us food. Do I look scrumptious to you? Does my body ignite wild fantasies of sinful feasting? I think not. Mice and rats refuse to respect us because they see us as midnight munchies.

(4) I don't ask for much—a home, some food, and maybe an occasional pat on the head. If I can't have these simple things, I would prefer somebody simply step on me. A fast, hard crunch would do—no spraying me with roach spray, no Roach Motel. I may be on the lower end of the species chain, but that doesn't mean I'm not entitled to live out my dreams. I am roach and hear me roar!

(5) When you humans kill each other off with nuclear bombs, we will still be around. With luck on our side, we will grow into big monsters because of exposure to radiation. Then I don't think those of you who remains will enjoy being chased around by giant, glowing roaches—all because you humans didn't want to hug a roach when you had the chance.

(6) One more thing: Stop trying to kill us with that pine-scented roach spray. It doesn't kill us it just makes us smell bad. If I want to smell like pine trees, I will go and frolic in some wood, naked and free. You people really tick me off.

—Israel Vasquez (Student)

1. How effective is Mr. Vasquez's essay?

   _____ Strong thesis statement? _____ Good supporting details?

   _____ Logical organization? _____ Effective conclusion?

2. Discuss your underlinings. What details or lines in the essay did you like the most? Explain as exactly as possible why you like something or why it made you laugh.

3. Mr. Vasquez's sense of humor comes through to readers. Does he also achieve his goal of presenting a roach's point of view?

4. Would you suggest any revisions? Is this essay effective or offensive? Why? Does the final paragraph provide a strong and humorous conclusion, or does it seem like an afterthought?

5. This essay contains several serious grammar errors. Can you find and correct them? What two error patterns does this fine writer need to watch out for?

GROUP WORK

In writing as in life, it is often easier to spot other people's errors than our own. In your group or class, discuss *your* particular error patterns and how you have learned to catch them. Do you have problems with comma splices, *-ed* verb endings, or prepositional phrases? Discuss any proofreading tricks and techniques you have learned to spot and correct those errors successfully in your own papers. Have someone jot down the best techniques that your group mates have used, and be prepared to share these with the class.

 ## WRITING AND REVISING IDEAS

1. Adopt a new point of view; discuss your life as a bird, animal, insect, or object.

2. Write as a person of another gender, ethnic group, or period in history.

Strengthening Your Spelling

CHAPTER 37

Spelling

PART A   Suggestions for Improving Your Spelling

Accurate spelling is an important ingredient of good writing. No matter how interesting your ideas are, if your spelling is poor, your writing will not be effective.

Some Tips for Improving Your Spelling

■ **Look closely at the words on the page.** Use any tricks you can to remember the right spelling. For example, "The *a*'s in *separate* are separated by an *r*," or "*Dessert* has two *s*'s because you want two desserts."

■ **Use a dictionary.** Even professional writers frequently check spelling in a dictionary. As you write, underline the words you are not sure of and look them up when you write your final draft. If locating words in the dictionary is a real problem for you, consider a "poor speller's dictionary."

■ **Use a spell checker.** If you write on a computer, make a habit of using the spell-check software. See Part B for tips and cautions about spell checkers.

■ **Keep a list of the words you misspell.** Look over your list whenever you can and keep it handy as you write.

■ **Look over corrected papers for misspelled words** (often marked *sp.*). Add these words to your list. Practice writing each word three or four times.

■ **Test yourself.** Use flash cards or have a friend dictate words from your list or from this chapter.

■ **Review the basic spelling rules explained in this chapter.** Take time to learn the material; don't rush through the entire chapter all at once.

■ **Study the spelling list on page 471,** and test yourself on these words.

■ **Read through Chapter 38, "Look-Alikes/Sound-Alikes,"** for commonly confused words (*their, there,* and *they're,* for instance). The practices in that chapter will help you eliminate some common spelling errors from your writing.

PART B   Computer Spell Checkers

Almost all word-processing programs are equipped with a spell checker. A spell checker picks up spelling errors and gives you alternatives for correcting them. Get in the habit of using this feature as your first and last proofreading task.

Depending on your program and the paper you are writing, determine the best ways to use the spell checker. For example, if your paper repeats an unusual name, use the "ignore all" feature rather than check the name each time it appears. If the name appears when you're using "ignore all," you've spelled the name differently that time.

What a spell checker cannot do is think. If you've mistyped one word for another—*if* for *it,* for example—the spell checker cannot bring it to your attention. If you've written *then* for *than,* the spell checker cannot help. Proofread your paper after using the spell checker. For questions about words that sound the same but are spelled differently, check Chapter 38, "Look-Alikes/Sound-Alikes." Run spell check again after you've made all your corrections. If you've introduced a new error, the spell checker will let you know.

PRACTICE 1

With a group of four or five classmates, read this poem, which "passed" spell check. Can your group find and correct all the errors that the spell check missed?

Eye halve a spelling check her,

It came with my pea see.

It clearly marques four my revue,

Miss steaks eye can knot sea.

I've run this poem threw it.

Your Shirley please too no

Its letter perfect in it's weigh.

My checker tolled me sew.

PART C   Spotting Vowels and Consonants

To learn some basic spelling rules, you must know the difference between vowels and consonants.

The **vowels** are *a, e, i, o,* and *u.*

The **consonants** are *b, c, d, f, g, h, j, k, l, m, n, p, q, r, s, t, v, w, x,* and *z.*

The letter *y* can be either a vowel or a consonant, depending on its sound:

daisy   sky

■ In each of these words, *y* is a vowel because it has a vowel sound: an *ee* sound in *daisy* and an *i* sound in *sky.*

yellow   your

■ In both *yellow* and *your, y* is a consonant because it has the consonant sound of *y.*

PRACTICE 2

Write *v* for vowel and *c* for consonant in the space on top of each word. Be careful of the *y.*

EXAMPLE

c	v	c	v	c
h	o	p	e	d

1.
_	_	_	_
h	a	l	l

2.
_	_	_	_
r	e	l	y

3.
_	_	_	_	_	_	_
p	e	r	h	a	p	s

4.
_	_	_	_
y	a	w	n

5.
_	_	_	_	_	_	_
i	n	s	t	e	a	d

6.
_	_	_	_
j	u	m	p

7.
_	_	_	_	_	_	_
q	u	a	l	i	f	y

8.
_	_	_	_	_	_
h	i	d	d	e	n

9.
_	_	_	_	_
f	o	r	g	e

10.
_	_	_	_	_	_	_	_	_
b	y	s	t	a	n	d	e	r

PART D   Doubling the Final Consonant (in Words of One Syllable)

When you add a suffix or an ending that begins with a vowel (like *-ed, -ing, -er, -est*) to a word of one syllable, double the final consonant *if* the last three letters of the word are *consonant-vowel-consonant* or *c-v-c.*

plan + ed = planned   swim + ing = swimming

thin + est = thinnest   light + er = lighter

■ *Plan, swim,* and *thin* all end in *cvc;* therefore, the final consonants are doubled.

■ *Light* does not end in *cvc;* therefore, the final consonant is not doubled.

PRACTICE 3

Which of the following words should double the final consonant? Check to see whether the word ends in *cvc.* Then add the suffixes *-ed* and *-ing.*

	Word	Last Three Letters	-ed	-ing
EXAMPLE	drop	cvc	dropped	dropping
	boil	vvc	boiled	boiling
1.	tan			
2.	brag			
3.	rip			
4.	mail			
5.	stop			
6.	peel			
7.	shift			
8.	wrap			
9.	ask			
10.	chat			

PRACTICE 4

Which of the following words should double the final consonant? Check for *cvc.* Then add the suffixes *-er* or *-est.*

	Word	Last Three Letters	-er	-est
EXAMPLE	wet	cvc	wetter	wettest
	cool	vvc	cooler	coolest
1.	deep			
2.	short			
3.	fat			
4.	slim			

Word	Last Three Letters	-er	-est
5. red	_____	_____	_____
6. green	_____	_____	_____
7. moist	_____	_____	_____
8. clean	_____	_____	_____
9. dim	_____	_____	_____
10. bright	_____	_____	_____

PART E   Doubling the Final Consonant (in Words of More Than One Syllable)

When you add a suffix that begins with a vowel to a word of more than one syllable, double the final consonant *if*

(1) the last three letters of the word are *cvc, and*

(2) the accent or stress is on the *last* syllable.

> **begin + ing = beginning   control + ed = controlled**

■ *Begin* and *control* both end in *cvc.*

■ In both words, the stress is on the last syllable: *be-gin', con-trol'*. (Pronounce the words aloud and listen for the correct stress.)

■ Therefore, *beginning* and *controlled* double the final consonant.

> **listen + ing = listening   visit + ed = visited**

■ *Listen* and *visit* both end in *cvc.*

■ However, the stress is *not* on the last syllable: lis'-ten, vis'-it.

■ Therefore, *listening* and *visited do not* double the final consonant.

PRACTICE 5

Which of the following words should double the final consonant? First, check for *cvc;* then check for the final stress. Then add the suffixes *-ed* and *-ing*.

	Word	Last Three Letters	-ed	-ing
EXAMPLE	repel	cvc	repelled	repelling
	enlist	vcc	enlisted	enlisting
	1. expel	_____	_____	_____
	2. happen	_____	_____	_____
	3. polish	_____	_____	_____

Word	Last Three Letters	-ed	-ing
4. admit	_____	_____	_____
5. offer	_____	_____	_____
6. prefer	_____	_____	_____
7. commit	_____	_____	_____
8. pardon	_____	_____	_____
9. compel	_____	_____	_____
10. answer	_____	_____	_____

PART F   Dropping or Keeping the Final *E*

When you add a suffix that begins with a vowel (like *-able, -ence, -ing*), drop the final *e*.

When you add a suffix that begins with a consonant (like *-less, -ment, -ly*), keep the final *e*.

move + ing = moving   **pure + ity = purity**

■ *Moving* and *purity* both drop the final *e* because the suffixes *-ing* and *-ity* begin with vowels.

home + less = homeless   **advertise + ment = advertisement**

■ *Homeless* and *advertisement* keep the final *e* because the suffixes *-less* and *-ment* begin with consonants.

Here are some exceptions to memorize:

argument	judgment	truly
awful	knowledgeable	simply
courageous	manageable	

PRACTICE 6

Add the suffix shown to each word.

EXAMPLE   hope + ing = _hoping_

hope + ful = _hopeful_

1. love + able = _____

2. love + ly = _____

3. pure + ly = _____

4. pure + er = _____

5. complete + ing = _____

6. complete + ness = _____

7. enforce + ment = _____

8. enforce + ed = _____

9. arrange + ing = _____

10. arrange + ment = _____

PRACTICE 7

Add the suffix shown to each word.

EXAMPLE | come + ing = _coming_

rude + ness = _rudeness_

1. guide + ance = _____   6. sincere + ly = _____

2. manage + ment = _____   7. like + able = _____

3. dense + ity = _____   8. response + ible = _____

4. complete + ly = _____   9. judge + ment = _____

5. motive + ation = _____   10. fame + ous = _____

PART G   Changing or Keeping the Final Y

When you add a suffix to a word that ends in -*y*, change the *y* to *i* if the letter before the *y* is a consonant.

Keep the final *y* if the letter before the *y* is a vowel.

happy + ness = happiness   portray + ed = portrayed

■ The *y* in *happiness* is changed to *i* because the letter before the *y* is a consonant, *p*.

■ The *y* in *portrayed* is not changed because the letter before it is a vowel, *a*.

However, when you add -*ing* to words ending in *y*, always keep the *y*:

copy + ing = copying   delay + ing = delaying

Here are some exceptions to memorize:

day + ly = daily   pay + ed = paid

lay + ed = laid   say + ed = said

PRACTICE 8

Add the suffix shown to each of the following words.

EXAMPLE | marry + ed = _married_

buy + er = _buyer_

1. try + ed = _____   6. wealthy + est = _____

2. vary + able = _____   7. day + ly = _____

3. worry + ing = _____   8. duty + ful = _____

4. pay + ed = _____   9. display + s = _____

5. enjoy + able = _____   10. occupy + ed = _____

Add the suffix in parentheses to each word.

1. beauty　(fy)　_____　　4. angry　(er)　_____

　　　　　　(ful)　_____　　　　　　　(est)　_____

　　　　　　(es)　_____　　　　　　　(ly)　_____

2. lonely　(er)　_____　　5. study　(es)　_____

　　　　　　(est)　_____　　　　　　　(ous)　_____

　　　　　　(ness)　_____　　　　　　　(ing)　_____

3. betray　(ed)　_____　　6. busy　(ness)　_____

　　　　　　(ing)　_____　　　　　　　(er)　_____

　　　　　　(al)　_____　　　　　　　(est)　_____

PART H　Adding -S or -ES

Nouns usually take an -s or an -es ending to form the plural. Verbs take an -s or -es in the third person singular (*he, she,* or *it*).

Add -es instead of -s if a word ends in *ch, sh, ss, x,* or *z* (the -es adds an extra syllable to the word):

box + es = boxes　　　**crutch + es = crutches**　　　**miss + es = misses**

Add -es instead of -s for most words that end in *o:*

do + es = does　　　**hero + es = heroes**

echo + es = echoes　　　**tomato + es = tomatoes**

go + es = goes　　　**potato + es = potatoes**

Here are some exceptions to memorize:

pianos　　sopranos

radios　　solos

When you change the final *y* to *i* in a word,* add -es instead of -s:

fry + es = fries　　　**marry + es = marries**　　　**candy + es = candies**

Add -s or -es to the following nouns and verbs, changing the final *y* to *i* when necessary.

_____

* See Part G of this chapter for more on changing or keeping the final *y*.

EXAMPLE | sketch _sketches_

echo _echoes_

1. watch _____   6. piano _____

2. tomato _____   7. donkey _____

3. reply _____   8. dictionary _____

4. company _____   9. boss _____

5. bicycle _____   10. hero _____

PART I   Choosing *IE* or *EI*

Write *i* before *e*, except after *c* or in an *ay* sound like *neighbor* or *weigh*.

achieve, niece   deceive   vein

■ *Achieve* and *niece* are spelled *ie*.

■ *Deceive* is spelled *ei* because of the preceding *c*.

■ *Vein* is spelled *ei* because of its *ay* sound.

However, words with a *shen* sound are spelled with an *ie* after the *c: ancient, conscience, efficient, sufficient.*

Here are some exceptions to memorize:

either   seize

neither   society

foreign   their

height   weird

PRACTICE 11

Pronounce each word out loud. Then fill in either *ie* or *ei*.

1. bel __ __ vc   9. rec __ __ ve

2. __ __ ght   10. fr __ __ nd

3. effic __ __ nt   11. consc __ __ nce

4. n __ __ ther   12. h __ __ ght

5. cash __ __ r   13. ach __ __ ve

6. th __ __ r   14. v __ __ n

7. ch __ __ f   15. for __ __ gn

8. soc __ __ ty   16. perc __ __ ve

Review

Test your knowledge of the spelling rules in this chapter by adding suffixes to the following words. If you have trouble, the part in which the rule appears is shown in parentheses.

		Part			Part
1. nerve + ous	_____	(F)	11. carry + ing	_____	(G)
2. feed + ing	_____	(D)	12. tomato + s/es	_____	(H)
3. beach + s/es	_____	(H)	13. admit + ing	_____	(E)
4. drop + ed	_____	(D)	14. test + er	_____	(D)
5. hope + ing	_____	(F)	15. tasty + est	_____	(G)
6. study + s/es	_____	(H)	16. sip + ing	_____	(D)
7. busy + ness	_____	(G)	17. believe + able	_____	(F)
8. manage + ment	_____	(F)	18. commit + ment	_____	(E)
9. radio + s/es	_____	(H)	19. deny + al	_____	(G)
10. occur + ed	_____	(E)	20. day + ly	_____	(G)

Review

Circle the correctly spelled word in each pair.

1. writting, writing
2. receive, recieve
3. begining, beginning
4. greif, grief
5. relaid, relayed

6. piece, peice
7. resourceful, resourcful
8. argument, arguement
9. marries, marrys
10. thier, their

PART J   Spelling Lists

Commonly Misspelled Words

Following is a list of words that are often misspelled. As you can see, they are words that you might use daily in speaking and writing. The trouble spot, the part of each word that is usually spelled incorrectly, has been put in bold type.

To help yourself learn these words, you might copy each one twice, making sure to underline the trouble spot, or copy the words on flash cards and have someone test you.

1. across	26. grammar	51. possible
2. address	27. height	52. prefer
3. answer	28. illegal	53. prejudice
4. argument	29. immediately	54. privilege
5. athlete	30. important	55. probably
6. beginning	31. integration	56. psychology
7. behavior	32. intelligent	57. pursue
8. calendar	33. interest	58. reference
9. career	34. interfere	59. rhythm
10. conscience	35. jewelry	60. ridiculous
11. crowded	36. judgment	61. separate
12. definite	37. knowledge	62. similar
13. describe	38. maintain	63. since
14. desperate	39. mathematics	64. speech
15. different	40. meant	65. strength
16. disappoint	41. necessary	66. success
17. disapprove	42. nervous	67. surprise
18. doesn't	43. occasion	68. taught
19. eighth	44. opinion	69. temperature
20. embarrass	45. optimist	70. thorough
21. environment	46. particular	71. thought
22. exaggerate	47. perform	72. tired
23. familiar	48. perhaps	73. until
24. finally	49. personnel	74. weight
25. government	50. possess	75. written

Personal Spelling List

In your notebook, keep a list of words that *you* misspell. Add words to your list from corrected papers and from the exercises in this chapter. First, copy each word as you misspelled it, underlining the trouble spot; then write the word correctly. Study your list often. Use this form:

	As I Wrote It	**Correct Spelling**
1.	probly	probably
2.	_____	_____
3.	_____	_____

4. _____   _____

5. _____   _____

Proofread the following essay for spelling errors. (Be careful: There are misspelled words from both the exercises in this chapter and the spelling list.) Correct any errors by writing above the lines.

The Cell Phone Explosion

(1) Cellular phones, those lightwieght telephones people carry with them, are becoming more popular all the time. (2) About fifty million people in the United States use them, sometimes at odd times—for example, when they are seated in a restaurant or standing in a crowdded elevator. (3) As digital technology keeps improveing, even more cell phones probly will appear—in even odder places.

(4) Although analog phones—the older, more familar type—transmit voices that usually come accross more clearly, digital phones have several advantages. (5) For one thing, they protect your privacy. (6) Calls made with analog phones can be picked up by radioes, other cellular sets, and even old televisions if they are lockked on the right frequency. (7) Digital technology, however, can prevent people from eavesdroping on your conversation.

(8) New digital wireless phone networks also simplify the process of useing cell phones outside your home area. (9) A digital network dosen't charge you for calls made in other citys or states.

(10) Digital cell phones are growing more high tech every day. (11) Some let you recieve messages. (12) Others combine a phone, pager, and two-way radio in one unit. (13) Some cell phones even fax, send e-mail, and browse the Web. (14) Furthermore, the phones are definately geting more fashionable. (15) Some cell phones can be worn like jewlery, prehaps clipped to a belt or straped on an arm.

CHAPTER 38

Look-Alikes/ Sound-Alikes

A/an/and

1. *A* is used before a word beginning with a consonant or a consonant sound.

   a **man**   *a* **house**
   a **union** (*u* in *union* is pronounced like the consonant *y*)

2. *An* is used before a word beginning with a vowel (*a, e, i, o, u*) or silent *h*.

   an **igloo**   *an* **apple**
   an **hour** (*h* in *hour* is silent)

3. *And* joins words or ideas together.

   Edward *and* **Ralph are taking the same biology class.**
   He is very honest, *and* **most people respect him.**

PRACTICE 1

Fill in *a*, *an*, or *and*.

1. The administration building is _____ old brick house on top of _____ hill.

2. _____ artist _____ two students share that studio.

3. The computer in my office has _____ amber screen _____ _____ hard-disk drive.

4. Joyce _____ Luis bought _____ lovely old rocker at the garage sale.

5. For lunch, Ben ate _____ ham sandwich, _____ apple, _____ two bananas.

473

Accept/except

1. *Accept* means to receive.

   That college *accepts* only women.   I *accepted* his offer of help.

2. *Except* means other than or excluding.

   Everyone *except* Ron thinks it's a good idea.

Fill in *accept* or *except*.

1. Jan has read all of Shakespeare's comedies _____ one.

2. Please _____ my apologies.

3. Unable to _____ defeat, the boxer protested the decision.

4. Sam loves all his courses _____ chemistry.

5. _____ for Elizabeth, all of my friends went home after the inter-
   mission.

Affect/effect

1. *Affect* (verb) means to have an influence on or to change.

   Her father's career as a lawyer *affected* her decision to go to law school.

2. *Effect* (noun) means the result of a cause or an influence.

   **Careful proofreading had a positive *effect* on the grades Carl received for
   his compositions.**

3. *Effect* is also a verb that means to cause.

   The U.S. Senate is attempting to *effect* changes in foreign policy.

Fill in *affect* or *effect*.

1. You are mistaken if you think alcohol will not _____ your judgment.

2. Attractive, neat clothing will have a positive _____ on an employment interviewer.

3. Your cigarette smoke _____ my ability to think straight.

4. Hot, humid summers always have the _____ of making me lazy.

5. We will not be able to _____ these changes without the cooperation of the employees and the union.

Been/being

1. *Been* is the past participle form of *to be*. *Been* is usually used after the helping verb *have, has,* or *had.*

   I *have been* to that restaurant before.

   She *has been* a poet for ten years.

2. *Being* is the *-ing* form of *to be*. *Being* is usually used after the helping verb *is, are, am, was,* or *were.*

   They *are being* helped by the salesperson.

   Rhonda *is being* foolish and stubborn.

PRACTICE 4

Fill in *been* or *being.*

1. Have you _____ to Rib Heaven yet?

2. Pete thinks his phone calls are _____ taped.

3. Are you _____ secretive, or have I _____ imagining it?

4. Yoko has never _____ to Omaha!

5. _____ a dynamic teacher is Jenny's goal.

Buy/by

1. *Buy* means to purchase.

   She *buys* new furniture every five years.

2. *By* means near, by means of, or before.

   He walked right *by* and didn't say hello.

   ***By* sunset, we had finished the harvest.**

PRACTICE 5

Fill in *buy* or *by.*

1. You can't _____ happiness, but many people try.

2. Lee _____ sand _____ the ton for his masonry business.

3. Please drop _____ the video store and _____ some blank tapes; I want to tape the football game.

4. _____ _____ out his partners, Joe became sole owner of the firm.

5. _____ the time he is thirty, Emil will have earned his M.A.

It's/its

1. *It's* is a contraction of *it is* or *it has*. If you cannot substitute *it is* or *it has* in the sentence, you cannot use *it's*.

   It's a ten-minute walk to my house.   It's been a nice party.

2. *Its* is a possessive and shows ownership.

   The kitten rolled playfully on *its* side.

   Industry must do *its* share to curb inflation.

Fill in *it's* or *its*.

1. Put the contact lens in ＿＿＿＿＿＿＿ case, please.

2. ＿＿＿＿＿＿＿ about time H.T. straightened up the rubble in his room.

3. Dan's truck has a dent in ＿＿＿＿＿＿＿ fender.

4. The company offered some of ＿＿＿＿＿＿＿ employees an early retirement option.

5. You know ＿＿＿＿＿＿＿ cold when the pond has ice on ＿＿＿＿＿＿＿ surface.

Know/knew/no/new

1. *Know* means to have knowledge or understanding.

2. *Knew* is the past tense of the verb *know*.

   Carl *knows* he has to finish by 6 P.M.

   The police officer *knew* the quickest route to the pier.

3. *No* is a negative.

   He is *no* longer dean of academic affairs.

4. *New* means recent, fresh, unused.

   I like your *new* hat.

Fill in *know, knew, no,* or *new*.

1. I ＿＿＿＿＿＿＿ he's ＿＿＿＿＿＿＿ in town, but this is ridiculous.

2. If I ＿＿＿＿＿＿＿ then what I ＿＿＿＿＿＿＿ now, I wouldn't have made so many mistakes when I was young.

3. Abe and Gabe ＿＿＿＿＿＿＿ that they have ＿＿＿＿＿＿＿ chance of winning the marathon.

4. Fran _____ when she bought this _____ chair that it was too big for the room.

5. _____, I don't _____ the way to Grandma's house, you hairy weirdo.

Lose/loose

1. *Lose* means to misplace or not to win.

   Be careful not to *lose* your way on those back roads.

   George hates to *lose* at cards.

2. *Loose* means too large, not tightly fitting.

   That shirt is not my size; it's *loose*.

PRACTICE 8

Fill in *lose* or *loose*.

1. When Ari studies in bed, he _____ the _____ change from his pockets.

2. Several layers of _____ clothing can warm you in winter.

3. Whenever my dog Rover gets _____ in the streets, all the neighborhood cats stay in hiding.

4. Don't _____ any sleep over tomorrow's exam.

5. If you _____ that _____ screw, the handle will fall off.

Past/passed

1. *Past* is that which has already occurred; it is over with.

   His *past* work has been satisfactory.

   Never let the *past* interfere with your hopes for the future.

2. *Passed* is the past tense of the verb *to pass.*

   She *passed* by and nodded hello.　The wild geese *passed* overhead.

PRACTICE 9

Fill in *past* or *passed*.

1. As Jake _____ the barn, he noticed a man talking to the reindeer.

2. To children, even the recent _____ seems like ancient history.

3. Mia _____ up the opportunity to see a friend from her _____.

4. The quarterback _____ the ball fifty yards for a touchdown.

5. This Bible was _____ down to me by my mother; it contains records of our family's _____.

Quiet/quit/quite

1. *Quiet* means silent, still.

   The woods are *quiet* tonight.

2. *Quit* means to give up or to stop doing something.

   Last year I *quit* drinking.

3. *Quite* means very or exactly.

   He was *quite* tired after playing handball for two hours.

   That's not *quite* right.

PRACTICE 10

Fill in *quiet, quit,* or *quite.*

1. The cottage is a _____ and beautiful place to study.

2. Nora is _____ dedicated to her veterinary career.

3. Don't _____ your job, even though you aren't _____ happy with the working conditions.

4. Each day when he _____ work, Dan visits a _____ spot in the park.

5. She made _____ an impression in red fake fur and a blond wig.

Rise/raise

1. *Rise* means to get up by one's own power.
   The past tense of *rise* is *rose.*
   The past participle of *rise* is *risen.*

   The sun *rises* at 6 A.M.

   Daniel *rose* early yesterday.

   He has *risen* from the table.

2. *Raise* means to lift an object or to grow or increase.
   The past tense of *raise* is *raised.*
   The past participle of *raise* is *raised.*

Raise your right hand.

She *raised* the banner over her head.

We have *raised* one thousand dollars.

PRACTICE 11

Fill in the correct form of *rise* or *raise*.

1. The loaves of bread have _____ perfectly.

2. The new mayor _____ his arms in a victory salute.

3. Once the sun has _____, Pete _____ the shades and opens the window.

4. We all _____ as the bride walked down the aisle.

5. The money we have _____ will help build a shelter.

Sit/set

1. *Sit* means to seat oneself.
   The past tense of *sit* is *sat*.
   The past participle of *sit* is *sat*.

   Sit up straight!

   He *sat* down on the porch and fell asleep.

   She has *sat* reading that book all day.

2. *Set* means to place or put something down.
   The past tense of *set* is *set*.
   The past participle of *set* is *set*.

   Don't *set* your books on the dining room table.

   She *set* the package down and walked off without it.

   She had *set* the timer on the stove.

PRACTICE 12

Fill in *sit* or *set*.

1. Please _____ your briefcase here. Would you like to _____ down?

2. Have they _____ in on a rehearsal before?

3. Tom _____ the chair by the window and _____ down.

4. Maria _____ her alarm clock for 6:30 A.M.

5. Sorry, I wouldn't have _____ here if I had known you were returning.

Suppose/supposed

1. *Suppose* means to assume or guess.
   The past tense of *suppose* is *supposed.*
   The past participle of *suppose* is *supposed.*

   Brad *supposes* that the teacher will give him an *A*.

   We all *supposed* she would win first prize.

   I had *supposed* Dan would bring his trumpet.

2. *Supposed* means ought to or should; it is followed by *to.*

   He is *supposed* to meet us after class.

   You were *supposed* to wash and wax the car.

   Remember: When you mean *ought to* or *should,* always use the *-ed* ending—*supposed.*

Fill in *suppose* or *supposed.*

1. Why do you ＿＿＿＿＿＿＿＿ wolves howl at the moon?

2. I ＿＿＿＿＿＿＿＿ you enjoy reggae.

3. Detective Baker is ＿＿＿＿＿＿＿＿ to address the Citizens' Patrol tonight.

4. Wasn't Erik ＿＿＿＿＿＿＿＿ to meet us at five?

5. Ms. Ita says we're not ＿＿＿＿＿＿＿＿ to guess in computer science class;

   we're ＿＿＿＿＿＿＿＿ to know.

Their/there/they're

1. *Their* is a possessive and shows ownership.

   They couldn't find *their* wigs.   ***Their* children are charming.**

2. *There* indicates a direction.

   I wouldn't go *there* again.   **Put the lumber down *there*.**

   There is also a way of introducing a thought.

   ***There* is a fly in my soup.**

   ***There* are two ways to approach this problem.**

3. *They're* is a contraction: *they* + *are* = *they're.* If you cannot substitute *they are* in the sentence, you cannot use *they're.*

   ***They're* the best tires money can buy.**   **If *they're* coming, count me in.**

PRACTICE 14

Fill in *their, there,* or *they're.*

1. If _____ not _____ on time, we will have to leave without them.

2. _____ two of the most amusing people I know.

3. _____ are two choices you can make, and _____ both risky.

4. Two mail carriers left _____ mail bags _____ on the post office steps.

5. Is _____ a doctor in the house?

6. The motorcycles roared _____ way into town.

7. _____ phone usually rings seven or eight times before they answer.

8. Don't worry about _____ performance in the race because _____ both tough.

Then/than

1. *Then* means afterward or at that time.

   First we went to the theater, and *then* we went out for a pizza and champagne.

   I was a heavyweight boxer *then*.

2. *Than* is used in a comparison.

   She is a better student *than* I.

PRACTICE 15

Fill in *then* or *than.*

1. First, Cassandra kicked off her shoes; _____ she began to dance.

2. Jupiter's diameter is eleven times larger _____ Earth's.

3. If you're more familiar with this trail _____ I, _____ you should lead the way.

4. Fran lived in Chicago _____; now she lives in Miami.

5. If he is better prepared _____ you, what will you do _____?

Through/though

1. *Through* means in one side and out the other, finished, or by means of.

    The rain came *through* the open window.

    We should be *through* soon.

    ***Through* practice, I can do anything.**

2. *Though* means although. Used with *as, though* means as if.

    ***Though* he rarely speaks, he writes terrific letters.**

    It was as *though* I had never ridden a bicycle before.

PRACTICE 16

Fill in *through* or *though*.

1. _____ study and perseverance, Charelle earned her degree in three years.

2. Dee usually walks to work _____ she sometimes rides the bus.

3. Julio strode _____ the bank as _____ he owned it.

4. Clayton is a Texan _____ and _____.

5. I'm not really hungry; I will have an apple, _____.

To/too/two

1. *To* means toward.

    We are going *to* the stadium.

    To can also be combined with a verb to form an infinitive.

    Where do you want *to go* for lunch?

2. *Too* means also or very.

    Roberto is going to the theater *too*.

    They were *too* bored to stay awake.

3. *Two* is the number 2.

    There are *two* new accounting courses this term.

PRACTICE 17

Fill in *to, too,* or *two*.

1. Please take my daughter _____ the movies _____.

2. We'd like a table for _____ with a view of the sea.

3. Dan, _____, took _____ hours _____ complete the exam.

4. Luis went _____ Iowa State for _____ semesters.

5. This curry is _____ hot _____ eat and _____

good _____ resist.

Use/used

1. *Use* means to make use of.
   The past tense of *use* is *used.*
   The past participle of *use* is *used.*

   Why do you *use* green ink?

   He *used* the wrong paint in the bathroom.

   I have *used* that brand of toothpaste myself.

2. *Used* means in the habit of or accustomed to; it is followed by *to.*

   I am not *used* to getting up at 4 A.M.   **They got *used* to the good life.**

Remember: When you mean *in the habit of* or *accustomed to,* always use the *-ed* ending—*used.*

PRACTICE 18

Fill in *use* or *used.*

1. Marie _____ to drive a jalopy that she bought at a _____ car lot.

2. We will _____ about three gallons of paint on this shed.

3. Can you _____ a _____ computer?

4. Pam _____ to _____ a pick to strum her guitar.

5. Shall I _____ contrast or illustration to develop this essay?

Weather/whether

1. *Weather* refers to atmospheric conditions.
   In June, the *weather* in Spain is lovely.

2. *Whether* implies a question.
   Whether or not you pass depends on you.

PRACTICE 19

Fill in *weather* or *whether.*

1. In fine _____, we take long walks in the woods.

2. _____ or not you like Chinese food, you'll love this dish.

3. The _____ person never said _____ or not it would snow.

4. I can't recall _____ you prefer tea or coffee.

5. In 1870 a national _____ service was established.

Where/were/we're

1. *Where* implies place or location.

   Where have you been all day?   **Home is *where* you hang your hat.**

2. *Were* is the past tense of *are*.

   We *were* on our way when the hurricane hit.

3. *We're* is a contraction: *we + are = we're*. If you cannot substitute *we are* in the sentence, you cannot use *we're*.

   We're going to leave now.   **Since *we're* in the city, let's go to the zoo.**

PRACTICE 20

Fill in *where, were,* or *we're*.

1. _____ going to Hawaii _____ the sun always shines.

2. _____ you standing _____ we agreed to meet?

3. _____ working out three times a week.

4. There _____ two high-rise apartment houses _____ the ballpark used to be.

5. _____ determined to attend college though we don't yet know _____.

Whose/who's

1. *Whose* implies ownership and possession.

   Whose term paper is that?

2. *Who's* is a contraction of *who is* or *who has*. If you cannot substitute *who is* or *who has*, you cannot use *who's*.

   Who's knocking at the window?

   Who's seen my new felt hat with the red feathers?

PRACTICE 21

Fill in *whose* or *who's*.

1. _____ Probe convertible is this?

2. Tanya, _____ in my history class, will join us for dinner.

3. We need someone in that position _____ dependable, someone

_____ abilities have already been proven.

4. _____ biology textbook is this?

5. _____ going to clean the oven?

Your/you're

1. *Your* is a possessive and shows ownership.

   Your knowledge astonishes me!

2. *You're* is a contraction: *you + are = you're*. If you cannot substitute *you are* in the sentence, you cannot use *you're*.

   You're the nicest person I know.

PRACTICE 22

Fill in *your* or *you're*.

1. _____ sitting on _____ hat.

2. When _____ ready to begin _____ piano lesson, we'll leave.

3. Let _____ adviser help you plan _____ course schedule.

4. When _____ with _____ friends, _____ a different person.

5. If you think _____ lost, why not use _____ map?

Personal Look-Alikes/Sound-Alikes List

In your notebook, keep a list of look-alikes and sound-alikes that *you* have trouble with. Add words to your list from corrected papers and from the exercises in this chapter; consider such pairs as *adapt/adopt, addition/edition, device/devise, stationery/stationary,* and so forth.

First, write the word you used incorrectly; then write its meaning or use it correctly in a sentence, whichever best helps you remember. Now do the same with the word you meant to use.

Word	Meaning
1. though	means although
through	I drove through the woods.
2. _____	_____
_____	_____

PRACTICE 23

Write ten sentences using as many of the look-alikes and sound-alikes as possible. Exchange sentences with a classmate and check each other's work.

PRACTICE 24   Review

The following essay contains a number of look-alike/sound-alike errors. Proofread for these errors, writing the correct word above the line.

Isabel Allende

(1) Possibly the best-known female writer of Latin-American literature, Isabel Allende has survived many political and personal tragedies. (2) Most of those events have found there way into her books. (3) Allende was born in Chile in 1942, but she fled after her uncle, President Salvador Allende, was killed during a military coup in 1973. (4) For the next seventeen years, she lived in Venezuela, were she couldn't find work and felt trapped in a unhappy marriage.

(5) Eventually, Allende started writing a letter to her grandfather, who was still in Chile; when he died, that letter grew until it became her first novel. (6) Still her most famous book, *The House of the Spirits* established Allende's style of writing, which combines political realism and autobiography with dreams, spirits, an magic. (7) The novel, which was banned in Chile, was translated into more then twenty-five languages and in 1994 was made into a movie.

(8) Buy 1988, Allende had moved to northern California, divorced, remarried, and written her fifth novel, *The Infinite Plan,* which is her second husband's story. (9) Her next book traced the profound affect on Allende of the death of her daughter, Paula. (10) The book *Paula,* like *The House of the Spirits,* was suppose to be a letter, this time two her daughter, who lay in a coma in a Madrid hospital.

(11) After *Paula* was published, Allende stopped writing for several years. (12) She started again in 1996, on January 8, the same day of the year that she had begun every one of her books. (13) The result was *Aphrodite.* (14) A nonfiction book about food and sensuality, *Aphrodite* was quiet different from anything Allende had written in the passed.

(15) Isabel Allende is famous for been a passionate storyteller who's writing captures both the Latin-American and the universal human experience. (16) As the first Latina to write a major novel in the mystical tradition, she not only created a sensation, but she paved the way for other female Hispanic writers, including Julia Alvarez and Sandra Cisneros.

Discuss a Time When Diverse People Were United

Some writers are naturally good spellers, and others are not. If you belong to the latter group, this unit has given you some techniques and tools for overcoming your spelling problems.

In your group or class, read this student's essay, aloud if possible. Underline the ideas and sentences you find especially effective. If you spot any spelling errors, correct them.

A Community of Fishermen

(1) Although City Island is probably best known for it's seafood restaurants, it's just before dinnertime that I most enjoy the island. That's when the fishing boats leave: the *Riptide*, *Apache*, and *Daybreak* all cruise out of their slips and head for the hot spot of the day. These large vessels can pack up to a hundred passengers on board, and the crowd is usualy more diversifyd than all the fish being hoisted over the railing.

(2) Anglers from all walks of life compete for the prize money that is awarded for catching the bigest fish. The anglers are black, white, brown, and yellow, but they leave any thoughts about their skin pigment back at the dock alongside there problems. What these fishermen do for a living, where they come from, and what kind of car they'll drive home that night are concepts of little importance. The things that count now are catching big fish, learning new tricks to catch them, and above all, having a good time. Men of all diffrent races and religions now have something in common; they are all fishermen.

(3) The passengers might be culturally diverse, but with the exception of an ocasional girlfriend or wife, they're all men. Grandfathers show sons and grandsons the ropes. Veterans give tips to the newer guys next to them, and as they hold their fishing poles over the side of the boat, elbow to elbow, they link together in a chain of masculinity.

(4) It's an eight-hour trip, and with a couple of hours down, you'll actually observe the passengers coming together. Almost everyone is drinking beer, and everyone likes to team up and tease land-lovers who get seasick. Salty old men swap fish tales and complain that the fishing is not what it used to be. Fathers talk shop and exchange jokes and busness cards. Younger men play pranks, like sliping bait into an old-timer's pocket when he's not looking. Naturally, they'll take things too far and get found out, but old-timers were not always old and will usually find humor in the gag. Toward the end of the trip, everyone congratulates the winner of the pool and slips in the last few jokes. Clearly, the conflicts that are so common in life are almost nonexistant when your out on a boat in the middle of Long Island Sound.

(5) Something about sharing close quarters and a passion for the same sport makes men feel like equals. The unity seen on a fishing boat is proof that people can blend without having problems as long as they have something in common. As Anna Quindlen writes in her essay "Melting Pot," "We melt together, then draw apart."

—Paul La Valle (Student)

1. How effective is Mr. La Valle's essay?

   _____ Strong thesis statement?   _____ Good supporting details?

   _____ Logical organization?   _____ Effective conclusion?

2. Discuss your underlinings. What details or lines in the essay did you like the most? Explain as exactly as possible why something struck you as interesting or moving.

3. What is the main idea of paragraph 2? Which sentence, if any, is the topic sentence? What is the main idea of paragraph 3? What is the main idea of paragraph 4?

4. This student ends his essay with a correctly punctuated quotation. Who is the source of the quotation? Does it provide a strong conclusion for the essay? Why or why not?

5. Give examples of times when or places where diverse people have united to become a true community.

6. This student's spelling errors are distracting in an otherwise thoughtful and very well written essay. What suggestions would you make to him for improving his spelling?

GROUP WORK

In your group, find and correct the spelling errors in this essay. See if your group can find every error. Hint: There are eleven misspelled or confused words.

 ## WRITING AND REVISING IDEAS

1. Discuss a time when diverse people were united.

2. Write an essay that concludes with a quotation. Use Anna Quindlen's words, "We melt together, then draw apart," or choose another quotation from the Quotation Bank at the end of this book or elsewhere.

UNIT 8

Reading Selections

Reading Strategies for Writers

We hope you will enjoy the reading selections that follow. These essays deal with many of the concerns you have as a student, as a worker, and as a member of a family. Your instructor may ask you to read and think about a selection for class discussion or for a composition either at home or in class.

The more carefully you read these selections, the better you will be able to discuss and write about them. Below are ten strategies that can help you become a more effective reader and writer:

1. **Note the title.** A title, of course, is your first clue as to what the selection is about. For example, the title "Strike Out Little League" lets you know that the selection will discuss negative aspects of organized sports for children.

    A title may also tell you which method of development the author is using. For instance, a selection entitled "Husbands and Wives: Different as Night and Day" might be a comparison/contrast essay; one entitled "Using the Library—Electronically" might be a process piece explaining how to use a computerized library catalogue.

2. **Underline main ideas.** If you read a long or difficult selection, you may forget some of the important ideas soon after you have finished the essay. However, underlining or highlighting these key ideas as you read will later help you review more easily. You may wish to number main ideas to help you follow the development of the author's thesis.

3. **Write your reactions in the margins.** Feel free to express your agreement or disagreement with the ideas in a selection by commenting "yes," "no," "Important—compare with Alice Walker's essay," or "Is he kidding?" in the margins.

    You will often be asked to write a "reaction paper," a composition explaining your thoughts about or reaction to the author's ideas. The comments that you have recorded in the margins will help you formulate a response.

4. **Prepare questions.** As you tackle more difficult reading selections, you may come across material that is hard to follow. Of course, reread the passage to see if a second reading helps. If it does not, put a question mark in the margin.

    Ask a friend or the instructor to help answer your questions. Do not be embarrassed to ask for explanations in class. Instructors appreciate careful readers who want to be sure that they completely understand what they have read.

5. **Note possible composition topics.** As you read, you may think of topics for compositions related to the ideas in the selection. Jot these topics in the margins or write about them in your journal. They may become useful if your instructor asks you for an essay based on the selection.

6. **Note effective writing.** If you are particularly moved by a portion of the selection—a phrase, a sentence, or an entire paragraph—underline or highlight it. You may wish to quote it later in class or use it in your composition.

7. **Circle unfamiliar words.** As you read, you will occasionally come across unfamiliar words. If you can guess what the word means from its context— from how it is used in the sentence or in the passage—do not interrupt your reading to look it up. Interruptions can cause you to lose the flow of ideas in the selection. Instead, circle the word and check it in a dictionary later.

8. **Vary your pace.** Some essays can be read quickly and easily. Others may require more time if the material is difficult or if much of the subject matter is unfamiliar to you. Be careful not to become discouraged, skimming a particularly difficult section just to get through with it. Extra effort will pay off.

9. **Reread.** If possible, budget your time so you can read the selection a second or even a third time. One advantage of rereading is that you will be able to discuss or write about the essay with more understanding. Ideas that were unclear may become obvious; you may even see new ideas that you failed to note the first time around.

   Another advantage is that by the second or third reading, your responses may have changed. You may agree with ideas you rejected the first time; you may disagree with ones you originally agreed with. Rereading gives you a whole new perspective!

10. **Do not overdo it.** Marking the selection as you read can help you become a better reader and writer. However, too many comments may defeat your purpose. You may not be able to decipher the mass—or mess—of underlinings, circles, and notes that you have made. Be selective.

The following essay has been marked, or annotated, by a student. Your responses might be different. Use this essay as a model to help you annotate other selections in this book—and reading material for your other courses as well.

How Sunglasses Spanned the World

Could be a process essay

Like many of the world's inhabitants, you probably own at least one pair of sunglasses, chosen as much for the image they project as for their ability to protect your eyes from the sun. In fact, sunglasses have become a staple in almost every country; it is no longer surprising to spot sunglasses on robed Arabian sheiks, Bolivian grandmothers, or Inuit fishermen tramping Arctic snows. The process by which sunglasses have gained worldwide popularity is a fascinating one that began, surprisingly, in the justice system of medieval China.   1

staple—standard item

Inuit—Eskimo

Step 1—really Stage 1

Dark glasses with smoke-tinted quartz lenses existed for centuries in China prior to 1430, but they were not used for sun protection. Chinese judges wore the darkened lenses in court to conceal their eye expressions and keep secret their reactions to evidence until the end of a trial. In 1430, when vision-correcting glasses were introduced into China from Italy, these lenses, too, were smoke-tinted, but almost entirely for judicial use. Some people wore the darkened lenses for sun protection, but the idea never really caught on.   2

This is a great idea. judicial—relating to court

Stage 2—aviator glasses invented

Five hundred years passed before the popularity of sunglasses began to grow. In the 1930s, the U.S. Army Air Corps asked the optical firm of Bausch & Lomb to produce a highly effective spectacle that would protect pilots from the dangers of high-altitude glare. Company scientists perfected a special dark-green tint that absorbed yellow light from the spectrum. They also designed a slightly drooping metal frame to protect the aviator's eyes, which repeatedly glanced down at the plane's instrument panel.   3   *I wonder why . . .*

I own a pair just like this!

spectrum— range or band (light breaks into a series of colors)

Stage 3

Soon this type of sunglasses was offered to the public as Ray Ban aviators, scientifically designed to ban the sun's rays. For the first time in history, large numbers of people began to purchase sunglasses.

4

Stage 4—sunglasses are chic

The next step in the process—making sunglasses chic—was the result of a clever 1960s advertising campaign by the firm of Foster Grant. Determined to increase its share of the sunglass market, the company began to feature the faces of Hollywood celebrities wearing sunglasses above a slogan that read, "Isn't that . . . behind those Foster Grants?" Big stars of the day like Peter Sellers, Anita Ekberg, and Elke Sommer posed for the ads, and the public love affair with sunglasses took off. Behind those Foster Grants, everyone now could feel like a movie star.

5 Ah, yes. What makes anything span the world? Advertising.

Stage 5—designer shades

In the 1970s, the trend escalated further when well-known fashion designers and Hollywood stars introduced their own brand-name lines, charging high prices for status sunglasses in the latest styles. A giant industry developed where only a few decades earlier none had existed, and shades became big business.

6 True. I know people who spend $200 for wrap-arounds to wear dancing— at night!

Stage 6

parasol—umbrella for the sun

Today sunglasses—like blue jeans and Coca Cola—circle the globe. Protection against solar radiation is just part of their appeal. As women in ancient times had hidden seductively behind an expanded fan or a tipped parasol, modern women and men all over the world have discovered the mystery, sex appeal, and cosmopolitan cool of wearing sunglasses.

7

Writing ideas—
• Research the development of origin of another popular item.
• Think more about the power of advertising to influence us.
• Observe sunglass wearers and write about them.

Only Daughter

Sandra Cisneros

Sandra Cisneros is one of a growing number of Hispanic writers in English. The author of *The House on Mango Street* and other books, she often writes in prose and poetry about the experience of being bicultural, bilingual, and female. In this essay, she explores the ways in which her birth family helped define who she is—and is not. Today Cisneros lives in San Antonio, Texas, in a large Victorian house that she has painted purple.

Once, several years ago, when I was just starting out my writing career, I was 1 asked to write my own contributor's note for an anthology I was part of. I wrote: "I am the only daughter in a family of six sons. *That* explains everything."

Well, I've thought about that ever since, and yes, it explains a lot to me, 2 but for the reader's sake I should have written: "I am the only daughter in a *Mexican* family of six sons." Or even: "I am the only daughter of a Mexican father and a Mexican-American mother." Or: "I am the only daughter of a working-class family of nine." All of these had everything to do with who I am today.

I was/am the only daughter and *only* a daughter. Being an only daughter 3 in a family of six sons forced me by circumstance to spend a lot of time by myself because my brothers felt it beneath them to play with a *girl* in public. But that aloneness, that loneliness, was good for a would-be writer—it allowed me time to think and think, to imagine, to read and prepare myself.

Being only a daughter for my father meant my destiny would lead me to 4 become someone's wife. That's what he believed. But when I was in the fifth grade and shared my plans for college with him, I was sure he understood. I remember my father saying, "*Que bueno, mi'ja,* that's good." That meant a lot to me, especially since my brothers thought the idea hilarious. What I didn't realize was that my father thought college was good for girls—good for finding a husband. After four years in college and two more in graduate school, and still no husband, my father shakes his head even now and says I wasted all that education.

In retrospect, I'm lucky my father believed daughters were meant for hus- 5 bands. It meant it didn't matter if I majored in something silly like English. After all, I'd find a nice professional eventually, right? This allowed me the liberty to putter about embroidering my little poems and stories without my father interrupting with so much as a "What's that you're writing?"

But the truth is, I wanted him to interrupt. I wanted my father to under- 6 stand what it was I was scribbling, to introduce me as "My only daughter, the writer." Not as "This is only my daughter. She teaches." *Es maestra*—teacher. Not even *profesora.*

In a sense, everything I have ever written has been for him, to win his 7 approval even though I know my father can't read English words, even though my father's only reading includes the brown-ink *Esto* sports maga- zines from Mexico City and the bloody *¡Alarma!* magazines that feature yet another sighting of *La Virgen de Guadalupe* on a tortilla or a wife's revenge on her philandering[1] husband by bashing his skull in with a *molcajete* (a kitchen mortar made of volcanic rock). Or the *fotonovelas*, the little picture paperbacks with tragedy and trauma erupting from the characters' mouths in bubbles.

My father represents, then, the public majority. A public who is uninter- 8 ested in reading, and yet one whom I am writing about and for, and privately trying to woo.

---

1. philandering: unfaithful

When we were growing up in Chicago, we moved a lot because of my 9 father. He suffered bouts of nostalgia. Then we'd have to let go our flat, store the furniture with mother's relatives, load the station wagon with baggage and bologna sandwiches and head south. To Mexico City.

We came back, of course. To yet another Chicago flat, another Chicago 10 neighborhood, another Catholic school. Each time, my father would seek out the parish priest in order to get a tuition break, and complain or boast: "I have seven sons."

He meant *siete hijos,* seven children, but he translated it as "sons." "I have 11 seven sons." To anyone who would listen. The Sears Roebuck employee who sold us the washing machine. The short-order cook where my father ate his ham-and-eggs breakfasts. "I have seven sons." As if he deserved a medal from the state.

My papa. He didn't mean anything by that mistranslation, I'm sure. But 12 somehow I could feel myself being erased. I'd tug my father's sleeve and whisper: "Not seven sons. Six! and *one daughter.*"

When my oldest brother graduated from medical school, he fulfilled my 13 father's dream that we study hard and use this—our heads, instead of this— our hands. Even now my father's hands are thick and yellow, stubbed by a history of hammer and nails and twine and coils and springs. "Use this," my father said, tapping his head, "and not this," showing us those hands. He always looked tired when he said it.

Wasn't college an investment? And hadn't I spent all those years in col- 14 lege? And if I didn't marry, what was it all for? Why would anyone go to college and then choose to be poor? Especially someone who had always been poor.

Last year, after ten years of writing professionally, the financial rewards 15 started to trickle in. My second National Endowment for the Arts Fellowship. A guest professorship at the University of California, Berkeley. My book, which sold to a major New York publishing house.

At Christmas, I flew home to Chicago. The house was throbbing, same as 16 always; hot *tamales* and sweet *tamales* hissing in my mother's pressure cooker, and everybody—my mother, six brothers, wives, babies, aunts, cousins—talking too loud and at the same time, like in a Fellini[2] film, because that's just how we are.

I went upstairs to my father's room. One of my stories had just been 17 translated into Spanish and published in an anthology of Chicano writing, and I wanted to show it to him. Ever since he recovered from a stroke two years ago, my father likes to spend his leisure hours horizontally. And that's how I found him, watching a Pedro Infante movie on Galavisión and eating rice pudding.

There was a glass filmed with milk on the bedside table. There were sev- 18 eral vials of pills and balled Kleenex. And on the floor, one black sock and a plastic urinal that I didn't want to look at but looked at anyway. Pedro Infante was about to burst into song, and my father was laughing.

I'm not sure if it was because my story was translated into Spanish, or 19 because it was published in Mexico, or perhaps because the story dealt with Tepeyac, the *colonia* my father was raised in and the house he grew up in, but at any rate, my father punched the mute button on his remote control and read my story.

I sat on the bed next to my father and waited. He read it very slowly. As if 20 he were reading each line over and over. He laughed at all the right places and read lines he liked out loud. He pointed and asked questions: "Is this So-and-so?" "Yes," I said. He kept reading.

---

2. Fellini: an Italian movie director whose films were full of strange, unforgettable characters

When he was finally finished, after what seemed like hours, my father 21
looked up and asked: "Where can we get more copies of this for the relatives?"

Of all the wonderful things that happened to me last year, that was the 22
most wonderful.

Discussion and Writing Questions

1. In what two ways can the title of this essay, "Only Daughter," be inter-
   preted?

2. What expectations did the author's father have for his daughter? Did his
   limited expectations create any advantages for her? Why did the father's
   comment "I have seven sons" bother her so much?

3. In paragraphs 16 through 18, Cisneros describes one of her trips home. She
   includes vivid details that help the reader "see" and "feel" life inside her
   parents' house. Which details do you find especially effective? Although
   the home is in Chicago, which details capture the family's Mexican heritage?

4. For years, the author wanted her father's attention and approval. Why do
   you think he finally appreciated her achievement as a writer?

Writing Assignments

1. In a group with three or four classmates, share statements about your
   personal history like those in Cisneros's opening paragraphs. First, take
   five minutes working on your own, and then define yourself, using a

   two- or three-sentence pattern: "I am _____

   _____.

   That explains everything."
       Revise your sentences until you feel they capture a truth about you.
   Now share and discuss these statements with your group. What is most
   and least effective or intriguing about each? Use your definition as the
   main idea for a paper to be written at home.

2. Have you (or has someone you know) wanted another person's approval
   so badly that it influenced how you conducted your life? Who was the
   person whose approval you sought, and why was that approval so important? What did you do to please him or her and what happened? Was it
   worth it?

3. What were your family's expectations for you as you grew up, and how
   did those expectations affect your life choices? Were the expectations high
   or low? Did your gender or place in the family (oldest, middle, youngest)
   affect them? Did you accept or reject the family's vision for you?

My Outing[1]

Arthur Ashe

Arthur Ashe was the first African American male to become a great tennis champion. After a heart attack ended his career, he contracted AIDS through a tainted blood transfusion. He kept his illness private for years while he pursued many business interests and human-rights projects. Then the possibility of a newspaper report forced him to reveal his condition to the public. The press conference he refers to in the essay was held in April 1992. Ashe died on February 6, 1993.

The day after my press conference, I made sure to keep the two appointments on my calendar because I was anxious to see how people would respond to me after the announcement. I was thinking not only about the people I knew personally, even intimately, but also about waiters and bartenders, doormen and taxi drivers. I knew all the myths and fears about AIDS. I also understood that if I hadn't been educated in the harshest possible way—by contracting the disease and living with it—I would probably share some of those myths and fears. I knew that I couldn't spread the disease by coughing or breathing or using plates and cups in a restaurant, but I knew that in some places my plates and cups would receive special attention, perhaps some extra soap and hot water. Perhaps they would be smashed and thrown away.

That morning, I accompanied Donald M. Stewart, head of the College Board Testing Service, on a visit to the offices of the New York Community Trust. We were seeking a grant of $5,000 to support the publication of a handbook aimed at student-athletes. The appointment went well; we got the money. And in the evening, I went in black tie to a gala dinner to celebrate the eightieth birthday of a man I had known for thirty years and regarded as one of my key mentors in New York City, Joseph Cullman III, a former chairman of Philip Morris. At the event, which took place at the Museum of Natural History in Manhattan, I felt anxiety rising as our taxi drew up to the curb. How would the other guests respond to me? The first person I saw was an old friend, John Reese. An investment banker now, in his youth John had been an up-and-coming star with me in junior tennis. He saw me, and hurried over. There was no mistaking the warmth of his greeting, his genuine concern but also his understanding of my predicament. We walked inside together and I had a fine time at the celebration. . . .

I was glad, in this context, that I had not concealed my condition from certain people. I had reminded myself from the outset[2] that I had an obligation to tell anyone who might be materially hurt by the news when it came out. I have been both proud of my commercial connections and grateful to the people who had asked me to represent them or work for them in some other way. Several of them had taken a chance on me when they knew full well, from the most basic market research in the early 1970s, that having an African American as a spokesman or an officer might cost them business.

Among these organizations, the most important were the Aetna Life and Casualty Company, where I was a member of the board of directors; Head USA, the sports-equipment manufacturer that had given me my first important commercial endorsement, a tennis racquet with my very own autograph on it; the Doral Resort and Country Club in Florida, where I had directed the tennis program; Le Coq Sportif, the sports-clothing manufacturer; Home Box Office (HBO), the cable-television network for which I worked as an analyst

---

1. "Outing" someone usually means revealing publicly, without permission, that he or she is homosexual. Although Ashe was not gay, he was "outed" as a person with AIDS.

2. outset: beginning

at Wimbledon;[3] and ABC Sports, for which I also served as a commentator.

Not one of these companies had dropped me after I quietly revealed to 5
their most important executives that I had AIDS. Now those executives had
to deal with the response of the public. I would have to give them a chance to
put some distance between their companies and me because I now carried the
most abominable and intimidating medical virus of our age. In business,
image is everything. And one would have to go back to leprosy, or the plague,
to find a disease so full of terrifying implications as AIDS carries. AIDS was a
scientific mystery that defied our vaunted[4] claims for science, and also a religious or spiritual riddle—at least to those who insisted on thinking of it as
possibly a punishment from God for our evil on earth, as more than one person had publicly suggested. . . .

I waited for the phone calls and the signs that my services were no longer 6
needed. None came.

I read somewhere that in the two weeks following his announcement that he 7
was HIV-positive, Earvin "Magic" Johnson received thousands of pieces of
mail, and that months later he was still receiving hundreds of letters a week.
Well, I received nothing approaching that volume of correspondence following my press conference, but I certainly had a mountain of reading and writing to do in its aftermath. And every time I appeared on one of the few television interview shows I agreed to do, such as with Barbara Walters or Larry
King, there was another surge of correspondence. I heard from the famous
and the completely unknown, people I knew and people I had never met.

The most moving letters, without a doubt, came from people who had 8
lived through an AIDS illness, either their own or that of a loved one. Often
the loved one was now dead. These writers, above all, understood why I had
made such a fuss about the issue of privacy. Many probably understood better than I did, because they were more vulnerable than I am, and had suffered
more. One Manhattan woman wrote to tell me about her father, who had
received HIV-tainted blood, as I had, through a blood transfusion following
heart surgery. Without knowing it, he had passed the infection on to her
mother. For some years, they had kept their illness a secret from their daughter. After they could keep the secret from her no longer, she in turn had
worked to keep their secret from other family members and friends, and from
the world. Although both parents were now dead, she wrote, "I share your
anger at that anonymous person who violated either your trust or their professional ethics." . . .

A grandmother in New England, HIV-positive after a transfusion, shared 9
with me her terror that the company she worked for would dismiss her if
they found out; she was awaiting the passage of a law that might protect her.
From Idaho, a mother told me about her middle-aged son, who had tried to
keep his AIDS condition a secret even from her. "My son kept it to himself for
six months before he told me and I'll never forget that day as we cried together." His ordeal included dementia,[5] forced incarceration in a state asylum, and
ostracism[6] by relatives and friends. But mother and son had spent his last
"four difficult months" together. "I'm so thankful to have had those days with
him."

I heard from people whom I had not thought of in years, and some of them 10
had been touched by their own tragedy. A woman I remembered as a stunningly
beautiful UCLA coed, as we called them in those days, told me about her
younger brother, who had been diagnosed with full-blown AIDS about five

---

3. Wimbledon: London, England, district where a major tennis tournament is held each year

4. vaunted: boastful

5. dementia: insanity

6. ostracism: exclusion, banishment

years before. "He is gay," she reported, "and I saw how he lost so much self-esteem and hope" because of intolerance. "No one can speak as eloquently[7] as you and Magic to allow the stigma[8] to disperse[9] regarding this situation." Another letter illustrated the power of the stigma. Signed simply, "Sorry I can't identify myself, but you understand," it came from a man who had been diagnosed with HIV three years ago. "I'm the father of six children and many grandchildren. I'm not into needles or the gay life. Don't know where it came from (really)."

As for my daughter, Camera, more than one writer underscored my fears 11 about what she might have to undergo from insensitive people in the future. A woman whose son had died of AIDS about a year before, following the death of his wife, was now bringing up their young son: "I struggle with how this little child is going to deal with the insults and rejections that people will inflict on him when they find out that his father died from AIDS." . . .

Needless to say, I am grateful to all those who have taken the trouble to 12 write. Most of the letters left me humbled.

Discussion and Writing Questions

1. In paragraph 3, Ashe says that he had told some business associates about his illness early on. Why had he done that? How had they reacted? Why, then, was Ashe concerned about the business community's reaction to his *public* announcement?

2. How did the general public react to Ashe's announcement? Which letters did Ashe find most moving? Why?

3. The privacy issue was extremely important to Ashe, who felt that he had been forced by the press to make an announcement he had not wanted to make. One letter he received said, "I share your anger at that anonymous person who violated either your trust or their professional ethics" (paragraph 8). What did the letter writer mean by this statement?

4. Arthur Ashe called his life story *Days of Grace.* On the basis of this essay, why do you think he chose that title? What example or examples of "grace" did he tell about?

Writing Assignments

1. Have you ever prepared yourself for the worst—the ending of a relationship, a frightening medical test result, or other bad news—only to find that the worst did not happen? Discuss such a time: why you expected the worst, what you did to prepare, and what really happened.

2. Serious illness can force people to reevaluate their lives—their aspirations and their goals. Have you, or has someone you know, looked at life differently because of an illness or accident? Write a short account of your own or the other person's experience.

3. In a group with three or four classmates, discuss Ashe's belief that no newspaper had the right to tell the world that he had AIDS. Do you think the press was justified in revealing Ashe's condition? Why or why not? Ashe believed that his right to privacy was greater than the public's need to know. The press argued that Ashe was a public figure and that

---

7. eloquently: skillfully, persuasively

8. stigma: mark of disgrace

9. disperse: disappear

whenever a public figure is ill, his or her condition is legitimate news. Write your own essay about this issue, based on the conclusions you come to after your group's discussion.

The Lady of the Ring

Rene Denfeld

What happens when a woman enters a traditionally male arena—specifically, a boxing ring? Rene Denfeld did just that, but the experience was far different from what she had expected. This article was first published in the *New York Times Magazine*.

I started boxing as a lark, a fantasy. I saw myself becoming glistening, fit and tough—a woman fighter. I saw myself rising from the canvas and fighting back, delivering amazing combinations until my opponent fell among the ropes, vanquished. 1

My first week in the gym in a run-down neighborhood in Portland, Ore., squashed my fantasy as I began to understand the long, difficult training regimen ahead of me. But I fell in love with the sport: the sound of the timer and the guys talking; the flying, hissing jump ropes; the punishment of the heavy bags, and, above all, the relationships between the fighters and our trainer, Jess Sandoval. 2

When I first went into the gym, Jess was in his 70s and increasingly infirm. He had lost his own professional career when he shipped out during World War II, but taught the sport afterward. He was shy around me, his only female fighter. We were all drawn close to Jess, though, an uneasy group, grieving in advance for the frail, titular[1] head of our family. 3

Most of the other fighters were Mexican immigrants like Jess. Sometimes, when they were away for a while, Jess would make sad remarks about prison. Still, their lives were not the easy, cheap simplifications about laziness and crime that many Americans believe about immigrants and illegal aliens. The younger ones seemed touchingly self-conscious despite their macho baggy pants and careful gang attire. Alberto worked at McDonald's and attended school. Bob supported his family by working as a janitor, while his wife sewed satin trunks for the fighters—$25 a pair. 4

Immigration got Ernesto, Jess told us grimly. But one day Ernesto was back. He snuck in, Jess said, triumphant. I still think about how hard it must be for these young men, who are torn between a love for their native country (he changed flags, they said contemptuously of one Mexican fighter who trains under a gringo[2] coach) and a longing to be wanted and appreciated right here. 5

I understand. As a woman in a boxing gym, I had changed flags, too. I'm sure Jess never imagined training a woman, and I'm sure the other fighters never imagined having to spar with one. Ernesto would hit me as hard as he would a man—hard enough to bruise my ribs, water my eyes, cut my lips and make my nose bleed. He had to, you see: if he didn't hit back, I would beat him. This is the dilemma I forced on these men. Hitting a woman? They think that only a bully, a wife beater, does that. But the prospect of being beaten by a woman? Only a sissy, a punk. And yet we found a way to manage. There in that safe place, we had an unspoken truce. 6

Sparring with men, I felt liberated from generations of fear, self-doubt, 7

---

1. titular: existing in name, or title, only

2. gringo: in Latin America, slang for a person from the United States or England (offensive)

finger-waving and genteel[3] restrictions: men aren't so tough, I found, once you get close enough. Perhaps women's fear has been misplaced, conferring a malignant power on those who neither deserve nor desire it.

In entering this world, I lost more than superficial fantasy and gained more than physical self-confidence. My perceptions of the sexes have been altered, and this has affected nearly every aspect of my life. I feel differently when I walk down the street alone—stronger, less fearful. No longer do I assume that I am less capable of handling anger and conflict.

But the greatest challenge was to the male fighters. I imagined their worries: What will she think of us when she realizes we are not as tough, as cold or as mean as women everywhere have been led to believe? Will she breathe a sigh of relief, or laugh in contempt?

A boxing gym is only one of many places where the myth of male superiority in strength and aggressiveness remains unquestioned. But it is also a place where the myth can begin to unravel. Just as I have always been strong, and never realized it, men have always been vulnerable and complicated.

Now the fighter of my dreams is replaced by myself, in honest memory, leaning over the ropes at the Golden Gloves after having won the title. My opponent was already receding, like a vapor[4] behind me, while the men from the gym cheered in the audience. But there was only me, and Jess, and I was kissing his face, in thanks.

Not long ago, Jess passed away. When I heard the news, I put down the phone and cried, thinking, with surprise, I've lost my father. I had gone into a boxing gym to learn how to be tough. But I also found affection, sincerity and caring—and the deep bond between athlete and coach. Boxing has, in the end, left me softer.

Discussion and Writing Questions

1. What was Denfeld's first fantasy about becoming a boxer (paragraph 1)? What replaced that fantasy?

2. What did boxing teach Denfeld about men? What did boxing teach her about herself?

3. What do the Mexican fighters mean when they say someone has "changed flags" (paragraph 5)? Why, according to the author, would someone do that? What does she mean when she says, "As a woman in a boxing gym, I had changed flags, too" (paragraph 6)?

4. Denfeld ends her narrative with Jess's death (paragraph 12). This event is *foreshadowed,* or hinted at, beforehand. Where in the article does Denfeld foreshadow Jess's death?

Writing Assignments

1. Did you ever participate in a sport, take a class, or work on a project that liberated you from "fear" and "self-doubt," as boxing liberated Denfeld? What kind of person were you before? What specifically gave you confidence? In what specific ways did this sport, class, or project change your life?

2. Jess was a hero, a role model, and possibly a father figure for Denfeld. Did you ever know someone who functioned in one or more of these ways for you or someone else? Write about that person and discuss the role he or she played in another's life.

---

3. genteel: polite, refined

4. vapor: mist, smoke

3. In a group with three or four classmates, discuss possible reasons why a boxing gym might be a place where sexual stereotypes can be faced and dropped. Did new understanding happen because of the place, the activity of boxing, the particular people?

Have you ever been in a situation or place where you were able to see through some stereotype—about gender, race, money, or academic achievement—to the truth? List the places and situations that your group members discuss. On your own, write a paper in which you describe a situation or place where stereotypes were set aside. Where and how did this happen?

Neat People Versus Sloppy People

Suzanne Britt

Suzanne Britt is a humorist and writer who likes to analyze people's behavior. In this essay from her book *Show and Tell*, she turns the commonly accepted judgments about neatness and sloppiness upside down.

1

I've finally figured out the difference between neat people and sloppy people. The distinction is, as always, moral. Neat people are lazier and meaner than sloppy people.

2

Sloppy people, you see, are not really sloppy. Their sloppiness is merely the unfortunate consequence of their extreme moral rectitude.[1] Sloppy people carry in their mind's eye a heavenly vision, a precise plan, that is so stupendous, so perfect, it can't be achieved in this world or the next.

3

Sloppy people live in Never-Never Land. Someday is their métier.[2] Someday they are planning to alphabetize all their books and set up home catalogs. Someday they will go through their wardrobes and mark certain items for tentative mending and certain items for passing on to relatives of similar shape and size. Someday sloppy people will make family scrapbooks into which they will put newspaper clippings, postcards, locks of hair, and the dried corsage from their senior prom. Someday they will file everything on the surface of their desks, including the cash register receipts from coffee purchases at the snack shop. Someday they will sit down and read all the back issues of *The New Yorker*.

4

For all these noble reasons and more, sloppy people never get neat. They aim too high and wide. They save everything, planning someday to file, order, and straighten out the world. But while these ambitious plans take clearer and clearer shape in their heads, the books spill from the shelves onto the floor, the clothes pile up in the hamper and closet, the family mementos accumulate in every drawer, the surface of the desk is buried under mounds of paper and the unread magazines threaten to reach the ceiling.

5

Sloppy people can't bear to part with anything. They give loving attention to every detail. When sloppy people say they're going to tackle the surface of the desk, they really mean it. Not a paper will go unturned; not a rubber band will go unboxed. Four hours or two weeks into the excavation, the desk looks exactly the same, primarily because the sloppy person is meticulously[3] creating new piles of papers with new headings and scrupulously[4] stopping to read all the old book catalogs before he throws them away. A neat person would just bulldoze the desk.

---

1. rectitude: righteousness, correctness
2. métier: specialty; work for which someone is especially suited
3. meticulously: very carefully
4. scrupulously: conscientiously

Neat people are bums and clods at heart. They have cavalier[5] attitudes 6 toward possessions, including family heirlooms. Everything is just another dust-catcher to them. If anything collects dust, it's got to go and that's that. Neat people will toy with the idea of throwing the children out of the house just to cut down on the clutter.

Neat people don't care about process. They like results. What they want 7 to do is get the whole thing over with so they can sit down and watch the rasslin' on TV. Neat people operate on two unvarying principles: Never handle any item twice, and throw everything away.

The only thing messy in a neat person's house is the trash can. The 8 minute something comes to a neat person's hand, he will look at it, try to decide if it has immediate use and, finding none, throw it in the trash.

Neat people are especially vicious with mail. They never go through their 9 mail unless they are standing directly over a trash can. If the trash can is beside the mailbox, even better. All ads, catalogs, pleas for charitable contributions, church bulletins and money-saving coupons go straight into the trash can without being opened. All letters from home, postcards from Europe, bills and paychecks are opened, immediately responded to, then dropped in the trash can. Neat people keep their receipts only for tax purposes. That's it. No sentimental salvaging[6] of birthday cards or the last letter a dying relative ever wrote. Into the trash it goes.

Neat people place neatness above everything, even economics. They are 10 incredibly wasteful. Neat people throw away several toys every time they walk through the den. I knew a neat person once who threw away a perfectly good dish drainer because it had mold on it. The drainer was too much trouble to wash. And neat people sell their furniture when they move. They will sell a La-Z-Boy recliner while you are reclining in it.

Neat people are no good to borrow from. Neat people buy everything in 11 expensive little single portions. They get their flour and sugar in two-pound bags. They wouldn't consider clipping a coupon, saving a leftover, reusing plastic non-dairy whipped cream containers or rinsing off tin foil and draping it over the unmoldy dish drainer. You can never borrow a neat person's newspaper to see what's playing at the movies. Neat people have the paper all wadded up and in the trash by 7:05 A.M.

Neat people cut a clean swath[7] through the organic[8] as well as the inor- 12 ganic[9] world. People, animals, and things are all one to them. They are so insensitive. After they've finished with the pantry, the medicine cabinet, and the attic, they will throw out the red geranium (too many leaves), sell the dog (too many fleas), and send the children off to boarding school (too many scuffmarks on the hardwood floors).

Discussion and Writing Questions

1. Britt says that the difference between neat and sloppy people is "moral" (paragraph 1). Which type of person does she claim to believe is superior? Is she serious about this? How do you know?

2. What does Britt mean when she says that "someday" is the "métier" for sloppy people (paragraph 3)?

_____

5. cavalier: showing disregard; not having respect

6. salvaging: rescuing, saving

7. swath: path, strip

8. organic: living

9. inorganic: nonliving

3. The author characterizes neat people as "bums and clods" (paragraph 6). In what ways does she see neat people as heartless?

4. From her contrast essay, do you think Suzanne Britt is a neat or a sloppy person? Why do you think so?

Writing Assignments

1. Are you neat or sloppy? If Britt does not accurately describe the reasons behind your behavior, write about those reasons. Alternatively, you might want to write a defense of neatness. Explain from a neat person's point of view why neat people do what they do and how they are more "moral" than sloppy people.

2. Contrast the different personalities of two people you know. For instance, you might discuss two members of your study group, one a careless worker and one a perfectionist. You might contrast twins, one of whom is almost a hermit while the other is very sociable. You might want to describe the differences between your mountain-climbing aunt and her stay-at-home husband. Use humor if you wish.

3. Write a one- or two-paragraph summary of "Neat People Versus Sloppy People." Refer to Chapter 18 on summary writing. Be sure to include Britt's main idea and her most important supporting points, all in your own words. Remember, you are summarizing Britt's ideas, not adding your own.

How to Get the Most Out of Yourself

Alan Loy McGinnis

Why are some persons successful and productive while others struggle along unhappily? Alan Loy McGinnis, a psychotherapist, believes that the answer lies in self-image. In this essay, he presents numerous ways people can strengthen their self-image.

Our success at business, sports, friendship, love—nearly every enterprise we attempt—is largely determined by our own self-image. People who have confidence in their personal worth seem to be magnets for success and happiness. Good things drop into their laps regularly, their relationships are long-lasting, their projects are usually carried to completion. To use the imagery of English poet William Blake, they "catch joy on the wing." 1

Conversely, some people seem to be magnets for failure and unhappiness. Their plans go awry,[1] they have a way of torpedoing their own potential successes, and nothing seems to work out for them. As a counselor, I see many such persons. Their problems usually stem from a difficulty with self-acceptance. When I am able to help them gain more confidence, often their troubles take care of themselves. 2

I believe that anyone can change his self-perception. A person with low self-image is not doomed to a life of unhappiness and failure. It *is* possible to 3

---

1. go awry: go off course

get rid of negative attitudes and gain the healthy confidence needed to realize one's dreams. Here's how:

Focus on your potential—not your limitations. When Helen Hayes was a 4 young actress, producer George Tyler told her that, were she four inches taller, she could become one of the great actresses of her time. "I decided," she says, "to lick my size. A string of teachers pulled and stretched till I felt I was in a medieval torture chamber. I gained nary[2] an inch—but my posture was military-straight. I became the tallest five-foot woman in the world. And my refusal to be limited by my limitations enabled me to play Mary of Scotland, one of the tallest queens in history."

Helen Hayes succeeded because she chose to focus on her strong points, 5 not her weak ones.

Many clients tell me that because they are not as smart or good-looking or 6 witty as others, they feel inferior. Probably no habit chips away at our self-confidence quite so effectively as that of scanning the people around us to see how we compare. And when we find that someone is indeed smarter, better-looking or wittier, it diminishes our sense of self-worth.

The Hasidic rabbi Zusya was asked on his deathbed what he thought the 7 kingdom of God would be like. "I don't know," he replied. "But one thing I *do* know. When I get there I am not going to be asked, 'Why weren't you Moses? Why weren't you David?' I am only going to be asked, 'Why weren't you Zusya? Why weren't you fully you?'"

Devote yourself to something you do well. There is nothing so common as 8 unsuccessful people with talent. Usually the problem lies not in discovering our natural aptitude but in developing that skill.

Young surgeons practice skills for months on end, such as tying knots in 9 a confined space or suturing. The refining of these skills is the surgeon's main method of improving total performance.

Many of us get interested in a field, but then the going gets tough, we see 10 that other people are more successful, and we become discouraged and quit. But it is often the boring, repetitive sharpening of our skills that will ultimately enable us to reach our goals.

Horace Bushnell, the great New England preacher, used to say, "Some- 11 where under the stars God has a job for you to do, and nobody else can do it." Some of us must find our place by trial and error. It can take time, with dead ends along the way. But we should not get discouraged because others seem more skilled. Usually it is not raw talent but drive that makes the difference.

See yourself as successful. If I could plug into the minds of my patients and 12 listen to the statements they make to themselves, I am convinced that the majority of them would be negative: "I'm running late again—as usual." "My hair looks terrible this morning." "That was a stupid remark I made—she probably thinks I'm a dummy." Since thousands of these messages flash across our brains every day, it is small wonder that the result is a diminished self-image.

One daily exercise for building self-confidence is called "imaging" or 13 "visualization." In order to succeed, you must *see* yourself succeeding. Picture yourself approaching a difficult challenge with poise[3] and confidence. Athletes often visualize a move over and over in their minds; they see themselves hitting the perfect golf or tennis shot. When we burn such positive images into our minds deeply enough, they become a part of the unconscious, and we begin to expect to succeed.

Author and editor Norman Cousins wrote: "People are never more inse- 14 cure than when they become obsessed with their fears at the expense of their

---

2. nary: not even one

3. poise: a look and feeling of self-assurance, calmness

dreams." There is no doubt that if we can envision beneficial things happening, they have a way of actually occurring.

Break away from other people's expectations. It is a liberating step when we 15 decide to stop being what other people want us to be. Although opera singer Risë Stevens performed onstage with great poise, the self-confidence she felt before audiences evaporated in social situations. "My discomfort," she says, "came from trying to be something I was not—a star in the drawing room as well as onstage. If a clever person made a joke, I tried to top it—and failed. I pretended to be familiar with subjects I knew nothing of."

Stevens finally had a heart-to-heart talk with herself: "I realized that I 16 simply wasn't a wit or an intellectual and that I could succeed only as myself. I began listening and asking questions at parties instead of trying to impress the guests. When I spoke, I tried to contribute, not to shine. Almost at once I started to feel a new warmth in my social contacts. They liked the real me better."

If we are true to our instincts, most of us will find that we naturally devel- 17 op certain trademarks. The discovery and expression of that uniqueness is one reason we are on this planet. Resisting conformity and developing some small eccentricities[4] are among the steps to independence and self-confidence.

Build a network of supportive relationships. Many of my clients scramble to 18 shore up[5] their self-images with various techniques, overlooking the source from which they will get help most readily—good friendships.

One of the surest ways to improve confidence is to make certain you have 19 lots of love in your life, to go to whatever lengths are necessary to construct a network of sustaining and nurturing relationships. In building such supportive relationships, most of my patients think their problem is in meeting new people. But the answer, really, is in deepening the friendships you presently have.

The extended family can be a major source of support and nurture. A 20 friend who is 45 tells me that visiting her parents in Indiana is always "a mixed bag." She makes connections with some relatives she'd just as soon not see anymore, and she usually has at least one blow-up with her parents. "But it's important to be around my family," she says. "I always come back feeling that I have a clearer idea of who I am, where I came from, and where I want to go."

She is a wise woman. Such connections with our heritage make our iden- 21 tities more secure. As author John Dos Passos said, "A sense of continuity with the generations gone before can stretch like a lifeline across the scary present."

The distribution of talents in this world should not be our concern. Our 22 responsibility is to take the talents we have and ardently parlay them[6] to the highest possible achievement.

When Yoshihiko Yamamoto of Nagoya City, Japan, was six months old, 23 physicians told his parents that he was mentally retarded. With a hearing loss that strangled his speech and an I.Q. that tested very low, Yamamoto faced a bleak future.

But a new special-education teacher, Takashi Kawasaki, took a special 24 interest in the boy. Gradually Yamamoto began to smile in class. He learned to copy the characters from the blackboard and cartoons from magazines. One day, Yamamoto drew an accurate sketch of Nagoya Castle. Kawasaki had the boy transfer his design to a wood block and encouraged him to concentrate

---

4. eccentricities: unusual or quirky personality traits or behavior

5. shore up: support, strengthen

6. parlay them: turn them into

on printmaking. Eventually Yamamoto won first prize in an art contest. Today, his work is much sought after.

It is not important that Yoshihiko Yamamoto has limitations. The impor- 25 tant thing is that he has capitalized on his potential.

Self-confidence, like happiness, is slippery when we set out to grab it for 26 its own sake. Usually it comes as a by-product. We lose ourselves in service or work, friendship or love, and suddenly one day we realize that we are confident and happy.

Discussion and Writing Questions

1. McGinnis discusses several ways of overcoming poor self-esteem. What are these ways? Can you think of any he doesn't mention?

2. Which of these ways do you think is the most effective? The least effective? Why?

3. Identify the paragraphs in which McGinnis uses an anecdote, or brief story, to illustrate the topic sentence(s) of the paragraph. Choose one or two of these paragraphs and illustrate the topic sentence with anecdotes from your own experience.

4. What is the most important point McGinnis illustrates with Yamamoto's story (paragraphs 23–26)?

Writing Assignments

1. Write about someone you consider successful. What qualities or characteristics distinguish this person from others? The person need not be someone you know directly; he or she could be a politician, a rock star, a local personality, or a teacher. Be sure to choose someone about whom you know interesting details, so that your writing will engage your reader.

2. Choose one of the methods the author presents for improving self-esteem and restate the method as a topic sentence. Then write a paragraph that fully develops that topic sentence. For example, you could restate "Break away from other people's expectations" (paragraph 15) this way: "In order for me to break away from other people's expectations, I have to concentrate on what I want in life." The supporting details would then show how you concentrate on what you want. Remember to use details that clearly support the topic sentence.

3. Write a one- or two-paragraph summary of "How to Get the Most Out of Yourself." Refer to Chapter 18 on summary writing. Be sure to include McGinnis's main idea and his most important points so that someone who has not read the essay will know what it is about. Remember, you are summarizing McGinnis's ideas, not adding your own ideas or opinions.

Beauty:
When the Other Dancer Is the Self

Alice Walker

Being physically injured can be terrifying; coming to terms with a permanent disability can be a painful, difficult process. Alice Walker, a noted fiction writer, poet, and author of *The Color Purple*, tells of her feelings and experiences before, during, and after an injury that changed her life.

It is a bright summer day in 1947. My father, a fat, funny man with beautiful 1 eyes and a subversive wit,[1] is trying to decide which of his eight children he will take with him to the county fair. My mother, of course, will not go. She is knocked out from getting most of us ready: I hold my neck stiff against the pressure of her knuckles as she hastily completes the braiding and then beribboning of my hair.

My father is the driver for the rich old white lady up the road. Her name 2 is Miss Mey. She owns all the land for miles around, as well as the house in which we live. All I remember about her is that she once offered to pay my mother thirty-five cents for cleaning her house, raking up piles of her magnolia leaves, and washing her family's clothes, and that my mother—she of no money, eight children, and a chronic earache—refused it. But I do not think of this in 1947. I am two and a half years old. I want to go everywhere my daddy goes. I am excited at the prospect of riding in a car. Someone has told me fairs are fun. That there is room in the car for only three of us doesn't faze[2] me at all. Whirling happily in my starchy frock, showing off my biscuit-polished patent-leather shoes and lavender socks, tossing my head in a way that makes my ribbons bounce, I stand, hands on hips, before my father. "Take me, Daddy," I say with assurance; "I'm the prettiest!"

Later, it does not surprise me to find myself in Miss Mey's shiny black car, 3 sharing the back seat with the other lucky ones. Does not surprise me that I thoroughly enjoy the fair. At home that night I tell the unlucky ones all I can remember about the merry-go-round, the man who eats live chickens, and the teddy bears, until they say: that's enough, baby Alice. Shut up now, and go to sleep.

It is Easter Sunday, 1950. I am dressed in a green, flocked, scalloped-hem 4 dress (handmade by my adoring sister, Ruth) that has its own smooth satin petticoat and tiny hot-pink roses tucked into each scallop. My shoes, new T-strap patent leather, again highly biscuit-polished. I am six years old and have learned one of the longest Easter speeches to be heard that day, totally unlike the speech I said when I was two: "Easter lilies / pure and white / blossom in / the morning light." When I rise to give my speech I do so on a great wave of love and pride and expectation. People in the church stop rustling their new crinolines. They seem to hold their breath. I can tell they admire my dress, but it is my spirit, bordering on sassiness (womanishness), they secretly applaud.

"That girl's a little *mess*," they whisper to each other, pleased. 5

Naturally I say my speech without stammer or pause, unlike those who 6 stutter, stammer, or, worst of all, forget. This is before the word "beautiful" exists in people's vocabulary, but "Oh, isn't she the *cutest* thing!" frequently floats my way. "And got so much sense!" they gratefully add . . . for which thoughtful addition I thank them to this day.

---

1. subversive wit: sarcastic, sharp sense of humor
2. faze: discourage

It was great fun being cute. But then, one day, it ended.   7

I am eight years old and a tomboy. I have a cowboy hat, cowboy boots, check-   8
ered shirt and pants, all red. My playmates are my brothers, two and four years
older than I. Their colors are black and green, the only difference in the way we
are dressed. On Saturday nights we all go to the picture show, even my mother;
Westerns are her favorite kind of movie. Back home, "on the ranch," we pretend
we are Tom Mix, Hopalong Cassidy, Lash LaRue (we've even named one of our
dogs Lash LaRue); we chase each other for hours rustling cattle, being outlaws,
delivering damsels from distress. Then my parents decide to buy my brothers
guns. These are not "real" guns. They shoot "BBs," copper pellets my brothers
say will kill birds. Because I am a girl, I do not get a gun. Instantly I am relegated
to[3] the position of Indian. Now there appears a great distance between us. They
shoot and shoot at everything with their new guns. I try to keep up with my
bow and arrows.

One day while I am standing on top of our makeshift "garage"—pieces of   9
tin nailed across some poles—holding my bow and arrow and looking out
toward the fields, I feel an incredible blow in my right eye. I look down just in
time to see my brother lower his gun.

Both brothers rush to my side. My eye stings, and I cover it with my   10
hand. "If you tell," they say, "we will get a whipping. You don't want that to
happen, do you?" I do not. "Here is a piece of wire," says the older brother,
picking it up from the roof; "say you stepped on one end of it and the other
flew up and hit you." The pain is beginning to start. "Yes," I say. "Yes, I will
say that is what happened." If I do not say this is what happened, I know my
brothers will find ways to make me wish I had. But now I will say anything
that gets me to my mother.

Confronted by our parents we stick to the lie agreed upon. They place me   11
on a bench on the porch and I close my left eye while they examine the right.
There is a tree growing from underneath the porch that climbs past the railing
to the roof. It is the last thing my right eye sees. I watch as its trunk, its
branches, and then its leaves are blotted out by the rising blood.

I am in shock. First there is intense fever, which my father tries to break   12
using lily leaves bound around my head. Then there are chills: my mother
tries to get me to eat soup. Eventually, I do not know how, my parents learn
what has happened. A week after the "accident" they take me to see a doctor.
"Why did you wait so long to come?" he asks, looking into my eye and shak-
ing his head. "Eyes are sympathetic,[4]" he says. "If one is blind, the other will
likely become blind too."

This comment of the doctor's terrifies me. But it is really how I look that   13
bothers me most. Where the BB pellet struck there is a glob of whitish scar tissue, a hideous cataract, on my eye. Now when I stare at people—a favorite
pastime, up to now—they will stare back. Not at the "cute" little girl, but at
her scar. For six years I do not stare at anyone, because I do not raise my head.

Years later, in the throes[5] of a mid-life crisis, I ask my mother and sister   14
whether I changed after the "accident." "No," they say, puzzled. "What do
you mean?"

What do I mean?   15

I am eight, and, for the first time, doing poorly in school, where I have   16
been something of a whiz since I was four. We have just moved to the place
where the "accident" occurred. We do not know any of the people around us

---

3. relegated to: assigned

4. sympathetic: closely connected

5. throes: a condition of struggle

because this is a different county. The only time I see the friends I knew is when we go back to our old church. The new school is the former state penitentiary. It is a large stone building, cold and drafty, crammed to overflowing with boisterous,[6] ill-disciplined children. On the third floor there is a huge circular imprint of some partition that has been torn out.

"What used to be there?" I ask a sullen girl next to me on our way past it 17 to lunch.

"The electric chair," says she. 18

At night I have nightmares about the electric chair, and about all the people 19 reputedly[7] "fried" in it. I am afraid of the school, where all the students seem to be budding criminals.

"What's the matter with your eye?" they ask, critically. 20

When I don't answer (I cannot decide whether it was an "accident" or 21 not), they shove me, insist on a fight.

My brother, the one who created the story about the wire, comes to my 22 rescue. But then brags so much about "protecting" me, I become sick.

After months of torture at the school, my parents decide to send me back to 23 our old community, to my old school. I live with my grandparents and the teacher they board. But there is no room for Phoebe, my cat. By the time my grandparents decide there *is* room, and I ask for my cat, she cannot be found. Miss Yarborough, the boarding teacher, takes me under her wing, and begins to teach me to play the piano. But soon she marries an African—a "prince," she says—and is whisked away to his continent.

At my old school there is at least one teacher who loves me. She is the 24 teacher who "knew me before I was born" and bought my first baby clothes. It is she who makes life bearable. It is her presence that finally helps me turn on the one child at the school who continually calls me "one-eyed bitch." One day I simply grab him by his coat and beat him until I am satisfied. It is my teacher who tells me my mother is ill.

My mother is lying in bed in the middle of the day, something I have never 25 seen. She is in too much pain to speak. She has an abscess in her ear. I stand looking down on her, knowing that if she dies, I cannot live. She is being treated with warm oils and hot bricks held against her cheek. Finally a doctor comes. But I must go back to my grandparents' house. The weeks pass but I am hardly aware of it. All I know is that my mother might die, my father is not so jolly, my brothers still have their guns, and I am the one sent away from home.

"You did not change," they say. 26

Did I imagine the anguish of never looking up? 27

I am twelve. When relatives come to visit I hide in my room. My cousin Bren- 28 da, just my age, whose father works in the post office and whose mother is a nurse, comes to find me. "Hello," she says. And then she asks, looking at my recent school picture, which I did not want taken, and on which the "glob," as I think of it, is clearly visible, "You still can't see out of that eye?"

"No," I say, and flop back on the bed over my book. 29

That night, as I do almost every night, I abuse my eye. I rant and rave at 30 it, in front of the mirror. I plead with it to clear up before morning. I tell it I hate and despise it. I do not pray for sight. I pray for beauty.

"You did not change," they say. 31

I am fourteen and baby-sitting for my brother Bill, who lives in Boston. He is 32

----

6. boisterous: rowdy and noisy
7. reputedly: supposedly

my favorite brother and there is a strong bond between us. Understanding my feelings of shame and ugliness he and his wife take me to a local hospital, where the "glob" is removed by a doctor named O. Henry. There is still a small bluish crater where the scar tissue was, but the ugly white stuff is gone. Almost immediately I become a different person from the girl who does not raise her head. Or so I think. Now that I've raised my head I win the boyfriend of my dreams. Now that I've raised my head I have plenty of friends. Now that I've raised my head classwork comes from my lips as faultlessly as Easter speeches did, and I leave high school as valedictorian, most popular student, and *queen,* hardly believing my luck. Ironically, the girl who was voted most beautiful in our class (and was) was later shot twice through the chest by a male companion, using a "real" gun, while she was pregnant. But that's another story in itself. Or is it?

"You did not change," they say.   33

It is now thirty years since the "accident." A beautiful journalist comes to visit 34 and to interview me. She is going to write a cover story for her magazine that focuses on my latest book. "Decide how you want to look on the cover," she says. "Glamorous, or whatever."

Never mind "glamorous," it is the "whatever" that I hear. Suddenly all I 35 can think of is whether I will get enough sleep the night before the photography session: if I don't, my eye will be tired and wander, as blind eyes will.

At night in bed with my lover I think up reasons why I should not appear 36 on the cover of a magazine. "My meanest critics will say I've sold out," I say. "My family will now realize I write scandalous books."

"But what's the real reason you don't want to do this?" he asks.   37

"Because in all probability," I say in a rush, "my eye won't be straight."   38

"It will be straight enough," he says. Then, "Besides, I thought you'd 39 made your peace with that."

And I suddenly remember that I have.   40

I remember: 41

I am talking to my brother Jimmy, asking if he remembers anything unusu- 42 al about the day I was shot. He does not know I consider that day the last time my father, with his sweet home remedy of cool lily leaves, chose me, and that I suffered and raged inside because of this. "Well," he says, "all I remember is standing by the side of the highway with Daddy, trying to flag down a car. A white man stopped, but when Daddy said he needed somebody to take his little girl to the doctor, he drove off."

I remember: 43

I am in the desert for the first time. I fall totally in love with it. I am so 44 overwhelmed by its beauty, I confront for the first time, consciously, the meaning of the doctor's words years ago: "Eyes are sympathetic. If one is blind, the other will likely become blind too." I realize I have dashed about the world madly, looking at this, looking at that, storing up images against the fading of the light. *But I might have missed seeing the desert!* The shock of that possibility—and gratitude for over twenty-five years of sight—sends me literally to my knees. Poem after poem comes—which is perhaps how poets pray.

On Sight

I am so thankful I have seen
The Desert
And the creatures in the desert
And the desert Itself.

The desert has its own moon
Which I have seen

With my own eye.
There is no flag on it.

Trees of the desert have arms
All of which are always up
That is because the moon is up
The sun is up
Also the sky
The stars
Clouds
None with flags.
If there *were* flags, I doubt
the trees would point.
Would you?

But mostly, I remember this: 45

I am twenty-seven, and my baby daughter is almost three. Since her birth   46
I have worried about her discovery that her mother's eyes are different from
other people's. Will she be embarrassed? I think. What will she say? Every
day she watches a television program called "Big Blue Marble." It begins with
a picture of the earth as it appears from the moon. It is bluish, a little battered-
looking, but full of light, with whitish clouds swirling around it. Every time
I see it I weep with love, as if it is a picture of Grandma's house. One day
when I am putting Rebecca down for her nap, she suddenly focuses on
my eye. Something inside me cringes, gets ready to try to protect myself. All
children are cruel about physical differences, I know from experience, and
that they don't always mean to be is another matter. I assume Rebecca will be
the same.

But no-o-o-o. She studies my face intently as we stand, her inside and me   47
outside her crib. She even holds my face maternally between her dimpled little hands. Then, looking every bit as serious and lawyerlike as her father, she
says, as if it may just possibly have slipped my attention: "Mommy, there's a
world in your eye." (As in, "Don't be alarmed, or do anything crazy.") And
then, gently, but with great interest: "Mommy, where did you *get* that world
in your eye?"

For the most part, the pain left then. (So what, if my brothers grew up to   48
buy even more powerful pellet guns for their sons and to carry real guns
themselves. So what, if a young "Morehouse man" once nearly fell off the
steps of Trevor Arnett Library because he thought my eyes were blue.) Crying
and laughing I ran to the bathroom, while Rebecca mumbled and sang herself
to sleep. Yes indeed, I realized, looking into the mirror. There *was* a world in
my eye. And I saw that it was possible to love it: that in fact, for all it had
taught me of shame and anger and inner vision, I *did* love it. Even to see it
drifting out of orbit in boredom, or rolling up out of fatigue, not to mention
floating back at attention in excitement (bearing witness, a friend has called
it), deeply suitable to my personality, and even characteristic of me.

That night I dream I am dancing to Stevie Wonder's song "Always" (The   49
name of the song is really "As," but I hear it as "Always"). As I dance,
whirling and joyous, happier than I've ever been in my life, another bright-
faced dancer joins me. We dance and kiss each other and hold each other
through the night. The other dancer has obviously come through all right, as I
have done. She is beautiful, whole and free. And she is also me.

Discussion and Writing Questions

1. When did the author stop being "cute"? Is she happy about this change?

2. Why do you think her family insists that she did not change after the shooting?

3. Until her operation at age fourteen, Walker speaks of hating her injured eye. By the end of the essay, she dances with another "dancer," who is "beautiful, whole and free. And she is also me." What makes the author change her mind about her "deformity"?

4. The author uses particular words and phrases to indicate time or chronological order in her narrative. Find the words that indicate time order. At one point in her narrative, she breaks this time order to skip back into the past. In which paragraph does this flashback occur?

Writing Assignments

1. Write about an unpleasant event or experience that resulted in personal growth for you. Your writing need not focus on something as painful as Alice Walker's injury. What is important is how you came to terms with the experience and what you ultimately learned from it.

2. Tell a story about being thrust into a completely unfamiliar situation. You might describe your reaction to attending a new school, starting a new job, or moving to a new city. Present concrete details of your experience. Organize the story around your most vivid memories, like meeting new classmates for the first time, or your first few days on the new job.

3. In a group with three or four classmates, discuss the accident that injured Walker's eye and the children's cover-up (paragraphs 8–11). Her brothers, ten and twelve, were given BB guns. How did these guns change the relationships among siblings even before the accident? Why did this happen? Are BB guns "real guns"? Have you known someone injured by "gun play"? How can such accidents be prevented? Write a paper on your own in which you present one to three ways in which Walker's injury—or one that you know about—could have been prevented.

Hunger of Memory

Richard Rodriguez

Growing up in California as a second-generation Mexican American, Richard Rodriguez wanted to understand the lives of *los pobres*, the poor Mexican laborers he saw around him. In this selection from *Hunger of Memory*, he tells of taking a summer job as a laborer and of learning about himself in the process.

It was at Stanford, one day near the end of my senior year, that a friend told 1 me about a summer construction job he knew was available. I was quickly alert. Desire uncoiled[1] within me. My friend said that he knew I had been looking for summer employment. He knew I needed some money. Almost apologetically he explained: It was something I probably wouldn't be interested in, but a friend of his, a contractor, needed someone for the summer to do

---

1. uncoiled: loosened, unwound

menial[2] jobs. There would be lots of shoveling and raking and sweeping. Nothing too hard. But nothing more interesting either. Still, the pay would be good. Did I want it? Or did I know someone who did?

I did. Yes, I said, surprised to hear myself say it.   2

In the weeks following, friends cautioned that I had no idea how hard   3 physical labor really is. ("You only *think* you know what it is like to shovel for eight hours straight.") Their objections seemed to me challenges. They resolved the issue. I became happy with my plan. I decided, however, not to tell my parents. I wouldn't tell my mother because I could guess her worried reaction. I would tell my father only after the summer was over, when I could announce that, after all, I did know what "real work" is like.

The day I met the contractor (a Princeton graduate, it turned out), he   4 asked me whether I had done any physical labor before. "In high school, during the summer," I lied. And although he seemed to regard me with skepticism,[3] he decided to give me a try. Several days later, expectant, I arrived at my first construction site. I would take off my shirt to the sun. And at last grasp desired sensation. No longer afraid. At last become like a *bracero*.[4] "We need those tree stumps out of here by tomorrow," the contractor said. I started to work.

I labored with excitement that first morning—and all the days after. The   5 work was harder than I could have expected. But it was never as tedious as my friends had warned me it would be. There was too much physical pleasure in the labor. Especially early in the day, I would be most alert to the sensations of movement and straining. Beginning around seven each morning (when the air was still damp but the scent of weeds and dry earth anticipated the heat of the sun), I would feel my body resist the first thrusts of the shovel. My arms, tightened by sleep, would gradually loosen; after only several minutes, sweat would gather in beads on my forehead and then—a short while later—I would feel my chest silky with sweat in the breeze. I would return to my work. A nervous spark of pain would fly up my arm and settle to burn like an ember in the thick of my shoulder. An hour, two passed. Three. My whole body would assume regular movements; my shoveling would be described by identical, even movements. Even later in the day, my enthusiasm for primitive sensation would survive the heat and the dust and the insects pricking my back. I would strain wildly for sensation as the day came to a close. At three-thirty, quitting time, I would stand upright and slowly let my head fall back, luxuriating[5] in the feeling of tightness relieved.

Some of the men working nearby would watch me and laugh. Two or   6 three of the older men took the trouble to teach me the right way to use a pick, the correct way to shovel. "You're doing it wrong, too hard," one man scolded. Then proceeded to show me—what persons who work with their bodies all their lives quickly learn—the most economical way to use one's body in labor.

"Don't make your back do so much work," he instructed. I stood impa-   7 tiently listening, half listening, vaguely watching, then noticed his work-thickened fingers clutching the shovel. I was annoyed. I wanted to tell him that I enjoyed shoveling the wrong way. And I didn't want to learn the right way. I wasn't afraid of back pain. I liked the way my body felt sore at the end of the day.

I was about to, but, as it turned out, I didn't say a thing. Rather it was at   8

---

2. menial: lowly, lacking status

3. skepticism: doubt

4. *bracero*: a Mexican living and working in the United States for a period of time

5. luxuriating: enjoying with deep pleasure

that moment I realized that I was fooling myself if I expected a few weeks of labor to gain me admission to the world of the laborer. I would not learn in three months what my father had meant by "real work." I was not bound to this job; I could imagine its rapid conclusion. For me the sensations of exertion and fatigue could be savored. For my father or uncle, working at comparable jobs when they were my age, such sensations were to be feared. Fatigue took a different toll on their bodies—and minds.

It was, I know, a simple insight. But it was with this realization that I took my first step that summer toward realizing something even more important about the "worker." In the company of carpenters, electricians, plumbers, and painters at lunch, I would often sit quietly, observant. I was not shy in such company. I felt easy, pleased by the knowledge that I was casually accepted, my presence taken for granted by men (exotics[6]) who worked with their hands. Some days the younger men would talk and talk about sex, and they would howl at women who drove by in cars. Other days the talk at lunchtime was subdued;[7] men gathered in separate groups. It depended on who was around. There were rough, good-natured workers. Others were quiet. The more I remember that summer, the more I realize that there was no single *type* of worker. I am embarrassed to say I had not expected such diversity. I certainly had not expected to meet, for example, a plumber who was an abstract painter in his off hours and admired the work of Mark Rothko. Nor did I expect to meet so many workers with college diplomas. (They were the ones who were not surprised that I intended to enter graduate school in the fall.) I suppose what I really want to say here is painfully obvious, but I must say it nevertheless: The men of that summer were middle-class Americans. They certainly didn't constitute[8] an oppressed society. Carefully completing their work sheets; talking about the fortunes of local football teams; planning Las Vegas vacations; comparing the gas mileage of various makes of campers—they were not *los pobres*[9] my mother had spoken about.

On two occasions, the contractor hired a group of Mexican aliens. They were employed to cut down some trees and haul off debris. In all, there were six men of varying age. The youngest in his late twenties; the oldest (his father?) perhaps sixty years old. They came and they left in a single old truck. Anonymous men. They were never introduced to the other men at the site. Immediately upon their arrival, they would follow the contractor's directions, start working—rarely resting—seemingly driven by a fatalistic[10] sense that work which had to be done was best done as quickly as possible.

I watched them sometimes. Perhaps they watched me. The only time I saw them pay me much notice was one day at lunchtime when I was laughing with the other men. The Mexicans sat apart when they ate, just as they worked by themselves. Quiet. I rarely heard them say much to each other. All I could hear were their voices calling out sharply to one another, giving directions. Otherwise, when they stood briefly resting, they talked among themselves in voices too hard to overhear.

The contractor knew enough Spanish, and the Mexicans—or at least the oldest of them, their spokesman—seemed to know enough English to communicate. But because I was around, the contractor decided one day to make me his translator. (He assumed I could speak Spanish.) I did what I was told. Shyly I went over to tell the Mexicans that the *patrón*[11] wanted them

---

6. exotics: people who are quite unfamiliar

7. subdued: quiet, constrained

8. constitute: make up

9. *los pobres:* the poor people

10. fatalistic: believing events to be predetermined; yielding to one's fate

11. *patrón:* boss

to do something else before they left for the day. As I started to speak, I was afraid with my old fear that I would be unable to pronounce the Spanish words. But it was a simple instruction I had to convey. I could say it in phrases.

The dark sweating faces turned toward me as I spoke. They stopped their 13 work to hear me. Each nodded in response. I stood there. I wanted to say something more. But what could I say in Spanish, even if I could have pronounced the words right? Perhaps I just wanted to engage them in small talk, to be assured of their confidence, our familiarity. I thought for a moment to ask them where in Mexico they were from. Something like that. And maybe I wanted to tell them (a lie, if need be) that my parents were from the same part of Mexico.

I stood there. 14

Their faces watched me. The eyes of the man directly in front of me 15 moved slowly over my shoulder, and I turned to follow his glance toward *el patrón* some distance away. For a moment I felt swept up by that glance into the Mexicans' company. But then I heard one of them returning to work. And then the others went back to work. I left them without saying anything more.

When they had finished, the contractor went over to pay them in cash. 16 (He later told me that he paid them collectively—"for the job," though he wouldn't tell me their wages. He said something quickly about the good rate of exchange "in their own country.") I can still hear the loudly confident voice he used with the Mexicans. It was the sound of the *gringo*[12] I had heard as a very young boy. And I can still hear the quiet, indistinct sounds of the Mexican, the oldest, who replied. At hearing that voice I was sad for the Mexicans. Depressed by their vulnerability. Angry at myself. The adventure of the summer seemed suddenly ludicrous. I would not shorten the distance I felt from *los pobres* with a few weeks of physical labor. I would not become like them. They were different from me.

Discussion and Writing Questions

1. Why does the author decide to take the summer construction job?

2. Why does Rodriguez say he didn't mind shoveling the wrong way? As he says this, what does he realize about the men he works with?

3. Why does the experience with the Mexican laborers have such an impact on Rodriguez?

4. Rodriguez might have written his essay using comparison or contrast, discussing his feelings before and after his work on the summer construction crew. Why do you think he chose to write it as a narrative?

Writing Assignments

1. Retell Rodriguez's narrative from the point of view of one of the Mexican laborers. You could retell the story Rodriguez tells about speaking with the men, but this time from *your* point of view as a laborer, or you could describe a typical day working for the *patrón*, doing various jobs at the construction site.

2. Tell what it is like to do a particular kind of work. You may choose, like

---

12. gringo: in Latin America, slang for a person from the United States or England (offensive)

Rodriguez, to describe hard, manual labor, or you may have a less strenuous form of work in mind. Whatever work you tell about, be sure to describe it in detail, so that your audience can picture exactly what the job involves.

3. In a group with three or four classmates, discuss the work of someone who was born a generation before you. What kind of work did he or she do? Consider that person's job opportunities or lack of them. Then write your own essay about that person and his or her work.

Some Thoughts About Abortion

Anna Quindlen

Since the *Roe vs. Wade* Supreme Court decision of 1973, the issue of abortion has gripped the United States as perhaps never before. In this essay, noted *New York Times* columnist Anna Quindlen describes her own mixed feelings about the subject and at the same time gives persuasive reasons for keeping abortion legal.

It was always the look on their faces that told me first. I was the freshman 1 dormitory counselor and they were the freshmen at a women's college where everyone was smart. One of them would come into my room, a golden girl, a valedictorian, an 800 verbal score on the S.A.T.'s, and her eyes would be empty, seeing only a busted future, the devastation of her life as she knew it. She had failed biology, messed up the math; she was pregnant.

That was when I became pro-choice. 2

It was the look in his eyes that I will always remember, too. They were as 3 black as the bottom of a well, and in them for a few minutes I thought I saw myself the way I had always wished to be—clear, simple, elemental, at peace. My child looked at me and I looked back at him in the delivery room, and I realized that out of a sea of infinite possibilities it had come down to this: a specific person, born on the hottest day of the year, conceived on a Christmas Eve, made by his father and me miraculously from scratch.

Once I believed that there was a little blob of formless protoplasm[1] in 4 there and a gynecologist went after it with a surgical instrument, and that was that. Then I got pregnant myself—eagerly, intentionally, by the right man, at the right time—and I began to doubt. My abdomen still flat, my stomach roiling with morning sickness, I felt not that I had protoplasm inside, but, instead, a complete human being in miniature to whom I could talk, sing, make promises. Neither of these views was accurate; instead, I think, the reality is something in the middle. And that is where I find myself now, in the middle—hating the idea of abortions, hating the idea of having them outlawed.

For I know it is the right thing in some times and places. I remember sit- 5 ting in a shabby clinic far uptown with one of those freshmen, only three months after the Supreme Court had made what we were doing possible, and watching with wonder as the lovely first love she had had with a nice boy unraveled[2] over the space of an hour as they waited for her to be called,

---

1. protoplasm: living matter
2. unraveled: came apart

degenerated[3] into sniping[4] and silences. I remember a year or two later seeing them pass on campus and not even acknowledge each other because their conjoining had caused them so much pain, and I shuddered to think of them married, with a small psyche in their unready and unwilling hands.

I've met fourteen-year-olds who were pregnant and said they could not 6 have abortions because of their religion, and I see in their eyes the shadows of twenty-two-year-olds I've talked to who lost their kids to foster care because they hit them or used drugs or simply had no money for food and shelter. I read not long ago about a teenager who said she meant to have an abortion but she spent the money on clothes instead: now she has a baby who turns out to be a lot more trouble than a toy. The people who hand out those execrable[5] little pictures of dismembered fetuses at abortion clinics seem to forget the extraordinary pain children may endure after they are born when they are unwanted, even hated, or simply tolerated.

I believe that in a contest between the living and the almost living, the lat- 7 ter must, if necessary, give way to the will of the former. That is what the fetus is to me, the almost living. These questions began to plague me—and, I've discovered, a good many other women—after I became pregnant. But they became even more acute after I had my second child, mainly because he is so different from his brother. On two random nights eighteen months apart the same two people managed to conceive, and on one occasion the tumult[6] within turned itself into a curly-haired brunet with merry black eyes who walked and talked late and loved the whole world, and on another it became a blond with hazel Asian eyes and a pug nose who tried to conquer the world almost as soon as he entered it.

If we were to have an abortion next time for some reason or another, 8 which infinite possibility becomes, not a reality, but a nullity?[7] The girl with the blue eyes? The improbable redhead? The natural athlete? The thinker? My husband, ever at the heart of the matter, put it another way. Knowing he is finding two children somewhat more overwhelming than he expected, I asked if he would want me to have an abortion if I accidentally became pregnant again right away. "And waste a perfectly good human being?" he said.

Coming to this quandary[8] has been difficult for me. In fact, I believe the 9 issue of abortion is difficult for all thoughtful people. I don't know anyone who has had an abortion who has been casual about it. If there is one thing I find intolerable about most of the so-called right-to-lifers, it is that they try to portray abortion rights as something that feminists thought up on a slow Saturday over a light lunch. That is nonsense. I also know that some people who support abortion rights are most comfortable with a monolithic[9] position because it seems the strongest front against the smug and sometimes violent opposition.

But I don't feel all one way about abortion anymore, and I don't think it 10 serves a just cause to pretend that many of us do. For years I believed that a woman's right to choose was absolute, but now I wonder. Do I, with a stable home and marriage and sufficient stamina and money, have the freedom to choose abortion because a pregnancy is inconvenient just now? Legally I do have the right; legally I want always to have that right. It is the morality of exercising it under those circumstances that makes me wonder.

_____

3. degenerated: became worse
4. sniping: bickering, arguing
5. execrable: disgusting
6. tumult: energetic movement
7. nullity: nonexistence
8. quandary: tough spot, predicament
9. monolithic: unified and solid

Technology has foiled[10] us. The second trimester has become a time of res- 11
urrection; a fetus at six months can be one woman's late abortion, another's
premature, viable[11] child. Photographers now have film of embryos the size of
a grape, oddly human, flexing their fingers, sucking their thumbs. Women
have amniocentesis[12] to find out whether they are carrying a child with birth
defects that they may choose to abort. Before the procedure, they must have a
sonogram, one of those fuzzy black-and-white photos like a love song heard
through static on the radio, which shows someone is in there.

I have taped on my VCR a public television program in which somehow, 12
inexplicably,[13] a film is shown of a fetus *in utero*[14] scratching its face, seemingly putting up a tiny hand to shield itself from the camera's eye. It would make
a potent weapon in the arsenal of the antiabortionists. I grow sentimental
about it as it floats in the salt water, part fish, part human being. It is almost
living, but not quite. It has almost turned my heart around, but not quite
turned my head.

Discussion and Writing Questions

1. Quindlen describes two positions she has taken about abortion. What are
   they?

2. In which paragraph does the author begin to express doubts about abortion? Why does she have these doubts?

3. By the end of her essay, how does Quindlen feel about abortion?

4. What types of proof does the author use in her argument?

Writing Assignments

1. Write on an issue about which you are, like Quindlen, undecided.
   Choose a topic you know fairly well so that you can present solid arguments for both sides. Be objective, but let your reader know which side
   you finally find more persuasive.

2. Do you believe that teenagers should be required to inform their parents
   before obtaining an abortion? Argue in favor of or against this position.

3. Quindlen first gained experience with the abortion issue as a freshman
   dorm counselor. Write about a time that you once counseled, or gave
   advice, to a friend in need. Your friend might have been contemplating an
   abortion, like some of the young women Quindlen describes. She or he
   may have been fighting with a mate or having a problem with money,
   career decisions, or school.

---

10. foiled: blocked, confused

11. viable: able to live

12. amniocentesis: a medical procedure for checking the amniotic fluid in the uterus

13. inexplicably: unexplainably

14. *in utero*: in the mother's uterus

Food for Thought

Dave Barry

Humorist Dave Barry writes that he was "born in Armonk, NY, in 1947 and has been steadily growing older ever since without ever actually reaching maturity." He is a Pulitzer Prize–winning columnist for the *Miami Herald*. Although Barry's columns and books often make us laugh out loud, his humor always has a point. Here he takes on science fair projects.

1   It's getting late on a school night, but I'm not letting my son go to bed yet, because there's serious work to be done.

2   "Robert!" I'm saying, in a firm voice. "Come to the kitchen right now and blow-dry the ant!"

3   We have a large ant, about the size of a mature raccoon, standing on our kitchen counter. In fact, it *looks* kind of like a raccoon, or possibly even a mutant[1] lobster. We made the ant out of papier-mâché, a substance you create by mixing flour and water and newspapers together into a slimy goop that drips down and gets licked up by your dogs, who operate on the wise survival principle that you should immediately eat everything that falls onto the kitchen floor, because if it turns out not to be food, you can always throw it up later.

4   The ant, needless to say, is part of a Science Fair project. We need a big ant to illustrate an important scientific concept, the same concept that is illustrated by *all* Science Fair projects, namely: "Look! I did a Science Fair project!"

5   (I know how we can solve our national crisis in educational funding: Whenever the schools needed money, they could send a letter to all the parents saying: "Give us a contribution right now, or we're going to hold a Science Fair." They'd raise billions.)

6   Our Science Fair project is due tomorrow, but the ant is still wet, so we're using a hair dryer on it. Science Fair judges *hate* a wet ant. Another problem is that our ant is starting to sag, both in the front (or, in entomological[2] terms, the "prognosis") and in the rear (or "butt"). It doesn't look like one of those alert, businesslike, "can-do" ants that you see striding briskly around. It looks depressed, like an ant that has just been informed that all 86,932 members of its immediate family were crushed while attempting to lift a Tootsie Roll.

7   While Robert is drying the ant, I get a flashlight and go outside to examine the experiment portion of our project, which is entitled "Ants and Junk Food." On our back fence we put up a banner that says, in eight-inch-high letters, WELCOME ANTS. Under this is a piece of cardboard with the following snack substances scientifically arranged on it: potato chips, a spicy beef stick, a doughnut, a Snickers candy bar, chocolate-filled cookies, Cheez Doodles, Cocoa Krispies, and Screaming Yellow Zonkers. If you were to eat this entire experiment, you would turn into a giant pimple and explode.

8   We figured this experiment would attract ants from as far away as Indonesia, and we'd note which junk foods they preferred, and this would prove our basic scientific point ("Look! I did a Science Fair project!"). Of course you veteran parents know what actually happened: The ants didn't show up. Nature has a strict rule against cooperating with Science Fair projects. This is why, when you go to a Science Fair, you see 200 projects designed to show you how an electrical circuit works, and not one of them can actually make the little bulb light up. If you had a project that was supposed to demonstrate the law of gravity using heavy lead weights, they would fall *up*.

1. mutant: biologically changed or altered
2. entomological: having to do with the scientific study of insects

So when the ants saw our banner, they said: "Ah-hah! A Science Fair project! Time for us to act in a totally unnatural manner and stay away from the food!"

The irony is, I knew where some ants were: in my office. They live in one of the electrical outlets. I see them going in there all day long. I think maybe they're eating electrons, which makes me nervous. I seriously considered capturing one of the office ants and carrying it out to the science experiment, and if necessary giving it broad hints about what to do ("Yum! Snickers!"). But I was concerned that if I did this, the ants might become dependent on me, and every time they got hungry they'd crawl onto my desk and threaten to give me electrical stings if I didn't carry them to a snack.

Fortunately, some real outdoor ants finally discovered our experiment, and we were able to observe their behavior at close range. I had been led to believe, by countless public-television nature shows, that ants are very organized, with the colony divided into specialized jobs such as drones, workers, fighters, bakers, consultants, etc., all working together with high-efficiency precision. But the ants that showed up at our experiment were total morons. You'd watch one, and it would sprint up to a Cocoa Krispie, then stop suddenly, as if saying: "Yikes! Compared with me, this Cocoa Krispie is the size of a Buick!" Then it would sprint off in a random direction. Sometimes it would sprint back; sometimes it would sprint to another Cocoa Krispie and act surprised again. But it never seemed to *do* anything. There were thousands of ants behaving this way, and every single time two of them met, they'd both stop and exchange "high-fives" with their antennas, along with, I assume, some kind of ant pleasantries ("Hi Bob!" "No, I'm Bill!" "Sorry! You look just like Bob!"). This was repeated *millions of times*. I watched these ants for two days, and they accomplished nothing. It was exactly like highway construction. It wouldn't have surprised me if some ants started waving orange flags to direct other insects around the area.

But at least there were ants, which meant we could do our project and get our results. I'd tell you what they were, but I really think you should do your own work. That's the whole point of a Science Fair, as I keep telling my son, who has gone to bed, leaving me to finish blow-drying the ant.

Discussion and Writing Questions

1. Although Dave Barry writes humorously, his essay makes a serious point. What is he really saying about science fair projects?

2. Which do you think are the funniest lines in this essay? Explain as specifically as possible why you think those sentences are so funny. What words does Barry use to add to the humor? For example, in paragraph 3, he describes the large ant as "about the size of a mature raccoon."

3. Barry's piece is filled with *irony:* his words express something other than their literal meaning. One such example appears in paragraph 4, where he writes that a *big* ant is needed to illustrate the importance of the scientific concept—as if *big* had anything to do with importance. What other examples of irony do you find?

4. Have you ever been assigned a project at school or work that seemed meaningless at first, yet later you found a way to make it interesting or meaningful? What was the project, and what did you do to make it work?

Writing Assignments

1. Have you ever taken on a serious project—sewing or building something, starting a fitness program, throwing a party—only to have it turn out

very differently from what you imagined? Using humor if you wish, describe your initial goal, the steps you took to achieve it, and the ways in which it all went wrong.

2. When parents help their children complete a school project or homework assignment, is this cheating? Write an essay advising parents how to help their child learn without doing the work for the child. You might wish to present your advice in three or four steps or guidelines. Or you might take a particular homework assignment and explain the difference between helping and cheating.

3. In a group with three or four classmates, discuss Barry's attitude toward science fair projects. Do you agree with Barry about the futility of such projects—or do you see value in them? Write your own essay, incorporating ideas from your group discussion if you wish, that either agrees with or contradicts Barry's argument.

One More Lesson

Judith Ortiz Cofer

Judith Ortiz Cofer attended Augusta College, Florida Atlantic University, and Oxford University in England. Here she contrasts her memories of holidays in her native Puerto Rico and of later school experiences in Paterson, New Jersey, telling what she learned about love, prejudice, and the power of words. Her essay sheds light, too, on her decision to become a writer.

1 I remember Christmas on the Island by the way it felt on my skin. The temperature dropped into the ideal seventies and even lower after midnight when some of the more devout Catholics, mostly older women, got up to go to church—*misa del gallo,* they called it; mass at the hour when the rooster crowed for Christ. They would drape shawls over their heads and shoulders and move slowly toward town. The birth of Our Savior was a serious affair in our town.

2 At Mamá's house, food was the focal point of *Navidad.* There were banana leaves brought in bunches by the boys, spread on the table, where the women would pour coconut candy steaming hot, and the leaves would wilt around the sticky lumps, adding an extra tang of flavor to the already irresistible treat. Someone had to watch the candy while it cooled, or it would begin to disappear as the children risked life and limb for a stolen piece of heaven. The banana leaves were also used to wrap the traditional food of holidays in Puerto Rico: *pasteles,* the meat pies made from grated yucca[1] and plantain[2] and stuffed with spiced meats.

3 Every afternoon during the week before Christmas Day, we would come home from school to find the women sitting around in the parlor with bowls on their laps, grating pieces of coconut, yuccas, plantains, cheeses—all the ingredients that would make up our Christmas Eve feast. The smells that filled Mamá's house at that time have come to mean anticipation and a sensual joy during a time in my life, the last days of my early childhood, when I could absorb joy through my pores—when I had not yet learned that light is followed by darkness, that all of creation is based on that simple concept, and maturity is a discovery of that natural law.

---

1. yucca: a thick-stemmed tropical plant
2. plantain: a banana-like fruit

It was in those days that the Americans sent baskets of fruit to our **4**
barrio[3]—apples, oranges, grapes flown in from the States. And at night, if you
dared to walk up to the hill where the mango tree stood in the dark, you
could see a wonderful sight: a Christmas tree, a real pine, decorated with
lights of many colors. It was the blurry outline of this tree you saw, for it was
inside a screened-in porch, but we had heard a thorough description of it
from the boy who delivered the fruit, a nephew of Mamá's, as it had turned
out. Only, I was not impressed, since just the previous year we had put up a
tree ourselves in our apartment in Paterson.

Packages arrived for us in the mail from our father. I got dolls dressed in **5**
the national costumes of Spain, Italy, and Greece (at first we could not decide
which of the Greek dolls was the male, since they both wore skirts); my brother got picture books; and my mother, jewelry that she would not wear,
because it was too much like showing off and might attract the Evil Eye.

Evil Eye or not, the three of us were the envy of the pueblo.[4] Everything **6**
about us set us apart, and I put away my dolls quickly when I discovered that
my playmates would not be getting any gifts until *Los Reyes*—the Day of the
Three Kings, when Christ received His gifts—and that even then it was more
likely that the gifts they found under their beds would be practical things like
clothes. Still, it was fun to find fresh grass for the camels the night the Kings
were expected, tie it in bundles with string, and put it under our beds along
with a bowl of fresh water.

The year went by fast after Christmas, and in the spring we received a **7**
telegram from Father. His ship had arrived in Brooklyn Navy Yard. He gave
us a date for our trip back to the States. I remember Mother's frantic packing,
and the trips to Mayagüez for new clothes; the inspections of my brother's
and my bodies for cuts, scrapes, mosquito bites, and other "damage" she
would have to explain to Father. And I remember begging Mamá to tell me
stories in the afternoons, although it was not summer yet and the trips to the
mango tree had not begun. In looking back I realize that Mamá's stories were
what I packed—my winter store.

Father had succeeded in finding an apartment outside Paterson's "verti- **8**
cal barrio," the tenement Puerto Ricans called *El Building*. He had talked a
candy store owner into renting us the apartment above his establishment,
which he and his wife had just vacated after buying a house in West Paterson,
an affluent suburb. Mr. Schultz was a nice man whose melancholy[5] face I was
familiar with from trips I had made often with my father to his store for cigarettes. Apparently, my father had convinced him and his brother, a look-alike
of Mr. Schultz who helped in the store, that we were not the usual Puerto
Rican family. My father's fair skin, his ultra-correct English, and his Navy
uniform were a good argument. Later it occurred to me that my father had
been displaying me as a model child when he took me to that store with him.
I was always dressed as if for church and held firmly by the hand. I imagine
he did the same with my brother. As for my mother, her Latin beauty, her
thick black hair that hung to her waist, her voluptuous[6] body which even the
winter clothes could not disguise, would have been nothing but a hindrance
to my father's plans. But everyone knew that a Puerto Rican woman is her
husband's satellite; she reflects both his light and his dark sides. If my father
was respectable, then his family would be respectable. We got the apartment
on Park Avenue.

---

3. barrio: district or neighborhood
4. pueblo: town or community
5. melancholy: sad
6. voluptuous: having a rounded, full shape

Unlike El Building, where we had lived on our first trip to Paterson, our   9
new home was truly in exile. There were Puerto Ricans by the hundreds only
one block away, but we heard no Spanish, no loud music, no mothers yelling
at children, nor the familiar *¡Ay Bendito!*, that catch-all phrase of our people.
Mother lapsed into silence herself, suffering from *La Tristeza*, the sadness that
only place induces and only place cures. But Father relished[7] silence, and we
were taught that silence was something to be cultivated and practiced.

Since our apartment was situated directly above where the Schultzes   10
worked all day, our father instructed us to remove our shoes at the door and
walk in our socks. We were going to prove how respectable we were by being
the opposite of what our ethnic group was known to be—we would be quiet
and inconspicuous.[8]

I was escorted each day to school by my nervous mother. It was a long   11
walk in the cooling air of fall in Paterson and we had to pass by El Building
where the children poured out of the front door of the dilapidated[9] tenement
still answering their mothers in a mixture of Spanish and English: "Sí, Mami,
I'll come straight home from school." At the corner we were halted by the
crossing guard, a strict woman who only gestured her instructions, never
spoke directly to the children, and only ordered us to "halt" or "cross" while
holding her white-gloved hand up at face level or swinging her arm sharply
across her chest if the light was green.

The school building was not a welcoming sight for someone used to the   12
bright colors and airiness of tropical architecture. The building looked func-
tional. It could have been a prison, an asylum, or just what it was: an urban
school for the children of immigrants, built to withstand waves of change,
generation by generation. Its red brick sides rose to four solid stories. The
black steel fire escapes snaked up its back like an exposed vertebra. A chainlink fence surrounded its concrete playground. Members of the elite safety
patrol, older kids, sixth graders mainly, stood at each of its entrances, wearing
their fluorescent white belts that criss-crossed their chests and their metal
badges. No one was allowed in the building until the bell rang, not even on
rainy or bitter-cold days. Only the safety-patrol stayed warm.

My mother stood in front of the main entrance with me and a growing   13
crowd of noisy children. She looked like one of us, being no taller than the
sixth-grade girls. She held my hand so tightly that my fingers cramped. When
the bell rang, she walked me into the building and kissed my cheek. Apparently my father had done all the paperwork for my enrollment, because the
next thing I remember was being led to my third-grade classroom by a black
girl who had emerged from the principal's office.

Though I had learned some English at home during my first years in   14
Paterson, I had let it recede deep into my memory while learning Spanish in
Puerto Rico. Once again I was the child in the cloud of silence, the one who
had to be spoken to in sign language as if she were a deaf-mute. Some of the
children even raised their voices when they spoke to me, as if I had trouble
hearing. Since it was a large troublesome class composed mainly of black and
Puerto Rican children, with a few working-class Italian children interspersed,[10] the teacher paid little attention to me. I re-learned the language
quickly by the immersion method.[11] I remember one day, soon after I joined

---

7. relished: enjoyed

8. inconspicuous: hard to notice

9. dilapidated: run-down

10. interspersed: mixed in

11. immersion method: method of learning a new language in which the student is surrounded
     only by speakers of that language

the rowdy class, when our regular teacher was absent and Mrs. D., the sixth-grade teacher from across the hall, attempted to monitor both classes. She scribbled something on the chalkboard and went to her own room. I felt a pressing need to use the bathroom and asked Julio, the Puerto Rican boy who sat behind me, what I had to do to be excused. He said that Mrs. D. had written on the board that we could be excused by simply writing our names under the sign. I got up from my desk and started for the front of the room when I was struck on the head hard with a book. Startled and hurt, I turned around expecting to find one of the bad boys in my class, but it was Mrs. D. I faced. I remember her angry face, her fingers on my arms pulling me back to my desk, and her voice saying incomprehensible things to me in a hissing tone. Someone finally explained to her that I was new, that I did not speak English. I also remember how suddenly her face changed from anger to anxiety. But I did not forgive her for hitting me with that hard-cover spelling book. Yes, I would recognize that book even now. It was not until years later that I stopped hating that teacher for not understanding that I had been betrayed by a classmate, and by my inability to read her warning on the board. I instinctively understood then that language is the only weapon a child has against the absolute power of adults.

I quickly built up my arsenal[12] of words by becoming an insatiable[13] reader of books.   15

Discussion and Writing Questions

1. Cofer writes that at some point after her early childhood she "learned that light is followed by darkness" (paragraph 3). What do you suppose she means by this?

2. How does the author seem to feel about her memories of Christmas in Puerto Rico? Is this feeling different from the one that she seems to have about her memories of Paterson?

3. Why does Cofer title her essay "One More Lesson"? What lesson does she learn? Why do you think she responded to her school experience by becoming a reader (and later, a writer) when another child might have learned to hate school?

4. Cofer uses rich description in this essay. Choose one paragraph that you think contains excellent description. What words and details help you "see" Cofer's young world?

Writing Assignments

1. Compare two places that have been important to you. You may want to concentrate on the people in those two places, or you might discuss the smells and sounds or other physical details of each location. Focus on the most important details.

2. Write about a lesson you learned, especially an experience of prejudice, misunderstanding, or achievement that strongly affected your attitude toward English class, reading, or school.

---

12. arsenal: stockpile of weapons
13. insatiable: unable to be satisfied

3. In a group of three or four classmates, discuss how English should be taught to speakers of other languages. Some educators believe in bilingual education, in which students are taught in their native language as well as in English. Others believe in the "immersion method" that Cofer writes about. Then write your own essay. Take a stand for bilingual education or for the immersion method. Which do you think is better for students in the long run?

A Brother's Murder

Brent Staples

Brent Staples grew up in a rough, industrial city. He left to become a successful journalist, but his younger brother remained. Staples's story of his brother is a reminder of the grim circumstances in which so many young black men of the inner city find themselves today.

It has been more than two years since my telephone rang with the news that 1 my younger brother Blake—just twenty-two years old—had been murdered. The young man who killed him was only twenty-four. Wearing a ski mask, he emerged from a car, fired six times at close range with a massive .44 Magnum, then fled. The two had once been inseparable friends. A senseless rivalry— beginning, I think, with an argument over a girlfriend—escalated[1] from posturing,[2] to threats, to violence, to murder. The way the two were living, death could have come to either of them from anywhere. In fact, the assailant had already survived multiple gunshot wounds from an accident much like the one in which my brother lost his life.

As I wept for Blake I felt wrenched backward into events and circum- 2 stances that had seemed light-years gone. Though a decade apart, we both were raised in Chester, Pennsylvania, an angry, heavily black, heavily poor, industrial city southwest of Philadelphia. There, in the 1960s, I was introduced to mortality, not by the old and failing, but by beautiful young men who lay wrecked after sudden explosions of violence. The first, I remembered from my fourteenth year—Johnny, brash lover of fast cars, stabbed to death two doors from my house in a fight over a pool game. The next year, my teenage cousin, Wesley, whom I loved very much, was shot dead. The summers blur. Milton, an angry young neighbor, shot a crosstown rival, wounding him badly. William, another teenage neighbor, took a shotgun blast to the shoulder in some urban drama and displayed his bandages proudly. His brother, Leonard, severely beaten, lost an eye and donned a black patch. It went on.

I recall not long before I left for college, two local Vietnam veterans—one 3 from the Marines, one from the Army—arguing fiercely, nearly at blows about which outfit had done the most in the war. The most killing, they meant. Not much later, I read a magazine article that set that dispute in a context. In the story, a noncommissioned officer—a sergeant, I believe—said he would pass up any number of affluent, suburban-born recruits to get hard-core soldiers from the inner city. They jumped into the rice paddies with "their manhood

---

1. escalated: increased

2. posturing: trying to appear tough

on their sleeves," I believe he said. These two items—the veterans arguing and the sergeant's words—still characterize for me the circumstances under which black men in their teens and twenties kill one another with such frequency. With a touchy paranoia born of living battered lives, they are desperate to be *real* men. Killing is only machismo taken to the extreme. Incursions[3] to be punished by death were many and minor, and they remain so: they include stepping on the wrong toe, literally; cheating in a drug deal; simply saying "I dare you" to someone holding a gun; crossing territorial lines in a gang dispute. My brother grew up to wear his manhood on his sleeve. And when he died, he was in that group—black, male and in its teens and early twenties—that is far and away the most likely to murder or be murdered.

I left the East Coast after college, spent the mid- and late 1970s in Chicago 4 as a graduate student, taught for a time, then became a journalist. Within ten years of leaving my hometown, I was overeducated and "upwardly mobile," ensconced[4] on a quiet, tree-lined street where voices raised in anger were scarcely ever heard. The telephone, like some grim umbilical, kept me connected to the old world with news of deaths, imprisonings and misfortune. I felt emotionally beaten up. Perhaps to protect myself, I added a psychological dimension to the physical distance I had already achieved. I rarely visited my hometown. I shut it out.

As I fled the past, so Blake embraced it. On Christmas of 1983, I traveled 5 from Chicago to a black section of Roanoke, Virginia, where he then lived. The desolate public housing projects, the hopeless, idle young men crashing against one another—these reminded me of the embittered town we'd grown up in. It was a place where once I would have been comfortable, or at least sure of myself. Now, hearing of my brother's forays[5] into crime, his scrapes with police and street thugs, I was scared, unsteady on foreign terrain.[6]

I saw that Blake's romance with the street life and the hustler image had 6 flowered dangerously. One evening that late December, standing in some Roanoke dive among drug dealers and grim, hair-trigger losers, I told him I feared for his life. He had affected the image of the tough he wanted to be. But behind the dark glasses and the swagger, I glimpsed the baby-faced toddler I'd once watched over. I nearly wept. I wanted desperately for him to live. The young think themselves immortal, and a dangerous light shone in his eyes as he spoke laughingly of making fools of the policemen who had raided his apartment looking for drugs. He cried out as I took his right hand. A line of stitches lay between the thumb and index finger. Kickback from a shotgun, he explained, nothing serious. Gunplay had become part of his life.

I lacked the language simply to say: Thousands have lived this for you 7 and died. I fought the urge to lift him bodily and shake him. This place and the way you are living smells of death to me, I said. Take some time away, I said. Let's go downtown tomorrow and buy a plane ticket anywhere, take a bus trip, anything to get away and cool things off. He took my alarm casually. We arranged to meet the following night—an appointment he would not keep. We embraced as though through glass. I drove away.

As I stood in my apartment in Chicago holding the receiver that evening 8 in February 1984, I felt as though part of my soul had been cut away. I questioned myself then, and I still do. Did I not reach back soon enough or earnestly enough for him? For weeks I awoke crying from a recurrent dream in which I chased him, urgently trying to get him to read a document I had, as though reading it would protect him from what had happened in waking life.

---

3. incursions: attacks, violations

4. ensconced: settled comfortably

5. forays: undertakings, trips

6. terrain: ground

His eyes shining like black diamonds, he smiled and danced just beyond my grasp. When I reached for him, I caught only the space where he had been.

Discussion and Writing Questions

1. Staples says that he was "introduced to mortality" in Chester, Pennsylvania, in the 1960s (paragraph 2). What does he mean?

2. What does the author mean when he says his brother grew up to "wear his manhood on his sleeve" (paragraph 3)? Does he imply that there are other ways of expressing masculinity?

3. Staples speaks of a dream in which he holds a document for his brother to read (paragraph 8). What do you suppose that document might say? What does this dream seem to say about communication between the two brothers?

4. Staples begins his narrative by describing the moment at which he hears of Blake's death. Why does he *start* with this event, instead of moving toward it?

Writing Assignments

1. Write a narrative about a shocking incident that took place in your neighborhood. Like Staples, you may want to start with the incident, and then narrate the smaller events in the story that led up to it. Or you can follow time order and end with the incident.

2. Do you think Brent Staples could have done more to change his brother? Can we really influence others to change their lives?

3. In a group with three or four classmates, discuss the most significant problem facing young people in the inner city today. Is it crime? Drugs? Lack of educational or employment opportunities? Choose one problem and decide how it can be solved. Your instructor may ask you to share your solution with the class. Then write your own paper, discussing the problem you think is most significant and proposing a solution.

In Search of Bruce Lee's Grave

Shanlon Wu

Most young people need heroes to respect or imitate. In this essay, Shanlon Wu discusses the lack of Asian heroes as he grew up in suburban New York in the 1950s. Then he saw his first Bruce Lee movie.

It's Saturday morning in Seattle, and I am driving to visit Bruce Lee's grave. I 1 have been in the city for only a couple of weeks and so drive two blocks past the cemetery before realizing that I've passed it. I double back and turn through the large wrought-iron gate, past a sign that reads: "Open to 9 P.M. or dusk, whichever comes first."

It's a sprawling cemetery, with winding roads leading in all directions. I 2 feel silly trying to find his grave with no guidance. I think that my search for his grave is similar to my search for Asian heroes in America.

I was born in 1959, an Asian-American in Westchester County, N.Y. Dur- 3 ing my childhood there were no Asian sports stars. On television, I can recall only that most pathetic of Asian characters, Hop Sing, the Cartwright family houseboy on "Bonanza." But in my adolescence there was Bruce.

I was 14 years old when I first saw "Enter the Dragon," the granddaddy 4 of martial-arts movies. Bruce had died suddenly at the age of 32 of cerebral edema, an excess of fluid in the brain, just weeks before the release of the film. Between the ages of 14 and 17, I saw "Enter the Dragon" 22 times before I stopped counting. During those years I collected Bruce Lee posters, putting them up at all angles in my bedroom. I took up Chinese martial arts and spent hours comparing my physique with his.

I learned all I could about Bruce: that he had married a Caucasian, Linda; 5 that he had sparred with Kareem Abdul-Jabbar; that he was a buddy of Steve McQueen and James Coburn, both of whom were his pallbearers.

My parents, who immigrated to America and had become professors at 6 Hunter College, tolerated my behavior, but seemed puzzled at my admiration of an "entertainer." My father jokingly tried to compare my obsession with Bruce to his boyhood worship of Chinese folk-tale heroes.

"I read them just like you read American comic books," he said.   7

But my father's heroes could not be mine; they came from an ancient lit- 8 erary tradition, not comic books. He and my mother had grown up in a land where they belonged to the majority. I could not adopt their childhood and they were wise enough not to impose it upon me.

Although I never again experienced the kind of blind hero worship I felt 9 for Bruce, my need to find heroes remained strong.

In college, I discovered the men of the 442d Regimental Combat Team, a 10 United States Army all-Japanese unit in World War II. Allowed to fight only against Europeans, they suffered heavy casualties while their families were put in internment camps. Their motto was "Go for Broke."

I saw them as Asians in a Homeric epic, the protagonists[1] of a Shake- 11 spearean tragedy; I knew no Eastern myths to infuse them with.[2] They embodied my own need to prove myself in the Caucasian world. I imagined how their American-born flesh and muscle must have resembled mine: epicanthic folds[3] set in strong faces nourished on milk and beef. I thought how much they had proved where there was so little to prove.

After college, I competed as an amateur boxer in an attempt to find my 12 self-image in the ring. It didn't work. My fighting was only an attempt to copy Bruce's movies. What I needed was instruction on how to live. I quit boxing after a year and went to law school.

I was an anomaly[4] there: a would-be Asian litigator.[5] I had always liked to 13 argue and found I liked doing it in front of people even more. When I won the first-year moot court competition in law school, I asked an Asian classmate if he thought I was the first Asian to win. He laughed and told me I was probably the only Asian to even compete.

The law-firm interviewers always seemed surprised that I wanted to liti- 14 gate.

"Aren't you interested in Pacific Rim trade?" they asked.   15

"My Chinese isn't good enough," I quipped.   16

My pat response seemed to please them. It certainly pleased me. I thought 17 I'd found a place of my own—a place where the law would insulate[6] me from

---

1. protagonists: main characters

2. infuse them with: put into them

3. epicanthic folds: folds of the upper eyelid skin found in many Asian people

4. anomaly: oddity, unusual person

5. litigator: one who argues legal matters

6. insulate: isolate and protect

the pressure of defining my Asian maleness. I sensed the possibility of merely being myself.

But the pressure reasserted itself. One morning, the year after graduating 18 from law school, I read the obituary of Gen. Minoru Genda—the man who planned the Pearl Harbor attack. I'd never heard of him and had assumed that whoever did that planning was long since dead. But the general had been alive all those years—rising at 4 every morning to do his exercises and retiring every night by 8. An advocate of animal rights, the obituary said.

I found myself drawn to the general's life despite his association with the 19 Axis powers. He seemed a forthright, graceful man who died unhumbled. The same paper carried a front-page story about Congress's failure to pay the Japanese-American internees their promised reparation[7] money. The general, at least, had not died waiting for reparations.

I was surprised and frightened by my admiration for General Genda, by 20 my still-strong hunger for images of powerful Asian men. That hunger was my vulnerability manifested,[8] a reminder of my lack of place.

The hunger is eased this gray morning in Seattle. After asking directions 21 from a policeman—Japanese—I easily locate Bruce's grave. The headstone is red granite with a small picture etched into it. The picture is very Holly-wood—Bruce wears dark sunglasses—and I think the calligraphy[9] looks a bit sloppy. Two tourists stop but leave quickly after glancing at me.

I realize I am crying. Bruce's grave seems very small in comparison to his 22 place in my boyhood. So small in comparison to my need for heroes. Seeing his grave, I understand how large the hole in my life has been, and how desperately I'd sought to fill it.

I had sought an Asian hero to emulate.[10] But none of my choices quite fit 23 me. Their lives were defined through heroic tasks—they had villains to defeat and wars to fight—while my life seemed merely a struggle to define myself.

But now I see how that very struggle has defined me. I must be my own 24 hero even as I learn to treasure those who have gone before.

I have had my powerful Asian male images: Bruce, the men of the 442d 25 and General Genda; I may yet discover others. Their lives beckon like fireflies on a moonless night, and I know that they—like me—may have been flawed by foolhardiness and even cruelty. Still, their lives were real. They were not houseboys on "Bonanza."

Discussion and Writing Questions

1. Why did Wu see *Enter the Dragon* so many times?

2. Why did the author need so badly to find heroes? How did his situation differ from that of his parents?

3. Does Wu conclude his search for heroes?

4. This narrative begins in the present, then switches to the past, and then ends in the present. Why does the author switch tenses this way?

---

7. reparation: compensation

8. manifested: revealed, made apparent

9. calligraphy: art of fine handwriting

10. emulate: imitate

Writing Assignments

1. Write about a longing you felt as a child that was important in your development as a person—perhaps to have friends, to play music, or to make your parents happy. Was this longing ever filled? Do you think this longing has helped shape the person you are today?

2. Discuss how it feels to be a stranger or an outsider. Perhaps you have felt like an outsider because your interests or ways of dressing are different from those of your classmates or neighbors; perhaps you have felt left out by your coworkers; or perhaps you have been treated as "different" because of your ethnic group or even your gender.

3. Write a one- or two-paragraph summary of "In Search of Bruce Lee's Grave." Refer to Chapter 18 on summary writing. Be sure to include Wu's main idea and his most important supporting points, all in your own words.

The Plot Against People

Russell Baker

Have you ever suspected that your appliances *plan* their breakdowns for the sole purpose of driving you crazy? Here, the Pulitzer Prize–winning author and humorist Russell Baker argues an absurd thesis: objects are out to defeat us.

Inanimate[1] objects are classified scientifically into three major categories—   1
those that break down, those that get lost, and those that don't work.

The goal of all inanimate objects is to resist man and ultimately to defeat   2
him, and the three major classifications are based on the method each object
uses to achieve its purpose. As a general rule, any object capable of breaking
down at the moment when it is most needed will do so. The automobile is
typical of the category.

With the cunning peculiar to its breed, the automobile never breaks down   3
while entering a filling station which has a large staff of idle mechanics. It
waits until it reaches a downtown intersection in the middle of the rush hour,
or until it is fully loaded with family and luggage on the Ohio Turnpike. Thus
it creates maximum inconvenience, frustration, and irritability, thereby reducing its owner's lifespan.

Washing machines, garbage disposals, lawn mowers, furnaces, TV sets,   4
tape recorders, slide projectors—all are in league with the automobile to take
their turn at breaking down whenever life threatens to flow smoothly for their
enemies.

Many inanimate objects, of course, find it extremely difficult to break   5
down. Pliers, for example, and gloves and keys are almost totally incapable of
breaking down. Therefore, they have had to evolve[2] a different technique for
resisting man.

They get lost. Science has still not solved the mystery of how they do it,   6

---

1. inanimate: nonliving
2. evolve: develop

and no man has ever caught one of them in the act. The most plausible[3] theory is that they have developed a secret method of locomotion which they are able to conceal from human eyes.

It is not uncommon for a pair of pliers to climb all the way from the cellar 7 to the attic in its single-minded determination to raise its owner's blood pressure. Keys have been known to burrow three feet under mattresses. Women's purses, despite their great weight, frequently travel through six or seven rooms to find hiding space under a couch.

Scientists have been struck by the fact that things that break down virtu- 8 ally never get lost, while things that get lost hardly ever break down. A furnace, for example, will invariably break down at the depth of the first winter cold wave, but it will never get lost. A woman's purse hardly ever breaks down; it almost invariably chooses to get lost.

Some persons believe this constitutes evidence that inanimate objects are 9 not entirely hostile to man. After all, they point out, a furnace could infuriate a man even more thoroughly by getting lost than by breaking down, just as a glove could upset him far more by breaking down than by getting lost.

Not everyone agrees, however, that this indicates a conciliatory[4] attitude. 10 Many say it merely proves that furnaces, gloves and pliers are incredibly stupid.

The third class of objects—those that don't work—is the most curious of 11 all. These include such objects as barometers, car clocks, cigarette lighters, flashlights and toy-train locomotives. It is inaccurate, of course, to say that they *never* work. They work once, usually for the first few hours after being brought home, and then quit. Thereafter, they never work again.

In fact, it is widely assumed that they are built for the purpose of not 12 working. Some people have reached advanced ages without ever seeing some of these objects—barometers, for example—in working order.

Science is utterly baffled by the entire category. There are many theories 13 about it. The most interesting holds that the things that don't work have attained the highest state possible for an inanimate object, the state to which things that break down and things that get lost can still only aspire.[5]

Discussion and Writing Questions

1. Part of the humor in this essay comes from Baker's imitation of scientific writing. Which sentence introduces the "scientific tone"? Which words establish that tone? Why is the end of that sentence funny?

2. How does Baker classify objects? That is, according to Baker, what are the three major categories into which objects can be divided?

3. Which category does Baker suggest is the "highest" of the three? Why?

4. "Objects" are nonliving things, but Baker constantly refers to them as "*inanimate* objects"—as if he needs to remind us that the objects are not alive. Why would he want to do that? How does he also suggest that the objects really are alive? What is his purpose in doing so?

---

3. plausible: likely, apparently true

4. conciliatory: trying to be friendly

5. aspire: hope to achieve

Writing Assignments

1. Have you had any frustrating experiences with objects such as Baker describes? Write about one object that always seems to get the better of you. What problems do you have with it? Do you ever feel that it has a mind of its own?

2. Have you developed a creative technique for finding lost or misplaced objects? For example, some people ask themselves where they might go if they were their own missing car keys. Describe a situation in which you lost something and then were able to find it by using an unusual or imaginative process.

3. Write a one- or two-paragraph summary of "The Plot Against People." Refer to Chapter 18 on summary and quotation. Be sure to include Baker's main idea and his most important supporting points and categories, all in your own words.

Road Rage

Andrew Ferguson

Although the term *road rage* only recently entered our language, many of us already have experienced it firsthand—either in ourselves or in another driver who has targeted us as the enemy. In this *Time* magazine story, Andrew Ferguson examines the causes of this new tragedy—and insanity—on our highways.

It's a jungle out there. Well, not really: it's worse than a jungle. It's a stretch of 1 roadway anywhere in America, and in place of the ravenous tigers and stampeding rhinos and slithery anacondas are your friends and neighbors and co-workers, that nice lady from the church choir and the cheerful kid who bags your food at the local Winn Dixie—even Mom and Dad and Buddy and Sis. They're in a hurry. And you're in their way. So step on it! That light is not going to get any greener! Move it or park it! Tarzan had it easy. Tarzan didn't have to drive to work.

It may be morning in America—crime down, incomes up, inflation 2 nonexistent—but it's high noon on the country's streets and highways. This is road recklessness, auto anarchy,[1] an epidemic of wanton[2] carmanship. Almost everyone from anywhere has a story about it, as fresh as the memory of this morning's commute. And no wonder. Incidents of "road rage" were up 51% in the first half of the decade, according to a report from the AAA Foundation for Traffic Safety. Some occurrences are grisly enough to make the headlines. Last year a high-speed racing duel on the George Washington Memorial Parkway outside Washington killed two innocent commuters, including a mother of two, traveling in the opposite direction.

More often the new road anarchy manifests itself in the mundane:[3] the 3 unsignaled lane change by the driver next to you, the guy who tailgates you if you go too slow, and the person ahead who brakes abruptly if you go too fast—each transgression[4] accented by a flip of the bird or a blast of the horn. Sixty-four percent of respondents to a recent Coalition for Consumer Health

---

1. anarchy: chaos, disorder
2. wanton: reckless
3. mundane: common, everyday
4. transgression: a violation of law

and Safety poll say people are driving less courteously and more dangerously than they were five years ago.

And the enemy is us. Take a ride with "Anne," a 40-year-old mother of three who would rather we not use her real name, as she steers her $2\frac{1}{2}$-ton black Chevy Suburban out of her driveway on a leafy street in residential Washington. The clock on the dashboard reads 2:16. She has 14 minutes to make it to her daughter's game. Within a block of her house she has hit 37 m.p.h., taking stop signs as suggestions rather than law. She has a lot on her mind. "I'm not even thinking of other cars," Anne admits cheerfully as she lays on the horn. An oldster in an econo box ahead of her has made the near fatal mistake of slowing at an intersection with no stop sign or traffic light. Anne swears and peels off around him.

Anne has a clean driving record with scarcely even a fender bender to her name. But when she takes to the highway, even her kids join the fun. "Make him move over!" they shout as she bears down on a 55-m.p.h. sluggard in the fast lane. She flashes her headlights. The kids cheer when the unlucky target gives in and moves aside. Back in town, Anne specializes in near misses. "Jeez, I almost hit that woman," she chirps, swinging the Suburban into the right lane to pass a car turning left at an intersection. She makes the game two minutes late. "I don't think I'm an aggressive driver," Anne says. "But there are a lot of bad drivers out there."

Residents of late 20th century America are arguably the luckiest human beings in history: the most technologically pampered, the richest, the freest things on two legs the world has ever seen. Then why do we drive like such jerks? The most common answer: What do you mean we, Kemo Sabe? Of course, you don't drive like a jerk. Very few drivers admit to being an obnoxious road warrior. There seem to be only three types of people on the road these days: the insane (those who drive faster than you), the moronic (those who drive slower than you) and . . . you. But this merely confuses the issue. Surely someone is doing all that speeding, tailgating, headlight flashing and abrupt lane changing, not to mention the bird flipping and horn blasting.

Aggressive driving, of course, has been around since the early decades of this century, from the moment when the average number of automobiles on any given roadway rose from 1 to 2. It is partly a matter of numbers. There are 17% more cars in America than there were 10 years ago, while the number of drivers is up 10%. More to the point: the number of miles driven has increased 35% since 1987, while only 1% more roads have been built.

But as the quantity of cars has risen, the nature of the problem has changed qualitatively as well. Maybe the congestion is making everyone cranky. Americans are famously attached to their cars; it's just the driving they can't stand. "Driving and habitual road rage have become virtually inseparable," says Leon James, a professor of psychology at the University of Hawaii who specializes in the phenomenon.

In the most comprehensive national survey on driving behavior so far, a Michigan firm, EPIC-MRA, found that an astounding 80% of drivers are angry most or all of the time while driving. Simple traffic congestion is one cause of irritation, but these days just about anything can get the average driver to tap his horn. More than one-third of respondents to the Michigan survey said they get impatient at stoplights or when waiting for a parking space; an additional 25% can't stand waiting for passengers to get in the car. And 22% said they get mad when a multi-lane highway narrows.

So not only are roads more crowded than ever, but they are crowded with drivers whom science has now discovered to be extremely touchy. Modern life offers plenty of ready-made excuses for bad driving, and here as elsewhere time seems to be of the essence: there's just not enough of it.

So many miles, so little time. For Ron Remer, 47, a soft-spoken salesman, offensive driving was simply part of the job. From his home in New Haven,

Conn., he logged 30,000 miles a year selling promotional products. "People on the road were an impediment[5] to my progress," he says. "If I was late, it would reflect badly on me. Maybe the customer wouldn't want the products, and I'd be out of a sale. Getting there was the only thing that was important. If I met you in person, I might invite you for coffee or something. But on the road, you were in my way."

Remer says he's reformed now. He was stopped one night on the narrow 12 and unlighted Merritt Parkway in Connecticut after a high-speed race with another car, and soon thereafter he enrolled in a seminar for aggressive drivers. "I was lucky to recognize my problem and try to fix it," he says.

Other road warriors are unrepentant. Alan Carter, 43, a computer special- 13 ist from North Carolina and a self-described "aggressive driver," has his own vision of a perfect commute: one with no other cars in sight. "I don't want anyone in front of me. Any time. I think maybe this type of thinking has its roots in the minutiae[6] of territorial rights and typical American individualism. But I don't really think about the deeper meanings. I just know that someone else is in my space or in the space I want."

Carter doesn't have to search for deeper meanings; that is a job for paid 14 professionals, of whom, in America, there are many. Their theories range from the sociological to the psychological to the quasi political. "There is a greater diversity of road users now than at any other time in history," says Hawaii's James. "Therefore streets are not reserved for the optimum, skilled driver but accommodate a variety of driver groups with varying skill, acuity[7] and emotional control"—jerks, in nontechnical lingo. And unlike in previous generations, the willingness to be a jerk on the road is no longer confined to a single sex.

Ed Sarpolus, the head researcher for the Michigan study of driving 15 behavior, was struck by the gender breakdown of aggressive drivers: 53% of them are women. "There is a tremendous cultural shift taking place," he says. "Men still outnumber women in pure numbers, but women are not only increasing, they are not falling off as they get older. Women have fought to be equal in the workplace and in society, and now they're fighting to be equal behind the wheel. [Our] data are full of soccer moms."

This democratization of the highway has occurred simultaneously [with] 16 a decline in traditional driver's education, once a near universal part of the curriculum in America's secondary schools—and a course beloved by generations of high schoolers, since the only way you could fail was by running over the instructor's cat. Some states have backed off mandatory driver training altogether, and elsewhere most courses demand no more than six hours behind the wheel.

Driving is a curious combination of public and private acts. A car isolates 17 a driver from the world even as it carries him through it. The sensation of personal power is intoxicating. Sealed in your little pod, you control the climate with the touch of a button, from Arctic tundra to equatorial tropic. The cabin is virtually soundproof. Your "pilot's chair" has more positions than a Barcalounger. You can't listen to that old Sammy Davis Jr. tape at home because your kids will think you're a dweeb, but in the car, the audience roars as you belt out I've Gotta Be Me. Coffee steams from the cup holder, a bag of Beer Nuts sits open at your side, and God knows you're safe. The safety belt is strapped snugly across your body, and if that fails, the air bag will save your life—if it doesn't decapitate you. Little bells and lights go off if you make a mistake: don't forget to buckle up! Change your oil, you sleepyhead!

---

5. impediment: blockage, obstruction
6. minutiae: small details
7. acuity: sharpness of vision

The illusions—of power, of anonymity,[8] of self-containment—pile up. You are the master of your domain. Actually driving the car is the last thing you need to worry about. So you can pick your nose, break wind, fantasize to your heart's content. Who's to know?

The fantasies are shaped not only by the comforts of the cars but by their sheer tonnage as well. Affluent Americans of the 1990s—so responsible at home, so productive in the workplace—want a car designed for war. With its four-wheel drive and tons of torque and booster-rocket horsepower, today's sports-utility vehicle would have come in handy at the Battle of the Bulge. "There is a real illusion of anonymity combined with potency because you have a machine you can command," says Jack Levin, a sociologist at Northeastern University's Program for the Study of Violence. "Top it off with the stress of work and people perhaps feeling insecure there, or with troubles at home, and it can make for a dangerous combination." [18]

Road-rage experts have come up with various solutions to the anarchy of our streets and highways. We could legislate it (lower speed limits, build more roads to relieve congestion), adjudicate it (more highway cops, stiffer penalties), regulate it (more elaborate licensing procedures) or educate it away (mandatory driver's ed). Others suggest an option perhaps more typical of America circa 1998: therapize it. [19]

"The road-rage habit can be unlearned," says James of the University of Hawaii, "but it takes more than conventional driver's ed." He calls for a new driver's ed program from kindergarten on—to teach "a spirit of cooperation rather than competition"—and grass-roots organizations called Quality Driving Circles. These, he told a radio station, would be "small groups of people meeting regularly together to discuss their driving problems and help one another do driving-personality makeovers." [20]

Will it work? A better question might be, Do we want it to? Road-rage therapists come perilously close to calling for a transformation of the national character—remaking our rough-and-tumble, highly individualistic country into a large-scale version of a college town where everyone recycles kitty litter, drinks latte, listens to Enya[9] and eats whole grains. Is that really what we want? For all its dangers, road rage may simply be a corruption of those qualities that Americans have traditionally, and rightly, admired: tenacity,[10] energy, competitiveness, hustle—something, in other words, to be contained and harnessed by etiquette and social censure rather than eradicated[11] outright. Until then, alas, anyone braving the streets and highways of America would be well advised to employ a technique older than therapy: prayer. [21]

Discussion and Writing Questions

1. According to Andrew Ferguson, what kinds of people are affected by road rage? Do they consider themselves dangerous drivers?

2. What are the main causes of road rage?

3. Ferguson uses illustration well to strengthen and humanize his argument; examples of drivers include "Anne," Ron Remer, Alan Carter, and others. Which examples did you find most effective? Explain why, as specifically as possible.

---

8. anonymity: the state of being unknown, unnamed
9. Enya: New Age singer
10. tenacity: persistence, refusal to give up
11. eradicated: eliminated

4. Paragraphs 17 and 18 skillfully describe driving as a "curious combination of public and private acts." What details does Ferguson include that especially capture the isolation, enjoyment, and power of driving alone in one's car? Do you agree with Ferguson that Americans "want a car designed for war"?

5. What kinds of solutions have been proposed for road rage? Will they work?

Writing Assignments

1. Have you or has someone you know experienced road rage? Describe what happened. Were you able to control your anger? How did you do so?

2. Ferguson says that cars give drivers a dangerous and false sense of control and power. Guns too can give a false sense of control and power, with similarly deadly results. Does wielding a deadly weapon give us real power? Many religions tell us that real power lies in kindness, forgiveness, and serenity. Who is right?

3. In a group with three or four classmates, discuss how you and others you know have handled road rage. Discuss any programs you know of and their procedures and results. Then write your own paper on solutions for road rage. You can use information you learned from your group, as well as anecdotes, examples, or research (studies, experts' opinions, statistics, and so on).

Quotation Bank

This collection of wise and humorous statements has been assembled for you to read, enjoy, and use in a variety of ways as you write. You might choose quotations that you particularly agree or disagree with and use them as the basis of journal entries and writing assignments. Sometimes when writing a paragraph or an essay, you may find it useful to include a quotation to support a point you are making. Alternatively, you may simply want to read through these quotations for ideas and for fun. As you come across other intriguing statements by writers, add them to the list—or write some of your own.

Education

Knowledge is power.   1
—*Francis Bacon*

Everyone is ignorant, only on different subjects.   2
—*Will Rogers*

The children need the bread of the mind.   3
—*Rafael Cordero y Molina*

Never be afraid to sit awhile and think.   4
—*Lorraine Hansberry*

A mind stretched by a new idea can never go back to its original dimensions.   5
—*Oliver Wendell Holmes, Jr.*

The contest between education and TV . . . has been won by television.   6
—*Robert Hughes*

Our minds are lazier than our bodies.   7
—*François, Duc de la Rochefoucauld*

This thing called "failure" is not the falling down, but the staying down.   8
—*Mary Pickford*

Tell me what you pay attention to, and I will tell you who you are.   9
—*José Ortega y Gasset*

Wisdom consists of anticipating the consequences.   10
—*Norman Cousins*

We learn something by doing it. There is no other way.   11
—*John Holt*

Work and Success

He who does not hope to win has already lost.   12
—*José Joaquin de Olmedo*

The harder you work, the luckier you get.   13
—*Gary Player*

Float like a butterfly, sting like a bee.   **14**
—*Muhammad Ali*

All glory comes from daring to begin.   **15**
—*Anonymous*

Have a vision not clouded by fear.   **16**
—*Old Cherokee saying*

Show me a person who has never made a mistake, and I'll show you a person **17**
who has never achieved much.
—*Joan Collins*

To me, success means effectiveness in the world, that I am able to carry out **18**
my ideas and values into the world—that I am able to change it in positive
ways.
—*Maxine Hong Kingston*

Nice guys finish last.   **19**
—*Leo Durocher*

Do as the bull in the face of adversity: charge.   **20**
—*José de Diego*

Life is a succession of moments. To live each one is to succeed.   **21**
—*Corita Kent*

Should you not find the pearl after one or two divings, don't blame the ocean! **22**
Blame your diving! You are not going deep enough.
—*P. Yogananda*

It is good to have an end to journey towards, but it is the journey that matters **23**
in the end.
—*Ursula K. LeGuin*

Nothing is really work unless you would rather be doing something else.   **24**
—*J. M. Barrie*

I merely took the energy it takes to pout and wrote some blues.   **25**
—*Duke Ellington*

I write when I'm inspired, and I see to it that I'm inspired at nine o'clock **26**
every morning.
—*Peter De Vries*

Love

    27
If you want to be loved, be lovable.
—*Ovid*

    28
After ecstasy, the laundry.
—*Zen saying*

    29
The first duty of love is to listen.
—*Paul Tillich*

The way is not in the sky. The way is in the heart. 30
—*Dhammapada*

A successful marriage requires falling in love many times, always with the 31
same person.
—*Mignon McLaughlin*

Love is a fire, but whether it's going to warm your hearth or burn down your 32
house, you can never tell.
—*Dorothy Parker*

The old Lakota was wise. He knew that man's heart away from nature 33
becomes hard.
—*Standing Bear*

The way to love anything is to realize that it might be lost. 34
—*G. K. Chesterton*

It's like magic. When you live by yourself, all your annoying habits are gone! 35
—*Merrill Marko*

Love does not consist in gazing at each other but in looking together in the 36
same direction.
—*Antoine de Saint-Exupéry*

The story of a love is not important—what is important is that one is capable 37
of love. It is perhaps the only glimpse we are permitted of eternity.
—*Helen Hayes*

To deserve a people's love, you must know them. You must learn to appreci- 38
ate their history, their culture, their values, their aspirations for human
advancement and freedom.
—*Jesus Colon*

Friends and Family

Love is blind; friendship closes its eyes. 39
—*Anonymous*

Friendship with oneself is all important because without it one cannot be 40
friends with anyone else in the world.
—*Eleanor Roosevelt*

What is a friend? A single soul dwelling in two bodies. 41
—*Aristotle*

You do not know who is your friend and who is your enemy until the ice 42
breaks.
—*Eskimo proverb*

What's more important? Building a bridge or taking care of a baby? 43
—*June Jordan*

Your children need your presence more than your presents. 44
—*Jesse Jackson*

The peace and stability of a nation depend upon the proper relationships 45
established in the home.
—*Jade Snow Wong*

How times change: it used to be kids would ask where they came from. Now 46
they tell you where to go.
—*Ann Landers*

Children need love, especially when they do not deserve it. 47
—*Harold S. Hulbert*

Ourselves in Society

America is not a melting pot. It is a sizzling cauldron. 48
—*Barbara Ann Mikulski*

When spider webs unite, they can tie up a lion. 49
—*Ethiopian proverb*

We can do no great things, only small things with great love. 50
—*Mother Teresa*

A smile is the shortest distance between two people. 51
—*Victor Borge*

Whether we're laughing or crying, the reality of the streets persists. 52
—*Roberto Santiago*

Freedom does not always win. This is one of the bitterest lessons of history. 53
—*A. J. P. Taylor*

If you think you're too small to have an impact, try going to bed with a mos- 54
quito.
—*Anita Koddick*

Courage isn't the absence of fear; it is action in the face of fear. 55
—*S. Kennedy*

Racism is still a major issue because it is a habit. 56
—*Maya Angelou*

What women want is what men want: they want respect. 57
—*Marilyn Vos Savant*

The same heart beats in every human breast. 58
—*Matthew Arnold*

Basically people are people . . . but it is our differences which charm, delight, 59
and frighten us.
—*Agnes Newton Keith*

I can think of no greater honor than to help others fight to survive. 60
—*Helen Cahlakee Burgess*

Wisdom for Living

Look within! The secret is inside you!   **61**
—*Hui Neng*

One who wants a rose must respect the thorn.   **62**
—*Persian proverb*

To live a creative life, we must lose our fear of being wrong.   **63**
—*Joseph Chilton Pearce*

Laughter can be more satisfying than honor, more precious than money, more   **64**
heart cleansing than prayer.
—*Harriet Rochlin*

People who keep stiff upper lips find that it's damn hard to smile.   **65**
—*Judith Guest*

The way to get things done is not to mind who gets the credit of doing them.   **66**
—*Benjamin Jowett*

Self-pity in its early stages is as snug as a feather mattress. Only when it hard-   **67**
ens does it become uncomfortable.
—*Maya Angelou*

When three people call you a donkey, put on a saddle.   **68**
—*Spanish proverb*

Never criticize a man until you have walked a mile in his moccasins.   **69**
—*Native American proverb*

Everyone is a moon and has a dark side which he never shows to anybody.   **70**
—*Mark Twain*

Self-examination—if it is thorough enough—is always the first step towards   **71**
change.
—*Thomas Mann*

If you can't change your fate, change your attitude.   **72**
—*Amy Tan*

Time is a dressmaker specializing in alterations.   **73**
—*Faith Baldwin*

Money can't buy friends, but you can get a better class of enemy.   **74**
—*Spike Milligan*

Living in the lap of luxury isn't bad, except you never know when luxury is   **75**
going to stand up.
—*Orson Welles*

Egoist. A person of low taste, more interested in himself than me.   **76**
—*Ambrose Bierce*

Envy is a kind of praise.   **77**
—*John Gay*

What doesn't destroy me strengthens me.   78
—*Friedrich Nietzsche*

Life shrinks and expands in proportion to one's courage.   79
—*Anaïs Nin*

I'm not afraid to die. I just don't want to be there when it happens.   80
—*Woody Allen*

Acknowledgments

(continued from copyright page)

Pages 494–496: "Only Daughter" © 1990 by Sandra Cisneros. First published in *Glamour*, November 1990. Reprinted by permission of Susan Bergholz Literary Services, New York. All rights reserved.

Pages 497–499: "My Outing" from *Days of Grace* by Arthur Ashe and Arnold Rampersad. Copyright © 1993 by Jeanne Moutoussamy-Ashe and Arnold Rampersad. Reprinted by permission of Alfred A. Knopf, Inc.

Pages 500–501: "The Lady of the Ring" by Rene Denfeld. Rene Denfeld is the author of "The New Victorians" and "Kill the Body, The Head Will Fall."

Pages 502–503: "Neat People Versus Sloppy People" by Suzanne Britt. Copyright © 1993 by Suzanne Britt. Reprinted by permission of the author.

Pages 504–507: "How to Get the Most out of Yourself" from *Confidence: How to Succeed at Being Yourself* by Alan Loy McGinnis. Copyright © 1987 Augsburg Publishing House. Used by permission of Augsburg Fortress and from the March 1988 Reader's Digest.

Pages 508–512: "Beauty: When the Other Dancer Is the Self" from *In Search of Our Mothers' Gardens: Womanist Prose*, copyright © 1983 by Alice Walker, reprinted by permission of Harcourt Brace & Company and David Hingham Associates.

Pages 513–516: From *Hunger of Memory* by Richard Rodriguez. Copyright © 1982 by Richard Rodriguez. Reprinted by permission of David R. Godine, Publisher.

Pages 517–519: "Some Thoughts About Abortion" from *Living Out Loud* by Anna Quindlen. Copyright © 1987 by Anna Quindlen. Reprinted by permission of Random House, Inc. and International Creative Management.

Pages 520–521: "Food for Thought" from *Dave Barry Is Not Making this Up* by Dave Barry. Copyright © 1994 by Dave Barry. Reprinted by permission of Crown Publishers, Inc.

Pages 522–525: "One More Lesson" by Judith Ortiz Cofer is reproduced with permission from the publisher of *Silent Dancing: A Partial Remembrance of a Puerto Rican Childhood* (Houston: Arte Publico Press-University of Houston, 1990).

Pages 526–528: "A Brother's Murder" by Brent Staples. Copyright © 1986 by The New York Times. Reprinted by permission.

Pages 528–530: "In Search of Bruce Lee's Grave" by Shanlon Wu. Copyright © 1990 by The New York Times. Reprinted by permission.

Pages 531–532: "The Plot Against People" by Russell Baker. Copyright © 1968 by The New York Times. Reprinted by permission.

Pages 533–536: "Road Rage" by Andrew Ferguson. Copyright © 1998 Time, Inc. Reprinted by permission.

ESL Reference Guide

Index

Rhetorical Index

The following index first classifies the paragraphs and essays in this text according to rhetorical mode and then according to rhetorical mode by chapter. (Those paragraphs with built-in errors for students to correct are not included.)

Rhetorical Modes

Rhetorical Modes by Chapter

2 Prewriting to Generate Ideas

Description

Mr. Martin, the reason, 8
Noises in My Village, 16

Mixed Modes

Two weeks ago, 14

3 The Process of Writing Paragraphs

Illustration

At local noontime, 22
John Bryant is, 35

Persuasion

Something strange and wonderful, 21
Eating sugar can be worse, 21

Mixed Modes

I allow the spiders, 20
The summer picnic gave ladies, 21
Pete's sloppiness, 38

4 Achieving Coherence

Illustration

Louis Pasteur is revered, 51
El Niño, an unusual, 52
I have always considered my father, 56
According to sports writer, 58
More important perhaps, 65
Making Mittens Out of Sweaters, 66

Narration

In 1905, a poor washerwoman, 44
James Escalante, 63

Description

We lived on the top floor, 47
On my right a woods, 48
On September 10, 1990, 57
Rocky Mountain bighorn sheep, 58
Mrs. Zajac seemed to have, 64

Process

Most Westerners are fascinated, 44
More important perhaps, 65

Definition

A grand jury is an investigative body, 55

Comparison and Contrast

Zoos in the past, 60
Christopher Reeve's story, 59

Cause and Effect

El Niño, an unusual, 52

Mixed Modes

When Lewis and Clark, 58
The blues is the one truly American, 64

5 Illustration

Illustration

Great athletes, 69, 70

Description

The Day of the Dead, 202
Two Childhoods, 209

Process

How to Prepare for a Final Exam, 204

Definition

Winning, 207

Comparison and Contrast

Two Childhoods, 209

Cause and Effect

Why I Stayed and Stayed, 213

Classification

The Potato Scale, 211

Persuasion

Stopping Youth Violence: An Inside Job, 216

16 The Introduction, the Conclusion, and the Title

Illustration

Lisette Flores-Nieves, 221

Comparison and Contrast

Almost all of us, 222
Speech is silver, 223

Persuasion

Few Americans stay put, 221
Millions of law-abiding Americans, 222
Speech is silver, 223
Thus, bird watchers, 224
Students who follow their hearts, 224
Illness related to, 224

18 Special College Skills: Summary and Quotation

Illustration

In most cultures, 244

Definition

Besides the nine known planets, 246

Cause and Effect

Identical twins, 245

Persuasion

It's Great to Get Old, 248

19 Revising for Consistency and Parallelism

Illustration

Immortality in Wax, 260

Narration

It was 1850, 253
On the night of December 2, 1777, 254
Nelly Bly, 265

Description

The tension built, 254

Process

It was 1850, 253
A Quick History of Chocolate, 255

Persuasion

The salesperson is crucial, 260

20 Revising for Sentence Variety

Narration

Little Richard, the King of Rock'n'Roll, 291

Description

I recall being told, 268
Little Richard, the King of Rock'n'Roll, 291

Cause and Effect

One cause of the falling crime rate, 268

Persuasion

Try to imagine using failure, 269

Rhetorical Modes in the Reading Selections

SELECTED READINGS for Middle Tennessee State University

The Story of an Hour

Kate Chopin

Knowing that Mrs. Mallard was afflicted with a heart trouble, great care was taken 1
to break to her as gently as possible the news of her husband's death.

It was her sister Josephine who told her, in broken sentences, veiled hints that 2
revealed in half concealing. Her husband's friend Richards was there, too, near her.
It was he who had been in the newspaper office when intelligence of the railroad
disaster was received, with Brently Mallard's name leading the list of "killed."
He had only taken the time to assure himself of its truth by a second telegram, and
had hastened to forestall any less careful, less tender friend in bearing the sad
message.

She did not hear the story as many women have heard the same, with a par- 3
alyzed inability to accept its significance. She wept at once, with sudden, wild
abandonment, in her sister's arms. When the storm of grief had spent itself she
went away to her room alone. She would have no one follow her.

There stood, facing the open window, a comfortable, roomy armchair. Into 4
this she sank, pressed down by a physical exhaustion that haunted her body and
seemed to reach into her soul.

She could see in the open square before her house the tops of trees that were 5
all aquiver with the new spring life. The delicious breath of rain was in the air. In
the street below a peddler was crying his wares. The notes of a distant song which
some one was singing reached her faintly, and countless sparrows were twitter-
ing in the eaves.

There were patches of blue sky showing here and there through the clouds that 6
had met and piled each above the other in the west facing her window.

She sat with her head thrown back upon the cushion of the chair quite motion- 7
less, except when a sob came up into her throat and shook her, as a child who has
cried itself to sleep continues to sob in its dreams.

She was young, with a fair, calm face, whose lines bespoke repression and 8
even a certain strength. But now there was a dull stare in her eyes, whose gaze was
fixed away off yonder on one of those patches of blue sky. It was not a glance of
reflection, but rather indicated a suspension of intelligent thought

There was something coming to her and she was waiting for it, fearfully. What 9
was it? She did not know; it was too subtle and elusive to name. But she felt it,
creeping out of the sky, reaching toward her through the sounds, the scents, the
color that filled the air.

Now her bosom rose and fell tumultuously. She was beginning to recognize 10
this thing that was approaching to possess her, and she was striving to beat it back
with her will—as powerless as her two white slender hands would have been.

When she abandoned herself a little whispered word escaped her slightly 11
parted lips. She said it over and over under her breath: "Free, free, free!" The
vacant stare and the look of terror that had followed it went from her eyes. They
stayed keen and bright. Her pulses beat fast, and the coursing blood warmed and
relaxed every inch of her body.

She did not stop to ask if it were not a monstrous joy that held her. A clear and 12
exalted perception enabled her to dismiss the suggestion as trivial.

She knew that she would weep again when she saw the kind, tender hands 13
folded in death; the face that had never looked save with love upon her, fixed and
gray and dead. But she saw beyond that bitter moment a long procession of years.
to come that would belong to her absolutely. And she opened and spread her arms
out to them in welcome.

There would be no one to live for during those coming years; she would live 27 for herself There would be no powerful will bending her in that blind persistence with which men and women believe they have a right to impose a private will upon a fellow creature. A kind intention or a cruel intention made the act seem no less a crime as she looked upon it in that brief moment of illumination.

And yet she had loved him—sometimes. Often she had not. What did it matter! What could love, the unsolved mystery, count for in face of this possession of self-assertion which she suddenly recognized as the strongest impulse of her being.

"Free! Body and soul free!" she kept whispering. 28

Josephine was kneeling before the closed door with her lips to the keyhole, imploring for admission. "Louise, open the door! I beg; open the door—you will make yourself ill. What are you doing, Louise? For heaven's sake open the door."

"Go away. I am not making myself ill." No; she was drinking in a very elixir of life through that open window.

Her fancy was running riot along those days ahead of her. Spring days, and summer days, and all sort of days that would be her own. She breathed a quick prayer that life might be long. It was only yesterday she had thought with a shudder that life might be long.

She arose at length and opened the door to her sister's importunities. There was a feverish triumph in her eyes, and she carried herself unwittingly like a goddess of Victory. She clasped her sister's waist, and together they descended the stairs. Richards stood waiting for them at the bottom.

Some one was opening the front door with a latchkey. It was Brently Mallard who entered, a little travel-stained, composedly carrying his gripsack and umbrella. He had been far from the scene of accident, and d not even know there 29 had been one. He stood amazed at Josephine piercing cry; at Richards' quick motion to screen him from the view his wife.

But Richards was too late. 30

When the doctors came they said she had died of heart disease—joy that kills. 31

32

Letter from Birmingham Jail

Martin Luther King, Jr.

April 16, 1963
My Dear Fellow Clergymen:
While confined here in Birmingham city jail, I came across your recent statement 33 calling my present activities "unwise and untimely." Seldom do I pause to answer criticism of my work and ideas. If I sought to answer all the criticisms that cross my desk, my secretaries would have little time for anything other than such correspondence in the course of the day, and I would have no time for constructive work. But since I feel that you are men of genuine good will and that your criticisms are sincerely set forth, I want to try to answer your statement in what I hope will be patient and reasonable terms.

I think I should indicate why I am here in Birmingham, since you have been influenced by the view which argues against "outsiders coming in." I have the honor of serving as president of the Southern Christian Leadership Conference, an organization operating in every southern state, with headquarters in Atlanta, 1 Georgia. We have some eighty-five affiliated organizations across the South, and one of them is the Alabama Christian Movement for Human Rights. Frequently we share staff, educational and financial resources with our affiliates. Several months ago the affiliate here in Birmingham asked us to be on call to engage in a nonviolent direct-action program if such were deemed necessary. We readily consented, and when the hour came we lived up to our promise. So I, along with several members of my staff, am here because I was invited here. I am here because I have organizational ties here.

But more basically, I am in Birmingham because injustice is here. Just as the prophets of the eighth century B.C. left their villages and carried their "thus saith the Lord" far beyond the boundaries of their home towns, and just as the Apostle Paul left his village of Tarsus and carried the gospel of Jesus Christ to the far corners of the Greco-Roman world, so am I compelled to carry the gospel of freedom beyond my own home town. Like Paul, I must constantly respond to the Macedonian call for aid.

Moreover, I am cognizant of the interrelatedness of all communities and states. I cannot sit idly by in Atlanta and not be concerned about what happens to Birmingham. Injustice anywhere is a threat to justice everywhere. We are caught in an inescapable network of mutuality, tied in a single garment of destiny. Whatever affects one directly, affects all indirectly. Never again can we afford to live with the narrow, provincial "outside agitator" idea. Anyone who lives inside the United States can never be considered an outsider anywhere within its bounds.

You deplore the demonstrations taking place in Birmingham. But your statement, I am sorry to say, fails to express a similar concern for the conditions that brought about the demonstrations. I am sure that none of you would want to rest content with the superficial kind of social analysis that deals merely with effects and does not grapple with underlying causes. It is unfortunate that demonstrations are taking place in Birmingham, but it is even more unfortunate that the city's white power structure left the Negro community with no alternative.

In any nonviolent campaign there are four steps: collection of the facts to determine whether injustices exist; negotiation; self-purification; and direct action. We have gone through all these steps in Birmingham. There can be no gain saying the fact that racial injustice engulfs this community. Birmingham is probably the most thoroughly segregated city in the United States. Its ugly record of brutality is widely known. Negroes have experienced grossly unjust treatment in the courts. There have been more unsolved bombings of Negro homes and churches in Birmingham than in any other city in the nation. These are the hard brutal facts of the case. On the basis of these conditions, Negro leaders sought to negotiate with the city fathers. But the latter consistently refused to engage in good-faith negotiation.

Then, last September, came the opportunity to talk with leaders of Birmingham economic community. In the course of negotiations, certain promises were made by the merchants—for example, to remove the stores' humiliating racial signs. On the basis of these promises, the Reverend Fred Shuttlesworth and the leaders of the Alabama Christian Movement for Human Rights agreed to a moratorium on all demonstrations. As the weeks and months went by, we realized that we were the victims of a broken promise. A few signs, briefly removed, returned; the others remained.

As in so many past experiences, our hopes had been blasted, and the shadow of deep disappointment settled upon us. We had no alternative except to prepare for direct action, whereby we would present our very bodies as a means of laying our case before the conscience of the local and the national community. Mindful of the difficulties involved, we decided to undertake a process of self-purification. We began a series of workshops on nonviolence, and we repeatedly asked ourselves: "Are you able to accept blows without retaliating?" "Are you able to endure the ordeal of jail?" We decided to schedule our direct-action program for the Easter season, realizing that except for Christmas, this is the main shopping period of the year. Knowing that a strong economic-withdrawal program would be the by-product of direct action, we felt that this would be the best time to bring pressure to bear on the merchants for the needed change.

Then it occurred to us that Birmingham's mayoralty election was coming up in March, and we speedily decided to postpone action until after election day. When we discovered that the Commissioner of Public Safety, Eugene "Bull" Connor, had piled up enough votes to be in the run-off, we decided again to postpone action until the day after the run-off so that the demonstrations could not be used to cloud the issues. Like many others, we waited to see Mr. Connor defeated, and to this end we endured postponement after postponement. Having aided in this community need, we felt that our direct-action program could be delayed no longer.

You may well ask: "Why direct action? Why sit-ins, marches and so forth? Isn't negotiation a better path?" You are quite right in calling for negotiation. Indeed, this is the very purpose of direct action. Nonviolent direct action seeks to create such a crisis and foster such a tension that a community which has constantly refused to negotiate is forced to confront the issue. It seeks so to dramatize the issue that it can no longer be ignored. My citing the creation of tension as part 9 of the work of the nonviolent-resister may sound rather shocking. But I must confess that I am not afraid of the word "tension." I have earnestly opposed violent tension, but there is a type of constructive nonviolent tension which is necessary for growth. Just as Socrates felt that it was necessary to create a tension in the mind so that individuals could rise from the bondage of myths and half-truths to the unfettered realm of creative analysis and objective appraisal, so must we see the need for nonviolent gadflies to create the kind of tension in society that will help men rise from the dark depths of prejudice and racism to the majestic heights 10 of understanding and brotherhood.

The purpose of our direct-action program is to create a situation so crisis-packed that it will inevitably open the door to negotiation. I therefore concur with you in your call for negotiation. Too long has our beloved Southland been bogged down in a tragic effort to live in monologue rather than dialogue.

One of the basic points in your statement is that the action that I and my associates have taken in Birmingham is untimely. Some have asked: "Why didn't you give the new city administration time to act?" The only answer that I can give to this query is that the new Birmingham administration must be prodded about as much as the outgoing one, before it will act. We are sadly mistaken if we feel that the election of Albert Boutwell as mayor will bring the millennium to Birmingham. While Mr. Boutwell is a much more gentle person than Mr. Connor, they are both segregationists, dedicated to maintenance of the status quo. I have hope that Mr. Boutwell Will be reasonable enough to see the futility of massive resistance to desegregation. But he will not see this without pressure from devotees of civil rights. My friends, 11 I must say to you that we have not made a single gain in civil rights without determined legal and nonviolent pressure. Lamentably, it is an historical fact that privileged groups seldom give up their privileges voluntarily. Individuals may see the moral light and voluntarily give up their unjust posture; but, as Reinhold Niebuhr 12 has reminded us, groups tend to be more immoral than individuals.

We know through painful experience that freedom is never voluntarily given by the oppressor; it must be demanded by the oppressed. Frankly, I have yet to engage in a direct-action campaign that was "well timed" in the view of those who have not suffered unduly from the disease of segregation. For years now I have heard the word "Wait!" It rings in the ear of every Negro with piercing familiarity. This "Wait" has almost always meant "Never." We must come to see, with one of our distinguished jurists, that "justice too long delayed is justice denied."

We have waited for more than 340 years for our constitutional and God-given rights. The nations of Asia and Africa are moving with jetlike speed toward gaining political independence, but we still creep at horse-and-buggy pace toward gaining a cup of coffee at a lunch counter. Perhaps it is easy for those who have never felt the stinging darts of segregation to say, "Wait." But when you have seen vicious mobs lynch your mothers and fathers at will and drown your sisters and brothers at whim; when you have seen hate-filled policemen curse, kick and even kill your black brothers and sisters; when you see the vast majority of your 20 mil- 13 lion Negro brothers smothering in an airtight cage of poverty in the midst of an affluent society; when you suddenly find your tongue twisted and your speech stammering as you seek to explain to your 6-year-old daughter why she can't go to the public amusement park that has just been advertised on television, and see tears welling up in her eyes when she is told that Fun town is closed to colored children, and see ominous clouds of inferiority beginning to form in her little mental sky, and see her beginning to distort her personality by developing an unconscious bitterness toward white people; when you have to concoct an answer for a 5-year-old son who is asking: "Daddy, why do white people treat colored people so mean?"; when you take a cross-country drive and find it necessary to sleep night after night in the uncomfortable corners of your automobile because no motel will accept you; when you are humiliated day in and day out by nagging signs reading "white" and "colored"; when your first name becomes "nigger," your middle name becomes "boy" (however old you are) and your last name becomes "John," and your wife and mother are never given the respected tide "Mrs."; when you are harried by day and haunted by night by the fact that you are a Negro, living constantly at tiptoe stance, never quite knowing what to expect next, and are plagued with inner fears and outer resentments; when you are forever fighting a degenerating sense of "nobodiness"—then you will understand why we find it difficult to wait. There comes a time when the cup of endurance runs over, and men are no longer willing to be plunged into the abyss of despair. I hope, sirs, you can understand our legitimate and unavoidable impatience. 14

You express a great deal of anxiety over our willingness to break laws. This is certainly a legitimate concern. Since we so diligently urge people to obey the Supreme Court's decision of 1954 outlawing segregation in the public schools, at first glance it may seem rather paradoxical for us consciously to break laws. One may well ask: "How can you advocate breaking some laws and obeying others?" The answer lies in the fact that there are two types of laws: just and unjust I would be the first to advocate obeying just laws. One has not only a legal but a moral responsibility to obey just laws. Conversely, one has a moral responsibility to disobey unjust laws. I would agree with St. Augustine that "an unjust law is no law at all."

Now, what is the difference between the two? How does one determine whether a law is just or unjust? A just law is a man-made code that squares with the moral law or the law of God. An unjust law is a code that is out of harmony with the moral law. To put it in the terms of St. Thomas Aquinas: An unjust law is a human law that is not rooted in eternal law and natural law. Any law that 15 uplifts human personality is just. Any law that degrades human personality is unjust. All segregation statutes are unjust because segregation distorts the soul and damages the personality. It gives the segregator a false sense of superiority and the segregated a false sense of inferiority. Segregation, to use the terminology of the Jewish philosopher Martin Buber, substitutes an "I-it" relationship for an "I-thou" relationship and ends up relegating persons to the status of things. Hence segregation is not only politically, economically and sociologically unsound, it is morally wrong and sinful. Paul Tillich has said that sin is separation. Is not segregation an existential expression of man's tragic separation, his awful estrangement, his terrible sinfulness? Thus it is that I can urge men to obey 16 the 1954 decision of the Supreme Court, for it is morally right; and I can urge them to disobey segregation ordinances, for they are morally wrong.

Let us consider a more concrete example of just and unjust laws. An unjust law is a code that a numerical or power majority group compels a minority group to obey but does not make binding on itself. This is *difference* made legal. By the same token, a just law is a code that a majority compels a minority to follow and that it is willing to follow itself. This is *sameness* made legal.

Let me give another explanation. A law is unjust if it is inflicted on a minority that, as a result of being denied the right to vote, had no part in enacting or devising the law. Who can say that the legislature of Alabama which set up that state's segregation laws was democratically elected? Throughout Alabama all sorts of devious methods are used to prevent Negroes from becoming registered voters, and there are some counties in which even though Negroes constitute a majority of the population, not a single Negro is registered. Can any law enacted under such circumstances be considered democratically structured?

Sometimes a law is just on its face and unjust in its application. For instance, I have been arrested on a charge of parading without a permit. Now, there is nothing wrong in having an ordinance which requires a permit for a parade. But such an ordinance becomes unjust when it is used to maintain segregation and to deny citizens the First Amendment privilege of peaceful assembly and protest.   17

I hope you are able to see the distinction I am trying to point out. In no sense do I advocate evading or defying the law, as would the rabid segregationist. That would lead to anarchy. One who breaks an unjust law must do so openly, lovingly, and with a willingness to accept the penalty. I submit that an individual who breaks a law that conscience tells him is unjust, and who willingly accepts the penalty of imprisonment in order to arouse the conscience of the community over its injustice, is in reality expressing the highest respect for law.   18

Of course, there is nothing new about this kind of civil disobedience. It was evidenced sublimely in the refusal of Shadrach, Meshach and Abednego to obey the laws of Nebuchadnezzar, on the ground that a higher moral law was at stake. It was practiced superbly by the early Christians, who were willing to face hungry lions and the excruciating pain of chopping blocks rather than submit to certain unjust laws of the Roman Empire. To a degree, academic freedom is a reality today because Socrates practiced civil disobedience. In our own nation, the Boston Tea Party represented a massive act of civil disobedience.   19   20

We should never forget that everything Adolf Hitler did in Germany was "legal" and everything the Hungarian freedom fighters did in Hungary was illegal." It was "illegal" to aid and comfort a Jew in Hitler's Germany. Even so, I am sure that, had I lived in Germany at the time, I would have aided and comforted my Jewish brothers. If today I lived in a Communist country where certain principles dear to the Christian faith are suppressed, I would openly advocate disobeying that country's anti-religious laws.   21

I must make two honest confessions to you, my Christian and Jewish brothers. First, I must confess that over the past few years I have been gravely disappointed with the white moderate. I have almost reached the regrettable conclusion that the Negro's great stumbling block in his stride toward freedom is not the White Citizen's Counciler or the Ku Klux Klanner, but the white moderate, who is more devoted to "order" than to justice; who prefers a negative peace which is the absence of tension to a positive peace which is the presence of justice; who constantly says: "I agree with you in the goal you seek, but I cannot agree with your methods of direct action"; who paternalistically believes he can set the timetable for another man's freedom; who lives by a mythical concept of time and who constantly advises the Negro to wait for a "more convenient season." Shallow understanding from people of good will is more frustrating than absolute misunderstanding from people of ill will. Lukewarm acceptance is much more bewildering than outright rejection.   22

I had hoped that the white moderate would understand that law and order exist for the purpose of establishing justice and that when they fail in this purpose they become the dangerously structured dams that block the flow of social progress. I had hoped that the white moderate would understand that the present tension in the South is a necessary phase of the transition from an obnoxious negative peace, in which the Negro passively accepted his unjust plight, to a substantive and positive peace, in which all men will respect the dignity and worth of human personality. Actually, we who engage in nonviolent direct action are not the creators of tension. We merely bring to the surface the hidden tension that is already alive. We bring it out in the open, where it can be seen and dealt with. Like a boil that can never be cured so long as it is covered up but must be opened with all its ugliness to the natural medicines of air and light, injustice must be exposed, with all the tension its exposure creates, to the light of human conscience and the air of national opinion before it can be cured.   23

In your statement you assert that our actions, even though peaceful, must be 24 condemned because they precipitate violence. But is this a logical assertion? Isn't this like condemning a robbed man because his possession of money precipitated the evil act of robbery? Isn't this like condemning Jesus because his unique God-consciousness and never-ceasing devotion to God's will precipitated the evil act of crucifixion? We must come to see that, as the federal courts have consistently affirmed, it is wrong to urge an individual to cease his efforts to gain his basic constitutional rights because the quest may precipitate violence. Society must protect the robbed and punish the robber.

I had also hoped that the white moderate would reject the myth concerning time in relation to the struggle for freedom. I have just received a letter from a white brother in Texas. He writes: "All Christians know that the colored people will receive equal rights eventually, but it is possible that you are in too great a religious hurry. It has taken Christianity almost two thousand years to accomplish what it has. The teachings of Christ take time to come to earth." Such an attitude stems 25 from a tragic misconception of time, from the strangely irrational notion that there is something in the very flow of time that will inevitably cure all ills. Actually, time itself is neutral; it can be used either destructively or constructively. More and more I feel that the people of ill will have used time much more effectively than have the people of good will. We will have to repent in this generation not merely for the hateful words and actions of the bad people but for the appalling silence of the good people. Human progress never rolls in on wheels of inevitability; it comes through the tireless efforts of men willing to be coworkers with God, and without this hard work, time itself becomes an ally of the forces of social stag- 26 nation. We must use time creatively, in the knowledge that the time is always ripe to do right. Now is the time to make real the promise of democracy and transform our pending national elegy into a creative psalm of brotherhood. Now is the time to lift our national policy from the quicksand of racial injustice to the solid rock of human dignity.

You speak of our activity in Birmingham as extreme. At first I was rather disappointed that fellow clergymen would see my nonviolent efforts as those of an extremist. I began thinking about the fact that I stand in the middle of two opposing forces in the Negro community. One is a force of complacency, made up in part of Negroes who, as a result of long years of oppression, are so drained of self-respect and a sense of' 'somebodiness" that they have adjusted to segregation; and in part of a few middle-class Negroes who, because of a degree of academic and economic security and because in some ways they profit by segregation, have become insensitive to the problems of the masses. The other force is one of bitterness and hatred, and it comes perilously close to advocating violence. It is expressed in the various black nationalist groups that are springing up across the nation, the largest and best-known being Elijah Muhammad's Muslim movement. Nourished by the Negro's frustration over the continued existence of racial discrimination, this movement is made up of people who have lost faith in America, who have absolutely repudiated Christianity, and who have concluded that the 27 white man is an incorrigible "devil."

I have tried to stand between these two forces, saying that we need emulate neither the "do-nothingism" of the complacent nor the hatred and despair of the black nationalist. For there is the more excellent way of love and nonviolent protest. I am grateful to God that, through the influence of the Negro church, the way of nonviolence became an integral part of our struggle.

If this philosophy had not emerged, by now many streets of the South would, I am convinced, be flowing with blood. And I am further convinced that if our white brothers dismiss as "rabble-rousers" and "outside agitators" those of us who employ nonviolent direct action, and if they refuse to support our nonviolent efforts, millions of Negroes will, out of frustration and despair, seek solace and security in black-nationalist ideologies—a development that would inevitably lead to a frightening racial nightmare.

Oppressed people cannot remain oppressed forever. The yearning for freedom eventually manifests itself, and that is what has happened to the American Negro. Something within has reminded him that it can be gained. Consciously or uncon- 28 sciously, he has been caught up by the Zeitgeist, and with his black brothers of Africa and his brown and yellow brothers of Asia, South America and the Caribbean, the United States Negro is moving with a sense of great urgency toward the promised land of racial justice. If one recognizes this vital urge that has engulfed the Negro community, one should readily understand why public demonstrations 29 are taking place. The Negro has many pent-up resentments and latent frustrations, and he must release them. So let him march; let him make prayer pilgrimages to the city hall; let him go on freedom rides—and try to understand why he must do so. If his repressed emotions are not released in nonviolent ways, they will seek expression through violence; this is not a threat but a fact of history. So I have not said to my people: "Get rid of your discontent." Rather, I have tried to say that this normal and healthy discontent can be channeled into the creative outlet of nonvi- 30 olent direct action. And now this approach is being termed extremist.

But though I was initially disappointed at being categorized as an extremist, as I continued to think about the matter I gradually gained a measure of satisfaction from the label. Was not Jesus an extremist for love: "Love your enemies, bless them that curse you, do good to them that hate you, and pray for them which despitefully use you, and persecute you." Was not Amos an extremist for justice: "Let justice roll down like waters and righteousness like an ever-flowing stream." Was not Paul an extremist for the Christian gospel: "I bear in my body the marks of the Lord Jesus." Was not Martin Luther an extremist: "Here I stand; I cannot do otherwise, so help me God." And John Bunyan: "I will stay in jail to the end of my days before I make a butchery of my conscience." And Abraham Lincoln: "This nation cannot survive half slave and half free." And Thomas Jefferson:' 'We hold these truths to be self-evident, that all men are created equal. . . ." So the question is not whether we will be extremists, but what kind of extremists we will be. Will we be extremists for hate or for love? Will we be extremists for the preservation of injustice or for the extension of justice? In that dramatic scene on Calvary's Hill three men were crucified. We must never forget that all 30 three were crucified for the same crime—the crime of extremism. Two were extremists for immorality, and thus fell below their environment. The other, Jesus Christ, was an extremist for love, truth and goodness, and thereby rose above his environment Perhaps the South, the nation and the world are in dire need of creative extremists.

I had hoped that the white moderate would see this need. Perhaps I was too optimistic; perhaps I expected too much. I suppose I should have realized that few members of the oppressor race can understand the deep groans and passionate yearnings of the oppressed race, and still fewer have the vision to see that injustice must be rooted out by strong, persistent and determined action. I am thankful, however, that some of our white brothers in the South have grasped the meaning of this social revolution and committed themselves to it. They are still all too few in quantity, but they are big in quality. Some—such as Ralph McGill, Lillian Smith, Harry Golden, James McBride Dabbs, Ann Braden and Sarah Patton Boyle—have written about our struggle in eloquent and prophetic terms. Others have marched with us down nameless streets of the South. They have languished in filthy, roach-infested jails, suffering the abuse and brutality of policemen who view them as "dirty nigger-lovers." Unlike so many of their moderate brothers and sisters, they have recognized the urgency of the moment and sensed the need for powerful "action" antidotes to combat the disease of segregation. 31

Let me take note of my other major disappointment. I have been so greatly disappointed with the white church and its leadership. Of course, there are some notable exceptions. lam not unmindful of the fact that each of you has taken some significant stands on this issue. I commend you, Reverend Stallings, for your Christian stand on this past Sunday, in welcoming Negroes to your worship service on a nonsegregated basis. I commend the Catholic leaders of this state for integrating Spring Hill College several years ago.

But despite these notable exceptions, I must honestly reiterate that I have been disappointed with the church. I do not say this as one of those negative critics who can always find something wrong with the church. I say this as a minister of the gospel, who loves the church; who was nurtured in its bosom; who has been sustained by its spiritual blessings and who will remain true to it as long as the cord of life shall lengthen.

When I was suddenly catapulted into the leadership of the bus protest in Montgomery, Ala., a few years ago, I felt we would be supported by the white church. I felt that the white ministers, priests and rabbis of the South would be 32 among our strongest allies. Instead, some have been outright opponents, refusing to understand the freedom movement and misrepresenting its leaders; all too many others have been more cautious than courageous and have remained silent behind the anesthetizing security of stained-glass windows.

In spite of my shattered dreams, I came to Birmingham with the hope that the white religious leadership of this community would see the justice of our cause and, with deep moral concern, would serve as the channel through which our just 33 grievances could reach the power structure. I had hoped that each of you would understand. But again I have been disappointed.

I have heard numerous southern religious leaders admonish their worshipers to comply with a desegregation decision because it is the law, but I have longed to hear white ministers declare: "Follow this decree because integration is morally right and because the Negro is your brother." In the midst of blatant injustices 34 inflicted upon the Negro, I have watched white churchmen stand on the sideline and mouth pious irrelevancies and sanctimonious trivialities. In the midst of a mighty struggle to rid our nation of racial and economic injustice, I have heard many ministers say: "Those are social issues, with which the gospel has no real concern." And I have watched many churches commit themselves to a completely other-worldly religion which makes a strange, unBiblical distinction between body and soul, between the sacred and the secular. 35

I have traveled the length and breadth of Alabama, Mississippi and all the other southern states. On sweltering summer days and crisp autumn mornings I have looked at the South's beautiful churches with their lofty spires pointing heavenward. I have beheld the impressive outlines of her massive religious-education buildings. Over and over I have found myself asking: "What kind of people wor- 36 ship here? Who is their God? Where were their voices when the lips of Governor Barnett dripped with words of interposition and nullification? Where were they when Governor Wallace gave a clarion call for defiance and hatred? Where were their voices of support when bruised and weary Negro men and women decided to rise from the dark dungeons of complacency to the bright hills of creative protest?"

Yes, these questions are still in my mind. In deep disappointment I have wept over the laxity of the church. But be assured that my tears have been tears of love. There can be no deep disappointment where there is not deep love. Yes, I love the church. How could I do otherwise? I am in the rather unique position of being the son, the grandson and the great-grandson of preachers. Yes, I see the church 37 as the body of Christ. But, oh! How we have blemished and scarred that body through social neglect and through fear of being nonconformists.

There was a time when the church was very powerful—in the time when the early Christians rejoiced at being deemed worthy to suffer for what they believed. In those days the church was not merely a thermometer that recorded the ideas and principles of popular opinion; it was a thermostat that transformed the mores of society. Whenever the early Christians entered a town, the people in power became disturbed and immediately sought to convict the Christians for being "disturbers of the peace" and "outside agitators." But the Christians pressed on, in the conviction that they were "a colony of heaven," called to obey God rather

than man. Small in number, they were big in commitment. They were too God- 38
intoxicated to be "astronomically intimidated." By their effort and example they
brought an end to such ancient evils as infanticide and gladiatorial contests.

Things are different now. So often the contemporary church is a weak, inef-
fectual voice with an uncertain sound. So often it is an archdefender of the status
quo. Far from being disturbed by the presence of the church, the power structure
of the average community is consoled by the church's silent—and often even
vocal—sanction of things as they are. 39

But the judgment of God is upon the church as never before. If today's church
does not recapture the sacrificial spirit of the early church, it will lose its authen-
ticity, forfeit the loyalty of millions, and be dismissed as an irrelevant social club
with no meaning for the twentieth century. Every day I meet young people whose
disappointment with the church has turned into outright disgust.

Perhaps I have once again been too optimistic. Is organized religion too inex-
tricably bound to the status quo to save our nation and the world? Perhaps I must
turn my faith to the inner spiritual church, the church within the church, as the true
ekklesia and the hope of the world. But again I am thankful to God that some noble
souls from the ranks of organized religion have broken loose from the paralyzing
chains of conformity and joined us as active partners in the struggle for freedom. 40
They have left their secure congregations and walked the streets of Albany, Ga,
with us. They have gone down the highways of the South on tortuous rides for
freedom. Yes, they have gone to jail with us. Some have been dismissed from their
churches, have lost the support of their bishops and fellow ministers. But they
have acted in the faith that right defeated is stronger than evil triumphant. Their 41
witness has been the spiritual salt that has preserved the true meaning of the
gospel in these troubled times. They have carved a tunnel of hope through the
dark mountain of disappointment.

I hope the church as a whole will meet the challenge of this decisive hour. But
even if the church does not come to the aid of justice, I have no despair about the 42
future. I have no fear about the outcome of our struggle in Birmingham, even if
our motives are at present misunderstood. We will reach the goal of freedom in
Birmingham and all over the nation, because the goal of America is freedom.
Abused and scorned though we may be, our destiny is tied up with America's
destiny. Before the pilgrims landed at Plymouth, we were here. Before the pen of
Jefferson etched the majestic words of the Declaration of Independence across the
pages of history, we were here. For more than two centuries our forebears labored
in this country without wages; they made cotton king; they built the homes of
their masters while suffering gross injustice and shameful humiliation—and yet
out of a bottomless vitality they continued to thrive and develop. If the inex-
pressible cruelties of slavery could not stop us, the opposition we now face will
surely fail. We will win our freedom because the sacred heritage of our nation and
the eternal will of God are embodied in our echoing demands.

Before closing I feel impelled to mention one other point in your statement that 43
has troubled me profoundly. You warmly commended the Birmingham police
force for keeping "order" and "preventing violence." I doubt that you would have
so warmly commended the police force if you had seen its dogs sinking their teeth
into unarmed, nonviolent Negroes. I doubt that you would so quickly commend
the policemen if you were to observe their ugly and inhumane treatment of
Negroes here in the city jail; if you were to watch them push and curse old Negro
women and young Negro girls; if you were to see them slap and kick old Negro
men and young boys; if you were to observe them as they did on two occasions,
refuse to give us food because we wanted to sing our grace together. I cannot join
you in your praise of the Birmingham police department.

It is true that the police have exercised a degree of discipline in handling the
demonstrators. In this sense they have conducted themselves rather "nonviolently" in public. But for what purpose? To preserve the evil system of segregation.
Over the past few years I have consistently preached that nonviolence demands

that the means we use must be as pure as the ends we seek. I have tried to make clear that it is wrong to use immoral means to attain moral ends. But now I must affirm that it is just as wrong, or perhaps even more so, to use moral means to preserve immoral ends. Perhaps Mr. Connor and his policemen have been rather nonviolent in public, as was Chief Pritchett in Albany, Ga., but they have used the moral means of nonviolence to maintain the immoral end of racial injustice. As T. S. Eliot has said: 'The last temptation is the greatest treason: To do the right deed for the wrong reason.

I wish you had commended the Negro sit-inners and demonstrators of Birmingham for their sublime courage, their willingness to suffer and their amazing discipline in the midst of great provocation. One day the South will recognize its real heroes. They will be the James Merediths, with the noble sense of purpose that enables them to face jeering and hostile mobs, and with the agonizing loneliness that characterizes the life of the pioneer. They will be old, oppressed, battered Negro women, symbolized in a 72-year-old woman in Montgomery, Ala., who rose up with a sense of dignity and with her people decided not to ride segregated buses, and who responded with ungrammatical profundity to one who inquired about her weariness: "My feet is tired, but my soul is at rest." They will be the young high school and college students, the young ministers of the gospel and a host of their elders, courageously and nonviolently sitting in at lunch counters and willingly going to jail for conscience sake. One day the South will know that when these disinherited children of God sat down at lunch counters, they were in reality standing up for what is best in the American dream and for the most sacred values in our Judaeo-Christian heritage, thereby bringing our nation back to those great wells of democracy which were dug deep by the founding fathers in their formulation of the Constitution and the Declaration of Independence.

Never before have I written so long a letter. I'm afraid it is much too long to take your precious time. I can assure you that it would have been much shorter if I had been writing from a comfortable desk, but what else can one do when he is alone in a narrow jail cell, other than write long letters, think long thoughts and pray long prayers?

If I have said anything in this letter that overstates the truth and indicates an unreasonable impatience, I beg you to forgive me. If I have said anything that understates the truth and indicates my having a patience that allows me to settle for anything less than brotherhood, I beg God to forgive me.

I hope this letter finds you strong in the faith. I also hope that circumstances will soon make it possible for me to meet each of you, not as an integrationist or a civil-rights leader but as a fellow clergyman and a Christian brother. Let us all hope that the dark clouds of racial prejudice will soon pass away and the deep fog of misunderstanding will be lifted from our fear-drenched communities, and in some not too distant tomorrow the radiant stars of love and brotherhood will shine over our great nation with all their scintillating beauty.

The Fixed

Annie Dillard

I have just learned to see praying mantis egg cases. Suddenly I see them everywhere; a tan oval of light catches my eye, or I notice a blob of thickness in a patch of slender weeds. As I write I can see the one I tied to the mock orange hedge outside my study window. It is over an inch long and shaped like a bell, or like the northern hemisphere of an egg cut through its equator. The full length of one of

Excerpted from chapter 4 of *Pilgrim at Tinker Creek* (1974).

its long sides is affixed to a twig; the side that catches the light is perfectly flat. It has a dead straw, deadweed color, and a curious brittle texture, hard as varnish, but pitted minutely, like frozen foam. I carried it home this afternoon, holding it carefully by the twig, along with several others—they were light as air. I dropped 3 one without missing it until I got home and made a count.

Within the week I've seen thirty or so of these egg cases in a rose-grown field on Tinker Mountain, and another thirty in weeds along Carvin's Creek. One was on a twig of tiny dogwood on the mud lawn of a newly built house. I think the mail-order houses sell them to gardeners at a dollar apiece. It beats spraying, because each case contains between one hundred twenty-five to three hundred 4 fifty eggs. If the eggs survive ants, woodpeckers, and mice—and most do—then you get the fun of seeing the new mantises hatch, and the smug feeling of knowing, all summer long, that they're out there in your garden devouring gruesome numbers of fellow insects all nice and organically. When a mantis has crunched up the last shred of its victim, it cleans its smooth green face like a cat.

In late summer I often see a winged adult stalking the insects that swarm about my porch light. Its body is a clear, warm green; its naked, triangular head can revolve uncannily, so that I often see one twist its head to gaze at me as it were over its shoulder. When it strikes, it jerks so suddenly and with such a fearful clatter of raised wings, that even a hardened entomologist like J. Henri Fabre[1] confessed to being startled witless every time.

Adult mantises eat more or less everything that breathes and is small enough to capture. They eat honeybees and butterflies, including monarch butterflies. People have actually seen them seize and devour garter snakes, mice, and even *hummingbirds.* Newly hatched mantises, on the other hand, eat small 5 creatures like aphids and each other. When I was in elementary school, one of the teachers brought in a mantis egg case in a Mason jar. I watched the newly hatched mantises emerge and shed their skins; they were spidery and translucent, all over joints. They trailed from the egg case to the base of the Mason jar in a living bridge that looked like Arabic calligraphy, some baffling text from the Koran inscribed down the air by a fine hand. Over a period of several hours, during which time the teacher never summoned the nerve or the sense to release them, they ate each other until only two were left. Tiny legs were still kicking from the mouths of both. The two survivors grappled and sawed in the Mason jar; finally both died of injuries. I felt as though I myself should swallow the corpses, shutting my eyes and washing them down like jagged pills, so all that life wouldn't be lost.

When mantises hatch in the wild, however, they straggle about prettily, dodging ants, till all are lost in the grass. So it was in hopes of seeing an eventual hatch 6 that I pocketed my jackknife this afternoon before I set out to walk. Now that I can see the egg cases, I'm embarrassed to realize how many I must have missed all along. I walked east through the Adams' woods to the cornfield, cutting three undamaged egg cases I found at the edge of the field. It was a clear, picturesque day, a February day without clouds, without emotion or spirit, like a beautiful woman with an empty face. In my fingers I carried the thorny stems from which the egg cases hung like roses; I switched the bouquet from hand to hand, warming the free hand in a pocket. Passing the house again, deciding not to fetch gloves, I walked north to the hill by the place where the steers come to drink from Tinker Creek. There in the weeds on the hill I found another eight egg cases. I was 7 stunned—I cross this hill several times a week, and I always look for egg cases here, because it was here that I had once seen a mantis laying her eggs.

It was several years ago that I witnessed this extraordinary procedure, but I remember, and confess, an inescapable feeling that I was watching something not real and present, but a horrible nature movie, a "secrets-of-nature" short, 8

---

1. Noted French observer of the behavior of insects (1823–1915).

beautifully photographed in full color, that I had to sit through unable to look anywhere else but at the dimly lighted EMT signs along the walls, and that behind the scenes some amateur moviemaker was congratulating himself on having stumbled across this little wonder, or even on having contrived so natural a setting, as though the whole scene had been shot very carefully in a terrarium in someone's greenhouse.

I was ambling across this hill that day when I noticed a speck of pure white. The hill is eroded; the slope is a rutted wreck of red clay broken by grassy hillocks and low wild roses whose roots clasp a pittance of topsoil. I leaned to examine the white thing and saw a mass of bubbles like spittle. Then I saw something dark like an engorged leech rummaging over the spittle, and then I saw the pray- 9
ing mantis.

She was upside-down, clinging to a horizontal stem of wild rose by her feet which pointed to heaven. Her head was deep in dried grass. Her abdomen was swollen like a smashed finger; it tapered to a fleshy tip out of which bubbled a wet, whipped froth. I couldn't believe my eyes. I lay on the hill this way and that, my knees in thorns and my cheeks in clay, trying to see as well as I could. I poked near 10
the female's head with a grass; she was clearly undisturbed, so I settled my nose an inch from that pulsing abdomen. It puffed like a concertina, it throbbed like a bellows; it roved, pumping, over the glistening, clabbered surface of the egg case testing and patting, thrusting and smoothing. It seemed to act so independently that I forgot the panting brown stick at the other end. The bubble creature seemed to have two eyes, a frantic little brain, and two busy, soft hands. It looked like a hideous, harried mother slicking up a fat daughter for a beauty pageant, touching her up, slobbering over her, patting and hemming and brushing and stroking. 11

The male was nowhere in sight. The female had probably eaten him. Fabre says that, at least in captivity, the female will mate with and devour up to seven males, whether she has laid her egg cases or not. The mating rites of mantises are well known: a chemical produced in the head of the male insect says, in effect, "No, don't go near her, you fool, she'll eat you alive." At the same time a chemical in his abdomen says, "Yes, by all means, now and forever yes."

While the male is making up what passes for his mind, the female tips the balance in her favor by eating his head. He mounts her. Fabre describes the mating, which sometimes lasts six hours, as follows: "The male, absorbed in the performance of his vital functions, holds the female in a tight embrace. But the wretch has no head; he has no neck; he has hardly a body. The other, with her muzzle turned over her shoulder continues very placidly to gnaw what remains of the gentle swain. And, all the time, that masculine stump, holding on firmly, goes on with the business! . . . I have seen it done with my own eyes and have not yet recovered from my astonishment." 12

I watched the egg-laying for over an hour. When I returned the next day, the mantis was gone. The white foam had hardened and browned to a dirty suds; then, and on subsequent days, I had trouble pinpointing the case, which was only an inch or so off the ground. I checked on it every week all winter long. In the spring the ants discovered it; every week I saw dozens of ants scrambling over the sides, unable to chew a way in. Later in the spring I climbed the hill every day, hoping to catch the hatch. The leaves of the trees had long since unfolded, the butterflies were out, and the robins' first broods were fledged; still the egg case hung 13
silent and full on the stem. I read that I should wait for June, but still I visited the case every day. One morning at the beginning of June everything was gone. I couldn't find the lower thorn in the clump of three to which the egg case was fixed. I couldn't find the clump of three. Tracks ridged the clay, and I saw the lopped stems: somehow my neighbor had contrived to run a tractor-mower over that steep clay hill on which there grew nothing to mow but a few stubby thorns.

So. Today from this same hill I cut another three undamaged cases and carried them home with the others by their twigs. I also collected a suspiciously light cynthia moth cocoon. My fingers were stiff and red with cold, and my nose ran. I

had forgotten the Law of the Wild, which is, "Carry Kleenex." At home I tied the 14
twigs with their egg cases to various sunny bushes and trees in the yard. They're
easy to find because I used white string; at any rate, I'm unlikely to mow my own
trees. I hope the woodpeckers that come to the feeder don't find them, but I don't
see how they'd get a purchase on them if they did.

Night is rising in the valley; the creek has been extinguished for an hour, and now
only the naked tips of trees fire tapers into the sky like trails of sparks. The scene that
was in the back of my brain all afternoon, obscurely, is beginning to rise from night's
lagoon. It really has nothing to do with praying mantises. But this afternoon I threw 15
tiny string lashings and hitches with frozen hands, gingerly, fearing to touch the egg
cases even for a minute because I remembered the Polyphemus moth.[2]

I have no intention of inflicting all my childhood memories on anyone. Far less
do I want to excoriate my old teachers who, in their bungling, unforgettable way,
exposed me to the natural world, a world covered in chitin, where implacable
realities hold sway. The Polyphemus moth never made it to the past; it crawls in
that crowded, pellucid pool at the lip of the great waterfall. It is as present as this
blue desk and brazen lamp, as this blackened window before me in which I can
no longer see even the white string that binds the egg case to the hedge, but only
my own pale, astonished face.

Once, when I was ten or eleven years old, my friend Judy brought in a
Polyphemus moth cocoon. It was January; there were doily snowflakes taped to
the schoolroom panes. The teacher kept the cocoon in her desk all morning and
brought it out when we were getting restless before recess. In a book we found
what the adult moth would look like; it would be beautiful. With a wingspread of
up to six inches, the Polyphemus is one of the few huge American silk moths, 16
much larger than, say, a giant or tiger swallowtail butterfly. The moth's enormous
wings are velveted in a rich, warm brown, and edged in bands of blue and pink
delicate as a watercolor wash. A startling "eyespot," immense, and deep blue
melding to an almost translucent yellow, luxuriates in the center of each hind
wing. The effect is one of a masculine splendor foreign to the butterflies, a fragility
unfurled to strength. The Polyphemus moth in the picture looked like a mighty
wraith, a beating essence of the hardwood forest, alien—skinned and brown, with
spread, blind eyes. This was the giant moth packed in the faded cocoon. We closed 17
the book and turned to the cocoon. It was an oak leaf sewn into a plump oval bundle; Judy had found it loose in a pile of frozen leaves.

We passed the cocoon around; it was heavy. As we held it in our hands, the
creature within warmed and squirmed. We were delighted, and wrapped it tighter
in our fists. The pupa began to jerk violently, in heart-stopping knocks. Who's
there? I can still feel those thumps, urgent through a muffling of spun silk and
leaf, urgent through the swaddling of many years, against the curve of my palm.
We kept passing it around. When it came to me again it was hot as a bun; it jumped
half out of my hand. The teacher intervened. She put it, still heaving and banging,
in the ubiquitous Mason jar.   18

It was coming. There was no stopping it now, January or not. One end of the
cocoon dampened and gradually frayed in a furious battle. The whole cocoon
twisted and slapped around in the bottom of the jar. The teacher fades, the classmates fade, I fade: I don't remember anything but that thing's struggle to be a
moth or die trying. It emerged at last, a sodden crumple. It was a male; his long
antennae were thickly plumed, as wide as his fat abdomen. His body was very 19
thick, over an inch long, and deeply furred. A gray, furlike plush covered his head;
a long, tan furlike hair hung from his wide thorax over his brown-furred, seg-
mented abdomen. His multijointed legs, pale and powerful, were shaggy as a
bear's. He stood still, but he breathed.

---

2. Polyphemus. in classical mythology, was a one-eyed giant (a Cyclops) whom the hero Odysseus   20
blinded. (*Odyssey*, Book 9). A Polyphemus moth has a large eyespot on each hind wing.

He couldn't spread his wings. There was no room. The chemical that coated his wings like varnish, stiffening them permanently, dried, and hardened his wings as they were. He was a monster in a Mason jar. Those huge wings stuck on his back in a torture of random pleats and folds, wrinkled as a dirty tissue, rigid as leather. They made a single nightmare clump still wracked with useless, frantic convulsions.

The next thing I remember, it was recess. The school was in Shadyside, a busy residential part of Pittsburgh. Everyone was playing dodgeball in the fenced playground or racing around the concrete schoolyard by the swings. Next to the playground a long delivery drive sloped downhill to the sidewalk and street. Someone—it must have been the teacher—had let the moth out. I was standing in the driveway, alone, stock-still, but shivering. Someone had given the Polyphemus moth his freedom, and, he was walking away.

He heaved himself down the asphalt driveway by infinite degrees, unwavering. His hideous crumpled wings lay glued and rucked on his back, perfectly still now, like a collapsed tent. The bell rang twice; I had to go. The moth was receding down the driveway, dragging on. I went; I ran inside. The Polyphemus moth is still crawling down the driveway, crawling down the driveway hunched, crawling down the driveway on six furred feet, forever.

Soup

The New Yorker

When Albert Yeganeh says "Soup is my lifeblood," he means it. And when he says "I am extremely hard to please," he means that, too. Working like a demon alchemist in a tiny storefront kitchen at 259-A West Fifty-fifth Street, Mr. Yeganeh creates anywhere from eight to seventeen soups every weekday. His concoctions are so popular that a wait of half an hour at the lunchtime peak is not uncommon, although there are strict rules for conduct in line. But more on that later.

"I am psychologically kind of a health freak," Mr. Yeganeh said the other day, in a lisping staccato of Armenian origin. "And I know that soup is the greatest meal in the world. It's very good for your digestive system. And I use only the best, the freshest ingredients. I am a perfectionist. When I make a clam soup, I use three different kinds of clams. Every other place uses canned clams. I'm called crazy. I am not crazy. People don't realize why I get so upset It's because if the soup is not perfect and I'm still selling it, it's a torture. It's my soup, and that's why I'm so upset. First you clean and then you cook. I don't believe that ninety-nine per cent of the restaurants in New York know how to clean a tomato. I tell my crew to wash the parsley eight times. If they wash it five or six times, I scare them. I tell them they'll go to jail if there is sand in the parsley. One time, I found a mushroom on the floor, and I fired that guy who left it there." He spread his arms, and added, "This place is the only one like it in . . . in . . . the whole earth! One day, I hope to learn something from the other places, but so far I haven't. For example, the other day I went to a very fancy restaurant and had borscht. I had to send it back. It was *junk*. I could see all the chemicals in it. I never use chemicals. Last weekend, I had lobster bisque in Brooklyn, a very well-known place. It was *junk*. When I make a lobster bisque, I use a whole lobster. You know, I never advertise. I don't have to. All the big-shot chefs and the kings of the hotels come here to see what *I'm* doing."

As you approach Mr. Yeganeh's Soup Kitchen International from a distance, 5 the first thing you notice about it is the awning, which proclaims "Homemade Hot, Cold, Diet Soups." The second thing you notice is an aroma so delicious that it makes you want to take a bite out of the air. The third thing you notice, in front of the kitchen, is an electric signboard that flashes, saying, "Today's Soups . . . Chicken Vegetable . . . Mexican Beef Chili . . . Cream of Watercress . . . Italian Sausage . . . Clam Bisque . . . Beef Barley. Due to Cold Weather . . . For Most Efficient and Fastest Service the Line Must.. . Be Kept Moving . . . Please . . . Have Your Money. Ready . . . Pick the Soup of Your Choice . . . Move to Your Extreme . . . Left After Ordering."

"I am not prejudiced against color or religion," Mr. Yeganeh told us, and he jabbed an index finger at the flashing sign. "Whoever follows that I treat very well. My regular customers don't say anything. They are very intelligent and well educated. They know I'm just trying to move the line. The New York cop is very smart— 6 he sees everything but says nothing. But the young girl who wants to stop and tell you how nice you look and hold everyone *up—yah!*" He made a guillotining motion with his hand. "I tell you, I hate to work with the public. They treat me like a slave. My philosophy is: The customer is always wrong and I'm always right. I raised my prices to try to get rid of some of these people, but it didn't work."

The other day, Mr. Yeganeh was dressed in chefs' whites with orange smears across his chest, which may have been some of the carrot soup cooking in a huge pot on a little stove in one corner. A three-foot-long handheld mixer from France sat on the sink, looking like an overgrown gardening tool. Mr. Yeganeh spoke to two young helpers in a twisted Armenian-Spanish barrage, then said to us, "I have no overhead, no trained waitresses, and I have the cashier here." He pointed to himself theatrically. Beside the doorway, a glass case with fresh green celery, red and yellow peppers, and purple eggplant was topped by five big gray soup urns. 7 According to a piece of cardboard taped to the door, you can buy Mr. Yeganeh's soups in three sizes, costing from four to fifteen dollars. The order of any well-behaved customer is accompanied by little waxpaper packets of bread, fresh vegetables (such as scallions and radishes), fresh fruit (such as cherries or an orange), 8 a chocolate mint, and a plastic spoon. No coffee, tea, or other drinks are served.

"I get my recipes from books and theories and my own taste," Mr. Yeganeh said. 9 "At home, I have several hundreds of books. When I do research, I find that I don't know anything. Like cabbage is a cancer fighter, and some fish is good for your heart 10 but some is bad. Every day, I should have one sweet, one spicy, one cream, one veg- 11 etable soup—and they must change, they should always taste a little different" He added that he wasn't sure how extensive his repertoire was, but that it probably includes at least eighty soups, among them African peanut butter, Greek moussaka, hamburger, Reuben, B.L.T., asparagus and caviar, Japanese shrimp miso, chicken chili, Irish corned beef and cabbage, Swiss chocolate, French calf's brain, Korean beef ball, Italian shrimp and eggplant Parmesan, buffalo, ham and egg, short rib, Russian beef Stroganoff, turkey cacciatore, and Indian mulligatawny. "The chicken and the seafood are an addiction, and when I have French garlic soup I let people have 1 only one small container each," he said. "The doctors and nurses love that one."

A lunch line of thirty people stretched down the block from Mr. Yeganeh's doorway. Behind a construction worker was a man in expensive leather, who was in front of a woman in a fur hat. Few people spoke. Most had their money out and their orders ready.

At the front of the line, a woman in a brown coat couldn't decide which soup 5 to get and started to complain about the prices.

"You talk too much, dear," Mr. Yeganeh said, and motioned her to move to the left. "Next!"

"Just don't talk. Do what he says," a man huddled in a blue parka warned.

"He's downright rude," said a blond woman in a blue coat. "Even abusive. But you can't deny it, his soup is the best"

Because I Could Not Stop for Death

Emily Dickinson

Because I could not stop for Death—
He kindly stopped for me—
The Carriage held but just Ourselves—
And Immortality.

We slowly drove—He knew no haste
And I had put away
My labor and my leisure too,
For His Civility—

We passed the School, where Children strove
At Recess—in the Ring—
We passed the Fields of Gazing Grain—
We passed the Setting Sun—

Or rather—He passed Us—
The Dews drew quivering and chill—
For only Gossamer, my Gown —
My Tippet—only Tulle—

We paused before a House that seemed
A Swelling of the Ground—
The Roof was scarcely visible —
The Cornice—in the Ground—

Since then—'tis Centuries—and yet
Feels shorter than the Day
I first surmised the Horses' Heads
Were toward Eternity—

Nature

Emily Dickinson

1891

xxIv

A NARROW fellow in the grass
Occasionally rides;
You may have met him, — did you not,
His notice sudden is.

The grass divides as with a comb,
A spotted shaft is seen;

And then it closes at your feet
And opens further on.

He likes a boggy acre,
A floor too cool for corn.
Yet when a child, and barefoot,
I more than once, at morn,

1

Have passed, I thought, a whip-lash
Unbraiding in the sun, —
When, stooping to secure it,
It wrinkled, and was gone.

5

Several of nature's people
I know, and they know me;
I feel for them a transport
Of cordiality;

10

But never met this fellow,
Attended or alone,
Without a tighter breathing,
And zero at the bone.

13

Sonnet 18: Shall I Compare Thee to a Summer's Day?

1

William Shakespeare

Shall I compare thee to a summer's day?
Thou art more lovely and more temperate:
Rough winds do shake the darling buds of May,
And summer's lease hath all too short a date:
Sometime too hot the eye of heaven shines,
And often is his gold complexion dimmed,
And every fair from fair sometime declines,
By chance, or nature's changing course untrimmed:
But thy eternal summer shall not fade,
Nor lose possession of that fair thou ow'st,
Nor shall death brag thou wand'rest in his shade,
When in eternal lines LO time thou grow'st,
     So long as men can breathe or eyes can see,
     So long lives this, and this gives life to thee.

5

10

15

20

Mending Wall

Robert Frost

Something there is that doesn't love a wall,
That sends the frozen-ground-swell under it,
And spills the upper boulders in the sun;
And makes gaps even two can pass abreast.
The work of hunters is another thing:

25

I have come after them and made repair 30
Where they have left not one stone on a stone,
But they would have the rabbit out of hiding,
To please the yelping dogs. The gaps I mean,
No one has seen them made or heard them made,
But at spring mending-time we find them there. 35
I let my neighbor know beyond the hill;
And on a day we meet to walk the line
And set the wall between us once again.
We keep the wall between us as we go.
To each the boulders that have fallen to each. 40
And some are loaves and some so nearly balls
We have to use a spell to make them balance:
'Stay where you are until our backs are turned!'
We wear our fingers rough with handling them. 44
Oh, just another kind of outdoor game,
One on a side. It comes to little more:
There where it is we do not need the wall:
He is all pine and I am apple orchard.
My apple trees will never get across
And eat the cones under his pines, I tell him.
He only says, 'Good fences make good neighbors.'
Spring is the mischief in me, and I wonder
If I could put a notion in his head:
'Why do they make good neighbors? Isn't it
Where there are cows? But here there are no cows.
Before I built a wall I'd ask to know
What I was walling in or walling out,
And to whom I was like to give offense.
Something there is that doesn't love a wall,
That wants it down.' I could say 'Elves' to him,
But it's not elves exactly, and I'd rather
He said it for himself. I see him there
Bringing a stone grasped firmly by the top
In each hand, like an old-stone savage armed.
He moves in darkness as it seems to me,
Not of woods only and the shade of trees.
He will not go behind his father's saying,
And he likes having thought of it so well
He says again, 'Good fences make good neighbors.'

Revising and Proofreading Symbols

The following chart lists common writing errors and the symbols that instructors often use to mark them. For some errors, your instructor may wish to use symbols other than the ones shown. You may wish to write these alternate symbols in the blank column.

Standard Symbol	Instructor's Alternate Symbol	Error	For help, see Chapter
adj		Incorrect adjective form	32
adv		Incorrect adverb form	32
agr		Incorrect subject-verb agreement	26; 23
		Incorrect pronoun-antecedent agreement	30, Parts A and B
apos		Missing or incorrect apostrophe	33
awk		Awkward expression	3, Part F; 21
cap		Missing or incorrect capital letter	35, Parts A and B
case		Incorrect pronoun case	30, Part D
⊘		Missing or incorrect comma	34; 24, Parts A and B
coh		Lack of coherence	4
⊙		Missing or incorrect colon	35, Part D
con d		Inconsistent discourse	18, Part C
con p		Inconsistent person	19, Part B
con t		Inconsistent verb tense	19, Part A
coord		Incorrect coordination	24, Part A
cs		Comma splice	25, Part A
⊖		Missing or incorrect dash	35, Part D
dev		Incomplete paragraph or essay development	3, Parts C, D, and E; 14, Parts C, D, and E
dm		Dangling or confusing modifier	20, Part D
ed		Missing -ed, past tense or past participle	27, Part A; 28, Part A
frag		Sentence fragment	25, Part B; 20, Part D; 24, Part B
¶		Missing indentation for new paragraph	3, Part A
()		Missing or incorrect parenthesis	35, Part D
‖		Faulty parallelism	19, Part C
pl		Missing or incorrect plural form	29
pp		Incorrect past participle form	28
⊙ ! ?		Missing or incorrect end punctuation	20, Part B
quot		Missing or incorrect quotation marks	35, Part C
rep		Unnecessary repetition	3, Parts D and F
ro		Run-on sentence	25, Part A
⊙		Missing or incorrect semicolon	24, Parts C and D
sub		Incorrect subordination	24, Part B
sp		Spelling error	37
		Look-alike, sound-alike error	38
sup		Inadequate support	3, Part F
title		Title needed	16, Part C
trans		Transition needed	3, Part E; 14, Part D
trite		Trite expression	21, Part C
ts		Poor or missing topic sentence or thesis statement	3, Parts A and B; 14, Part B
u		Lack of paragraph or essay unity	3, Part F; 14, Parts C, D, and E
w		Unnecessary words	21, Part B
⌒		Too much space	
ꝯ		Words or letters to be deleted	
?		Unclear meaning	21, Part A
^		Omitted words	
~		Words or letters in reverse order	